Programming
with
ANSI C

B.J.Holmes BSc, MSc, CEng, MBCS, Cert Ed.

Principal Lecturer in the School of Computing and Mathematical Sciences,
Oxford Brookes University, Headington, Oxford, OX3 0BP

DP Publications Ltd
Aldine Place, 142/144 Uxbridge Road
Shepherds Bush Green, London W12
1995

Disclaimer

The programs presented in this book have been included for their instructional value. They have been computer-tested with considerable care and are not guaranteed for any particular purpose. The author does not offer any warranties or representations, nor does he accept any liabilities with respect to the programs.

Trademark Acknowledgements

DEC, digital, DECStation and ULTRIX are all trademarks of the Digital Equipment Corporation

IBM is a trademark of the International Business Machines Corporation

Microsoft Visual C++ is a trademark of the Microsoft Corporation

TopSpeed is a trademark of Jensen and Partners International

UNIX is a trademark of AT & T

A CIP catalogue record for this book is available from the British Library

First Edition 1995

ISBN 1 85805 117 7

Typeset and illustrated by B.J.Holmes

Printed by B.P.C Hazell Books Ltd, Aylesbury, England.

Contents

Preface

The need to teach C

It's a fact of life, the C language tends to dominate many programming applications these days. Just take a look at the job advertisements for programmers and it is clear that a large proportion of work requires at least a knowledge of C. However, many academic courses in universities and colleges, prescribe for good reason, languages such as Pascal, Modula-2 or Ada as the first language. Yet increasingly there is a pressure from both the computing industry and the student population to teach C.

C offers the programmer a freedom from many language restraints and virtually total control over the computer and how it executes programs. With this freedom and power must come responsibility, therefore, every C programmer must exercise proper care and attention to detail.

The C programs listed in this book, have been deliberately written in a style similar to that expected when using Pascal-like languages. The language is taught in a structured and readable manner, pointing out both good practice and possible areas for error that can occur when using C.

Why ANSI C?

ANSI C allows programs to be written for a wide range of computers. To demonstrate this versatility all the programs in this book have been compiled and tested using three different compilers on two different brands of computer under MSDOS and UNIX operating systems.

ANSI C is a subset of C++, therefore, the text should provide an invaluable foundation to anyone wanting to initially learn C, then extend their programming knowledge to C++ in the future.

Audience

The author has assumed that the reader has no prior knowledge of computer programming. The text is intended to be used on first-year undergraduate degree courses in computing, software engineering, information technology and allied engineering disciplines where a knowledge of programming is thought to be essential.

The book is equally suitable as a course text or as a self-instruction text, and may also be used as a suitable conversion course to C for those readers who can already program in other high-level languages.

Format

Chapters 1 to 8 provide the reader with a gradual introduction to the fundamentals of programming. Chapters 9 to 12 introduce elementary data structures and program development techniques. Finally chapters 13 to 16 explain about more advanced features of programming and data structures.

In addition to an exposition of the C language, the text contains a comprehensive appraisal of many important topics found in data structures - arrays, records, linked lists, queues, stacks and trees; in data processing - sorting, searching, merging, report writing and data validation; and in programming - modularity, recursion and data abstraction.

The emphasis throughout the book is on the use of carefully chosen examples that highlight the features of the language being studied. Explanation about the language follows from, and is put into context with, the example programs.

The development of the language statements and the programs are taken in manageable steps, to enable the reader to build a firm foundation of knowledge. The type of programming examples used are simple enough to give the reader confidence at each stage of learning to program in C.

A section on programming questions is found at the end of each chapter. These questions serve to test the reader's understanding of the topics and to reinforce the material of the chapter. The reader is advised to complete the answers to the questions before progressing to the next chapter. The answers to a selection of questions are given in appendix D. The answers to those question numbers found in brackets [ ] are available on a lecturers' supplement disk.

Lecturers' Supplement disk

A PC-compatible disk containing all the example programs and all the answers to the programming questions is available free of charge, from DP Publications Ltd, to lecturers adopting the book as a course text. This disk is also available at a small charge for readers who have chosen to use the text on a self-study basis.

Language and computer requirements

Studying from this book can be more effective and enjoyable if a computer is used for running both the example programs and the reader's own answers to the programming questions.

All the programs written for the examples and the answers, have been compiled using DEC C, JPI TopSpeed C and Microsoft Visual C++, to ensure their portability between UNIX (ULTRIX), MSDOS and Windows environments on a Digital Personal DEC Station and an IBM compatible computer.

In fact any C compiler that is compliant with ANSI/ISO 9899-1990 C can be used for the implementation of the programs found in this book.

BJH - Oxford June 1995

Chapter 1
Programming Environment

The purpose of this chapter is to provide the reader with enough background information to be able to understand a computing environment in which to work as a programmer. An introduction is given to the hardware and software that make up a typical computer system which may be used for the development of computer programs written in C. By the end of the chapter the reader should have an understanding of the following topics.

☐   The stages involved in writing a computer program.

☐   The purpose of a computer program and its relationship to data and results.

☐   The hardware units that make up a computer system.

☐   The different levels of computer languages.

☐   The need to translate languages into a form that the computer can recognise.

☐   The necessary stages in the implementation of a computer program.

1.1 What is programming?

Before a computer can be programmed to solve a problem, it is necessary for the programmer to first understand how to solve the problem. This solution is known as an algorithm, and programming is the technique of designing an algorithm then coding the algorithm, using a suitable computer language, into a corresponding computer program. However, this is not the whole story. At the stages of design and after coding the program, it is necessary to test the solution to the problem and verify that it does indeed function correctly. A computer program is not usually static. Over a period of time it may be changed, and indeed evolve as the computer project to which it contributes also evolves. For this reason programming must also involve documenting the purpose of the program, the method of solution, the stages of testing that it has undergone, and other necessary facts. Programming, therefore, contains the activities of designing an algorithm, coding a program from the algorithm, and testing and documenting the program, as illustrated in figure 1.1.

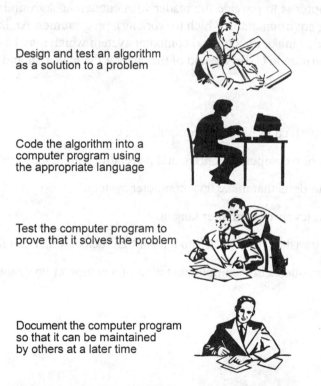

Design and test an algorithm
as a solution to a problem

Code the algorithm into a
computer program using
the appropriate language

Test the computer program to
prove that it solves the problem

Document the computer program
so that it can be maintained
by others at a later time

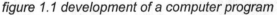

figure 1.1 development of a computer program

The methods used in programming will vary between organisations. The production of the algorithm can take several forms, however, the use of diagrams such as flowcharts, structure charts and even textual descriptions of a solution are most common. An algorithm is converted into a computer program by either hand-coding the solution into statements from the programming language being used, or with the aid of a program generator. Program generators take the design in pseudo-diagrammatic/ textual form and convert it into a computer program. The advantage of this technique is that it saves time in coding a program, and the design and program always match.

Programs can be tested, by either the programmer tracing through the program, or by peer-group inspection. The latter technique involves a small group of staff in reviewing the accuracy of a program and whether it meets the original specification. Further testing, using suitable test data, is always carried out with the program being run on a computer.

The documentation of a program will usually conform to the in-house standards of an organisation.

1.2 Program, data and results

A computer program is a coded algorithm, represented by a series of instructions for the computer to obey and provides a method for processing data. Data is the name given to facts represented by characters and quantities. For example, in a business the names of employees and the number of hours worked by the employees represent data. Data is input into a computer, processed under the direction of a program into results, that are output in the form of, say, a report on the wages for hourly paid staff.

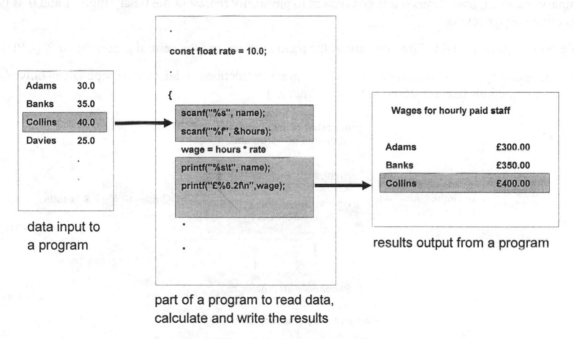

data input to a program

part of a program to read data, calculate and write the results

results output from a program

figure 1.2 an example of a segment of program

In figure 1.2 data has been represented by a list of names and the number of hours worked by employees in a business. The segment of computer program contains instructions to read the name of an employee *scanf("%s", name)* and the number of hours worked by an employee *scanf("%f", &hours)*. The gross weekly wage of an employee is then calculated by the instruction *wage = hours * rate*, where all employees are paid at the same hourly rate of £10 per hour, declared by the statement *const float rate = 10.0*. The result of this calculation can then be written to a report on the wages for hourly paid staff. The two instructions *printf("%s\t", name)* and *printf("£%6.2f\n", wage)* are used to write the name and gross weekly wage for one employee.

In this example the name *Collins,* who worked a *40* hour week, has been read into the computer by the program. The gross weekly wage for employee *Collins* was then calculated to be *£400.00*, on the basis that all employees are paid at the hourly rate of £10 per hour. The name of the employee and the gross weekly wage are then written to the report. This sequence of statements is repeated until there is no more data available.

The program has been used to input data into the computer, process the data, then output the results from the computer in the form of a report.

1.3 A digital computer

A digital computer is an electronic machine capable of storing instructions and obeying them at a very high speed. For example an instruction can be obeyed in one hundred millionth of one second. The term digital implies that all information is represented by numbers within the computer. The numbers are stored as binary numbers, base 2, since it is convenient to physically represent the binary digits 1 and 0 as two respective voltage levels.

A digital computer is divided into two areas, the main memory and the central processing unit (CPU).

The main memory is used to temporarily store program instructions and data. A computer can only obey program instructions that are stored in the main memory.

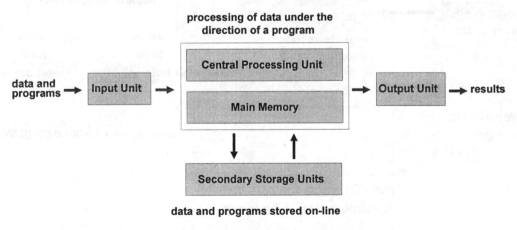

figure 1.3 a computer model

The CPU consists of two sub-units, the arithmetic and logic unit (ALU) and the control unit. The ALU performs the processes of arithmetic, logical operations and comparisons on data. Whereas the control unit fetches the instructions from main memory, interprets and obeys them, and co-ordinates the flow of information about the computer system.

Figure 1.3 illustrates a computer model containing the CPU, main memory and in addition three other units - input, secondary storage and output, known as peripheral units.

An input unit allows data and computer programs to be input into the computer model.

Since the main memory is only used to temporarily store programs and data, it is necessary to have secondary storage units to provide a permanent storage facility. Programs and data are transferred to and from the secondary storage units to the main memory only when they are required. The information is said to be on-line to the computer. The rate of transfer of information is fast and dependent upon the type of secondary storage unit being used.

In order to transfer results from the main memory and secondary storage units to the outside world it is necessary to provide an output unit.

1.4 Input and output units

The most popular input unit used in a computer system is a keyboard. The layout of a popular keyboard is depicted in figure 1.4. Notice that a modern keyboard contains other banks of keys in addition to the keys normally found on a typewriter. Both data and programs can be keyed into the computer by using such a keyboard.

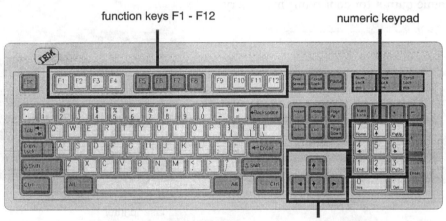

figure 1.4 the layout of a popular keyboard

A television screen or monitor can be used to simultaneously display the information that is being typed into a computer. Such a display is meant to provide a means of visually checking that the correct information is being entered. A monitor has a dual function, as well as displaying the information that is typed at a keyboard, information that has been processed by a computer can also be displayed on the screen. Figure 1.5 illustrates a typical monitor that is used in a computer system.

The major disadvantage of using a monitor as an output unit stems from the inability of the unit to provide a hard copy of the output. Because information on a printed page is so convenient, it is necessary to include a printer as another output unit. Printers vary in their speed of output and include matrix printers that print characters composed from dots at a rate of up to 150 characters per second and laser printers that print complete pages in seconds. Figure 1.6 illustrates both types of printers.

It is worth mentioning in passing that there are other types of input and output units, however, these units are for specialised use and do not normally form part of a program development environment. Input units,

figure 1.5 a monitor

for example bar code readers, are used to detect stock codes on supermarket merchandise. Magnetic ink character readers detect bank account numbers and branch codes on bank cheques. Optical character and mark readers are used to detect information written on documents. Similarly, output units are not only limited to monitors and printers but can include graph and map plotters, synthesised speech units and digital to analogue output for controlling machinery.

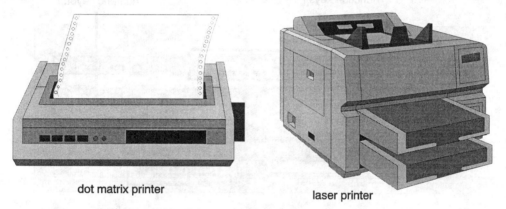

dot matrix printer

laser printer

figure 1.6 a selection of printers

1.5 Secondary storage units

These units can be broadly subdivided into:

(i) magnetic disk units with a storage capacity of up to many thousands of millions of characters; these are known colloquially as hard disks;

(ii) floppy disk units that have, depending upon their size and density, a storage capacity of up to several million characters, on one exchangeable magnetic disk;

(iii) optical and magneto/optical exchangeable disks with a storage capacity of up to hundreds of millions of characters on one exchangeable disk;

(iv) magnetic tape units with a storage capacity of up to a hundred million characters on one tape.

The magnetic and optical disk units transfer information to, and receive information from, the CPU at speeds of several millions of characters per second. When dealing with disk-based media access to the information is direct and fast. By comparison access speeds to information held on magnetic tape is slow, since the contents of the tape must be read sequentially before information can be retrieved.

3.5 inch disk with a storage capacity of 1.44 Mbytes

5.25 inch disk with a storage capacity of 360 Kbytes

figure 1.7 popular floppy disks

The most common form of secondary storage medium the reader will use is the floppy disk. Figure 1.7 illustrates two popular sizes of floppy disk. Access to information is slow in comparison with hard disks.

1.6 Computer configurations

The reader is likely to come across two different, but popular ways, in which computer equipment is configured. The first is a stand alone personal computer as shown in figure 1.8. This consists of an outer casing or box that contains the central processing unit, main memory, secondary storage devices such as a hard disk, and floppy disk drives, a power supply and various interface cards to permit linking the CPU to other devices. The personal computer has as standard a keyboard and monitor. In addition to these, a device known as a mouse is used to point at items displayed on the monitor, and the computer will probably be connected to a printer.

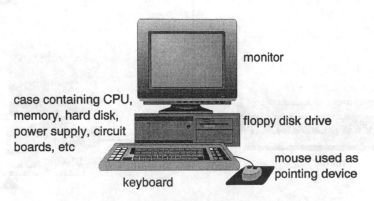

monitor

case containing CPU, memory, hard disk, power supply, circuit boards, etc

floppy disk drive

mouse used as pointing device

keyboard

figure 1.8 a stand-alone personal computer

A second configuration that is extremely popular is a network of computers. There are several ways in which the computers can be joined together on a network, but this is of little importance in this chapter. The main points to consider are that a network usually contains a larger more powerful computer known as a file server to which all the other computers are connected. The purpose of the file server is to store and distribute essential software and information that is of common use to all the users on the network. Each terminal on the network can be a personal computer with its own local processing power and capability to store information. In addition to sharing software a computer network can permit the sharing of other peripheral devices, such as printers and plotters. Figure 1.9 illustrates a small network in which three personal computers are connected to the file server in order to obtain access to commonly used computer software and a single printer.

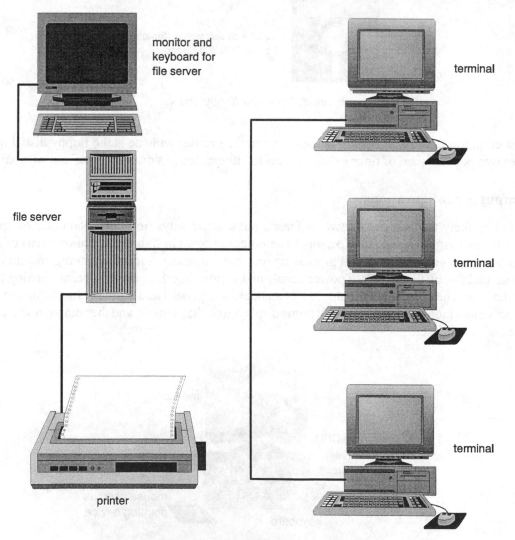

figure 1.9 a network of personal computers

1.7 Computer languages

A computer language is a set of instructions used for writing computer programs. There are essentially three levels of language, high, low and machine code.

C is a high-level language and was designed and implemented as far back as 1972, by Dennis Ritchie of Bell laboratories. However, it was as recent as 1990 that the first ANSI standard for the language was completed. The following segment of code illustrates several statements in a C program.

```
scanf("%f", &gross_pay);

if (gross_pay < 1000)
   tax = 0;
else
   tax = tax_rate * gross_pay;

printf("%8.2f", tax);
```

As this example illustrates, high-level languages contain statements that are written with English words and symbols. Such languages are not designed specifically for any one brand of computer.

The architecture of a computer may be defined as the type of CPU, memory size, and internal features of the hardware. A program written in C to run on one computer architecture, for example a Digital Personal DECstation, that also runs without modification on a different architecture, for example an IBM PC, is said to be portable between the two computers, if it produces exactly the same results.

Many computer languages are defined by respective standards for each language. A standard is essentially a definition of the format or grammar of the language statements, the meaning or semantics of the statements and sometimes recommendations on how the language should be implemented on a computer.

The version of C used in this book conforms to the ANSI/ISO 9899-1990 Standard. High-level languages will only remain portable between computers, if the language statements used, conform to those defined in the standard for the language. However, software manufacturers tend to enhance languages with different extra facilities, creating in effect a dialect of the language. Computers also differ in their CPU and memory architectures. The more dialects of a language that exist and the difference in word sizes between computers, the less portable the language is likely to be.

Low level languages contain statements that are written using mnemonic codes (codes suggesting their meaning and, therefore, easier to remember) to represent operations and addresses that relate to the main memory and storage registers of a computer. Each low level language has instructions which correspond closely to the in-built operations of a specific computer. Since different CPU architectures use different low level languages a program written for one CPU architecture will not run on a different CPU architecture. Despite the many low level languages in existence they all adhere to the same broad principles of language structure. An example of statements from a typical low level language is:

```
LDA 5000
ADD 6000
STA 5000
```

9

This program segment adds two numbers and stores the result in a memory location! This type of programming is obviously not as clear as writing **sum = sum + number;** which is the equivalent operation in C.

Machine level statements are even worse to mentally interpret. They are normally written using one of the number bases 2, 8 or 16. For example the following program segment coded in base 2 binary, would require the aid of a reference manual in order to decipher the meaning of each code.

```
11011101 1011011
01001100 1011100
11011100 1011011
```

1.8 Program implementation

There are four phases associated with the implementation of a program on a computer system. These phases are illustrated in figure 1.10, and are explained as follows.

Phase 1. In order to type a C program at the keyboard and save the program on a disk it will be necessary to run a program called an editor. In addition to program entry, an editor allows a program to be retrieved from disk and amended as necessary. A C program is stored in text mode so that the programmer can read the program as it was written. No translation of the C program to a machine recognisable form has been necessary at this stage. The input of a program using an editor in the Microsoft Visual C++ environment is shown in window <1> of figure 1.11.

Phase 2. A computer stores and uses information in a binary format, therefore, the computer cannot understand programs written in either high or low level languages. Program code written in either a high or low level language must be translated into a binary machine code that the computer can recognise. Translation is possible by using a supplied program to translate high or low level language statements into machine code.

Translation to machine code from a high level language is by compiler, and from a low level language by assembler. The translator, compiler or assembler, is resident in the main memory of the computer and uses the high or low level program code as input data. The output from the translator is a program in machine readable code. In addition to translation, a compiler or assembler will report on any grammatical errors made by the programmer in the language statements of the program.

Different compilers are normally associated with different computer architectures. For example a program written in C for an IBM PC computer would require translation using, say, a Microsoft Visual C++ compiler or a JPI TopSpeed C compiler. However, the same program, in text form, could be transferred to a Digital Personal DECstation and be translated into machine-oriented language using a DEC C compiler. Note the portability of the language only refers to the language in text mode not machine code. Since the three compilers all conform to the ANSI C Standard, programs written to the Standard are easily ported between PC compatibles and Digital Personal DECstations.

Phase 3. Before a compiled C program can be run or executed by the computer it must be converted into an executable form. One function of the link/loader is to take the machine oriented program and combine it with any necessary software (already in machine oriented form) to enable the program to be run. For example, input and output routines that are supplied by the system will need linking into the program to

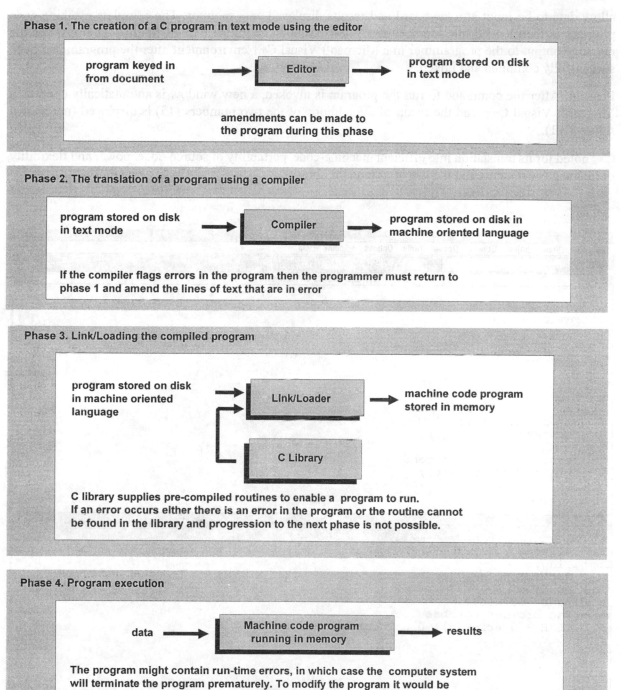

figure 1.10 four phases of program implementation

allow data to be input at a keyboard and results displayed on a monitor. The complete machine code program is then loaded into memory ready for execution. Window <2> of figure 1.11 illustrates the message output to the programmer in a Microsoft Visual C++ environment after the program had been successfully compiled and linked.

Phase 4. After the command to run the program is invoked, a new window is automatically opened in Microsoft Visual C++ and the result of the addition of the two numbers (15) is displayed (not shown figure 1.11).

C is noted for its translation into efficient machine-code, portability of source-code, power and flexibility of language statements and the use of a standard library.

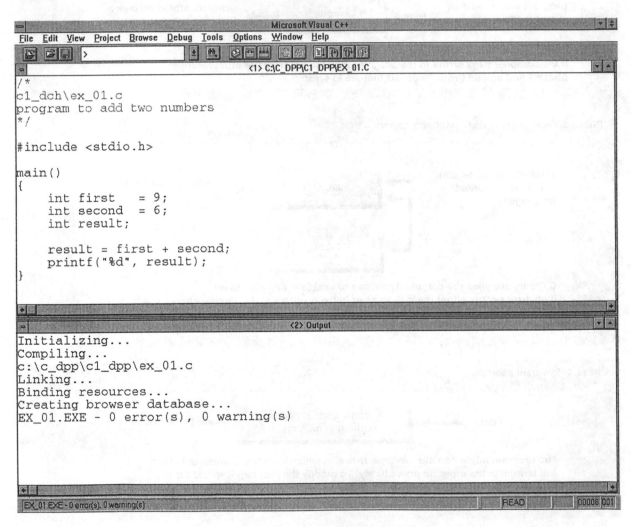

figure 1.11 Microsoft Visual C++ Environment

There exists a higher layer of software known as an operating system, above the user's program, that controls the computer system. The role of an operating system covers many areas, however, one important aspect is that of supervising the execution of user written programs. Such supervision includes the premature termination of user programs in the event of attempting to execute illegal operations, such as dividing a number by zero or reading from a data file that has not been opened.

Two popular operating systems are MSDOS and UNIX. Figure 1.11 refer to the implementation of a C program in a Microsoft Visual C++ Windows 3.1 environment under MSDOS. C program implementation under UNIX is covered in appendix C.

1.9 Summary

☐ Programming consists of designing an algorithm, coding the algorithm into a computer program, testing the computer program and finally supplying sufficient documentation with the program so that it can easily be understood and modified by others.

☐ Data is input to the computer and processed under the direction of a program to produce results at an output unit.

☐ A digital computer consists of input, output and secondary storage units that are peripheral to the central processing unit and main memory.

☐ Common input units are a keyboard and a mouse and common output units are a monitor and printer.

☐ Secondary storage media span the range of fixed hard disks, removable floppy disks, removable magneto/ optical disks and removable tapes.

☐ Secondary storage devices may also be considered as input/ output devices since many permit both reading and writing.

☐ Computers can either be stand-alone devices or be part of a computer network containing many workstations.

☐ The advantage of a network is that software and hardware can be shared between the network users and processing power distributed over the network.

☐ There are three levels of computer language, high (for example C), low (assembly level language) and machine code (binary representation).

☐ Programs written in a high-level language, such as C, must be compiled, linked and loaded into memory before they can be executed by a computer.

☐ The supervision of the running of a program on a computer is one of the tasks of the operating system.

1.10 Questions - *answers begin on page 461*

1. What are the activities associated with programming?

2. What are the five major hardware units of a digital computer system, and how are these represented in a typical personal computer? Discuss the relative capacities of the storage media.

3. List three input units and three output units. What are the most common input and output units in a C development environment ?

4. What are the major advantages of networking computers together?

5. Why is it necessary to translate a C program into a machine-oriented language ?

6. List the four phases that are necessary before a C program can be executed by a computer.

7. What is meant by program portability ? Why are low level languages not considered to be portable ?

Chapter 2
Data

This chapter contains information about data found in everyday life. It explores the different characteristics of data such as type, size and format, and introduces the reader to four data types *integer*, *real*, *character* and *string*. The methods of declaring these types of data and documenting their meaning in a C program is also examined. By the end of the chapter the reader should have an understanding of the following topics.

- ☐ How to recognise data and classify it by type.

- ☐ The format of data.

- ☐ How data is stored inside the memory of a computer.

- ☐ The identification of variables and constants.

- ☐ How to represent variables and constants in a program.

2.1 What is data?

The reader's first introduction to the meaning of data in this book was given in the first chapter, where data was defined as the name given to facts represented by characters and quantities. The word data has found its way into everyday language. The Concise Oxford Dictionary definition of data is "..1 known facts or things used as a basis for inference or reckoning. 2 quantities or characters operated on by a computer etc..". Put another way, data can be numbers and/ or groups of characters that represent facts. There are plenty of examples of data to be found. Consider the diagram of a road sign, figure 2.1, that you might come across when travelling through Wiltshire. The road sign contains the names of towns/ cities and distances to travel. A group of characters represents a name, for example Oxford, and a positive whole number represents a distance, for example 40.

Marlborough	**15**
Swindon	**25**
Oxford	**40**

figure 2.1 a road sign

Figure 2.2 illustrates a thermometer to indicate the temperature outside. The scale on the thermometer is graduated in both degrees Fahrenheit and degrees Celsius. From the illustration it is clear that the temperature is cold outside, and can be either $+14^\circ$ Fahrenheit or -10° Celsius. The temperature is represented by either a positive or a negative whole number.

Figure 2.3 illustrates a menu. The names of the items of food or drink are represented by groups of characters and the price of each item by a number containing a decimal fraction.

$^\circ$F	$^\circ$C
68	20
50	10
32	0
14	-10
-4	-20

Ben's Breakfast Bar
M E N U

Eggs - scrambled or fried	**£ 1.50**
Bacon	**£ 2.00**
Sausages	**£ 1.75**
Black Pudding	**£ 0.95**
Tomatoes	**£ 1.00**
Baked Beans	**£ 0.50**
Toast	**£ 0.75**
Cerial	**£ 1.00**
Tea or Coffee	**£ 0.75**
Hot Chocolate	**£ 0.95**

all prices exclude VAT

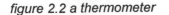

figure 2.2 a thermometer   *figure 2.3 a menu*

Figure 2.4 illustrates part of a railway timetable. The names of the stations are represented by groups of characters, the departure or arrival of a train by a single character **d** or **a**, and the times of departure or arrival of a train by numbers that represent the time of day.

Railway Timetable						
Crewe	d			0639	0724	
Macclesfield	d			0641		0741
Stoke-on-Trent	d			0701	0710	0801
Stafford	d			0721	0747	0822
Wolverhampton	d		0643	0740	0807	0840
Birmingham New Street	a	0323	0702	0803	0830	0903
Birmingham New Street	d	0427	0706	0806		0906
Birmingham International	d		0716	0816	0858	0916
Coventry	d		0729	0829	0909	0929
Leamington Spa	a		0743	0843		0943
Banbury	a		0803	0903		1003
Oxford	a	0540	0826	0924		1024

figure 2.4

Figure 2.5 illustrates a sales receipt. The name of the cashier is represented by a group of characters, the date is represented by whole numbers indicating day, month and year and the time of day by whole numbers for hours and minutes. The name of the purchases are represented by groups of characters and the quantities purchased by whole number. The unit cost, purchase price, sub total, value added tax, total, cash amount and change are all represented by numbers containing decimal fractions.

DIY SUPERSTORE		
JEANNETTE		14/10/94
		15:35
SALES RECEIPT		
paint	1 @ 8.99	8.99
brush	2 @ 2.49	4.98
SUB TOTAL AMOUNT		13.97
VAT		2.44
TOTAL AMOUNT		16.41
CASH AMOUNT:		20.00
CHANGE:		3.59
THANK YOU FOR YOUR CUSTOM		

figure 2.5

From these few examples it should be evident that data can take the form of whole numbers, such as distances, temperatures, hours, minutes, day, month and year; numbers with a decimal fraction, such as amounts of money; single characters such as **a** or **d** as codes for arrive or depart respectively; and finally groups of characters such as names of towns and cities, items of food and drink on a menu, names of people and names of purchases.

2.2 Types of data

Data can be classified into at least four types - *integer* (positive or negative whole numbers), *real* (numbers with a decimal fraction), *char* (a single character) and *string* (a group of characters). For example, in figure 2.1 the name of the city Oxford is composed from a group of characters and is known as a *string* data type. The distance to Oxford of 40 miles, is a whole number and is known as an *integer* data type.

The thermometer shown in figure 2.2 contains two different temperature scales. Both temperature scales use positive and negative numbers. If you assume that the accuracy of the scale is to a whole number of degrees, then the positive or negative whole numbers are of *integer* data type.

The menu shown in figure 2.3 contains a mixture of data, the names of items of food and drink are of the data type *string*; the prices contain a decimal fraction and are numbers of data type *real*.

The railway timetable shown in figure 2.4 contains the names of the towns and cities and are of data type *string*. The times are represented as whole numbers in a 24-hour clock format and are represented by *integers*. A single character **a** or **d** is used to denote arrive or depart respectively and is of data type *char*.

The sales receipt shown in figure 2.5 contains the name of the sales assistant and the names of the purchases and is of data type *string*. The date expressed as day, month and year are *integers*, and the time in hours and minutes are represented by *integers*. The quantity of goods purchased is a whole number and is of data type *integer*. The unit cost and purchase price of the goods, sub total, value added tax, total, cash amount and change are all numbers of data type *real*.

2.3 Data representation

The main memory of a computer is made up from many millions of storage cells called bytes. Each byte has a unique address in the memory of the computer and is capable of storing eight bits (binary digits) worth of information.

Integer Numbers

Integers are stored within a fixed number of bytes. A common size for integer storage is two bytes, which gives the range of integers that can be stored as -32768 to +32767. Any integer that lies outside this range cannot be stored in the memory of the computer as a two-byte integer. A representation of the integer 1225 in two bytes is given in figure 2.6.

This is known as a pure binary representation of the number. Each bit represents a multiple of 2, with the rightmost bit of byte 0 having a value of 1, the next bit a value of 2, the next a value of 4, the next a value of 8 and so on. Summing only those bits that are set at 1 results in $2^0+2^3+2^6+2^7+2^{10}$ =1+8+64+128+1024=1225. Notice that the leftmost bit of byte 1 is reserved as the sign bit. A sign bit set at 0 represents a positive number, and set at 1 represents a negative number. Negative numbers are stored using a 2's complement representation. For example the number -1225 will be stored using the following bit pattern.

+1225   = 00000100 11001001
1's complement   = 11111011 00110110 interchange 1's and 0's
2's complement   = 11111011 00110111 add 1 to rightmost bit

The result of this bit manipulation is a two byte representation of -1225. Notice that the sign bit has been automatically set to 1.

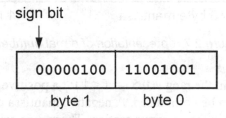

figure 2.6 a representation of an integer

In C the type *integer* can be described in three different formats:

> **short int**
> **int**
> **long int**

where each description may be qualified as being **unsigned** since all integers, by default are assumed to be signed. The range of integer values that can be stored in the memory of a computer is machine dependent. In a byte organised machine, such as a PC compatible computer, a typical range of values for the integers might be as follows:

short int (2 bytes)	-32768 .. +32767
unsigned short int (2 bytes)	0 .. 65535
int (2 bytes)	-32768 .. +32767
unsigned int (2 bytes)	0 .. +65535
long int (4 bytes)	-2147483648 .. + 2147483647
unsigned long int (4 bytes)	0 .. +4294967295

Notice there is no distinction in the range of short integers and integers on a PC compatible, however, distinctions may exist for other computer architectures.

Real Numbers

Real numbers are stored within a fixed number of bytes using a floating point representation of the number. The number of bytes can vary between four, eight and ten, however, four is common. Real numbers have two parts, a mantissa (the fractional part) and an exponent (the power to which the base of the number must be raised in order to give the correct value of the number when multiplied by the mantissa). For example 437.875 can be re-written as 0.437875×10^3, where 0.437875 is the mantissa, and 3 is the exponent.

The number +437.875 has a binary equivalent of 110110101.111 and when the binary point is floated to the left and exponent adjusted the number is represented as $0.110110101111 \times 2^9$. The organisation of this number in a floating point representation is shown in figure 2.7.

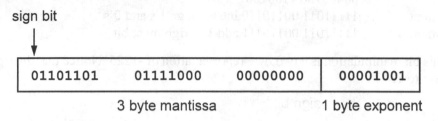

figure 2.7 representation of a real number

The mantissa (f) must always lie in the ranges $0.5 <= f < 1$ for a positive fraction and $-1 <= f < -0.5$ for a negative fraction. It is then said to be normalised. A negative mantissa can be represented using the 2's complement technique described in the previous section. There are various techniques for representing the exponent, however, a pure binary representation is shown here.

A four byte organisation of a real number will give a maximum value of 3.4×10^{38} and a minimum value of 1.17×10^{-38} with an accuracy of 6 decimal digits. The majority of decimal fractions do not convert exactly into binary fractions, therefore, the representation of a real number is not always accurate. The more storage space that is allocated to the mantissa, results in the real number being represented to a greater precision. When more storage space is allocated to the exponent the range of real numbers that can be stored will increase.

When the result of a computation is too large to be represented, the number has overflowed storage. Conversely, when a result is too small to be represented the number has underflowed storage and the computer will probably return the result as zero.

In C the type *real* can be described in three different formats:

float
double
long double

where float represents a single-precision floating-point number, double represents a double-precision floating-point number and long double represents an extended-precision floating-point number. The precision and approximate maximum and minimum values that can be represented by these three real types is machine dependent. Typical values for real numbers stored in a PC compatible computer are as follows.

float (4 bytes) precision 6 decimal digits, maximum value 3.4×10^{38} smallest value 1.17×10^{-38}
double (8 bytes) precision 15 decimal digits, maximum 1.79×10^{308} smallest value 2.22×10^{-308}
long double (10 bytes) precision 19 decimal digits, maximum 1.18×10^{4932} smallest value 3.36×10^{-4932}

Characters

A character is stored in a single byte of memory using a 7-bit binary code. For example, the character 'A' is coded 65, 'B' is coded 66, 'C' is coded 67 etc - see figure 2.8 The list of ASCII (American Standard Code for Information Interchange) character codes is given in figure 2.10. Notice that characters are not confined to letters of the alphabet, but can be digits and other symbols.

character	ASCII code	binary representation
A	65	01000001
B	66	01000010
C	67	01000011

figure 2.8 representation of characters

In C the type declaration **char** is used to denote a single character taken from the ASCII character set. A character is stored using its ASCII code, which is an integer in the range 0..127. ANSI C does not specify whether char is signed or unsigned.

Strings

The type declaration *string* is **not** implicitly defined as part of the C language. A *string* is stored as a set of characters within consecutive memory locations. Each character is stored as the binary representation of its ASCII code and occupies one byte of memory. The end of the string is denoted by the *null* character, which is automatically appended provided enough storage space has been allocated to store the string. Figure 2.9 illustrates how characters of a string are stored across consecutive memory locations.

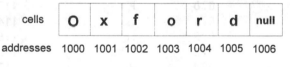

cells: O x f o r d null

addresses: 1000 1001 1002 1003 1004 1005 1006

figure 2.9

2.4 Syntax notation

As a means of understanding and expressing the format and structure of a computer language it is necessary to capture the components of a language using a notation. Within this and further chapters the notation used in the ANSI/ISO 9899-1990 Standard to define the syntax of ANSI C will be used. A complete description of the syntax of ANSI C can be found in appendix A.

Tokens are the simplest textual elements of C, and can be classified into *keywords*, *identifiers*, *constants*, *string-literals*, *operators* and *punctuators*. A formal notation can be used to describe how sequences of tokens are assembled to form programs. This notation consists of productions involving syntactical constructs and tokens. Each construct can have several productions associated with it, each expressing a possible expansion of the construct. For example a decimal constant might be defined as:

Code	Character	Code	Character	Code	Character
000	NUL	043	+	086	V
001	SOH	044	,	087	W
002	STX	045	-	088	X
003	ETX	046	.	089	Y
004	EOT	047	/	090	Z
005	ENQ	048	0	091	[
006	ACK	049	1	092	\
007	BEL	050	2	093	]
008	BS	051	3	094	^
009	HT	052	4	095	_
010	LF	053	5	096	`
011	VT	054	6	097	a
012	FF	055	7	098	b
013	CR	056	8	099	c
014	SO	057	9	100	d
015	SI	058	:	101	e
016	DLE	059	;	102	f
017	DC1	060	<	103	g
018	DC2	061	=	104	h
019	DC3	062	>	105	i
020	DC4	063	?	106	j
021	NAK	064	@	107	k
022	STN	065	A	108	l
023	ETB	066	B	109	m
024	AN	067	C	110	n
025	EM	068	D	111	o
026	SUB	069	E	112	p
027	ESC	070	F	113	q
028	FS	071	G	114	r
029	GS	072	H	115	s
030	RS	073	I	116	t
031	US	074	J	117	u
032	space	075	K	118	v
033	!	076	L	119	w
034	"	077	M	120	x
035	#	078	N	121	y
036	$	079	O	122	z
037	%	080	P	123	{
038	&	081	Q	124		
039	'	082	R	125	}
040	(	083	S	126	~
041	)	084	T	127	del
042	*	085	U		

figure 2.10 ASCII codes for characters

decimal-constant:
>> *nonzero-digit*
>> *decimal-constant   digit*

nonzero-digit: one of
>> **1   2   3   4   5   6   7   8   9**

digit: one of
>> **0   1   2   3   4   5   6   7   8   9**

where non-terminal syntactic categories are indicated by *italic* type; terminal symbols - literal words and character set members are indicated by **bold** type; a colon **:** following a non-terminal symbol introduces its definition; an optional symbol is indicated by the subscript " opt "; alternative definitions are listed on separate lines, except when prefaced by the words "one of ".

A floating constant can be represented as follows.

floating-constant:
>> *fractional-constant exponential-part opt floating-suffix opt*
>> *digit-sequence exponent-part floating-suffix opt*

fractional-constant:
>> *digit-sequence opt . digit-sequence*
>> *digit-sequence .*

exponent-part:
>> **e** *sign opt digit-sequence*
>> **E** *sign opt digit-sequence*

digit-sequence:
>> *digit*
>> *digit-sequence digit*

sign: one of
>> **+   -**

floating-suffix: one of
>> **f   l   F   L**

2.5 Variables

The main memory of a computer is made up from many millions of storage cells, each with a unique numeric address, as illustrated in figure 2.11.

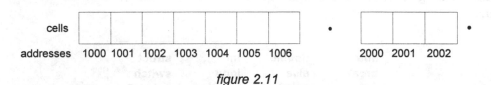

figure 2.11

Data may be thought of, as occupying areas of the computer's memory, in the same way as people occupy houses in a street. To distinguish different families in different houses we could use either the surname of the family or the number of the house. To distinguish data in different areas of memory we could give the data a name or use the numeric memory address where the data is stored.

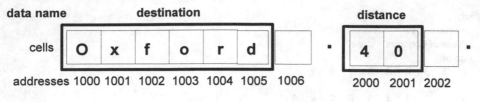

figure 2.12

In C it is much easier to refer to data by name and let the computer do the work of finding out where in memory the data is stored. Figure 2.12 illustrates how data can be stored across the storage cells and accessed by the names given to the groups of cells and not the addresses of the cells.

When a program that uses these data names is executed, the instructions may change the contents of some, if not all, of the groups of bytes. Because of this change or variation in the data the data names are known as *variables*. A programmer is required to compose many different types of names in a program, of which variables are just one type. The collective name given to all these names is identifiers. C uses the following rules for the composition of identifiers.

An identifier may contain combinations of letters of the alphabet (both upper case A-Z and lower case a-z), an underscore character _ and decimal digits, provided the identifier begins with a non-digit (either a letter or an underscore character). C distinguishes between the use of upper and lower case letters in an identifier. Identifiers can normally be of any length, however, the particular implementation of C being used may only recognise up to a certain number of characters. An identifier must not be the same as C keywords listed in figure 2.13. The syntax of an identifier can be re-expressed as:

identifier:

      nondigit
      identifier   nondigit
      identifier   digit

A programmer should always compose identifiers so they convey meaning. The identifiers *name, street, town, postcode* imply the meaning of the data that they represent, rather than using the non-descriptive identifiers *N, S, T* and *P*. When an identifier is constructed from more than one word, each word should either begin with an upper case letter, or be separated by an underscore, so that the identifier can be clearly read and its meaning understood. Examples of legal identifiers are *SubTotal, sales_tax, unit_cost, rate_of_pay*.

auto	double	int	struct
break	else	long	switch
case	enum	register	typedef
char	extern	return	union
const	float	short	unsigned
continue	for	signed	void
default	goto	sizeof	volatile
do	if	static	while

figure 2.13 Keywords

2.6 Variable declaration

When investigating the data that is to be used in a computer program it can be helpful to document this information on a data analysis form as shown in figure 2.14. The form has been completed from the study of the five everyday situations presented earlier in the chapter. A description of the data helps to provide a clearer meaning to the identifiers being used. The data type is established and approximate sizes of data recorded. Where sizes of data cannot be predicted the maximum size for the data type has been recorded.

A C program can be divided into two areas, data declarations and instructions. The data declarations must appear before the instructions since they describe the type of data used by the instructions.

If the values of the data in the storage cells can be changed by the instructions in a computer program, then the values of the data vary, and the data identifiers are known as *variable names*. A simplified syntax of a variable declaration follows. For a more detailed syntax see appendix A.

variable-declaration:
                type-specifier declarator-list ;
declarator-list:
                identifier
                declarator-list , *identifier*

For example the data declarations for the road sign shown in figure 2.1 might be:

```
char    destination[12];
int     distance;
```

Since the name of a destination was defined as a *string* it is necessary to declare it as type **char** having twelve consecutive memory locations set aside for storing the largest string. The string "Marlborough" has eleven characters but it is necessary to include a twelfth character for storing the end of string *null* terminator. This is automatically appended to the string, provided enough memory has been designated, hence the declaration **char destination[12]**.

Data declarations for the thermometer and the menu shown in figure 2.2 and 2.3 respectively might be:

```
int     temperature;
```

and

```
char    menu_item[26];
float   price;
```

The largest string in menu_item was "Eggs - scrambled or fried" which contains twenty-five characters including spaces, hence the declaration **char menu_item[26]**. Notice that the declaration of the name of the breakfast bar, the title and the last line of the menu and the currency sign have nor been included since these are not variable quantities. Only the items of food and drink, and the price will vary according to the data being used.

The data declarations for the railway timetable shown in figure 2.4 might be:

```
char    town[25];
int     time;
char    a_d_code;
```

DATA ANALYSIS FORM			
description	identifier	data type	size
town/ city	destination	char-string	<12 chars
distance to town in miles	distance	int	<=40
temperature either in F or C	temperature	int	<=68
item from menu	menu_item	char	<=26
price of item	price	float	<=2.00
name of town	town	char-string	<25
arrival or departure code	a_d_code	char	1 char
time of day - 24 hour format	time	int	<=2359
name of cashier	name	char-string	<10 chars
date - day	day	int	<=31
date - month	month	int	<=12
date - year	year	int	<=99
time - hours	hours	int	<=23
time - minutes	minutes	int	<=59
description of each purchase	description	char-string	<6 chars
quantity of each purchase	quantity	int	<=32767
unit cost of each purchase	unit_cost	float	$<10^{38}$
price of each purchase	price	float	$<10^{38}$
sub-total amount	sub_total	float	$<10^{38}$
value added tax	tax	float	$<10^{38}$
total amount	total	float	$<10^{38}$
cash amount	cash	float	$<10^{38}$
change given	change	float	$<10^{38}$

figure 2.14

Clearly the name of the town/ city and departure or arrival time does vary according to the data being used and are therefore variables. However, the heading does not change and is not declared as a variable.

The data declarations for the sales receipt shown in figure 2.5 follow. Once again information that does not change, for example the name of the store and informative text have not be declared as variables.

```
char     name[10];
int      day;
int      month;
int      year;
int      hours;
int      minutes;
char     description[6];
int      quantity;
float    unit_cost;
```

26

```
float   price;
float   sub_total;
float   tax;
float   total;
float   cash;
float   change;
```

To reduce the number of lines used in declaring variables it is permissible to group the declarations according to their data types. For example the previous list of declarations can be re-written on fewer lines as follows:

```
char    name[10], description[6];
int     day, month, year, hours, minutes, quantity;
float   unit_cost, price, sub_total, tax, total, cash, change;
```

When defining the lengths of strings it is only necessary to allocate enough memory to store the largest string plus the terminating *null* character. The reader might adopt the habit of allocating the same arbitrary amount of memory to every string. In the example relating to the sales receipt both the name of the cashier and the name of a product might have been allocated an arbitrary ten characters.

Variables can be initialised at the point of declaration. If "JEANNETTE" was the only cashier in the store it is permissible to declare:

```
char    name[10] = "JEANNETTE";
```

or

```
char    name[] = "JEANNETTE";
```

In this latter case it was not necessary to specify the amount of memory to allocate to the string since the number of characters found in the string "JEANNETTE" can be calculated at the time of compilation.

2.7 Constants

In many programs there will be data values that do not change, but remain constant during the running of the program. In the previous example if the name of the cashier was never to change during the running of the program then it could be declared as a constant. Other examples of items of data that remain constant could be the rate of value added tax at 17.5%, mathematical PI at 3.14159, and the Earth's gravitational constant (g) at the surface 9.80665 ms^{-2}. Such constants can be declared in a C program as :

```
const   char    name[]     = "JEANNETTE";
const   float   VAT        = 0.175;
const   float   PI         = 3.14159;
const   float   g          = 9.80065;
```

The syntax for a decimal constant has already been given in section 2.4 under the heading of syntax notation. However, a decimal constant is part of an integer constant described by the following syntax.

integer-constant:
        decimal-constant   integer-suffix opt
        octal-constant integer-suffix opt
        hexadecimal-constant   integer-suffix opt

integer-suffix:
        unsigned-suffix   long-suffix opt
        long-suffix   unsigned-suffix opt

unsigned-suffix: one of
     u U

long-suffix: one of
     l L

Integer constants can be represented in base 10, decimal; base 8, octal; or base 16, hexadecimal. Figure 2.15 illustrates the numbers 0 through 15 expressed as octal, decimal and hexadecimal numbers.

Octal	Decimal	Hexadecimal
0	0	0
1	1	1
2	2	2
3	3	3
4	4	4
5	5	5
6	6	6
7	7	7
10	8	8
11	9	9
12	10	A
13	11	B
14	12	C
15	13	D
16	14	E
17	15	F

figure 2.15

Decimal integer constants contain the digits 0..9 and must **not** begin with 0 (zero), for example 237, 18567, -789.

Octal integer constants contain the digits 0..7 and **must** begin with 0 (zero), for example 017, 05643, 0234. Each digit represents the base 8 raised to a power, with the least significant digit representing 8^0, the next most significant digit 8^1, the next most significant digit 8^2, and so on. For example the octal number 05643 is $5 \times 8^3 + 6 \times 8^2 + 4 \times 8^1 + 3 \times 8^0$ which is equivalent to 2979 in decimal.

Hexadecimal integer constants contain the digits 0..9 and the letters a..f, or A..F and **must** begin with 0x, for example 0x12FF, 0x56ABC, 0x89A345. Each digit represents the base 16 raised to a power, with the least significant digit representing 16^0, the next most significant digit 16^1, the next most significant 16^2, and so on. For example the hexadecimal number 0x12FF is $1\times16^3+2\times16^2+15\times16^1+15\times16^0$ which is equivalent to 4863 in decimal.

Integer constants can be defined as being long, if the letter L or l appears after the number, for example 12345678L.

Integer constants can be defined as being unsigned if the letter U or u appears after the number, for example 43456U.

Since integer constants can be both unsigned and long, both suffixes may appear after the number, for example 67543679UL.

A floating constant can be represented in either decimal notation or in scientific notation using the letter E or e to denote the exponent, for example 1234.56, 0.7865E+02.

Floating constants are, by default, stored in double precision. If either single precision or long double precision is required then either the letters f or l or (F or L) respectively, should appear after the number, for example 6.784f, 67812.87L, 0.456321E+05L.

A simplified syntax of a character constant is defined below. See appendix A for more detail.

character-constant:
>   ' *c-char-sequence* '

c-char-sequence:
>   *c-char*
>   *c-char-sequence c-char*

c-char:
>   any member of the source character set except the single quote, backslash or new-line character

Character constants are enclosed between single apostrophes, for example 'A', 'a', '5', and can be declared as follows:

```
const   char    letter = 'A';
```

Similarly a simplified syntax for a string literal is given below. See appendix A for more detail.

string-literal:
>   " *s-char-sequence opt* "

s-char-sequence:
>   *s-char*
>   *s-char-sequence   s-char*

s-char:
>   any member of the source character set except the double quote, backslash or new-line character

String literals (constants) are enclosed between double quotes, for example "abracadabra", and the compiler marks the end of the string with a *null* character. A constant string can be declared as follows:

```
const   char    magic[12] = "abracadabra";
```

Although the string "abracadabra" contains eleven characters it has been necessary to declare storage space for twelve characters to accommodate the end of string *null* character.

2.8 Summary

☐ Data is composed from numbers and characters that represent facts.

☐ There are at least four implicit data types in C, **int**, **float**, **double** and **char**.

☐ The data type *string* is not implicitly defined in the language and must be explicitly defined in a program as a variable or constant of type **char**, qualified by the amount of storage space to set aside for all the characters in the string plus the terminating *null* character.

☐ The size of data that can be stored in a computer's memory is limited by its type, and must fit between pre- defined ranges.

☐ Data must conform to set formats.

☐ A formal notation is used to denote the syntax or grammar of statements in a computer language.

☐ Data stored in the memory of a computer can be referenced through a data name invented by the programmer.

☐ Data names must conform to the rules for identifiers.

☐ All the variables used in a C program must be declared, before they can be used by instructions contained in the program.

☐ Variable data declaration specifies the type of data followed by the name of the data.

☐ Variables may be initialised at the point of declaration.

☐ Data values that do not change during the running of a program may be declared as constants.

2.9 Questions - *answers begin on page 462*

1. From the illustrations in figures 2.16, 2.17 and 2.18 of items found in everyday life, discuss what you consider to be data, and show how the data is classified by type as variables declared in a C program.

used cars for sale	
Astra 1.4 L, 5 door, 91 (H), blue	£6750
BMW 316, 2 door, 87 (E), black	£6590
BMW 320i SE, 4 door, 88 (E), blue	£7990
Escort 1.6 Ghia Estate, 91 (J), silver	£9750
Fiesta 1.1 LX, 5 door, 91 (H), white	£6490
Granada 2.0 LXI, 90 (H), white	£6390
Jaguar 2.9 Auto, ABS, air con, 90 (G), grey	£12990
Nissan Sunny 1.6 GSX, 4 door, 89 (F), white	£5690
Sierra Sapphire 1.8 LX, 89 (F), white	£4990
Toyota Corolla, 89 (G), silver	£3990
VW Golf 1.6, 5 door, 87 (E), blue	£4790

figure 2.16

World forecasts

City	Today
Acapulco	90/79 s
Athens	79/59 pc
Bangkok	90/78 pc
Beijing	62/38 pc
Berlin	63/51 r
Bermuda	81/74 pc
Budapest	72/52 pc
Buenos Aries	83/62 pc
Cairo	89/ 68 pc
Dublin	53/ 39 c
Frankfurt	63/56 sh
Hong Kong	84/74 s

figure 2.17

Note

The numbers refer to high and low temperatures in degrees Fahrenheit and the abbreviations to the following weather conditions.

s sunny
pc partial cloud
r rain
c cloud
sh showers

XYZ Bank plc

Mr A.N.Other

Market Place, Anytown, B1 6PT

Statement of Account

1993 sheet 90 Account No. 5678910	DEBIT	CREDIT	BALANCE Credit C Debit D
JAN18 BALANCE BROUGHT FORWARD			550.50 C
JAN21 cheque 100642	55.86		494.64 C
JAN26 cheque 100644	10.08		484.56 C
JAN27 SWEET HOME BUILDING SOCIETY	280.14		204.42 C
JAN28 cheque 100643	51.69		152.73 C
FEB 1 SALARY		650.00	802.73 C
FEB 4 cheque 100645	38.11		764.62 C
FEB 8 GAS COMPANY	32.00		732.62 C
FEB 9 ELECTRICITY COMPANY	22.00		710.62 C
FEB10 cheque 100647	10.08		700.54 C
FEB11 cheque 100648	41.96		658.58 C
FEB15 SUNDRIES		15.00	673.58 C
FEB18 BALANCE CARRIED FORWARD			673.58 C

figure 2.18

2. Identify the illegal variable names in the following list of identifiers. State why you think the names are illegal.

(a). PriceOfBricks (b). net-pay   (c). X1   (d). cost of paper
(e). INTEGER   (f). ?X?Y   (g). 1856AD   (h) float

3. Describe the types of the following items of data.

(a). "Lexington"   (b). ';'   (c). +156   (d). 2147483647
(e). 247.9   (f). 0.732E+01L   (g). 0173   (h). 0xAB0
(i). 2179U   (j). 23.96f

4. Using figure 2.10 what are the ASCII codes of the following characters? Derive an 8-bit binary representation of the characters.

(a). A   (b). M   (c). *   (d). a
(e). m   (f). NUL   (g). 9

5. Write the following numbers using the E notation for real numbers, such that there is only one non-zero digit to the left of the decimal point.

(a). -874.458   (b). +0.00123456   (c). 123456789.0

6. State, giving reasons, why the following numbers cannot be stored as numbers of type float within the ranges defined in this chapter. Suggest how you would change the data type so as to accommodate the numbers in the memory of the computer.

(a). 30.16E+38   (b). 1234567890.1234567   (c). -0.000456E-39

7. How would the integer +7384 be expressed in a pure binary form using 16 bits? What is the 16 bit representation of -7384 using 2's complement notation?

8. If a computer stored real numbers to an accuracy of 6 decimal digits and a signed 2 digit exponent in the range -38 to +38, indicate and comment where necessary, how the following numbers can be represented, assuming the magnitude of the mantissa is less than 1.

(a). 3.7948×10^{16}.   (b). -2.6394782   (c). 739.4621348
(d). $-17694.327 \times 10^{35}$ (e). $0.000000471 \times 10^{-34}$

9. Convert the following numbers into decimal values.

(a) 0234   (b) 0x56ABC   (c) 10110111(binary in two's complement format)

10. Using the syntax notation described in this chapter, derive productions that describe octal and hexadecimal numeric constants.

Chapter 3
Input and Output

This chapter looks at the routines available for the input of data from a keyboard into computer memory and the output of information to a screen from computer memory. In particular the following points are covered.

- ☐ The standard library.

- ☐ The limits for integers and reals.

- ☐ *Printf* routine to provide formatted output to a screen.

- ☐ *Scanf* routine to read data entered at a keyboard.

- ☐ The input and output of strings using the routines *gets* and *puts*.

- ☐ The input and output of characters using the routines *getchar* and *putchar*.

- ☐ The format of a C program.

3.1 Standard library

The ANSI C standard library is rich in pre-written routines that assist the programmer in developing software. The standard library is divided into fifteen parts, with each part described by a header. When routines from the standard library are to be used in a program, the programmer must ensure that the appropriate header name is included at the beginning of the program. The following list is a summary of the names of the headers and their applicability. Full details can be found in Appendix B.

```
<assert.h>       diagnostics
<ctype.h>        character handling
<errno.h>        errors
<float.h>        characteristics of floating types
<limits.h>       sizes of integral types
<locale.h>       localisation
<math.h>         mathematics
<setjmp.h>       non-local jumps
<signal.h>       signal handling
<stdarg.h>       variable arguments
<stddef.h>       common definitions
<stdio.h>        input/ output
<stdlib.h>       general utilities
<string.h>       string handling
<time.h>         date and time
```

The range of integer values that can be stored in the memory of a computer is machine dependent. The standard library contains a header file **<limits.h>** that contains the maximum and minimum values for each integer type for the computer system being used. The Jensen & Partners TopSpeed C compiler is designed for PC compatible computers and the contents of the <limits.h> header file reflects the fact that the smallest addressable memory cell will be 8 bits. A partial listing from the <limits.h> file follows.

```
#define SCHAR_MAX 127
#define SCHAR_MIN (-128)
#define UCHAR_MAX 255

#define SHRT_MAX 32767
#define SHRT_MIN (-32767-1)
#define USHRT_MAX 65535U

#define INT_MAX 32767
#define INT_MIN (-32767-1)
#define UINT_MAX 0xFFFFU

#define LONG_MAX 2147483647L
#define LONG_MIN (-2147483647L-1)
#define ULONG_MAX 4294967295UL
```

.
.

Prior to the compilation of a C program, a preprocessor is automatically invoked by the system. During preprocessing, the C program source text is modified according to the preprocessing directives that are embedded in the program. There are six categories of preprocessor directive of which **#define** is just one category. If the header <limits.h> is included in a program then any reference in the program to, say, INT_MAX would be replaced with the machine dependent value of 32767.

The range and precision for real numbers is given in the header file <float.h>. A partial listing of the Jensen & Partners TopSpeed C header file <float.h> follows.

```
#define FLT_DIG 6 /* number of decimal digits of precision */
#define FLT_GUARD 0
#define FLT_MANT_DIG 24 /* number of bits in mantissa */
#define FLT_MAX_10_EXP 38 /* maximum decimal exponent */
#define FLT_MAX_EXP 128 /* maximum binary exponent */
#define FLT_MIN_10_EXP -37 /* minimum decimal exponent */
#define FLT_MIN_EXP -125 /* minimum binary exponent */
#define FLT_NORMALIZE 0
#define FLT_RADIX 2 /* exponent radix */
#define FLT_ROUNDS 1 /* addition rounding chops */
#define FLT_EPSILON 1.192092896e-07 /* smallest such that 1.0+FLT_EPSILON != 1.0 */
#define FLT_MAX 3.402823466e+38 /* maximum value */
#define FLT_MIN 1.175494351e-38 /* minimum positive value */

#define DBL_DIG 15 /* number of decimal digits of precision */
#define DBL_MANT_DIG 53 /* number of bits in mantissa */
#define DBL_MAX_10_EXP 308 /* maximum decimal exponent */
#define DBL_MAX_EXP 1024 /* maximum binary exponent */
#define DBL_MIN_10_EXP -307 /* minimum decimal exponent */
#define DBL_MIN_EXP -1021 /* minimum binary exponent */
#define DBL_RADIX 2 /* exponent radix */
#define DBL_ROUNDS 1 /* addition rounding */
#define DBL_EPSILON 2.2204460492503131e-016 /* 1.0+DBL_EPSILON != 1.0 */
#define DBL_MAX 1.7976931348623151e+308 /* maximum value */
#define DBL_MIN 2.2250738585072014e-308 /* minimum positive value */

#define LDBL_DIG 19 /* number of decimal digits of precision */
#define LDBL_EPSILON 5.4210108624275221706e-20 /* smallest 1.0+LDBL_EPSILON != 1.0 */
#define LDBL_MANT_DIG 64 /* number of bits in mantissa */
#define LDBL_MAX 1.189731495357231765e+4932L /* maximum value */
#define LDBL_MAX_10_EXP 4932 /* maximum decimal exponent */
#define LDBL_MAX_EXP 16384 /* maximum binary exponent */
#define LDBL_MIN 3.36210314311120935063e-4932L /* minimum positive value */
#define LDBL_MIN_10_EXP (-4931) /* minimum decimal exponent */
#define LDBL_MIN_EXP (-16381) /* minimum binary exponent */
#define LDBL_RADIX 2 /* exponent radix */
#define LDBL_ROUNDS DBL_ROUNDS /* addition rounding */
```

Similarly if the header **<float.h>** was included in a program then any reference in the program to, say, FLT_MAX would be replaced by the preprocessor with the machine dependent value of 3.402823466e+38.

The reader may notice that the header file <float.h> contains text between the opening delimiter character-pair /* and the closing delimiter character-pair */. Such text is treated as a comment. Comments can be listed on the same line as language statements, or be listed on one or more lines. Comments cannot be nested one within another. The compiler ignores comments and replaces each comment by a single space character. Comments should be used throughout a program as an aid to documenting a program.

*Warning! If you forget to terminate a comment with a closing */, the compiler will ignore the lines in the program up to the next occurrence of a closing delimiter.*

In common with such languages as Ada and Modula-2, C contains no statements in the definition of the language for the input and output of data. These languages are supplied with libraries that contain routines for input and output as well as other routines. Whenever data is to be input or results output, the most appropriate routines from the libraries should be used.

The header **<stdio.h>** contains routines that permit input of data at a keyboard and output of information to a screen. The most common of these routines will now be described.

3.2 Output

The routine *printf* is found in the standard library header file <stdio.h>. The purpose of this function is to display in a formatted form, numbers and characters on a standard output device, which is normally the screen of a monitor.

The format of printf is:

```
printf("control string", arg1, arg2, ... argn);
```

where the control string inside the quotes is the actual output, and the arguments help to define the output. A control string may contain up to three different character sequences and any combination of these sequences. Descriptions of the three character sequences follows.

(i) A string of ordinary characters.

example

```
printf("computing is fun!");
```

will display the output as:

```
computing is fun!_
```

In processing the control string the string literal is displayed on the screen of a monitor or any other default output device and assuming the output device is a monitor, the cursor _ remains on the same line as the string.

36

(ii) Escape sequence characters, from the following set, can be represented in a control string:

\a   alert (bell)
\b   backspace
\f   form feed
\n   new line
\r   carriage return
\t   horizontal tab
\v   vertical tab
\\   backslash
\?   question mark
\'   single quote
\"   double quote
\ddd   where ddd is an octal number in the range 0 .. 377 and represents the ASCII code for the
         character
\xdd   where dd is a hexadecimal number in the range 0 .. FF and represents the ASCII code for the
         character

The value of ddd and dd in the last two escape sequences will depend upon the character set being used.

example

```
printf("WARNING\a");
```

will display the output as:

```
WARNING_
```

In processing the control string the string literal is displayed and an audible warning (bell) is sounded from the computer's speaker. The cursor _ remains on the same line as the string literal.

example

```
printf("C programming is easy\n");
```

will display the output as:

```
C programming is easy

_
```

In processing the control string the string literal is displayed and the cursor _ moves to the next line (\n) below the letter C.

example

```
printf("character whose octal code is 141 is \141 ");
```

will display the output as:

```
character whose octal code is 141 is a _
```

37

In processing the control string the string literal is displayed followed by the character **a** whose octal code is 141 (\141). The cursor _ remains on the same line as the string literal and character.

(iii) Format specifications corresponding to the list of arguments after the control string.

This will take the form *%width [. precision] type* where type is one of the following:

d, i	decimal integer
o	unsigned octal
x, X	unsigned hexadecimal
u	unsigned decimal integer
c	single character
s	string
f	floating-point number
e, E	floating-point number in exponential format
g, G	floating-point number in either fixed decimal or exponential format, whichever is more compact

The types d,o,x, X or u may be preceded by the letter l to indicate they are long integers.

The types e, E, f, g or G may be preceded by the letter L to indicate they are long double.

Width is a number that represents the minimum size of the field for displaying a number. The number is right-justified unless a negative width is used, in which case the number is displayed left justified. If the value to be printed is larger than the width specified, then the width is automatically expanded to accommodate the number. Regardless of the value of the width the displayed number will never be truncated. Thus no field width may be specified and a number will still be displayed.

The precision after the decimal point indicates the number of decimal places to display a number of type float, double or long float.

example

```
printf("alpha = %5d\n", alpha);
```

assuming alpha has the value 31678, printf will display the output as:

```
alpha = 31678
_
```

In processing the control string the string literal is displayed followed by the value of alpha in a field width of 5 digits (%5d). The cursor _ moves to the beginning of a new line below the letter **a** of alpha.

example

```
printf("beta = %-10.4f", beta);
```

assuming beta has the value 1.2345, printf will display the output as:

```
beta = 1.2345    _
```

In processing the control string the string literal is displayed followed by the value of beta, left justified in a field width of 10 characters and 4 decimal places (%-10.4f). The cursor _ remains on the same line as the output following the trailing spaces after the number.

example

```
printf("CASH AMOUNT\t\t%5.2f\n", cash);
```

assuming cash has the value 20, printf will display the output as:

```
CASH AMOUNT                    20.00
_
```

In processing the control string the string literal is displayed, the cursor moves through two tabulation positions (\t\t) and the value for cash is then displayed as a floating-point number having a field width of 5 characters with 2 decimal places (%5.2f). The cursor _ then moves to the beginning of the next line below the letter C.

example

```
printf("\t\t\t%2d:%2d %c\n", hours, minutes, am_pm);
```

assuming hours, minutes and am_pm are 2, 15 and p respectively, printf will display the output as:

```
                2:15 p
_
```

In processing the control string the cursor moves through three tabulation positions (\t\t\t) and the value of hours is displayed in a field width of 2 digits (%2d). A colon (:) is then displayed, since it forms part of the control string. The value of minutes is displayed in a field width of 2 digits (%2d). A space is then displayed, since this also forms part of the control string. A value for am_pm is displayed as a single character (%c). The cursor _ then moves down one line (\n).

example

```
printf("%s\t%d @ %4.2f\t%5.2f\n", article, quantity, unit_cost, price);
```

assuming article, quantity, unit_cost and price are brush, 2, 2.49 and 4.98 respectively, printf will display output as:

```
brush         2 @ 2.49         4.98
_
```

In processing the control string the value of article is displayed as a string (%s) and the cursor moves to the next tabulation position (\t). The value of quantity is displayed (%d). Note when the field width is omitted the number is displayed in a width suitable for the size of the number. The three characters space@space are displayed as part of the control string, followed by the value of unit_cost using a field width of 4 characters with 2 decimal places (%4.2f). The cursor _ moves through to the next tabulation position (\t) and the value of price is displayed on a field width of 5 characters with 2 decimal places (%5.2f). The cursor then moves down one line (\n), to below the letter b.

Warning! Printf will output the characters in a string until the null character is detected. If there is no null character in the string the printf function will continue to output the contents of memory addresses until a null character is eventually detected.

3.3 Address operator

The variables that have been introduced so far in the text have been associated with integer, float or char types. It is understood that a declaration of the form **int largest = INT_MAX**; implies that the identifier *largest* contains, or stores, the value of INT_MAX which happens to be 32767 using a 16 bit representation.

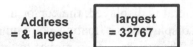

Address
= & largest

largest
= 32767

An illustration of an area of memory used to store
an integer, largest, where the address of this location
is &largest

figure 3.1

Pictorially *largest* might be seen as a box containing the value 32767 as shown in figure 3.1. This box represents an area of computer memory used for storing the integer largest. The *address* of this area of memory is denoted by **&largest**, where **&** is the *address operator*.

3.4 Input

When data is input at a keyboard it is normally stored in a temporary area of computer memory known as a keyboard buffer. When the return key is pressed this is a signal for the computer to scan the buffer for data.

The routine *scanf* is found in the standard library header file **<stdio.h>**. The purpose of the routine is to read characters from a standard input device, normally a keyboard (buffer), and store the converted data at the *addresses* given by the arguments. The arguments are *addresses* indicating where to store the converted input.

Warning! When using scanf to input a number or a single character the address of the variable is used and not simply the variable name.

The format of scanf is:

```
scanf("control string", arg1, arg2, ... argn);
```

where the control string defines how the input is to be converted.

A simplified version of the control string has the following structure *%[width] type* where width is the maximum number of characters to be scanned for the current argument. When the width is omitted *scanf* will read the characters being input, up to the first space, horizontal or vertical tab, form-feed or new-line character.

type refers to the following:

d   signed decimal integer
i   signed integer where the base is determined by the format of the number input:
         prefix 0 expects octal integer;
         prefix 0x expects hexadecimal integer;
         otherwise decimal integer
u   unsigned decimal integer
o   unsigned octal integer
x   unsigned hexadecimal integer using the digits 0 to 9 and either abcdef or ABCDEF
e, f, g signed floating point value
l   is used to prefix the types d, i, o u and x as long int or unsigned long int;
L   is used to prefix the types e, f and g as long double.

example

```
scanf("%d", &alpha);
```

will read a signed decimal integer value and store the result at the address of *alpha*.

example

```
scanf("%10f", &beta);
```

will read the first ten characters of a signed real number and store the value at the address of *beta*.

example

```
scanf("%le", &gamma);
```

will read a double, signed floating-point number and store the value at the address of *gamma*.

example

```
scanf("%o", &delta);
```

will read an unsigned octal integer and store the value at the address of *delta*.

example

```
scanf("%lx", &epsilon);
```

will read an unsigned long hexadecimal integer and store the value at the address of *epsilon*.

example

```
scanf("%u%u%u", &day, &month, &year);
```

will read three unsigned decimal integers and store the values at the addresses of *day, month* and *year* respectively.

example

```
scanf("%d%d%c", &hours, &minutes, &am_pm);
```

will read two signed decimal integers and a single character, and store the values at the addresses of *hours*, *minutes* and *am_pm* respectively.

example

```
scanf("%d%f%Le", &first, &second, &third);
```

will read a signed integer, a signed floating point real and a signed, long double precision floating point real, and store the values at the addresses of *first*, *second* and *third* respectively.

Input data does not need to appear on one line. The data for this example could be input as:

```
12345   0.9876
-6.3456789E-19
```

The *scanf* function regards white-space characters (space, horizontal and vertical tabs, form-feed and new-line characters) as field delimiters. Therefore, since a space separates the integer from the real number, the field for the integer number will contain 12345 and the field for the real number will contain 0.9876. A new-line character separates the two real numbers, therefore, the field for the floating-point number will contain -6.3456789E-19.

example

```
scanf("%s", article);
```

Scanf will ignore any leading white-space characters in a string and input the string up to the next white-space character. The string will be appended with a null character provided there is enough storage space declared for the string. If the maximum number of character to be input is known in advance, n say, then the control format can be modified to %ns.

Warning! Never use scanf if a string is to be input that contains white space-characters.

Strings can be input and output using *scanf* and *printf*, where %s is used in the control format.

Warning! The name of a string is the address of the first character in the string, therefore, there is no need to use the address of the string in the scanf statement.

3.5 String input/ output

An alternative to scanf for the input of a string is the function *gets*. All the characters, including white-space characters, will be stored until a newline character is input as a string terminator. For example, **gets(name)** where name has been declared as **char name[20]** will allow a string of less than 20 characters to be input. The system appends a string terminator at the end of the string.

A string can also be output using the function *puts*. This function will output the characters in a string up to the first null character, the function then outputs a newline character. For example **puts(name)** will display the value of the string *name*, followed by a new line character.

3.6 Assignment

A simplified format for an assignment statement follows. See appendix A for further detail.

assignment-statement:
      identifier = expression

where the symbol = is known as an assignment operator.

The destination of a result will always be on the left-hand side of an assignment. Therefore A=9 implies that A is assigned the value 9. The statement 9=A has no meaning since 9 is an illegal variable name. However, A=B would imply that A is assigned the value of B, whereas, B=A would imply that B is assigned the value of A.

In order to exchange the values of the two variables A and B it is necessary to introduce a third, temporary variable T. T=A duplicates the value of A in T, A=B overwrites the value of A with the value of B, B=T overwrites the value of B with the value of T, hence the original contents of A and B have been exchanged.

Type conversion can be implicit, in which case it is performed automatically when the type of the expression on the right-hand side of an assignment does not match the type of the variable on the left-hand side. In this case the value on the right-hand side of the assignment is converted to the type of the variable on the left- hand side.

Type conversion may also be explicit through the use of a *cast* operation. A cast expression has the form **(type name) expression** where the type name in parenthesis indicates the type to which the expression should be converted. For example,

```
float alpha;
int beta;

alpha = (float)beta;
```

(float)beta is used to convert beta in the expression to a number of type float, this does not imply that beta has changed its type from int to float, only the value of beta has been converted to type float in the expression.

3.7 Character input/ output

Although *scanf* and *printf* can be used for the input and output of single characters, there exists two routines which permit character input and character output. The routine *getchar()* will enable a single character to be input at a keyboard and stored as an integer corresponding to the ASCII code for the character. For example, **code = getchar();** where code is declared as **int code;** will store the ASCII code of the character being input into the integer variable *code*.

The data type **char** and the data type **int** both represent integers, although the range of integers of data of type char is much smaller than the range of integers of data type int. Compared to say, Ada or Pascal, C is a weakly typed language. It is possible to declare **char character**; and yet assign **character = getchar()**. Since the routine *getchar()* returns an integer value, this assignment would not be tolerated in other languages. To conform to the rules of strict typing it would be necessary to state **code = (int) character;**

and **character = (char) code;** using the cast operator, however, it might be viewed as being unnecessary to C programmers!

It is not always necessary to use the routine *getchar()* in an assignment statement. The routine can be used in isolation as a means of getting and discarding unwanted characters from the keyboard buffer. For example when the following statements are executed:

```
scanf ("%d" &age);
gets (name);
```

the keyboard buffer might contain

```
25<return>
```

in response to the *age*. The value 25 is stored at the address of *age*, however, the *<return>* character still remains in the keyboard buffer. This is not a problem if the next value to be input is a number, since scanf will ignore all leading white space characters when scanning for a number in the required format. However, if the next value to be input is a string, then the <return> character is taken to be the string delimiter, and the user never gets the opportunity of typing the value for the string.

The solution to the problem is to use the getchar() routine to remove the unwanted <return> character from the keyboard buffer, therefore the code is modified to:

```
scanf ("%d" &age);
getchar ();
gets (name);
```

The routine **putchar(code)** will display on a screen the character, whose corresponding ASCII integer code, is stored in the variable *code*.

3.8 Program format

The format of a C program may be viewed very simply as:

> **#include directive(s)**
>
> **main()**
> **{**
>   **declaration of constants and variables**
>
>   **sequence of instructions**
> **}**

The #include directive makes it possible to include any previously written character file in the source file. Since the routines *printf*, *scanf*, *puts*, *gets*, *getchar* and *putchar* are all defined in the header file <stdio.h>

it is necessary to write the directive **#include <stdio.h>** at the beginning of a program if any of these routines are to be used in the program. Notice that header files are always given the suffix .h by convention.

A C program is organised into routines (the routines are known as *functions* - these will be covered in a later chapter); main() represents the routine where program execution must begin, and as the name suggests is the main or controlling routine.

The declarations of constants and variables, and the language statements that make up the sequence of instructions contained within a function, are delimited by the opening brace { and closing brace }. The declarations and executable statements within the function are separated by semi-colons. However, there are no semi-colons after the function heading main(), or delimiting braces.

3.9 Worked examples

Problem - The first program in this section illustrates some of the different ways in which *printf* can be used to display numbers and strings. In the first example several variables have been declared and initialised and their respective values output using different control strings in the printf statements. Remember that the escape sequence \t provides a tabulation, \n a new line and any format specification that contains a negative width implies that the number will be left-justified.

```
/*
c3_dpp\ex_01.c
program to demonstrate some of the different ways in which printf can
be used to display numbers and strings
*/

#include <stdio.h>

main()
{
        int                 A = 32;
        unsigned long int   B = 123456789UL;
        long int            C = 0x56A7C;
        unsigned int        D = 0347;
        float               E = 67.123;
        double              F = 0.987654321E+20L;
        char                letter = 'Z';
        char                string[] = "Popocatapetl";

        printf("value of A\t %-10d\n", A);
        printf("          B\t %-15lu\n", B);
        printf("          C\t %10lX\n", C);
        printf("          D\t %o\n", D);
        printf("          E\t %10.4f\n", E);
        printf("          F\t %20.12G\n\n", F);
        printf("          letter\t %c\n", letter);
        printf("          string\t %s\n", string);
}
```

Results from program ex_01.c being run

```
value of A       32
        B        123456789
        C               56A7C
        D        347
        E             67.1230
        F               9.87654321E+19

        letter   Z
        string   Popocatapetl
```

Problem - In the second example *scanf* has been used to input values from a keyboard. The remainder of the program uses *printf* to display the values that had been input at the keyboard.

Repeated warning! When using scanf to input a number or a single character the address of the variable is used and not simply the variable name.

```c
/*
c3_dpp\ex_02.c
program to demonstrate the various uses of scanf
*/

#include <stdio.h>

main()
{
        int     alpha;
        float   beta;
        double  gamma;
        int     delta;
        long int epsilon;

        printf("input integer value for alpha ");
        scanf("%d", &alpha);
        printf("input float value (10 characters) for beta ");
        scanf("%10f", &beta);
        printf("input double value (15 characters) for gamma ");
        scanf("%le", &gamma);
        printf("input octal unsigned integer ");
        scanf("%o", &delta);
        printf("input hexadecimal unsigned integer ");
        scanf("%lx", &epsilon);

        printf("\n\n");
        printf("alpha   = %-5d\n", alpha);
```

```
        printf("beta    = %10.4f\n", beta);
        printf("gamma   = %15.4e\n", gamma);
        printf("delta   = %-10o\n", delta);
        printf("epsilon = %1X\n", epsilon);
}
```

Results from program ex_02.c being run

```
input integer value for alpha 31678
input float value (10 characters) for beta 1.23456789
input double value (15 characters) for gamma 9.876543210E-15
input octal unsigned integer 347
input hexadecimal unsigned integer AC3F

alpha   = 31678
beta    =       1.2346
gamma   =       9.8765e-15
delta   = 347
epsilon = AC3F
```

Notice that both the octal number (347) and the hexadecimal number (AC3F) have been input without using the **0** and **0x** prefixes respectively. These prefixes only apply to the specification of octal and hexadecimal constants in a program.

Problem - The third example is used to illustrate that a control string in a scanf statement can contain many arguments, and that the data corresponding to these arguments can be separated by white space characters.

```
/*
c3_dpp\ex_03.c
program to illustrate the control string of scanf with many arguments
*/

#include <stdio.h>

main()
{
        unsigned int         octal;
        unsigned long int    hex;
              float          number;

        scanf("%o%lx%f", &octal, &hex, &number);
        printf("\n\toctal %o\n", octal);
        printf("\thex     %1X\n", hex);
        printf("\tnumber  %f\n", number);
}
```

Results from program ex_03.c being run

```
567 5BDF
1.23456

        octal 567
        hex     5BDF
        number  1.234560
```

Problem - In the fourth example the printf routine is used to display the ranges for the data types introduced in the previous chapter. Since all ranges are given in the header files <limits.h> and <float.h> it is possible to include these files at the beginning of the program and display the constants defined in them.

```c
/*
c3_dpp\ex_04.c
program to illustrate the ranges for the data types:
char, int, long int, float, double
*/

#include <stdio.h>
#include <limits.h>
#include <float.h>
main()
{
        char            char_min, char_max, char_unsigned_max;
        int             int_min, int_max, int_unsigned_max;
        long int        long_int_min, long_int_max, long_int_unsigned;
        float           float_small, float_max;
        double          double_small, double_max;

        /* range of characters */
        char_min = SCHAR_MIN;
        char_max = SCHAR_MAX;
        char_unsigned_max = UCHAR_MAX;

        printf("char min: %d\n",char_min);
        printf("char max: %d\n",char_max);
        printf("char unsigned max: %u\n\n", char_unsigned_max);

        /* range of integers */
        int_min = INT_MIN;
        int_max = INT_MAX;
        int_unsigned_max = UINT_MAX;

        printf("int min: %d\n",int_min);
        printf("int max: %d\n",int_max);
        printf("int unsigned max: %u\n",int_unsigned_max);
```

48

```
        /* range of long integers */
        long_int_min = LONG_MIN;
        long_int_max = LONG_MAX;
        long_int_unsigned = ULONG_MAX;

        printf("long int min: %ld\n",long_int_min);
        printf("long int max: %ld\n",long_int_max);
        printf("long int unsigned max: %lu\n\n",long_int_unsigned);

        /* range of float */
        float_small = FLT_MIN;
        float_max = FLT_MAX;

        printf("float smallest: %15.9e\n",float_small);
        printf("float max: %15.9e\n\n",float_max);

        /* range of double */
        double_small = DBL_MIN;
        double_max = DBL_MAX;

        printf("double smallest: %25.16e\n",double_small);
        printf("double max: %25.16e\n\n",double_max);
}
```

Results from program ex_04.c being run on a PC under MSDOS

```
char min: -128
char max: 127
char unsigned max: 65535                [4294967295]

int min: -32768                         [-2147483648]
int max: 32767                          [+2147483647]
int unsigned max: 65535                 [4294967295]
long int min: -2147483648
long int max: 2147483647
long int unsigned max: 4294967295

float smallest: 1.175494351e-38
float max: 3.402823466e+38

double smallest:   2.2250738585072014e-308
double max:    1.7976931348623151e+308
```

Note the figures in brackets [ ] indicate the results when the program was run on a Digital Personal DEC station under UNIX.

Problem - In the final example of this section a program is written to demonstrate the use of the routines getchar and putchar. A single character is input from the keyboard and its ASCII code is displayed on a screen, followed by an ASCII code being input from the keyboard and its corresponding character is displayed on the screen.

```
/*
c3_dpp\ex_05.c
program to input a single character and display its ASCII code
then input an ASCII code and display the corresponding character
*/

#include <stdio.h>

main()
{
        char    character;
        int     code;

        printf("input a single character ");
        code = getchar();
        character = (char) code;
        printf("ASCII code for %c is %d\n\n", character, code);

        printf("input an ASCII code in the range 33 to 126 ");
        scanf("%d", &code);
        character = (char) code;
        printf("character with ASCII code %d is %c\n", code, character);
}
```

Results from program ex_05.c being run

```
input a single character R
ASCII code for R is 82

input an ASCII code in the range 33 to 126 64
character with ASCII code 64 is @
```

This program may be re-written to deliberately exclude the character variable and the cast operations, and still produce the same result. After examining the program do you understand why the output should be the same?

```
/*
c3_dpp\ex_06.c
re-written program to input a single character and display its ASCII code
then input an ASCII code and display the corresponding character
*/

#include <stdio.h>

main()
{
        int     code;

        printf("input a single character ");
        code = getchar();
        printf("ASCII code for %c is %d\n\n", code, code);

        printf("input an ASCII code in the range 33 to 126 ");
        scanf("%d", &code);
        printf("character with ASCII code %d is %c\n", code, code);
}
```

Remember the routine getchar always returns an integer value - the ASCII code for the character. The same code can be used in two different contexts in a control string of a printf statement - (%c) will display a character, (%d) will display an ASCII code.

Although the re-written program is slightly shorter, it may be argued that it is not as clearly written as the previous version.

3.10 Summary

- □ All input and output is dependent upon the use of the appropriate library routines.

- □ The routines *printf*, *scanf*, *gets*, *puts*, *getchar* and *putchar* are all found in the library file denoted by the header <stdio.h>.

- □ The appropriate header must be included at the beginning of a program if routines from the header file are to be used in the program.

- □ The header <limits.h> contains the machine dependent maximum and minimum values for each integer type.

- □ The header <float.h> contains the machine dependent range and precision for real numbers.

- □ The routine *printf* is used to display formatted numbers, together with strings and characters. The contents of the control string is used to format the information to be printed.

- □ The memory address of a variable can be obtained by using the *address operator* **&**

☐ The routine *scanf* is used to input data from the default input device, such as a keyboard. Particular care must be exercised when using *scanf* since the data being input must conform **exactly** to the requirements of the control string.

☐ The #include directive is used to include any previously written files into a program, such as library header files.

☐ A C program is organised into routines, with main() being the controlling routine from which program execution must begin.

☐ All the statements within a routine are bracketed by the use of braces.

☐ Statements within a routine are separated from each other by a semi-colon.

☐ Comments may be included within a program, either on a single line or spread over many lines. All comments must be delimited by the symbols /* and */ respectively.

☐ Type conversion is either implicit (right-hand side type converted to left-hand side type in assignment) or explicit through the use of a cast operation.

3.11 Questions - *answers begin on page 464*

1. Investigate the contents of the <limits.h> and <float.h> header files for the version of ANSI C on the computer system being used by you. Compare the values with those listed in this chapter. If they are significantly different then make a note of the specific differences. Re-run program c3_dpp\ex_04.c and compare the results with those listed.

2. How would you expect the following *printf* statements to display the information?

(a) printf("Hello World");
(b) printf("\tname: ");
(c) printf("\tname: %s\n", name); where name is declared as char name[] = "Mickey Mouse";
(d) printf("a=%d\tb=%d\tc=%d\n", a, b, c); where a = 3, b=4, and c=5.
(e) printf("area covered %f10.2\n", area); where area = 635.8658
(f) printf("alpha = %8o\tbeta = %10.4e\n", alpha, beta); where alpha = 01675 and beta = 1.3456E+16.

3. Discover the errors in the following statements.

(a) scanf("%d", &alpha); where alpha is a real number
(b) scanf("%f", beta); where beta is a real number
(c) scanf("%2d%2d", &day, & month, &year);
(d) scanf("%s", &name); where name is declared as char name[20];
(e) scanf("%Lx", &gamma); where gamma is declared as long int
(f) scanf("alpha = %-5d\n", alpha); where alpha is defined as an unsigned integer.

[4]. Write a program containing *printf* statements to test the full range of escape sequence characters described in section 3.2 (ii), embedded within control strings.

5. Write a program to input a message of your choice, at a keyboard, and display the message on a screen.

Chapter 4
Instruction Sequences

This chapter contains work on the following topics - arithmetic applied to variables and constants and the development of a sequence of instructions into a computer program. By the end of the chapter the reader should have an understanding of the following topics.

- ☐ The construction of arithmetic expressions for the purposes of calculation.

- ☐ The order of evaluation of arithmetic expressions.

- ☐ Designing and testing algorithms.

- ☐ The use of constants and variables in a program.

- ☐ The construction of sequences of instructions that form the basis of simple programs for the input and processing of data and the output of results.

4.1 Arithmetic

In section 2.5 of the second chapter it was shown that data can be referenced by name in the memory of a computer. Figure 4.1 illustrates numbers being referenced by names A, B and C in three separate locations in memory.

5	16	12
A	B	C

figure 4.1 numbers stored by name

The arithmetic operators + (addition) - (subtraction) * (multiplication) / (division) and % (remainder) can be used to make calculations on the stored numeric data. For example A = B + C would add the contents of B to the contents of C and store the result in A, destroying or overwriting the previous contents of A. Therefore, after the statement A = B + C had been executed by the computer the contents of A changed, and the result of the computation is shown in figure 4.2.

28	16	12
A	B	C

figure 4.2 result of the computation A=B+C

Similar before and after situations can be applied to other computations as illustrated in figure 4.3.

In the last example of figure 4.3 the expression counter = counter + 1 may seem a little unusual, since the variable counter appears on both sides of the expression. The statement should be read as follows. On the right-hand side of the expression the current value of counter (3) is increased by 1, giving a result of (4). This result is then assigned to the variable on the left-hand side of the expression, that also happens to be the variable counter. The old value of counter (3) is overwritten or destroyed by the new value (4). The effect of this statement has been to increase the value of the variable counter by 1.

The arithmetic operators in C can be divided into three categories:

unary operators

```
+ unary plus
- unary minus
```

binary multiplicative operators

```
* multiplication
/ division
% remainder
```

and *binary additive operators*

```
+ addition
- subtraction
```

54

before

15	2	3	4
A	B	C	D

after

9	2	3	4
A	B	C	D

result of computation

A = B+C+D

before

21	16	9
X	Y	Z

after

7	16	9
X	Y	Z

result of computation

X = Y- Z

before

1.5	20.0	0.05
tax	price	tax_rate

after

1.0	20.0	0.05
tax	price	tax_rate

result of computation

tax = price * tax_rate

before

50.0	120.0	60.0
time	distance	speed

after

2.0	120.0	60.0
time	distance	speed

result of computation

time = distance / speed

before

37	15	19
A	B	C

after

37	15	7
A	B	C

result of computation

C = A % B

before

3
counter

after

4
counter

result of computation

counter = counter +1

figure 4.3 results of various computations

4.2 Operator precedence

If an expression was written as A + B * C - D / E how would it be evaluated? There is a need to introduce a set of rules for the evaluation of such expressions. All operators have an associated hierarchy that determines the order of precedence for evaluating an expression.

The normal precedence rules, that are found in other high-level languages, apply to these operators. Unary operators have a higher order of precedence than multiplicative operators and multiplicative operators a higher order of precedence over additive operators.

Expressions are evaluated by taking the operators with a higher priority before those of a lower priority. Where operators are of the same priority the expression is evaluated from left to right.

Expressions in parenthesis will be evaluated before non-parenthesised expressions. Parenthesis, although not an operator, can be considered as having an order of precedence after unary operators.

The expression A + B * C - D / E can be evaluated by inspecting the operators and grouping operations according to the above rules. The numbers in figures 4.4 and 4.5 indicate the order of evaluation. The equivalent algebraic expression is given at each stage of the evaluation.

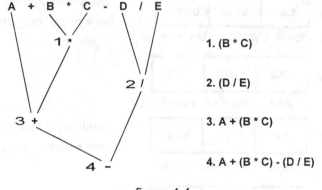

figure 4.4

The expression (X * X + Y * Y) / (A + B) can be evaluated in the same way as illustrated in figure 4.5.

The reader should adopt the habit of using parenthesis in order to make the meaning of an expression as clear as possible. For example, the algebraic expression: U.V / W.X is written in C as U*V/W/X however, (U*V)/(W*X) is easier to understand. Similarly, $X^2 + Y^2 + \dfrac{4}{Z^2}*(X + Y)$

would be written in C as: (X*X)+(Y*Y)+4*(X+Y)/(Z*Z).

The unary operators only require one operand, whereas the binary operators require two operands.

With the exception of the % remainder operator, which must have integer operands, all other operators can have integer or floating point operands or a mixture of both.

In a division if both the operands are integer then the result will have the fractional remainder truncated.

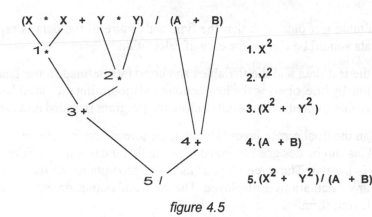

figure 4.5

When using either a division operator with two integer operands or a remainder operator, if one operand is a negative integer then the result is implementation dependent. For example, the value of -5 / 2 is -2 in TopSpeed C, however, it could be -3 in other implementations. Similarly, -5 % 2 is -1 and 5 % -2 is +1 in TopSpeed C (the sign of i % j is the same sign as the left operand). In other implementations the sign of i % j, when either i or j are negative, depends upon the implementation.

When operands are of different types, one or more of the operands must be converted before the operation can be performed. Type conversion can be implicit, in which case it is performed automatically. The operands are converted to the type that can safely accommodate both values. For example, an operation involving an integer type and a long integer type would cause the integer type to be promoted to the long integer type; an operation involving a float type and a double type would cause the float type to be promoted to a double type. Notice in the second example that float is promoted to double and not long double, since double can be used to store both operands without incurring any extra overhead of memory.

4.3 Program design

Having been through the fundamentals of the meaning of data, data types, input and output, assignment, arithmetic and the format of a program it is now possible to bring together these elements in designing and writing computer programs to solve a set of simple problems.

Firstly it is necessary to state a few guidelines before attempting to design and code a computer program. Under the following headings, the necessary stages involved in developing a computer program are explained.

Algorithm - Document in English, NOT C code, the sequence of operations that are necessary to solve the problem. This is in fact the algorithm or method of solving the problem, and is represented in a pseudo-code.

Data Dictionary - Determine the items of data required; show any calculations that will be used on this data. Classify this data into constants and variables, and specify the data type for each constant and variable.

Test Data - Invent suitable test data such that the type and nature of the data is representative of the problem. Numerical data should be chosen for ease of calculation.

Desk Check - Using the test data and the variables and constants defined in the data dictionary, trace through the algorithm line by line, obeying the instructions and modifying the variables as required. From this desk check it is possible to predict the results before the program is coded and run.

Screen Layout - Design the final screen layout showing the screen text, specimen data that will be used and expected results. This can be designed on ruled paper so that the column positions of each character in each line of output is known. The screen layout indicates prompts to the user for data and how the information related to any calculations is displayed. The input and output statements in a program can be coded directly from a layout form.

Coding - From the information documented by the algorithm, data dictionary and screen layout code the program using the C language.

Compile and link the program - Only if these two stages are successful can you run the program using the same test data, and inspect whether the results are the same as predicted by the desk check.

Problem - In this example a program is required that will allow a user to input a distance to travel, in miles, and the speed of travel, in m.p.h., from a town. The program is required to calculate the time it will take, in hours, to reach the town.

Algorithm - In programs that require calculations to be made on input data there is a set order to the instructions that will be used. These are basically:

input data
using the data calculate the information required
output the information

These three stages can be refined to produce a logical order of necessary operations for solving the problem.

input distance to travel
input speed of travel
calculate time using the expression time = distance / speed
display the time of travel

Data Dictionary - Three items of data can be identified in this problem, distance, speed and time. If distance and speed are whole numbers then because of the calculation of time (distance/speed), the data type for the time must be a real number. The declaration for the data in this problem would be:

```
int      distance;    /* distance to travel from town in miles */
int      speed;       /* speed of travel in mph */
float    time;        /* calculated time of travel = distance / speed */
```

Test data - the distance can be chosen as 15 miles and the speed as 45 mph.

Desk Check

variable	value
distance	15
speed	45
time	15/45 = 0.33

Ensure that the format of the *printf* routine caters for at least two decimal places, since any less will display an inaccurate result!

```
                        Screen Layout

12345678901234567890123456789012345678901234567890
input distance to town 15
input speed of travel 45
time taken to reach town is 0.33 hours
```

Warning! In coding this program typical errors that are made by beginners to programming have been deliberately introduced. Can you find the errors before the program is compiled?

```c
/*
o4_dpp\ex_01.c
program to calculate and output the time in hours, to travel a
distance input in miles, at an average speed input in mph
*/

#include <stdio.h>

main()
{
        int     distance;
        int     speed;
        float   time

        printf("input distance to town ");
        scanf("%d", distance);

        printf("input speed of travel );
        scanf("%d", &speed);

        time = distance / speed;

        printf("time taken to reach town is %4.2f hours\n", time);
}
```

4.4 Implementing a C program

Regardless of the programming environment being used, the following stages are necessary to implement the C program developed in the previous section. Having invoked the editor, it is now possible to type the program at the keyboard.

After the program has been typed it is saved to disk using the filename *ex_01.c*. The program is then compiled. The result of the compilation is that a number of errors and warnings are reported. By returning to the editor these errors can be corrected. The error and warning diagnostics are as follows.

Syntax error, expected: ; [(= , in relation to the line printf("input distance to town ");

This can be very misleading since the error occurred on the previous line. You may notice that the data declaration **float time** has not been separated from the **printf** statement by a semi-colon. Remember that the semicolon is used to separate statements in a program.

Error: Invalid string constant in relation to the line printf("input speed of travel);

All string literals or constants are delimited by matching inverted commas or double quotes. The right-hand inverted commas are missing in this string.

Warning: Possible use of 'distance' before assigned a value. This warning stems from the fact that the routine scanf requires the address of a variable and not the name of the variable. The address operator is missing before the variable *distance* in the line scanf("%d", distance);

After the errors are corrected the program is re-compiled, link/loaded and run. The results of the program execution follow.

Results from program ex_01.c being run

```
input distance to town 15
input speed of travel 45
time taken to reach town is 0.00 hours
```

In comparing this result with the expected result of 0.33, clearly something has gone wrong! Look again at the calculation. Both distance and speed are integer values. The integer result of dividing 15 / 45 is zero and not 0.33. It is the result zero that is converted to the type float on the left-hand side of the expression, which still results in zero.

In this example it is necessary to perform a type conversion on distance and speed, therefore, the expression is modified to *time = (float) distance / (float) speed;* after this modification the results from running the program are as expected.

4.5 Worked examples

This section contains five worked examples to illustrate how programs can be developed that contain a sequence of instructions.

Marlborough	15
Swindon	25
Oxford	40

Problem - The first example in this section is only a refinement of the previous example. Here the user is first invited to enter the name of the town, so that it can be used in future textual output. Both the distance and speed are input and the time taken to reach the town is calculated in the same manner as the previous example.

Algorithm

input name of town
input distance
input speed
calculate time using the expression distance / speed
display time

Data Dictionary - The only additional item of data is the name of a town which is of type string. The other variables remain the same as in the previous example.

```
char     town[12];     /* name of a town or city */
int      distance;     /* distance to travel from town in miles */
int      speed;        /* speed of travel in mph */
float    time;         /* calculated time of travel = distance / speed */
```

Test data - The value for town can be input as Marlborough, the distance and speed remain the same.

Desk Check

variable	value
town	Marlborough
distance	15
speed	45
time	0.33

```
                        Screen Layout

12345678901234567890123456789012345678901234567890
input name of town Marlborough
input distance to Marlborough 15
input speed of travel 45
time taken to reach Marlborough is 0.33 hours
```

```
/*
c4_dpp\ex_02.c
program to calculate and output the time in hours, to travel a
distance input in miles, at an average speed input in mph
*/

#include <stdio.h>

main()
{
        char    town[12];
        int     distance;
        int     speed;
        float   time;

        printf("input name of town ");
        gets(town);

        printf("input distance to %s ", town);
        scanf("%d", &distance);

        printf("input speed of travel ");
        scanf("%d", &speed);

        time = (float)distance / (float)speed;

        printf("time taken to reach %s is %4.2f hours\n", town, time);
}
```

Results from program ex_02.c being run

```
input name of town Marlborough
input distance to Marlborough 15
input speed of travel 45
time taken to reach Marlborough is 0.33 hours
```

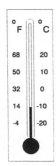

Problem - The thermometer illustrated in figure 2.2 shows two temperature scales, one in Fahrenheit and the other in Celsius. Write a program to input a temperature in degrees Fahrenheit and convert it to degrees Celsius.

The expression for conversion is Celsius = (Fahrenheit - 32) * 5 / 9.

Algorithm

input temperature in degrees Fahrenheit
convert temperature to degrees Celsius
display temperature in degrees Celsius

Data Dictionary - There are only two items of data in this example, a temperature in degrees Fahrenheit and its equivalent temperature in degrees Celsius. If both temperatures are recorded to an accuracy of one degree then both items of data are integers. The declaration of the data in this example is:

```
int Fahrenheit, Celsius;
```

Test data - A value for Fahrenheit can be chosen to be 14°F.

Desk Check

variable	value
Fahrenheit	14
Celsius	(14-32)*5/9 = -18*5/9 = -10

Screen Layout

```
12345678901234567890123456789012345678901234567890
input temperature in degrees F 14
equivalent temperature is -10 degrees C
```

```c
/*
c4_dpp\ex_03.c
program to input a temperature in degrees Fahrenheit and output the
temperature in degrees Celsius
*/

#include <stdio.h>

main()
{
        int     Fahrenheit;
        int     Celsius;

        printf("input temperature in degrees F ");
        scanf("%d", &Fahrenheit);
        Celsius = (Fahrenheit - 32) * 5 / 9;
        printf("equivalent temperature is %3d degrees C\n", Celsius);
}
```

Results from program ex_03.c being run

```
input temperature in degrees F 14
equivalent temperature is -10 degrees C
```

Problem - In the third example, if a person buys three newspapers, the Courier, Globe and Mercury; write a program to input the name and cost in pence of each newspaper, calculate the total cost and average cost in pence and display the result of these two computations.

Algorithm

input name of the first paper
input the price of the first paper
input name of the second paper
input the price of the second paper
input the name of the third paper
input the price of the third paper
calculate the total cost of all three papers
calculate the average cost of the three papers
display the total cost
display the average cost

Data Dictionary - The names of the three newspapers, the individual costs of the three newspapers, the total cost and average price are all items of data. The names of the newspapers are string variables, and the prices, total cost and average price are integer variables.

```
char    name_paper_1[10], name_paper_2[10], name_paper_3[10];
int     price_paper_1, price_paper_2, price_paper_3;
int     total_cost, average;
```

The total cost is the sum of the costs of the three newspapers:
total_cost = price_paper_1 + price_paper_2 + price_paper_3
and the average price is average = total_cost / 3

Test data - The names of the papers are the Globe, Mercury and Courier, and their respective costs are 40p, 50p and 60p.

Desk Check

variable	value
name_paper_1	Globe
price_paper_1	40
name_paper_2	Mercury
price_paper_2	50
name_paper_3	Courier
price_paper_3	60
total_cost	40+50+60 = 150
average	150 / 3 = 50

```
                        Screen Layout

12345678901234567890123456789012345678901234567890123456789012345678901234567890
name of first newspaper Globe
price of Globe 40
name of second newspaper Mercury
price of Mercury 50
name of third newspaper Courier
price of Courier 60
total cost of three newspapers is 150p
average cost of newspapers is 50p
```

In the following program notice the use of the getchar() statement to flush the keyboard buffer of the unwanted return character.

```c
/*
c4_dpp\ex_04.c
program to input the names and prices of three newspapers, calculate
and output the total cost and average price of the papers
*/

#include <stdio.h>

main()
{
        char    name_paper_1[10], name_paper_2[10], name_paper_3[10];
        int     price_paper_1, price_paper_2, price_paper_3;
        int     total_cost, average;

        printf("name of first newspaper ");
        gets(name_paper_1);
        printf("price of %s ", name_paper_1);
        scanf("%d", &price_paper_1); getchar();
```

```
        printf("name of second newspaper ");
        gets(name_paper_2);
        printf("price of %s ", name_paper_2);
        scanf("%d", &price_paper_2); getchar();

        printf("name of third newspaper ");
        gets(name_paper_3);
        printf("price of %s ", name_paper_3);
        scanf("%d", &price_paper_3);

        total_cost = price_paper_1 + price_paper_2 + price_paper_3;
        average = total_cost / 3;

        printf("total cost of three newspapers is %3dp\n", total_cost);
        printf("average price of newspapers is %2dp\n", average);
}
```

Results from program ex_04.c being run

```
name of first newspaper Globe
price of Globe 40
name of second newspaper Mercury
price of Mercury 50
name of third newspaper Courier
price of Courier 60
total cost of three newspapers is 150p
average price of newspapers is 50p
```

Problem - In the fourth example, write a program to solve the following problem. A rectangular living room has a total window area of 3 square metres and a total door area of 1.5 square metres. Write a program to input the length, width and height of the room and calculate the area of available wall space. If a 1 litre tin of paint will cover 25 square metres of wall, calculate and display the number of tins required to paint only the walls of the room. Note - the window and door areas, floor and ceiling are not to be painted.

Algorithm

input length
input width
input height
calculate wall area
calculate number of tins
display number of tins

Data Dictionary - In this problem the window and door areas, and area of coverage of a tin of paint can all be treated as constants. Since the problem requests that the dimensions of the room are to be input at the keyboard, the length, width and height should be treated as variables of type real. Before the number of tins of paint can be calculated it would be useful, but not necessary, to calculate the area of the walls to be painted. This variable will again be of type real. If it assumed that only 1 litre tins of paint can be used then the number of cans will be of type integer.

Three constants can be identified in this problem:

```
const  float  paint_cover = 25.0;
const  float  window_area = 3.0;
const  float  door_area   = 1.5
```

The variables are

```
float  length, width, height, wall_area;
int    tins;
```

In calculating the number of tins to purchase it will be necessary to adjust the result of dividing the wall area by paint coverage to give a whole number of tins, otherwise, the calculation will result in fractional parts of a tin of paint. A constant of 0.999 should be added to the theoretical number of tins before the result is truncated.

wall area = (2 * height * length) + (2 * height * width) - window area - door area
        = 2 * height * (length + width) - (window area + door area)
tins   = ((wall area / paint cover) + 0.999)

Since the variable tins is of type integer and it lies on the left-hand side of the assignment, the expression ((wall area / paint cover) + 0.999) will be truncated to the nearest integer value, however, since 0.999 has been added this has the effect of rounding the value of the expression to the next whole tin.

Test data -   Length 7.0 m, width 5.0 m and height 2.5m.

Desk Check

variable	values
length	7
width	5
height	2.5
wall_area	2*2.5*(7 + 5) - (3 + 1.5) = 5*12 - 4.5 = 55.5
tins	(55.5 / 25) + 0.999 = 2.22 + 0.999 = 3 |.219

Note because tins is an integer the decimal fraction 3.219 is truncated leaving a value of 3.

```
┌─────────────────────────────────────────────────────────────────┐
│                          Screen Layout                            │
├───────────────────────────────────────────────────────────────────┤
│ 12345678901234567890123456789012345678901234567890123456789012345678901234567890 │
│ input room dimensions                                             │
│ length? 7.0                                                       │
│ width? 5.0                                                        │
│ height? 2.5                                                       │
│ number of tins to purchase = 3                                    │
│                                                                   │
└─────────────────────────────────────────────────────────────────┘
```

```c
/*
c4_dpp\ex_05.c
program to calculate the amount of paint needed to paint the walls
of a room
*/

#include <stdio.h>

main()
{
        const   float   paint_cover     = 25.0;
        const   float   window_area     = 3.0;
        const   float   door_area       = 1.5;

                float   length, width, height;
                float   wall_area;
                int     tins;

        printf("input room dimensions\n");
        printf("length? "); scanf("%f", &length);
        printf("width? ");  scanf("%f", &width);
        printf("height? "); scanf("%f", &height);

        wall_area = 2 * height * (length + width) - (window_area + door_area);
        tins = (wall_area / paint_cover) + 0.999;

        printf("number of tins to purchase = %d\n", tins);
}
```

Results from program ex_05.c being run

```
input room dimensions
length? 7.0
width? 5.0
height? 2.5
number of tins to purchase  =  3
```

```
            DIY SUPERSTORE

        JEANNETTE          14/10/94
                             15:35

            SALES RECEIPT


    paint    1 @ 8.99        8.99
    brush    2 @ 2.49        4.98


    SUB TOTAL AMOUNT        13.97

    VAT                      2.44

    TOTAL AMOUNT            16.41

    CASH AMOUNT:           20.00

    CHANGE:                  3.59


    THANK YOU  FOR YOUR CUSTOM
```

Problem - In the last example of this section a program is written to display a sales receipt similar to that shown in chapter 2, figure 2.5. This example requires the date and time of the transaction to be input, together with the names of the articles purchased, the quantity and unit price of the articles and the amount of cash tendered for the purchase. The individual costs of the articles, sub total, value added tax, total and change are then calculated and displayed.

Algorithm

The solution to this problem breaks down into the three stages

input date and time of transaction
input details of first article purchased
input details of second article purchased
input amount of cash tendered

calculate cost of purchasing articles
calculate sub-total
calculate tax
calculate total
calculate change

display headings
display date and time of transaction
display sub-heading
display details of articles purchased
display sub-total
display tax
display total
display cash tendered
display change given
display final message

Data Dictionary - This will be similar to that described in sections 2.6 and 2.7, however, since there are two articles displayed on the sales receipt it will be necessary to declare two variables each for the name of the article, the quantity purchased and the unit price. It is assumed that the name of the cashier and the rate of value added tax are declared as constants.

```
const   float   VAT = 0.175;
const   char    name[] = "JEANNETTE";

        int     day, month, year;
        int     hours, minutes;
        char    article_1[10], article_2[10]; /* names of articles */
        int     quantity_1, quantity_2; /* quantities purchased */
        float   unit_cost_1, unit_cost_2; /* individual cost of articles */
        float   price_1, price_2; /* quantity * unit_cost */
        float   sub_total, tax, total, cash, change;
```

Test data - This can be taken directly from the illustration of the sales receipt.

Desk Check

variable	value
day	14
month	10
year	94
hours	15
minutes	35
article_1	paint
quantity_1	1
unit_cost_1	8.99
article_2	brush
quantity_2	2
unit_cost_2	2.49
cash	20.00
price_1	1 * 8.99 = 8.99
price_2	2 * 2.49 = 4.98
sub_total	8.99 + 4.98 = 13.97
tax	0.175 * 13.97 = 2.44
total	13.97 + 2.44 = 16.41
change	20.00 - 16.41 = 3.59

```
+--------------------------------------------------------------+
|                        Screen Layout                         |
|--------------------------------------------------------------|
| 12345678901234567890123456789012345678901234567890123456789  |
| input date as DD MM YY 14 10 94                              |
| input time as HH MM 15 35                                    |
| input name of first article paint                           |
| input quantity purchased 1                                  |
| input unit price 8.99                                       |
|                                                              |
| input name of second article brush                          |
| input quantity purchased 2                                  |
| input unit price 2.49                                       |
|                                                              |
| input amount of money tendered 20.00                        |
|                                                              |
|                                                              |
|     D I Y    S U P E R S T O R E                            |
|                                                              |
| JEANNETTE                   14/10/94                         |
|                             15:35                            |
|                                                              |
|          SALES RECEIPT                                       |
|                                                              |
|                                                              |
| paint   1 @ 8.99           8.99                             |
| brush   2 @ 2.49           4.98                             |
|                                                              |
| SUB TOTAL AMOUNT          13.97                             |
| VAT                        2.44                             |
| TOTAL AMOUNT              16.41                             |
| CASH AMOUNT              20.00                             |
| CHANGE                     3.59                             |
|                                                              |
| _____                                |
|                                                              |
|     THANK YOU FOR YOUR CUSTOM                                |
|                                                              |
+--------------------------------------------------------------+
```

```c
/*
c4_dpp\ex_06.c
program to produce a sales receipt
*/

#include <stdio.h>

main()
{
        const   float    VAT      = 0.175;
        const   char     name[] = "JEANNETTE";

                int      day, month, year;
                int      hours, minutes;
                char     article_1[10], article_2[10];
                int      quantity_1, quantity_2;
                float    unit_cost_1, unit_cost_2;
                float    price_1, price_2;
                float    sub_total, tax, total, cash, change;
```

71

```
/* input data */

printf("input date as DD MM YY ");
scanf("%d%d%d", &day, &month, &year);

printf("input time as HH MM ");
scanf("%d%d", &hours, &minutes);

printf("input name of first article "); scanf("%s", article_1);
printf("input quantity purchased "); scanf("%d",&quantity_1);
printf("input unit price "); scanf("%f",&unit_cost_1);

printf("\ninput name of second article "); scanf("%s", article_2);
printf("input quantity purchased "); scanf("%d",&quantity_2);
printf("input unit price "); scanf("%f",&unit_cost_2);

printf("\ninput amount of money tendered "); scanf("%f", &cash);
printf("\n\n");

/* calculate amounts for sales receipt */

price_1 = quantity_1 * unit_cost_1;
price_2 = quantity_2 * unit_cost_2;
sub_total = price_1 + price_2;
tax = VAT * sub_total;
total = tax + sub_total;
change = cash - total;

/* display sales receipt */

printf("  D I Y   S U P E R S T O R E\n\n");
printf("%s\t\t%2d/%2d/%2d\n",name, day, month, year);
printf("\t\t\t%2d:%2d\n\n", hours, minutes);
printf("\tSALES RECEIPT\n");
printf("_____\n\n");
printf("%s\t%d @ %4.2f\t%5.2f\n", article_1, quantity_1,
     unit_cost_1, price_1);
printf("%s\t%d @ %4.2f\t%5.2f\n\n", article_2, quantity_2,
     unit_cost_2, price_2);
printf("SUB TOTAL AMOUNT\t%5.2f\n", sub_total);
printf("VAT\t\t\t%5.2f\n", tax);
printf("TOTAL AMOUNT\t\t%5.2f\n", total);
printf("CASH AMOUNT\t\t%5.2f\n", cash);
printf("CHANGE\t\t\t%5.2f\n\n", change);
printf("_____\n\n");
printf("    THANK YOU FOR YOUR CUSTOM\n\n");
}
```

Results from program ex_06.c being run

```
input date as DD MM YY 14 10 94
input time as HH MM 15 35
input name of first article paint
input quantity purchased 1
input unit price 8.99

input name of second article brush
input quantity purchased 2
input unit price 2.49

input amount of money tendered 20.00

    D I Y    S U P E R S T O R E

JEANNETTE                14/10/94
                         15:35

       SALES RECEIPT

    _____

paint  1 @ 8.99          8.99
brush  2 @ 2.49          4.98

SUB TOTAL AMOUNT         13.97
VAT                       2.44
TOTAL AMOUNT             16.41
CASH AMOUNT             20.00
CHANGE                    3.59

    _____

    THANK YOU FOR YOUR CUSTOM
```

4.6 Summary

☐ Arithmetic can be used on the contents of the memory locations, allowing computations to be made on numeric data.

☐ Numbers can be added, subtracted, multiplied and divided by using the operators +, -, * and / respectively.

☐ With the exception of the % remainder operator, which must have integer operands, all other operators can have integer or real operands or a mixture of both.

☐ All operators are given a priority. Expressions are evaluated by taking the operators with the highest priority before those of a lower priority. Where operators are of the same priority the expression is evaluated from left to right.

☐ Expressions in parenthesis will be evaluated before non-parenthesised expressions.

☐ The result of a computation is assigned to a variable using the = assignment operator.

☐ When operands are of different types, one or more of the operands must be converted to the type that can safely accommodate the values, before the operation can be performed.

☐ When the types on both sides of an assignment do not match, the value on the right-hand side of the assignment is converted to the type of the variable on the left-hand side.

☐ All input and output is dependent upon the use of appropriate library routines.

☐ The names of the constants should be used in the program and not their literal values.

☐ All constants and variables must be declared before they can be used in the program.

☐ A semi-colon is used to separate statements in a C program.

4.7 Questions - *answers begin on page 465*

1. What are the values of the following variables after the execution of the respective assignments?

(a). B = A;
      C = A;
      D = A;

A	B	C	D
36	98	45	29

(b). D = A + B + C + D;

A	B	C	D
10	14	29	36

(c). A = B - 2;

A	B
17	50

(d). Y = X - Y;

X	Y
19	32

(e). Z = X * Y;

X	Y	Z
18	3	27

(f). B = B / A;

A	B
12.5	25.0

(g).   X = A / B;   A   B   X   (assume that A, B and X are integers)
                                      16   3   25

(h).   Y = C % D;   C   D   Y
                                      19   5   2

(i).   D = D + 1   D
                                      34

2. How are the following expressions written in C?

(a). $\dfrac{A+B}{C}$ (b). $\dfrac{W-X}{(Y+Z)}$ (c). $\dfrac{D-B}{2A}$ (d). $\dfrac{1}{2}(A^2+B^2)$

(e). (A - B).(C - D)   f. B.B - 4.A.C   g. A.X.X+B.X.X+C

3. Find the errors in the following C expressions.

(a). A.B   (b). X*-Y   (c). (64+B)/-6   (d). (A-B)(A+B)
(e). -2 / A + -6   (f). $\dfrac{1}{2}*(X-Y)$

4. Re-write the following C expressions as algebraic expressions.

(a). X + 2 / Y + 4   (b). A * B / (C + 2)   (c). U / V * W / X
(d). B * B - 4 * A * C   (e). A / B + C / D + E / F

5. Write a program to store the numbers 5 and 9 as integer variables A and B respectively. Compute the sum, difference, product, integer quotient and remainder of these variables taken in the order A+B, A-B, A*B, A / B, A % B, and display the results on a screen.

6. Write a program to input your name, height in inches and weight in pounds; convert the height to centimetres and weight to kilograms and display the following results. Note: 1 inch = 2.54 cm and 1 pound = 0.4546 Kg.

PERSONAL DETAILS
NAME: Henry Smithers
HEIGHT (cm): 180
WEIGHT (Kg): 75

7. Write a program to input the length and width of a rectangular-shaped garden, calculate the area of the lawn and the cost of turfing the lawn, if a 1.0 metre border is left around the perimeter of the garden. Assume the cost of turf is £2.00 per square metre. Display the result of these calculations.

8. Write a program to input an amount of money as a whole number, for example £157, and display an analysis of the minimum number of £20, £10 and £5 notes and £1 coins that make up this amount.

[9]. Write a program to input the length, width and depths at the deepest and shallowest ends of a rectangular swimming pool that has a constant gradient between two opposite ends of the pool. Calculate the volume of water required to fill the pool and display this volume.

10. Write a program to input a letter of the alphabet in upper case. Display in both octal and decimal the ASCII code for the character.

[11]. Write a program to input the radius of a sphere and calculate the surface area and volume of the sphere. The formulae for the surface area and volume of the sphere follow.

surface_area = 4.0 * pi * radius * radius

volume = surface_area * radius / 3

where pi may be taken as 3.14159.

[12]. Return to the illustration of *Ben's Breakfast Bar* menu in chapter 2, figure 2.3.

A customer is given a discount of 25% on the cost of any three items of food purchased. Write a program to input the names and prices of three items chosen from the menu and output a fully itemised bill, including value added tax at 17.5%.

Chapter 5
Selection

In chapter 4 the reader was introduced to programs that were based upon the input of data, calculations made using the data and the output of results. Programs written in this manner are fine for solutions to problems that require no more than the computer to follow a sequence of instructions, but are of little use if decisions are to be made within a program. This chapter introduces the reader to coding decisions and branching on the result of a decision to alternative statements in a program. By the end of the chapter the reader should have an understanding of the following topics.

- [ ] The syntax and use of the statements **if** and **if .. else.**

- [ ] The construction and evaluation of a conditional expression.

- [ ] Embedding selection statements one within another.

- [ ] The declaration of variables of enumerated type.

- [ ] The use of logical operators in the construction of conditional expressions.

- [ ] The conditional operator.

- [ ] The syntax and use of the **switch** statement.

5.1 If

Consider the following simple program which informs the user of what garment to wear depending on whether it is raining or not.

```
/*
c5_dpp\ex_01.c
program to demonstrate the if statement
*/

#include <stdio.h>
#include <string.h>

main()
{
    const   char    yes = 'Y';

            char    reply;
            char    garment[] = "overcoat";

            printf("is it raining outside? answer Y[es] or N[o] ");
            scanf("%c", &reply);

            if (reply == yes) strcpy(garment, "raincoat");

            printf("before you go out today take your %s\n", garment);
}
```

Results from program ex_01.c being run twice

```
is it raining outside? answer Y[es] or N[o] N
before you go out today take your overcoat

is it raining outside? answer Y[es] or N[o] Y
before you go out today take your raincoat
```

In tracing through the program the following operations take place. The string variable garment is initialised to the value *overcoat* in the declaration of garment. The user is then requested to input whether it is raining or not. If the answer to the question is **Y** *(yes)*, then the value of garment is changed to *raincoat*. However, if the answer to the question is **N** *(no)*, then the value of garment remains unaltered. Finally the user is advised of the garment to take before venturing outdoors.

In the program it has been possible to ask a question, and depending upon the answer, select an alternative statement for the computer to execute. This is possible by using the **if** statement

```
    if (reply == yes) strcpy(garment, "raincoat");
```

The expression *reply* == *yes* is known as a conditional expression, where the symbol == represents the relational operator *equal to*. The conditional expression will either equate to non-zero, when the reply is equal to yes, or zero, when the reply is **not** equal to yes, therefore by implication may be equal to no. Only when the expression equates to non-zero will the statement immediately after the conditional expression be executed by the computer. If the conditional expression equates to zero, the computer will ignore the statement after the conditional expression and branch to the next executable statement. The end of the if statement, as far as the computer is concerned, follows the ; (semicolon) after the statement *strcpy(garment, "raincoat")*.

Notice that other than in the string declaration it is **not** possible to assign a string literal to a string variable. A string must be copied into a variable using the routine *strcpy* from the <string.h> header found in the standard library. This is the reason why the header <string.h> has been included in the program.

In the conditional expression *reply == yes*, pay particular attention to the data types being used. The data type for reply is *char*, and the identifier *yes* is declared as a constant assigned the value 'Y'. This technique has been used to improve the readability of the program. An alternative method of coding the conditional expression could have been *reply == 'Y'*, which is not as clear.

Conditional expressions in many high level languages equate to either *false* or *true*. However, in C *false* and *true* are not keywords and conditions equate to either zero, corresponding to *false*, or non-zero, corresponding to *true*.

5.2 If .. else

The following syntax notation indicates that there is more to the if statement than was indicated in the previous section.

selection-statement:

        if (*expression*) *statement*
        if (*expression*) *statement* **else** *statement*

Consider the following modification to the previous program to include the statement if ..else.

```
/*
c5_dpp\ex_02.c
program to demonstrate the if .. else statement
*/

#include <stdio.h>
#include <string.h>

main()
{
        const   char    yes = 'Y';

                char    reply;
                char    garment[9];

        printf("is it raining outside? answer Y[es] or N[o] ");
        scanf("%c", &reply);
```

```
        if (reply == yes)
            strcpy(garment, "raincoat");
        else
            strcpy(garment, "overcoat");

            printf("before you go out today take your %s\n", garment);
}
```

The function of the program is exactly the same as before. If it was executed using the same data as the first program then there would be no change in the output.

There are two differences in the construction of the program. Firstly there has been no initial assignment to the string variable garment, and secondly an if ..else statement of the form

```
        if (reply == yes)
            strcpy(garment, "raincoat");
        else
            strcpy(garment, "overcoat");
```

has replaced the if statement in the previous program. The manner in which this statement functions is very straightforward. If the result of the conditional expression *reply == yes* is non-zero (*true*) then the statement *strcpy(garment,"raincoat")* will be executed. However, if the result of the conditional expression is zero (*false*), then the statement after **else** *strcpy(garment,"overcoat")* will be executed by the computer. In both cases the computer will then branch to the printf statement after the if .. else .. statement.

5.3 Nested if 's

The statement that follows the conditional expression and/or *else* can also be an *if* statement. In the previous examples if the weather had been warm then wearing either a raincoat or an overcoat could prove to be very uncomfortable. If a second item of data is included about the temperature then it is possible to more accurately specify what to wear whether it is raining or not.

Problem - If it is raining and the temperature is less than 60° Fahrenheit then wear a raincoat, otherwise if it is warmer then take an umbrella. However, if it is not raining and the temperature is less than 60° Fahrenheit then wear an overcoat, otherwise if it is warmer then wear a jacket. The program has been reconstructed to take these new facts into account. The outer if ..else statement is used to determine which path to take depending upon whether it is raining. The inner if ..else statements are used to determine which path to take depending upon the temperature.

Notice also the use of the relational operator in the expression *temperature < 60*. The relational operator < means *less than*. A list of relational operators that can be used in conditional expressions is given in figure 5.1.

operator	meaning
>	greater than
<	less than
==	equal to
>=	greater than or equal to
<=	less than or equal to
!=	not equal to

figure 5.1 relational operators

```
/*
c5_dpp\ex_03.c
program to demonstrate the if .. else statement
*/

#include <stdio.h>
#include <string.h>

main()
{
        const   char    yes = 'Y';

                char    reply;
                char    garment[9];
                int     temperature;

                printf("what is the temperature outside today? ");
                scanf("%d", &temperature); getchar();

                printf("is it raining outside? answer Y[es] or N[o] ");
                scanf("%c", &reply);

                if (reply == yes)

                    if (temperature < 60)
                        strcpy(garment, "raincoat");
                    else
                        strcpy(garment, "umbrella");

                else

                    if (temperature < 60)
                        strcpy(garment, "overcoat");
                    else
                        strcpy(garment, "jacket");


                printf("before you go out today take your %s\n", garment);
}
```

Results from program ex_03.c being run four times

```
what is the temperature outside today? 50
is it raining outside? answer Y[es] or N[o] Y
before you go out today take your raincoat

what is the temperature outside today? 50
is it raining outside? answer Y[es] or N[o] N
before you go out today take your overcoat

what is the temperature outside today? 60
is it raining outside? answer Y[es] or N[o] Y
before you go out today take your umbrella

what is the temperature outside today? 60
is it raining outside? answer Y[es] or N[o] N
before you go out today take your jacket
```

In the program, after both the *temperature* and *reply* have been input, if the conditional expression *reply* == *yes* is true, then the statement after the conditional expression will be obeyed. But this is another if statement! If the conditional expression *temperature < 60* is true then the statement *strcpy(garment "raincoat")* will be executed, however, if the conditional expression *temperature < 60* is false then the statement *strcpy(garment, "umbrella")* will be executed. In either case the computer will then branch to the next executable statement after the last statement in the outer if .. else statement. If the conditional expression *reply == yes* is false, then the statement after else, in the outer if ..else, will be obeyed, and if the conditional expression *temperature < 60* is true then the statement after the conditional expression *strcpy(garment, "overcoat")* will be executed, however, if the conditional expression *temperature < 60* is false then the statement *strcpy(garment, "jacket")* will be executed.

In the last example only one statement was executed whether the conditional expression evaluated to zero or non-zero. What if more than one statement is to be executed? The answer is to treat the group of statements as a compound statement by introducing braces { } , for example:

```
if (alpha == beta)
{
   A = B;
   C = D;
}
else
{
   A = D;
   C = B;
}
```

If .. else statements can be nested to any depth, however, you should pay particular attention to the use of indentation and the grouping of else statements. In the following example, to which *if* statement does the single *else* statement belong?

```
if (alpha == 3)
   if (beta == 4)
     printf("alpha 3 beta 4\n");
else
   printf("alpha beta not valid");
```

The indentation suggests that the else belongs to if (alpha == 3), however, as you might expect this is wrong. The rule in C regarding which else belongs to which if is simple. An else clause belongs to the nearest if statement that has not already been paired with an else. This example can be rewritten taking into account the correct indentation.

```
if (alpha == 3)
   if (beta == 4)
     printf("alpha 3 beta 4\n");
   else
     printf("alpha beta not valid");
```

If the else clause did belong to if (alpha == 3) then braces would be introduced into the coding thus:

```
if (alpha == 3)
{
   if (beta == 4)
     printf("alpha 3 beta 4\n");
}
else
   printf("alpha beta not valid");
```

5.4 Enumerated data type

In order to clarify the coding in a computer program it sometimes helps if integer values such as 0 and 1, are replaced by meaningful names. An enumeration is a collection of integer values that have been given names by the programmer. All enumerated constants start with the integer value 0, unless otherwise specified by the programmer, and successive constants have successive integer values. For example, a condition in an if statement is regarded as false if it evaluates to zero and true if it evaluates to non-zero. By stating **enum {false, true}** the names *false* and *true* become synonymous with the numbers 0 and 1, and can be used in place of 0 and 1.

A programmer is allowed to explicitly define a data type that is not implicit in the language by using **typedef**. The Boolean data type is common in many high-level languages with the exception of C. In this example a data type *boolean* has been defined that contains the enumerated constants false and true where false = 0 and true = 1.

```
typedef enum {false, true} boolean;
```

A variable can then be designated the data type *boolean*, and initialised to the value false. For example:

```
boolean error = false;
```

In program *c5_dpp\ex_03.c* how would the computer cater for data being input that did not match either *yes* or *no* in response to a reply? If the reply was neither **Y** or **N** then the conditional expression *reply ==* *yes* would be false and the computer would assign *overcoat* to the variable *garment* if the temperature was less than sixty degrees, or would assign *jacket* to the variable *garment* if the temperature was warmer. This is clearly an undesirable feature of the program, and it is the responsibility of the programmer to trap any invalid data and report the exceptional circumstances to the user of the program.

The next program traps and reports on data being input that does not conform to the reply *yes* or *no*. The program introduces the explicitly defined type *boolean* whose values are *false* or *true*. A variable *error*, has been declared as being *boolean*, which means that the values *false* or *true* can be assigned to it. In the program the variable *error* is initialised to *false* on the assumption that no invalid data will be input. However, as soon as invalid data is recognised, the value of *error* is changed to *true*.

Since *error* is of type *boolean* and only has the values *false* (zero) or *true* (non-zero) assigned to it, the variable may be used in place of a conditional expression. Notice in the last segment of the program code that if there has been an error, the message of what garment to take is suppressed and replaced by a data error message.

```
/*
c5_dpp\ex_04.c
program to demonstrate the use of an enumeration type
*/

#include <stdio.h>
#include <string.h>

main()
{
        typedef enum{false, true} boolean;

        const   char    yes = 'Y';
        const   char    no  = 'N';

                char    reply;
                char    garment[9];
                int     temperature;
                boolean error = false;

        printf("what is the temperature outside today? ");
        scanf("%d", &temperature); getchar();

        printf("is it raining outside? answer Y[es] or N[o] ");
        scanf("%c", &reply);

        if (reply == yes)

            if (temperature < 60)
```

```
                strcpy(garment, "raincoat");
        else
                strcpy(garment, "umbrella");

    else

        if (reply == no)

                if (temperature < 60)
                    strcpy(garment, "overcoat");
                else
                    strcpy(garment, "jacket");

        else
                error = true;


    if (error)
        printf("DATA ERROR - reply not input as either Y or N\n");
    else
        printf("before you go out today take your %s\n", garment);
}
```

Results from the program ex_04.c being run twice

```
what is the temperature outside today? 65
is it raining outside? answer Y[es] or N[o] Y
before you go out today take your umbrella

what is the temperature outside today? 65
is it raining outside? answer Y[es] or N[o] ?
DATA ERROR - reply not input as either Y or N
```

5.5 Conditional expressions

From the discussion so far it should be clear to the reader that conditional expressions can only equate to one of two values, either zero (false) or non-zero (true). Examples of conditional expressions given so far have been *temperature < 60, reply == yes, reply == no* and *error*.

Problem - The next example is a program that will input the name of a person and decide whether they are a suspect to a crime. It has been reported that the crime was committed by a person aged between 20 and 25 years, and between 66 to 70 inches tall. The program displays the name of the suspect if they fit this description.

```
/*
c5_dpp\ex_05.c
program to display the name of a suspect to a crime who is aged between
20 and 25 years and between 66 inches and 70 inches tall
*/

#include <stdio.h>

main()
{
    char      name[20];
    int       age;
    int       height;

    printf("input name of suspect "); gets(name);
    printf("age? "); scanf("%d", &age);
    printf("height? "); scanf("%d", &height);

    if (age >= 20 && age <= 25)

      if (height >= 66 && height <= 70)
         printf("%s is a suspect and should be interrogated\n", name);

}
```

Results from program ex_05.c being run

```
input name of suspect Artful Dodger
age? 23
height? 69
Artful Dodger is a suspect and should be interrogated
```

The conditions used in this program are (age >=20), (age <=25), (height >= 66) and (height <=70). It has been possible to combine these conditions into (age >= 20 && age <= 25), and (height >= 66 && height <= 70) by using the logical operator *and* (**&&**). A truth table for logical *and* is given in figure 5.2. This table can be interpreted as follows.

If the (age >= 20) is condition X and (age <= 25) is condition Y, then X && Y can only be *true* if both condition X is *true* and condition Y is *true*. In other words both conditions (age >= 20) and (age <= 25) must be *true* for the expression to be *true*. Therefore, if either condition X or condition Y or both, happen to be *false* the complete expression given by X && Y is *false*.

Similarly both conditions in the Boolean expression (height >= 66 && height <=70) must be *true* for the condition to be *true*. If either one condition or both conditions are *false* then the conditional expression is *false*.

condition X	condition Y	X && Y
FALSE	FALSE	FALSE
FALSE	TRUE	FALSE
TRUE	FALSE	FALSE
TRUE	TRUE	TRUE

figure 5.2 truth table for logical AND

In the program, if the age is between 20 and 25 years, then the computer executes the next **if** statement, and if the height is between 66 and 70 inches then the name of the suspect is printed. This program can be reconstructed, by omitting the second **if** statement, and combining the conditions for age and height as follows.

```
if (age >= 20 && age  <= 25 && height >= 66 && height  <= 70)
   printf("%s is a suspect and should be interrogated\n", name);
```

The same program can be reconstructed yet again using different conditions and the logical operator *or* (||). By considering the age and height to lie outside the ranges it is possible to construct the following conditional expressions:

```
(age < 20 || age > 25)
(height < 66 || height > 70)
```

From the truth table for logical *or*, given in figure 5.3, if (age < 20) is condition X, and (age >25) is condition Y, then X || Y is *true* if X is *true*, <u>or</u> Y is *true*, <u>or</u> both are *true*. Clearly both conditions cannot be true in this example.

Similarly, if (height < 66) is condition X, and (height > 70) is condition Y, then X || Y is *true* if X is *true*, or Y is *true*, or both are *true*. Once again both conditions cannot be true in this example. The conditions for age and height can also be combined into

```
(age < 20 || age > 25 || height < 66 || height  > 70)
```

Thus if any one of the conditions is *true* the entire conditional expression is *true*, and the suspect is released. However, if all the conditions are *false*, then the entire conditional expression must be *false*, the suspect is between 20 and 25 years of age and between 66 and 70 inches tall, and is held for interrogation, as depicted in the next program.

condition X	condition Y	X || Y
FALSE	FALSE	FALSE
FALSE	TRUE	TRUE
TRUE	FALSE	TRUE
TRUE	TRUE	TRUE

figure 5.3 truth table for logical OR

```
/*
c5_dpp\ex_06.c
program to display the name of a suspect to a crime who is aged between
20 and 25 years and between 66 inches and 70 inches tall
*/

#include <stdio.h>

main()
{
        char    name[20];
        int     age;
        int     height;

        printf("input name of suspect "); gets(name);
        printf("age? "); scanf("%d", &age);
        printf("height? "); scanf("%d", &height);

        printf("%s", name);

        if (age < 20 || age > 25 || height < 66 || height > 70)
            printf(" is not a suspect and should be released\n");
        else
            printf(" is a suspect and should be interrogated\n");
}
```

Results from program ex_06.c being run twice

```
input name of suspect Bill Sykes
age? 44
height? 68
Bill Sykes is not a suspect and should be released

input name of suspect Artful Dodger
age? 23
height? 69
Artful Dodger is a suspect and should be interrogated
```

5.6 Conditional operator

In an earlier example in this chapter, program *ex_04.c*, if a user had typed either the values **y** or **n**, without depressing the shift key, in response to the question *is is raining outside? answer Y[es] or N[o]* they would have been informed that the response was in error. However, the user had typed the correct letter, it was simply in lower case and not upper case as requested. What is required in the program is a means of converting the character to upper case, if it is a lower case letter of the alphabet. This is possible by using the following statement.

```
if ('a'<=reply && reply <='z') reply = reply - 32
```

If the value of reply is input as a lower case letter of the alphabet then the condition is true and the value 32 is deducted from the ASCII code of the character. This has the effect of changing the ASCII code for the character to the ASCII code for the corresponding upper case letter of the alphabet. If the condition is false then the value of reply remains unchanged.

An alternative method of expressing this statement is by the use of a *conditional operator* **? :** (the symbols ? and : are considered to be a single operator) and requires three operands in the format:

```
expression_1 ? expression_2 : expression_3
```

The expression is evaluated as follows: expression_1 is evaluated to either zero (false) or non-zero (true). If the value of expression_1 is non-zero (true), then the entire expression takes on the value of expression_2. However, if the value of expression_1 is zero (false) then the entire expression takes the value of expression_3. The if statement used to convert lower case letters to upper case may be replaced by:

```
reply = ('a' <= reply && reply <= 'z') ? reply - 32 : reply
```

however, it is questionable whether it is as easy to understand as the *if* statement it has replaced!

The program *ex_04.c*, defined in section 5.4 has been re-coded to include the following features.

(i) A statement containing a conditional operator for the conversion of a lower case character to an upper case character. (ii) The use of the logical operator **&&** to combine several conditions and reduce the complexity of the nested if statements.

```
/*
c5_dpp\ex_07.c
program to demonstrate the use of a condition operator and
logical operators
*/

#include <stdio.h>
#include <string.h>

main()
{
    typedef enum{false, true} boolean;
```

89

```
const    char    yes = 'Y';
const    char    no  = 'N';
char     reply;
char     garment[9];
int      temperature;
boolean error = false;

printf("what is the temperature outside today? ");
scanf("%d", &temperature); getchar();
printf("is it raining outside? answer Y[es] or N[o] ");
scanf("%c", &reply);

reply = ('a' <= reply && reply <= 'z') ? reply - 32 : reply;

if (reply == yes && temperature < 60)
      strcpy(garment, "raincoat");
else if (reply == yes && temperature >= 60)
      strcpy(garment, "umbrella");
else if (reply == no && temperature < 60)
      strcpy(garment, "overcoat");
else if (reply == no && temperature >= 60)
      strcpy(garment, "jacket");
else
      error = true;

if (error)
      printf("DATA ERROR - reply not input as either Y or N\n");
else
      printf("before you go out today take your %s\n", garment);
}
```

The results from running this program are very similar to those shown earlier. The only exception is that lower case **y** or **n** can now be input, in response to the question *is it raining outside? - answer Y[es] or N[o],* without resulting in an error.

5.7 Switch

An ordinal type has a value that belongs to an ordered set of items. For example integers are ordinal types since they belong to the set of values from -32768 to +32767. A character is an ordinal type since it belongs to the ASCII character set of values from the *null* character to the *del* character. Real numbers and strings are not ordinal types.

If selection is to be based upon an ordinal type then a **switch** statement can be used in preference to multiple **if..else** statements.

The syntax of the switch statement follows.

switch-statement:
>   **switch** (*expression*) *labelled-statement*

labelled-statement:

> *identifier* **:** *statement*
> **case** *constant-expression* **:** *statement*
> **default** **:** *statement*

The expression must evaluate to an ordinal value. Each possible ordinal value is represented as a case label, which indicates the statement to be executed corresponding to the value of the expression. Those values that are not represented by case labels will result in the statement after *default* being executed.

Problem - In the example that follows a user is invited to input a value for a motorway junction on the M2 in Kent. Depending upon the value of the junction from 1 to 7, the destination of the adjoining roads at that junction are displayed. If the value input is not in the range 1..7 the statement after the default will warn the user of the data error. Notice that every case statement list must be terminated with a break statement. Failure to comply with this requirement will cause the computer to test the remaining case labels in the switch statement. The break statement causes the computer to branch to the end of the switch statement.

```c
/*
C5_dpp\ex_08.c
program to demonstrate the use of switch and break statements
*/

#include <stdio.h>

main()
{
        int     junction_number;

        printf("input junction number on the M2 motorway ");
        scanf("%d", &junction_number);

        switch(junction_number)
        {
        case 1:  printf("A2 only\n"); break;
        case 2:  printf("A228 Snodland Rochester\n"); break;
        case 3:  printf("A229 Maidstone Chatham\n"); break;
        case 4:  printf("A278 Gillingham\n"); break;
        case 5:  printf("A249 Sittingbourne Sheerness\n"); break;
        case 6:  printf("A251 Ashford Faversham\n"); break;
        case 7:  printf("A2 Canterbury Dover/ A299 Margate Ramsgate\n");
                 break;
        default: printf("DATA ERROR - incorrect junction number\n");
        }
}
```

Results from program ex_08.c being run three times

```
input junction number on the M2 motorway 5
A249 Sittingbourne Sheerness

input junction number on the M2 motorway 3
A229 Maidstone Chatham

input junction number on the M2 motorway 66
DATA ERROR - incorrect junction number
```

By comparing the switch statement in the program with the syntax notation, the reader should note the following points.

An expression is any expression that will evaluate to an item of ordinal type. In this example the expression consists of a single variable *exit_number* of type integer, which evaluates to an integer in the range 1 .. 7.

A case label is any value that corresponds to the ordinal type in the expression. Case labels in this example represent the junction numbers 1, 2, 3, 4, 5, 6 and 7. Case labels must be unique.

The use of default is optional, and used for the purpose of trapping any values of the expression that are not represented as case labels.

5.8 Worked examples

This section contains two programs to further demonstrate the use of if, if ..else and switch statements.

Problem - The first program in this section validates a date as far as the year 2099. The format of the date is three integers representing day, month and year. The program checks that the number of months in a year should not exceed 12, and that the number of days in each month has not been exceeded. The program also reports on Leap Years.

Algorithm

input date in format day, month and year

validate the month in range 1..12
calculate the number of days in the month allowing for a Leap Year

if error in month or days in month then
    report error
else
    report date is valid

The validation of both month and the number of days in a month, together with determining a Leap Year can be incorporated into a switch statement. The syntax of the switch statement is not fully represented in the pseudo-code, however, the functionality of the switch statement remains the same.

switch month

1,3,5,7,8,10,12	:	*number of days in month is 31;*
4,6,9,11	:	*number of days in month is 30;*
2	:	*if leap year then*
		number of days in month is 29
		report on Leap year
		else
		number of days in month is 28
default	:	*error in month number;*

The method of determining a Leap Year has been to divide the year by 4, and to test for a zero remainder. For example, if the year is 1992, then 1992 % 4 is 498 after division with a remainder 0. Therefore the condition (1992 % 4 == 0) would be *true* for a Leap Year. Clearly if the year was 1993, then 1993 % 4 is 498 after division with a remainder 1. Therefore the condition (1993 % 4 == 0) would be *false* for a non Leap Year.

Data Dictionary - The numeric values for the day, month, year and number of days in a month are represented as integers. Notice the use of the boolean variable *error* to trap a possible error in the value for months.

```
typedef enum {false, true} boolean;

int     day, month, year;
int     number_of_days;
boolean error = false;
```

Test data - Dates should be chosen that fully test the algorithm, for example a valid date (18 3 1987), a Leap Year (12 2 1992) and either a month or a day that is out of range (30 2 1987).

Desk Check

variable	value(s)		
day	18	12	30
month	3	2	2
year	1987	1992	1987
number_of_days	31	29	28
error	false	false	true

```
                           Screen Layout
  12345678901234567890123456789012345678901234567890
  input a date in the format DD MM 19YY
  12 2 1992
  1992 is a Leap Year
  date checked and is valid
```

```c
/*
c5_dpp\ex_09.c
program to validate a date in the format DD MM YY
*/


#include <stdio.h>

main()
{
        typedef enum {false, true} boolean;

        int       day, month, year;
        int       number_of_days;
        boolean error = false;

        printf("input a date in the format DD MM 19YY\n");
        scanf("%d%d%d", &day, &month, &year);

        /* calculate the number of days in a month and check for a Leap Year */

        switch (month)
        {
        case 1: case 3: case 5: case 7: case 8: case 10: case 12:
        number_of_days = 31; break;

        case 4: case 6: case 9: case 11:
        number_of_days = 30; break;

        case 2:  {
                if (year % 4 == 0)
                {
                    number_of_days = 29;
                    printf("%d is a Leap Year\n", year);
                }
                else
                    number_of_days = 28;
                break;
                }
        default: error = true;
        }
```

```
        if (day > number_of_days || error)
            printf("DATA ERROR - check day or month\n");
        else
            printf("date checked and is valid\n");

}
```

Results from program ex_09.c being run three times

```
input a date in the format DD MM 19YY
18 3 1987
date checked and is valid

input a date in the format DD MM 19YY
12 2 1992
1992 is a Leap Year
date checked and is valid

input a date in the format DD MM 19YY
30 2 1987
DATA ERROR - check day or month
```

Problem - In the final example of this chapter, a program is written to mimic a simple calculator. The user is invited to type the value of two real numbers, and to state whether the numbers are to be added (+), subtracted (-), multiplied (*) or divided (/). A switch statement is used to select the appropriate calculation corresponding to the arithmetic operator that was input. Since the result of a division by zero will give a meaningless answer, the program includes an if...else statement to trap a zero divisor.

Algorithm

input first operand
input second operand
input operator

switch operator
'+'   :   add numbers;
'-'   :   subtract numbers;
''   :   multiply numbers;*
'/'   :   if second operand is zero then
*   error in attempting to divide by zero*
*   else*
*   divide numbers;*
default :   error wrong operator

95

if error then
    report on error
else
    display the result of the computation

Data Dictionary - The two operands and result are of type float. The operator is a single character, and the error condition is an enumerated type boolean.

```
typedef enum {false, true} boolean;

float   first, second;
float   result;
char    operator;
boolean error = false;
```

Test data - In practice it would be prudent to test every path, however, in this example it is enough to test a calculation and a deliberate attempt to divide by zero. Suitable test data might be 250.0 75.0 + and 35.0 0.0 /.

Desk Check

variable	value(s)	
first	250.0	35.0
second	75.0	0.0
operator	+	/
result	325.0	not calculated
error	false	true

```
┌─────────────────────────────────────────────────────────────┐
│                       Screen Layout                           │
├─────────────────────────────────────────────────────────────┤
│12345678901234567890123456789012345678901234567890123456 7890 │
│input first number 250.0                                       │
│input second number 75.0                                       │
│input operator +                                               │
│=        325.00                                                │
└─────────────────────────────────────────────────────────────┘
```

```
/*
c5_dch\ex_10.c
program to add, subtract, multiply or divide two numbers
*/

#include <stdio.h>

main()
{
  typedef enum {false, true} boolean;

  float    first, second;
  float    result;
  char     operator;
  boolean error = false;

  printf("input first number "); scanf("%f", &first);
  printf("input second number "); scanf("%f", &second);
  getchar(); /* flush return character from buffer */
  printf("input operator "); scanf("%c", &operator);
  switch(operator)
  {
  case '+':    result = first + second; break;
  case '-':    result = first - second; break;
  case '*':    result = first * second; break;
  case '/':    if (second == 0.0)
                   error = true;
               else
                   result = first / second;

               break;
  default :    error = true;
  }

  if (error)
    printf("DATA ERROR - illegal operator or attempt to divide by zero\n");
  else
    printf(" = %10.2f\n", result);
}
```

Results from program ex_10.c being run four times

```
input first number 250.0
input second number 75.0
input operator +
=       325.00
```

```
input first number 18.0
input second number 26.0
input operator *
=       468.00

input first number 35.0
input second number 0.0
input operator /
DATA ERROR - illegal operator or attempt to divide by zero

input first number 121.0
input second number 11.0
input operator x
DATA ERROR - illegal operator or attempt to divide by zero
```

5.9 Summary

- ☐ A conditional expression evaluates to either *zero* (false) or *non-zero* (true).

- ☐ Depending upon the result of the conditional expression it is possible for the computer to select different statements in an if statement.

- ☐ The values false and true can be defined as enumerated constants that are equivalent to the values 0 and 1 respectively.

- ☐ By explicitly defining an enumerated type, containing the enumerated constants false and true, it is possible to mimic the Boolean type found in other high-level languages.

- ☐ A programmer may change the default values of the enumerated constants by assigning new integer values at the time of the enumeration declaration.

- ☐ An explicit data type may be defined by the programmer using typedef.

- ☐ Conditional expressions can be combined into one expression by using the logical operators and **&&** and or **||**.

- ☐ If statements may be nested, one within another.

- ☐ An else clause belongs to the nearest if statement that has not already been paired with an else.

- ☐ When selection is based upon an ordinal type, a switch statement may be used.

- ☐ All case labels must be unique and of an ordinal type compatible with the selector type.

5.10 Questions - *answers begin on page 468*

1. If A=1, B= -2, C=3, D=4, E='S' and F='J' then state whether the following conditions are true or false.

(a). A = = B   (b). A > B   (c). (A < C && B < D)
(d). (A < C && B > D)   (e). (A > B || C < D)
(f). E > F   (g). ((A + C) > (B - D)) && ((B + C) < (D - A))

2. How would you code the following conditions in C?

(a).   X is equal to Y
(b).   X is not equal to Y
(c).   A is less than or equal to B
(d).   Q is not greater than T(e). X is greater than or equal to Y
(f).   X is less than or equal to Y and A is not equal to B
(g).   A is greater than 18 and H is greater than 68 and W is greater than 75
(h).   G is less than 100 and greater than 50
(i).   H is less than 50 or greater than 100.

3. Trace through the following segment of code for each new value of A,B and C, and state the output in each case.

(a). A=16, B=16, C=32   (b). A=16, B= -18, C=32
(c). A= -2, B= -4, C=16

```
if (A>0)
{
   if (B<0)
     putchar('x');
   else
     if C>20
       putchar('y');
}
else
   putchar('z');
```

4. Modify the suspect program *c5_dpp\ex_06.c* given in the chapter to cater for both sexes, and eliminate all women from the list of suspects.

5. A worker is paid at the hourly rate of £8 per hour for the first 35 hours worked. Thereafter overtime is paid at 1.5 times the hourly rate for the next 25 hours worked and 2 times the hourly rate for further hours worked. Write a program to input the number of hours worked per week, calculate and output the overtime paid.

[6]. A salesperson earns commission on the value of sales. Figure 5.4 shows the scale of the commission. Write a program to input a figure for the value of sales, calculate and output the commission.

value of sales	% commission
£1 - £999	1
£1000 - £9999	5
£10000 - £99999	10

figure 5.4

7. A barometer dial is calibrated into the following climatic conditions STORM RAIN CHANGE FAIR and DRY. Write a program that will input one of these readings abbreviated to the number assigned to the condition, and output what to wear from the following rules.

1	STORM	wear overcoat and hat.
2	RAIN	wear raincoat and take umbrella.
3	CHANGE	behave as for FAIR if it rained yesterday and as for RAIN if it did not.
4	FAIR	wear jacket and take umbrella.
5	DRY	wear jacket.

Hint - Create an enumeration **enum{STORM=1,RAIN=2,CHANGE=3,FAIR=4,DRY=5}** and use the numerical code as a selector in a switch statement with the corresponding enumerated constants as case labels in the same statement.

[8]. A bicycle shop in Oxford hires bicycles by the day at different rates throughout the year, according to the season - see figure 5.5. The proprietor also gives a discount on the number of days a bicycle is hired. If the hire period is greater than 7 days, then a reduction of 25% is made. For every bicycle hired a returnable deposit of £50 must be paid. Write a program to input the season and the number of days hire, calculate and display the cost of the hire including the returnable deposit.

season	charge
Spring	£5.00
Summer	£7.50
Autumn	£3.75
Winter	£2.50

figure 5.5

Hint. Use a similar technique to that described in the previous question for the selection on the season.

9. Modify your answer to question 10 in section 4.7 of the previous chapter, to output the ASCII code of an alphabetic character as a hexadecimal number.

Chapter 6
Repetition

In writing computer programs it is often necessary to repeat part of a program a number of times. One way of achieving this would be to write out that part of the program as many times as it was needed. This however, is a very impractical method, since it would produce a very lengthy computer program and the number of times part of the program is to be repeated, is not always known in advance. The purpose of this chapter is to introduce the reader to three methods for repetition that overcome the disadvantages just mentioned. These methods are based on the control structures known as **while, do..while** and **for**. By the end of the chapter the reader should have an understanding of the following topics.

- [ ] The syntax and use of *while*, *do..while* and *for* control statements.

- [ ] A knowledge of when it is appropriate to use each statement.

- [ ] The comparison of strings, using an imported library function, in a conditional expression.

- [ ] An introduction to l-values and prefix and postfix operators.

- [ ] The detection of characters input at a keyboard.

- [ ] Unconditional branching within a program.

101

6.1 While

A while loop will allow a statement to be repeated zero or more times. The syntax of the while loop is:

while-statement:
>**while** (*expression*) *statement*

Consider the use of a while loop to display numbers on a screen while the numbers are not zero. A segment of the program follows.

```
scanf("%d", &number);
while (number != 0)
{
   printf("%3d",number);
   scanf("%d", &number);
}
```

If the first number to be read is zero then the conditional expression *number != 0* will be false. The computer will not enter the loop but branch to the next executable statement after the end of the compound statement delimited by the braces { }. Since the loop was not entered the contents of the loop is said to have been repeated zero times.

However, if the first number to be read was non-zero, the conditional expression would be true, and the computer would execute the statements contained within the loop. To this end the number would be written on the screen and the next number input at the keyboard. The computer then returns to the line containing the conditional expression which is re-evaluated to test whether the new number is not zero. If the condition is true the computer continues to execute the statements in the loop. If the condition is false the computer will branch to the next executable statement after the end of the compound statement.

Restating the behaviour of the while loop, if the first number read is zero then the loop is not entered, the statements within the loop have been repeated zero times. If the second number to be read is zero the statements in the loop will have been repeated once. If the third number to be read is zero the statements in the loop will have been repeated twice, etc. Therefore, if the hundredth number to be read is zero the statements inside the loop will have been repeated ninety-nine times.

The outline program has been developed into the following C program.

```
/*
c6_dpp\ex_01.c
program to demonstrate a while loop
*/

#include <stdio.h>

main()
{
        int     number;

        printf("input an integer - terminate with 0 ");
        scanf("%d", &number);
```

```
        while (number != 0)
        {
                printf("%3d\n", number);
                printf("input an integer - terminate with 0 ");
                scanf("%d", &number);
        }
}
```

The specimen outputs from the program shows (i) the statements within the loop being repeated twice, and (ii) the statements within the loop not being repeated at all.

(i) Results from program ex_01.c being run

```
input an integer - terminate with 0 36
 36
input an integer - terminate with 0 18
 18
input an integer - terminate with 0 0
```

(ii) Results from program ex_01.c being run

```
input an integer - terminate with 0 0
```

The program *c5_dpp\ex_05.c*, taken from section 5.5 in the previous chapter, has been re-constructed to include a while loop to allow the program to be repeated many times without the need to re-run the program.

Before the while loop is entered the user is requested to input the name of a suspect. If the word END is input, then this is a cue to exit from the while loop. The reader might expect to construct the conditional expression *name != "END"* to control the while loop, for example, *while (name != "END")*. However, in C you cannot compare strings in this manner. There exists in the standard library a header file <string.h> that contains a routine *strcmp* that will allow two strings to be compared, and returns the value zero if both strings are the same, otherwise it returns the value non-zero. To compare the name with the string "END", it is necessary to construct the conditional expression *(strcmp(name, "END") == 0)*. If the contents of the string variable *name* is equal to the string "END", then the result is true. If this expression is to be used in a while loop it will be necessary to negate the condition, for example,

```
        while (strcmp(name, "END") != 0)
```

The while loop will then be exited only when the conditional expression *strcmp(name, "END")* is zero.

As long as the string "END" is not input in response to the prompt to input the name of a suspect, the computer will continue to process the details of all suspects to the crime.

```
/*
c6_dpp\ex_02.c
program to display the name of a suspect to a crime who is aged between
20 and 25 years and between 66 inches and 70 inches tall
*/

#include <stdio.h>
#include <string.h>

main()
{
    char    name[20];
    int     age;
    int     height;

    printf("input name of suspect - terminate with END ");
    gets(name);

    while (strcmp(name, "END") != 0)
    {
        printf("age? "); scanf("%d", &age);
        printf("height? "); scanf("%d", &height);
        getchar();

        if (age >= 20 && age <= 25)

            if (height >= 66 && height <= 70)
                printf("%s is a suspect and should be interrogated\n", name);

        printf("input name of suspect - terminate with END ");
        gets(name);
    }
}
```

Results from program ex_02.c being run

```
input name of suspect - terminate with END Smith
age? 20
height? 68
Smith is a suspect and should be interrogated
input name of suspect - terminate with END Jones
age? 26
height? 68
input name of suspect - terminate with END Evans
age? 25
height? 69
```

```
Evans is a suspect and should be interrogated
input name of suspect - terminate with END END
```

6.2 Do .. while

Unlike a while loop a *do..while* loop will permit the statements within the loop to be executed at least once by the computer. The syntax of the do..while loop is:

do-while:
>   do *statement* **while** (*expression*) ;

The program *c5_dpp\ex_08.c*, taken from section 5.7 in the previous chapter, has been re-constructed to include a do..while loop to allow the program to be repeated many times without the need to re-run the program. In this program the user is given the option to continue executing the statements in the loop until the reply to the question is 'N' *no*.

Notice that the computer enters the loop without any test for entry being made. Hence the contents of a do..while loop will always be executed at least once. There can be either a single statement or a compound statement between the reserved words do and while. If the reply to continue is 'N' *no* then the conditional expression, *reply == yes,* will be false and the computer will branch to the next executable statement after the conditional expression. However, if the reply is 'Y' *yes* then the conditional expression will be true and the computer will repeat all the statements within the loop.

In this example the conditional expression that controls the exit from the do..while loop compares the contents of a character variable with a character constant. The character constant *yes* had been declared as a constant in the program.

```
/*
C6_dpp\ex_03.c
program to demonstrate the use of the do..while statement
*/

#include <stdio.h>

main()
{
        const char yes = 'Y';

        int     junction_number;
        char    reply;

        do
        {
                printf("input junction number on the M2 motorway ");
                scanf("%d", &junction_number); getchar();
```

105

```
        switch(junction_number)
        {
        case 1:  printf("A2 only\n"); break;
        case 2:  printf("A228 Snodland Rochester\n"); break;
        case 3:  printf("A229 Maidstone Chatham\n"); break;
        case 4:  printf("A278 Gillingham\n"); break;
        case 5:  printf("A249 Sittingbourne Sheerness\n"); break;
        case 6:  printf("A251 Ashford Faversham\n"); break;
        case 7:  printf("A2 Canterbury Dover/ A299 Margate Ramsgate\n");
                 break;
        default: printf("DATA ERROR - incorrect junction number\n");
        }

        printf("continue? - answer Y[es] or N[o] ");
        scanf("%c", &reply);
        /* convert lower case to upper case */
        if ('a' <= reply && reply <= 'z') reply = reply - 32;
    }
    while (reply == yes);
}
```

Results from program ex_03.c being run

```
input junction number on the M2 motorway 5
A249 Sittingbourne Sheerness
continue? - answer Y[es] or N[o] Y
input junction number on the M2 motorway 7
A2 Canterbury Dover/ A299 Margate Ramsgate
continue? - answer Y[es] or N[o] y
input junction number on the M2 motorway 8
DATA ERROR - incorrect junction number
continue? - answer Y[es] or N[o] y
input junction number on the M2 motorway 1
A2 only
continue? - answer Y[es] or N[o] N
```

6.3 L-values

At this point in the chapter it is worth digressing to the topic of incrementing and decrementing values, in particular in the context of control variables found in loops.

An lvalue (pronounced el-value) and representing l(eft)value refers to an area of storage in computer memory. In practice lvalues are normally the names of simple variables, since these represent storage locations in computer memory.

In the first example in section 6.1 the variable *number* was an lvalue.

The C language contains increment and decrement operators, written as ++ and -- respectively, and are used to increase or decrease an lvalue. In other languages these might be functions INC and DEC. However, unlike other languages, these operators can be described as prefix or postfix operators depending upon whether they come before the lvalue or after the lvalue.

Prefix operators change an lvalue <u>before</u> the value is used, whereas postfix operators change an lvalue <u>after</u> the value is used. The following program serves to illustrate the use of prefix and postfix operators on an lvalue.

```
/*
c6_dpp\ex_04.c
program to demonstrate prefix and postfix operators
*/

#include <stdio.h>

main()
{
        int counter = 1;

        /* counter is increased to 2 */
        counter++;
        printf("%2d", counter);

        /* value of counter 2 and is increased to
        3 after printf executed */
        printf("%2d", counter++);
        printf("%2d", counter);

        /* counter is increased to 4 before printf is executed */
        printf("%2d\n", ++counter);

        /* counter is decreased to 3 */
        counter--;
        printf("%2d", counter);

        /* value of counter 3 and is decreased to
        2 after printf executed */
```

```
        printf("%2d", counter--);
        printf("%2d", counter);

        /* counter is decreased to 1 before printf is executed */
        printf("%2d\n", --counter);
}
```

Results from program ex_04.c being run

```
2 2 3 4
3 3 2 1
```

Do you understand why the results appear as they do? If you are not sure then look again at the comments within the program.

The increment and decrement prefix and postfix operators are useful within loops as the following program illustrates.

```
/*
c6_dpp\ex_05.c
program to demonstrate the use of prefix and postfix operators
within while loops and do..while loops
*/

#include <stdio.h>

main()
{
        int counter;

        counter = 1;
        while (counter < 4)
        {
            printf("%2d", counter);
            counter++;
        }
        printf("\n");

        counter = 1;
        while (counter < 4)
            printf("%2d", counter++);

        printf("\n");
```

```
        counter = 1;
        do
        {
                printf("%2d", counter);
                ++counter;
        }
        while (counter < 4);
}
```

Results from program ex_05.c being run

```
1 2 3
1 2 3
1 2 3
```

Clearly the three loops produce the same output. In the first loop the counter is incremented by 1 as a separate statement using a postfix operator.

In the second loop the postfix operator has been embedded within a printf statement. After the printf statement has been executed the value for counter will be increased by 1.

In the third loop the counter is incremented by 1 as a separate statement using a prefix operator.

6.4 For loop

The format of a *for* statement in C is:

for-statement:

                for (*expression-1 opt* ; *expression-2 opt* ; *expression-3 opt*) *statement*

where *expression-1* and *expression-3* are both assignment statements and *expression-2* is a conditional statement and can be regarded as a shorthand version of the following while loop.

```
expression_1;          /* initialisation of loop control variable */
while (expression_2) /* conditional expression */
{
    statement(s);
    expression_3    /* change value of loop control variable */
}
```

The following program serves to illustrate how for statements may be used. In other high-level languages it is common practice to state the range of values over which the loop control variable is applicable, however, in C only the initial value is given, followed by the condition under which loop execution continues, and the incremental or step value of the loop control variable.

```
/*
c6_dpp\ex_06.c
program to demonstrate the use of the for loop
*/

#include <stdio.h>

main()
{
    int counter;

    for (counter = 1; counter < 4; counter++)
        printf("%2d", counter);

    printf("\n");

    /* if expression_1 is omitted, then the initialisation of the
    control variable must take place outside the beginning of the loop
    */
    counter = 1;
    for (; counter < 4; counter++)
        printf("%2d", counter);

    printf("\n");

    /* if expression_2 is omitted then the loop does not terminate
    unless it contains a break statement
    */
    for (counter = 1;; counter++)
    {
        printf("%2d", counter);
        if (counter == 3) break;
    }
    printf("\n");

    /* if expression_3 is omitted then the loop control variable
    must be incremented (or decremented) within the body of the loop
    */
    for (counter = 1; counter < 4;)
        printf("%2d", counter++);

}
```

Results from program ex_06.c being run

```
1 2 3
1 2 3
1 2 3
1 2 3
```

By omitting all three expressions it is possible to set up an infinite loop!

```
for ( ; ; )
    printf("forever and ever ... ");
```

Notice that despite the expressions being omitted in for loops the semi-colon ; separators must be present.

By using a *comma* operator it is possible to initialise and increment/ decrement other variables in addition to the loop control variable. Either expression_1 and/ or expression_3 in a for statement can be composed from single expressions that are separated from each other by commas.

Consider the following program in which the positions of each of the letters in the alphabet is displayed. Comma operators in the for statement have been used to initialise the value of the index and letter, and increment both the value of the index and the letter.

```
/*
c6_dpp\ex_07.c
program to display the position of each letter of the alphabet
*/

#include <stdio.h>

main()
{
        char letter;
        int  counter;

        for (counter = 1, letter = 'A'; counter <= 26; counter++, letter++)
        {
            printf("%-3d%c\t", counter, letter);
            if  (counter % 2 == 0) printf("\n");
        }
}
```

Results from program ex_07.c being run

```
1  A       2   B
3  C       4   D
5  E       6   F
7  G       8   H
9  I       10  J
11 K       12  L
13 M       14  N
15 O       16  P
17 Q       18  R
19 S       20  T
21 U       22  V
23 W       24  X
25 Y       26  Z
```

Since some or all of the expressions that control the loop variable in a for statement can be omitted, and other expressions can be included that have no relationship with the loop variable it should be clear that there is no restriction placed on the three expressions that control the behaviour of the loop, and indeed these expressions need not involve the same variable.

Warning! Use both the comma operator and omitting expressions in a for statement, with great care! Indeed the for statement in C is very versatile, more versatile than in other high-level languages. You might produce very short, tight code, but can it be easily read and modified by someone else?

6.5 Worked examples

Problem - The following program illustrates how a sentence is input at the keyboard and the number of words in the sentence counted. It is assumed that only one space is used between words and the sentence is terminated by a full stop.

Algorithm

The complete sentence is stored in the keyboard buffer. The following algorithm assumes that the input buffer is scanned one character at a time, analysing the sentence before displaying the number of words.

initialise word count to zero
input character
while character not full stop
    if character is a space increase word count by 1
    input character
increase word count by one (since end of sentence)
display word count

Important note - the indented pseudo-code statements indicate the body of the loop

112

Data dictionary - The word delimiters, a space and a full stop, can be represented as constants in the program. These have been assigned the octal values of their respective ASCII codes. A single character is of type char, and the number of words in the sentence of type integer and initialised to zero.

```
const    char     space = 040;
const    char     full_stop = 056;

         char     character;
         int      number_of_words = 0;
```

Test data - The sentence stored in the buffer is *Have a nice day.*

Desk Check

character	number_of_words	full stop?	space?
H	0	false	false
a	0	false	false
v	0	false	false
e	0	false	false
<space>	1	false	true
a	1	false	false
<space>	2	false	true
n	2	false	false
i	2	false	false
c	2	false	false
e	2	false	false
<space>	3	false	true
d	3	false	false
a	3	false	false
y	3	false	false
. <full stop>	4	true	

```
┌──────────────────────────────────────────────────────────────┐
│                        Screen Layout                           │
├──────────────────────────────────────────────────────────────┤
│123456789012345678901234567890123456789012345678901234567890    │
│input a sentence on one line - terminate with a full stop       │
│Have a nice day.                                                │
│number of words in sentence is    4                             │
└──────────────────────────────────────────────────────────────┘
```

```
/*
c6_dpp\ex_08.c
program to count the number of words in a sentence
*/

#include <stdio.h>

main()
{
        const   char    space = 040;
        const   char    full_stop = 056;

                char    character;
                int     number_of_words = 0;

        printf("input a sentence on one line - terminate with a full stop\n");

        scanf("%c", &character);
        while (character != full_stop)
        {
                if (character == space) number_of_words++;
                scanf("%c", &character);
        }

        number_of_words++;
        printf("number of words in sentence is %d", number_of_words);
}
```

Result from program ex_08.c being run twice

```
input a sentence on one line - terminate with a full stop
Have a nice day.
number of words in sentence is  4

input a sentence on one line - terminate with a full stop
To be or not to be that is the question.
number of words in sentence is  10
```

In this example the end of the sentence was detected by using the full stop as a sentinel. However, it is possible to detect the end of a line of data by testing for the end of line character. This is given in the ASCII codes as LF with a decimal code of 10 or an octal code of 012.

Problem - In the second example of this section a program is to be written that will edit a single line of text. Within the input text will be found an opening parenthesis (, followed some characters later by a closing parenthesis). The text is to be output, with the characters between and including the parentheses removed. In this example you may assume that the character (always appears before the character), and both characters will always be present.

114

Algorithm

Once again it is assumed that the keyboard buffer contains the line of text, and the algorithm is applied to each character, in succession, in the buffer.

input character
while character not opening parenthesis '('
    display character
    input character

while character not closing parenthesis ')'
    input character

input character in order to consume closing parenthesis
while character is not end of line
    display character
    input character

Data dictionary - The end of line character can be stored as a character constant with value 012, and the character being examined from the input buffer as a variable of type char.

```
const    char    end_of_line = 012;

         char    character;
```

Test data - The line of text stored in the buffer is *printf("\n");*

Desk Check

character	(?	) ?	end_of_line?	output
p	false			p
r	false			r
i	false			i
n	false			n
t	false			t
f	false			f
(	true			
"		false		
\		false		
n		false		
"		false		
)		true		
;			false	;
<return>			true	

```
                        Screen Layout
    123456789012345678901234567890123456789012345678901234567890
    input one line of text
    printf("\n");
    printf;
```

```c
/*
c6_dpp\ex_09.c
program to input a line of text, edit a portion of the text and
output the edited text
*/

#include <stdio.h>

main()
{
        const   char    end_of_line = 012;

                char    character;

        printf("input one line of text\n");

        /* read and write characters up to ( */
        scanf("%c", &character);
        while (character != '(')
        {
                printf("%c", character);
                scanf("%c", &character);
        }

        /* read characters up to ) */
        while (character != ')' )
        {
                scanf("%c", &character);
        }

        /* read and write characters as far as the end of the line */
        scanf("%c", &character);
        while (character != end_of_line)
        {
                printf("%c", character);
                scanf("%c", &character);
        }
}
```

Results from program ex_09.c being run

```
input one line of text
printf("\n");
printf;
```

Problem - In the last worked example of this chapter, a program has been written to allow a sentence to be input at the keyboard. The sentence may be written over several lines, be punctuated by commas, semi-colons, colons, and spaces, and be terminated by a question mark, exclamation mark or full stop. The purpose of the program is to count the number of words in the sentence and display this value. The user is given the opportunity to type more than one sentence.

Every time a character is input, it is checked for being either a terminator (question mark, exclamation mark or full stop), or a word separator (comma, semi-colon, colon, space, carriage return CR or line feed LF). In response to both types of word-delimiter (terminator or separator), the word count must be increased by one. However, it is necessary to detect the occurrence of multiple spaces or two separators together, in which case the word count must not be increased again.

Algorithm

do
initialise word count to zero
input character
while character not a sentence terminator
if character is a word separator
increase word count by 1
input character
while character is space, CR or LF
input character

else
input character

increase word count by 1
display word count
ask user if there are more sentences
while more sentences to process

Data dictionary - The sentence terminators and word terminators can be represented as character constants. The character being examined from the input buffer and the user reply about more sentences, are variables of type char. The number of words in a sentence is a variable of type integer.

117

```
const    char    yes = 'Y';
const    char    question_mark = '?';
const    char    exclamation_mark = '!';
const    char    full_stop = '.';
const    char    comma = ',';
const    char    semi_colon = ';';
const    char    colon = ':';
const    char    space = ' ';
const    char    LF = 10;
const    char    CR = 13;

         char    character;
         int     words;
         char    reply;
```

Test data

The following lines of text are stored one after another in the keyboard buffer.

To be or not
to be,
that is the question!

Desk Check

character	words	terminator?	separator?	space, CR, LF?
	0			
T	0	false	false	
o	0	false	false	
\<space\>	1	false	true	
b	1	false	false	false
e	1	false	false	
\<space\>	2	false	true	
o	2	false	false	false
r	2	false	false	
\<space\>	3	false	true	
n	3	false	false	false
o	3	false	false	
t	3	false	false	
\<CR\>	4	false	true	
\<LF\>	4			true
t	4	false	false	false
o	4	false	false	
\<space\>	5	false	true	
b	5	false	false	false
e	5	false	false	
,	6	false	true	

character	words	terminator?	separator?	space, CR, LF?
<CR>	6	false		true
<LF>	6	false		true
t	6	false	false	false
h	6	false	false	
a	6	false	false	
t	6	false	false	
<space>	7	false	true	
i	7	false	false	false
s	7	false	false	
<space>	8	false	true	
t	8	false	false	false
h	8	false	false	
e	8	false	false	
<space>	9	false	true	
q	9	false	false	false
u	9	false	false	
e	9	false	false	
s	9	false	false	
t	9	false	false	
i	9	false	false	
o	9	false	false	
n	9	false	false	
!	10	true		

The output from this desk check is the number of words in the sentence which is 10.

```
+-----------------------------------------------------------------+
|                          Screen Layout                          |
+-----------------------------------------------------------------+
| 12345678901234567890123456789012345678901234567890123456789890  |
| input a sentence, terminate with ? ! or .                       |
| To be or not                                                    |
| to be,                                                          |
| that is the question!                                           |
|                                                                 |
| number of words in sentence 10                                  |
|                                                                 |
| more sentences - answer Y[es] or N[o] N                         |
|                                                                 |
+-----------------------------------------------------------------+
```

```
/*
c6_dpp\ex_10.c
program to count the number of words in a sentence
*/

#include <stdio.h>

main()
{
        const   char    yes = 'Y';
        const   char    question_mark = '?';
        const   char    exclamation_mark = '!';
        const   char    full_stop = '.';
        const   char    comma = ',';
        const   char    semi_colon = ';';
        const   char    colon = ':';
        const   char    space = ' ';
        const   char    LF = 10;
        const   char    CR = 13;

                char    character;
                int     words;
                char    reply;

        do
        {
                words = 0;
                printf("input a sentence, terminate with ? ! or .\n");
                scanf("%c", &character);

                /* test for terminator */
                while (character != question_mark &&
                        character != exclamation_mark &&
                        character != full_stop)
                    {

                        /* test for separator */
                        if (character == comma ||
                            character == semi_colon ||
                            character == colon ||
                            character == space ||
                            character == LF)
                        {
                                words++;
                                scanf("%c", &character);

                                /* ignore further separators */
                                while (character == space ||
                                        character == CR ||
```

```
                                  character == LF)
                          {
                                  scanf("%c", &character);
                          }
                  }
              else
                  scanf("%c", &character);
          }

          words++;

          /* flush input buffer */
          getchar();

          printf("\nnumber of words in sentence %d\n\n", words);
          printf("more sentences - answer Y[es] or N[o] ");
          scanf("%c",&reply);
          /* convert lower case to upper case */
          if ('a' <= reply && reply <= 'z') reply = reply - 32;

          /* flush input buffer */
          getchar();
      }
      while (reply == yes);
}
```

Results from program ex_10.c being run

```
input a sentence, terminate with ? ! or .
To be or not
to be,
that is the question!

number of words in sentence 10

more sentences - answer Y[es] or N[o] Y
input a sentence, terminate with ? ! or .
This is a test of the program,
a full sentence can be input
over
as many lines as are required,
and, full account, will be taken of all
punctuation.

number of words in sentence 29

more sentences - answer Y[es] or N[o] N
```

6.6 Unconditional branching

break statement

A break statement, first discussed in section 5.7, can be used in conjunction with an if statement anywhere in a loop to terminate the loop.

continue statement

A continue statement causes the computer to branch to the end of the last statement in a loop, but not outside the loop. If used in conjunction with an if statement, statements inside the loop can be by-passed if a particular condition happens to be true. Continue is different to break in so much as the computer remains in the loop, whereas with break the computer was taken outside the loop or selection statement.

goto statement

The author does not wish to get entangled in the age-old debate about goto statements. They of course allow for unconditional branching and should be avoided whenever possible. The break and continue statements all permit a restricted form of unconditional branching and it should not usually be necessary to use goto. However, the statement is part of the language and a brief mention is all it will receive. The format of a goto statement is: goto label; where the label is an identifier. A label must be followed by a statement and any statement can have more than one label. In the example that follows the label is *end* and it is followed by the statement printf("unconditional branch");

```
{
     .
    goto end;
     .
end: printf("unconditional branch");
     .
}
```

null statement

If the label in the last example had been at the end of the compound statement it would still require to be followed by a statement. The null statement is represented by a semi-colon ; and is used whenever a statement is required to complete the syntax, as in *end : ;*

A null statement can be used in the body of a loop if the body is required to be kept empty, for example:

```
    while ((character = getchar()) == space)
    ; /* this is the body of the loop and contains a null statement */
```

This loop will keep receiving input from a keyboard as long as the character is a space, or in other words, ignore all space characters.

Warning! Be very careful where you place null statements with regard to if, while and for statements.

6.7 Summary

- ☐ The statements within a *while* loop can be executed zero or more times.

- ☐ The statements within a *do..while* loop are executed at least once.

- ☐ Both loops use conditional expressions to control the amount of repetition.

- ☐ In a *while* loop and a *do..while* loop all statements within the loops will be executed while the conditional expression is true.

- ☐ An lvalue can be used as a loop counter, and can have its value changed by increment or decrement, prefix or postfix operators.

- ☐ Prefix operators change an lvalue before the value is used. Postfix operators change an lvalue after the value is used.

- ☐ A *for* loop is a generalised while loop and may contain up to three expressions.

- ☐ If the first expression, in a for loop is omitted, then the initialisation of the loop control variable can take place outside the loop.

- ☐ If the second expression, in a for loop is omitted, then the loop does not terminate unless it contains a break statement.

- ☐ If the third expression, in a for loop is omitted, then the loop control variable must be incremented/ decremented within the body of the loop.

- ☐ By omitting all three expressions from within a for loop it is possible to set up an infinite loop.

- ☐ By using the comma operator in a for loop it is possible to manipulate other variables/ expressions in addition to the loop expressions.

- ☐ A break statement in conjunction with an if statement can be used to terminate a loop.

- ☐ A continue statement in conjunction with an if statement can be used to branch within a loop.

- ☐ A goto statement permits unconditional branching and its use should be avoided if possible.

6.8 Questions - *answers begin on page 471*

1. Write a program to display the message 'Hello World' ten times on the screen.

2. Write a program to input a message of your choice and the number of times you want to repeat it, then repeatedly display the message.

3. Write a program to output a table of conversion from miles to kilometres. The table should contain column headings for miles and kilometres. Miles should be output as integer values between 1 to 50, in steps of 1 mile, with a new headings being printed at the beginning of the table and after 20 and 40 miles respectively. Note 1 mile = 1.609344 Km

4. Write a program using *while* loops to output:

(a). The odd integers in the range 1 to 29.

(b). The squares of even integers in the range 2 to 20.

(c). The sum of the squares of the odd integers between 1 to 13 inclusive.

(d). The alphabet in upper case.

[5]. Repeat question 4 using *for* loops.

[6]. Repeat question 4 using *do..while* loops.

7. Write a program to find and print the arithmetic mean of a list of non-zero numbers. The number of numbers is not known in advance. Terminate the sequence of numbers with zero.

8. Write a program to calculate and output the overtime pay for ten employees and the total overtime paid. Overtime is paid at £12.00 per hour for every hour worked over 40 hours per week. Assume that employees do not work for fractional parts of an hour.

9. Write a program to input a phrase and display the ASCII code for each character of the phrase.

10. Write a program to find and print the largest integer from ten integers input at the keyboard. Assume that numbers are input one per line.

[11]. Rewrite the program *c6_dpp\ex_09.c* listed in section 6.5, so that it will output the contents of the parentheses only.

[12]. Write a program to input a phrase on one line and perform a classification of the vowels. Display the number of vowels in each category.

Chapter 7
Functions

By now the reader has enough information to write small programs. At this stage it is important to explain how specifically programmed activities can be formed into building blocks known as functions. The functions can then be used as the basis for constructing larger programs. By the end of this chapter the reader should have a knowledge of the following topics.

☐ The construction of a function and its place within a program.

☐ How to call a function from within a program.

☐ How to pass data as an argument into a function.

☐ How to return a value from a function.

☐ The storage classes of data.

☐ The scope of constant, types and variables.

7.1 What is a function?

A function can be regarded as a group of self-contained declarations and executable statements that can be used to perform a specifically programmed activity. It is very important to stress the words self-contained, since a function can be written and tested in isolation from the final program. A function can be thought of as a building block. Different building blocks are written for different activities within a program. A complete program is built from many different building blocks or functions, each having been tested, before being used as part of the whole program.

Functions fall into one of two categories. Those pre-written routines that are supplied within libraries and used in a program, for example *getchar*, *putchar*, *gets*, *puts*, *printf, scanf,* etc, and programmer defined routines that are written as part of a program. Within this chapter the emphasis will be on the construction and use of programmer defined functions.

For the reader who can already program in other languages it is worth mentioning that C does not differentiate between procedures and functions. C uses only functions. Depending upon the function, it can be used either on its own (as a procedure call to execute a specific routine), or used in an assignment or output statement (as a function call returning a specific value).

7.2 Programmer defined functions

A C program normally consists of at least one function, the main function. In the program that follows a function has been introduced to display a character on the screen. This may appear somewhat of an over use of functions, since it is merely a library function within a programmer-defined function. The program illustrates how to define a function within a program and how to call the function so that it can be executed.

```
/*
c7_dpp\ex_01.c
program to demonstrate how to construct and call a function
*/

#include <stdio.h>

int     symbol;


void display(void)
{
        putchar(symbol);
}


main()
{
        symbol = getchar();
        display();
}
```

The main function is executed before any other function. In this example a character is input at the keyboard and assigned to the variable *symbol*. The computer then branches to the function *display* and the character represented by *symbol* is displayed on the screen. The computer then returns to the next statement after the function call in the main program, but this happens to be the end of the main function. The program then terminates.

Results from program ex_01.c being run

```
z
z
```

A general form of function definition is:

> **return-type function-name (formal-parameter list)**
> **{**
>   **declarations**
>   **statements**
> **}**

In the example program both the return-type and formal-parameter list for the function *display*, do not exist, and are replaced by the keyword **void**.

There are no declarations present in the function and the only statement is a call to the library function **putchar**.

The function is called from the main function by *display()* using the name of the function, followed by empty parenthesis, indicating there are no arguments to pass to the function.

Warning! Failure to include parenthesis in a function call causes the compiler to ignore the call.

If the declaration of the function *display* is to made after the function main, then the compiler will need a forward reference to the identifier *display*. This can be achieved by specifying the first line of the function before the function main. This declaration is known as a *function prototype* and has the format:

return-type function-name (formal-parameter list);

Apart from the terminating semi-colon used at the end of the function prototype, a function declaration must resemble the first line of a function definition.

```
/*
c7_dpp\ex_02.c
program to demonstrate the use of a forward reference to a function
*/

#include <stdio.h>

int     symbol;
```

```
/* function prototype */
void display(void);

main()
{
        symbol = getchar();
        display();
}

void display(void)
{
        putchar(symbol);
}
```

To enable *symbol* to be accessed by the function *display*, in both of the example programs, it has been necessary to declare it before the declaration of the two functions. The variable *symbol* has in effect become a *global* variable.

Global declarations are not new to the reader. All the constant, type and variable declarations that have been made, in all the programs that have been written prior to this chapter, have been global. The word global implies that the constants and variables can be accessed anywhere in the program.

Programs should never be built on global variables alone. The first program in this section can be modified so that the variable *symbol* remains local to the function *main*, yet can be passed across as an argument to the function *display*.

```
/*
c7_dpp\ex_03.c
program to demonstrate the use of a function that requires
a parameter, but does not return a value
*/

#include <stdio.h>

void display(int character)
{
        putchar(character);
}

main()
{
        int symbol;

        symbol = getchar();
        display(symbol);
}
```

In C, some arguments, depending upon their type, are passed by value. When a function is called, each actual parameter (argument) is evaluated and its value is assigned to the corresponding formal parameter found in the formal parameter list of the function. This means that a local copy of the value passed, is used by the function and not the original.

A function may be given a type. The type is the type assigned to a value associated with a **return** statement in the body of the function. If a function is written without a type being assigned, the function is assumed to have a default type of int (integer), unless the type is specifically described as being void.

The final program in this section shows how the function *display* can be modified to return the ASCII value of the symbol. The variable *value*, assigned to function display is then increased by 1, and the character having this new ASCII code is then displayed. In this last example the return statement has been used to return a value to the function and terminate the function. Notice that the function type has been declared as **int** and not **void** as in previous examples. Notice also that in this example the function has been used in its accepted sense of returning a value, *value = display(symbol)* and also later in the program in the context of a procedure call *display(value)*.

```
/*
c7_dpp\ex_04.c
program to demonstrate the use of a function that requires a parameter
and returns a value
*/

#include <stdio.h>

int display(int character)
{
        return putchar(character);
}



main()
{
        int symbol;
        int value;

        symbol = getchar();
        value  = display(symbol);

        /* increase the value of the ASCII code returned by 1 */
        value++;

        /* display the character having the ASCII code of value */
        display(value);
}
```

Results from program ex_04.c being run

```
A
AB
```

7.3 Storage classes

There are four storage classes that can be assigned to variables - *static*, *auto*, *extern* and *register*.

Static variables are allocated storage for the life of the program and not just the life of a function. In the following example the variable *character* has been described as being static. Although this value is initialised to 65 (the ASCII code for the character 'A') in the function *another_one*, repetitive calls to the function use the updated value of character *character++* and not the original value initialised to 65. The program will display the characters ABC.

```
/*
c7_dpp\ex_05.c
program to demonstrate the use of static storage
*/

#include <stdio.h>

void another_one(void)
{
      static int character = 65;

      putchar(character);
      character++;
}

main()
{
        another_one();
        another_one();
        another_one();
}
```

Result from program ex_05.c being run

```
ABC
```

Auto variables are declared inside a function after the opening brace and are allocated storage space whenever a function is called. In an earlier example both *symbol* and *value* were, by default, auto variables. When an auto variable is allocated storage space it contains garbage, unless specifically initialised. An auto variable only has a meaningful value for the life of a function. The next time a function is called the values of the auto variables cannot be determined unless they are re-initialised. Auto variables have the same meaning as *local* variables in other languages.

If the variable *character* was not declared as being static in the previous example, then by default it would be an auto variable, and upon every call to the function *another_one*, the value of character would be re-initialised to 65, and the output from the program would be AAA.

Global variables are also static by default, since their values are preserved for the life of a program, and not just the life of the functions.

A variable can also be accessed from another source file, by declaring the variable as **extern**. This implies that the variable has already been allocated storage in another source file, and is not allocated any additional storage. In the example that follows, two source files, *first.c* and *second.c* , contain function *main* and function *change_char* respectively. A variable *character* is declared and initialised in the file *first.c*, and the character is declared as being external in the file *second.c*. Both files are separately compiled then linked together to form one executable program. Separate compilation is covered in chapter 12.

Source file *first.c*

```
#include <stdio.h>
int character = 65;

main()
{
   putchar(character);
   change_char();
   putchar(character);
}
```

Source file *second.c*

```
extern int character;
/* extern implies that character has already been allocated storage space
in another file */

change_char()
{
   character = character + 1;
}
```

Results from program being run

AB

Warning! When declarations of the same variable appear in different files, the compiler cannot check that the declarations are consistent. It is not usually advisable to make variables global in this way.

When the same variables are frequently used, it might improve execution speed if the variables are stored in the *cpu* registers, by declaring them as **register** storage class. A variable declared as *register* storage class has the same properties as *auto* storage class.

Function declarations, like variable declarations, may include a storage class. The only options available are extern and static. The extern storage class indicates that a function may be called from other files. The static storage class indicates that a function may be called only within the file in which it is defined. If no class is specified then the function is assumed to be external, as was depicted in the last example where *change_char*, stored in *second.c*, was called from the function *main*, stored in first.c.

7.4 Scope

From the examples given in this chapter it should be clear to the reader that the body of a function is declared between open and closed braces { } known as a compound statement. When the compound statement contains declarations it is known as a block .

Variables declared between corresponding braces are by default *auto*. Storage is allocated to the variable when the block is entered and deallocated when the block is exited.

A variable can either have **block scope** (the variable is visible from its point of declaration to the end of the closing block) or **file scope** (the variable is visible from its point of declaration to the end of the enclosing file).

A variable declared at the beginning of a function is only accessible by that function.

The scope of an external variable is from the point it is declared to the end of the source file. It can be accessed from other source files by using the *extern* storage class.

When a declaration inside a block, names an identifier that is already visible, the new declaration temporarily hides the old declaration, and the identifier takes on a new meaning. At the end of the block the identifier regains its old meaning.

In the following example the variable *symbol* has been initialised to the ASCII code for the character Z, and should be visible throughout the function main. However, a new block has been defined within main, with symbol being assigned the ASCII code for the character A. According to the scope rules, the new declaration in the inner block hides the old declaration of symbol, so the letter A will be displayed. At the end of the inner block the old declaration of symbol is assumed and the character Z will be displayed.

```
/*
c7_dpp\ex_06.c
program to demonstrate scope rules
*/

#include <stdio.h>
int symbol = 90; /* static storage duration with file scope */
```

```
main()
{
        {
                int symbol = 65; /* auto storage with block scope */
                putchar(symbol); /* output the character A */
        }

        putchar(symbol); /* output the character Z */
}
```

Results from program ex_06.c being run

AZ

7.5 Parameters - copy or reference?

It was stated earlier in the chapter that in C some arguments, depending upon their type, are passed by value. Implying that other arguments not falling into this category must be passed by other means! There are two methods for passing arguments in C.

The first evaluates the argument and creates a local **copy** of the value, assigning it to the corresponding parameter in the function. Figure 7.1 illustrates the argument *symbol* being passed across to the parameter *character* in the function *display*. The one-way arrow head implies that whatever changes are made to *character* do not affect *symbol*.

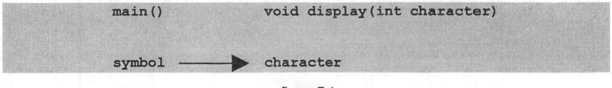

figure 7.1

However, if the argument is a character string, then a local copy of the string is NOT created. Instead the argument passes to the corresponding function parameter a **reference** to the original character string. Figure 7.2 illustrates the argument *information* being passed across to the parameter *message[]* in the function *display*. The two-way arrow head implies that whatever changes are made to *message[]* will also apply to *information*.

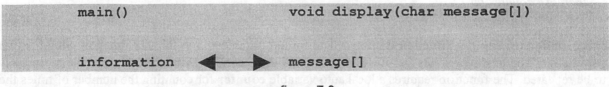

figure 7.2

133

If a character string, used as an argument, is not to be changed then the reserved word **const** must be appended to the declaration of the string in the formal parameter list. For example:

```
void display(const char message[])
```

When **const** is present, the compiler will check that no assignment is made to the character string in the body of the function. If such an assignment is attempted then the compiler will flag this as an error.

7.6 Worked examples

Problem - The first example requires a function to display a message a specified number of times on a screen. The message and the number of times the message is to be repeated are both passed from the main function to the function *display* as value parameters. For example if the information to be passed to the function was "Happy Birthday", and the number of times it was repeated was 5, then the message Happy Birthday would be repeatedly displayed over five lines as illustrated in the screen layout.

```
Screen Layout

12345678901234567890123456789012345678901234567890
input message Happy Birthday
repeat how many times? 5
Happy Birthday
Happy Birthday
Happy Birthday
Happy Birthday
Happy Birthday
```

Algorithm for function display

initialise counter to zero
while counter not equal to number of times of repetition
    display message
    increase counter by 1

Data dictionary for the function display - The formal parameter list for this function contains two parameters. The first represents the **message** string and the second the **number** of times the message is to be repeated. The function requires a local auto variable **counter** for counting the number of times the message is displayed. The function does not return a value and is therefore declared as void. Notice that it is not necessary to declare the size of the message string, since its size is taken to be that of the argument being passed to the function.

```
void    display(char message[], int number)
int     counter;
```

Algorithm for the function main

input message
input number of times message is to be printed
call function display

Data dictionary for the function main - The two arguments to be passed to the function display are a message string **information**, and the **number_of_times** the message is to be repeated. The size of the message string is such that it will cater for a line of text up to eighty characters in length.

```
char    information[80];
int     number_of_times;
```

Figure 7.3 illustrates the argument **information** is passed by reference to the parameter **message[]** and the argument **number_of_times** is passed as a local copy of value number_of_times, assigned to the parameter **number**.

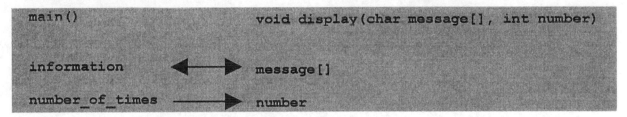

figure 7.3

Test data - *information* Happy Birthday   *number_of_times*   5

Desk Check of function display

message	number	counter	counter !=number ?	output
Happy Birthday	5			
		0	true	Happy Birthday
		1	true	Happy Birthday
		2	true	Happy Birthday
		3	true	Happy Birthday
		4	true	Happy Birthday
		5	false	

```
/*
c7_dpp\ex_07.c
program to illustrate the use of an argument being passed by value
*/

#include <stdio.h>

void display(char message[], int number)
/* function to display a message a number of times on a screen */
{
        int     counter = 0;

        while (counter != number)
        {
                printf("%s\n", message);
                counter++;
        }
}


main()
{

        char    information[80];
        int     number_of_times;

        printf("input message "); gets(information);
        printf("repeat how many times? "); scanf("%d", &number_of_times);
        display(information, number_of_times);
}
```

Results from program ex_07.c being run

```
input message Happy Birthday
repeat how many times? 5
Happy Birthday
Happy Birthday
Happy Birthday
Happy Birthday
Happy Birthday
```

Problem - The second example involves developing a function that will calculate a modulus-11 check digit for a four-digit number. It is common practice to provide account numbers, for example customer bank account numbers, with a check-digit. This digit becomes part of the account number and provides a means for the computer to check that the account number has been correctly entered into the computer and that the digits have not been transposed. As a result of a test done on modulus-11 it was discovered that it detected all transcription and transposition errors and 91% of random errors.

A modulus-11 check-digit, for a four-digit number, is calculated in the following way.

Using the account number 9118 as an example: multiply each digit by its associated weight, here we have the weights 5,4,3,2 and calculate the sum of the partial products.

$(5x9) + (4x1) + (3x1) + (2x8) = 68$

The sum 68 is then divided by 11 and the remainder 2 is then subtracted from 11, the result 9 is the check digit. The account number, including the check-digit as the last digit, becomes 91189. If the value of the check-digit is computed to be 10 this is replaced by the character X and a check-digit of 11 will be replaced by 0.

When the account number is input to the computer precisely the same calculation is carried out, using the weight of 1 for the rightmost check digit.

$(5x9) + (4x1) + (3x1) + (2x8) + (1x9) = 77$; divide by 11; 7 remainder 0.

If the remainder was not zero then an error would have been made in the input of the account number.

```
                        Screen Layout
12345678901234567890123456789012345678901234567890
input a four-digit number 3456
number with check digit 34568
```

Algorithm for function convert

isolate digits in number
calculate the sum of the partial products
return the value of the check digit

Data dictionary for the function convert - The formal parameter list for this function contains one item, an integer parameter to represent a four-digit number. The function returns an integer value that represents the value of the check-digit that must be appended to the four-digit number. The function will have auto integer variables that represents the four individual digits of the number and an integer auto variable to represent the sum of the partial products.

```
int convert(int number)
int d1,d2,d3,d4;
int sum;
```

Algorithm for the function main

input a four digit number
call function convert and assign the returned value to the check digit
display the value of the number
switch check digit
10   : display 'X';
11   : display '0';
default   : display check digit

Data dictionary for the function main - The only argument to be passed to the function convert is the integer four digit account_number. The value returned by the function convert is assigned to the integer variable check_digit.

```
int check_digit;
int account_number;
```

Figure 7.4 illustrates that the argument **account_number** is passed as a copy to the function **convert** and assigned to the to the parameter **number**. The function returns a value that is assigned to the variable **check_digit**.

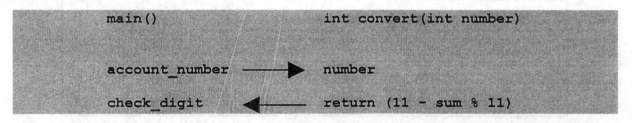

figure 7.4

Test Data - *account_number* 3456, 1001, 1234

Desk Check of function convert

number	d1	d2	d3	d4	sum	convert(number)
3456	3	4	5	6	58	8
1001	1	0	0	1	7	4
1234	1	2	3	4	30	3

138

```
/*
c7_dpp\ex_08.c
program to demonstrate the use of a value argument and a function return-
ing a value
*/

#include <stdio.h>

int convert(int number)
{
        int     d1,d2,d3,d4; /* four digits of number */
        int     sum; /* sum of partial products */

        /* isolate digits from number */
        d1 = number / 1000;
        d2 = (number % 1000) / 100;
        d3 = (number % 100) / 10;
        d4 = number % 10;

        /* calculate the sum of the partial products */
        sum = (5 * d1) + (4 * d2) + (3 * d3) + (2 * d4);
        return (11 - sum % 11);
}


main()
{
        int     check_digit;
        int     account_number;

        printf("input a four-digit number ");
        scanf("%d", &account_number);
        check_digit = convert(account_number);
        printf("number with check digit %4d", account_number);

        switch (check_digit)
        {
        case 10 : printf("X\n"); break;
        case 11 : printf("0\n"); break;
        default : printf("%d\n", check_digit);
        }
}
```

Results from program ex_08.c being run three times

```
input a four-digit number 3456
number with check digit 34568

input a four-digit number 1001
```

```
number with check digit 10014

input a four-digit number 1234
number with check digit 12343
```

Problem - In the third example of this section a function is written to calculate the number of pieces of wood that can be cut to a set size from a length of wood. The size of the pieces to be cut and the length of the wood used are passed to the function pieces as parameters. The function pieces returns an integer value that represents the number of pieces that can be cut to size. For example if the length of wood was 10 metres and the size of the pieces were 1.5 metres then the function would return the value 6, indicating that 6, 1.5 metre pieces can be cut from a 10 metre length of wood. The screen layout for this program is shown below. The reader would be correct in thinking that the use of a function is extravagant, since the number of pieces can be calculated as (int) (length_of_wood / size_of_pieces). However, the purpose of the exercise is to demonstrate passing arguments and returning a value from a function. It also helps to reinforce the use of a while loop and decrement operator.

Screen Layout

```
12345678901234567890123456789012345678901234567890
what is the length of the wood? 10.0
what size pieces do you want to cut? 1.5
number of pieces 6
```

Algorithm for the function pieces

initialise number of pieces to zero
while length is greater than or equal to the size to be cut
    decrease length of wood by size
    increase number of pieces by 1
return the number of pieces

Data dictionary for the function pieces - The formal parameter list for this function contains two items of type float, the first is the *size* of the wood to be cut and the second is the original *length* of the wood. The function returns an integer value that represents the number of pieces cut to size from the length of the wood.

The only auto variable required is of type integer and represents the *number_of_pieces* of wood cut.

140

```
int pieces(float size, float length)
int number_of_pieces;
```

Algorithm for the function main

input length of wood
input size of pieces to be cut from the wood
display number of pieces cut from the wood

Data Dictionary for the function main - The arguments to be passed to the function are the length_of_wood and the size_of_wood both of type float. There is no need to declare a separate variable for the number of pieces since this value is returned by the function pieces and can be displayed within a printf statement.

```
float length_of_wood;
float size_of_pieces;
```

Figure 7.5 illustrates that the arguments **size_of_pieces** and **length_of_wood** are both passed to the function **pieces** as copies and assigned to the parameters **size** and **length** respectively. The function returns the value of the local variable **number_of_pieces** that can be output in a printf statement without any further assignment being made.

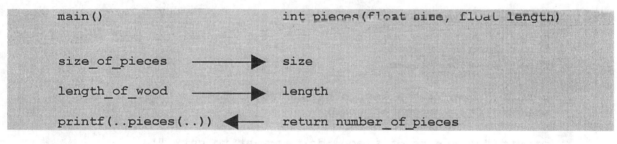

figure 7.5

Test Data - *length_of_wood* 10.0 *size_of_pieces* 1.5

Desk Check of function pieces

size	length	length >= size ?	number_of_pieces
1.5	10.0		0
		true	1
	8.5	true	2
	7.0	true	3
	5.5	true	4
	4.0	true	5
	2.5	true	6
	1.0	false	

```
/*
c7_dpp\ex_09.c
program to demonstrate the use of value arguments
*/

#include <stdio.h>

int pieces(float size, float length)
/*
function to calculate the number of pieces of wood that can be cut to a
set size from a length of wood
*/

{
        int number_of_pieces = 0;

        while (length >= size)
        {
            length = length - size;
            number_of_pieces++;
        }

        return number_of_pieces;
}

main()
{
        float length_of_wood;
        float size_of_pieces;

        printf("what is the length of the wood? ");
        scanf("%f", &length_of_wood);

        printf("what size of pieces do you want to cut? ");
        scanf("%f", &size_of_pieces);

        printf("number of pieces ");
        printf("%d\n", pieces(size_of_pieces, length_of_wood));
}
```

Results from program ex_09.c being run

```
what is the length of the wood? 10.0
what size pieces do you want to cut? 1.5
number of pieces 6
```

Problem - The fourth example involves writing a function to find the price of food at Ben's Breakfast Bar, see figure 2.3, section 2.1 in chapter 2. The name of an item of food or drink from the menu, is passed as an argument from the main function to the function price. This function returns a floating point value that represents the price of the item of food or drink. For example if the item of food was *bacon* then the function would return the value *2.00*. A sample screen layout follows.

```
                    Screen Layout

12345678901234567890123456789012345678901234567890

input an item of food from the following menu

eggs       bacon       sausages    black pudding
beans      cerial      toast       tomatoes
tea        coffee      chocolate

? bacon
£2.00
? black pudding
£0.95
? eggs
£ 1.50
? chocolate
£0.95
? water
```

Algorithm for the function price

if	*item is eggs return 1.50*
else if	*item is bacon return 2.00*
else if	*item is sausages return 1.75*
else if	*item is black pudding or chocolate return 0.95*
else if	*item is tomatoes or cerial return 1.00*
else if	*item is beans return 0.50*
else if	*item toast or tea or coffee return 0.75*
else	*return 0.0*

Data Dictionary for the function price - The formal parameter list for this function contains one item, the name of the item of food or drink, of data type character string. The function returns a floating point value that represents the price of the item of food or drink. If the value returned is zero this implies that the item was not listed in the menu and its price could not be found.

```
float price(char item[])
```

Algorithm for the function main

display the menu of food and drink
do
    input the name of an item of food or drink
    call the function price and assign the value returned to the cost of the item
    if the cost of the item is no-zero display the cost of the item
while cost of item is non-zero

Data Dictionary for the function main - The argument to be passed to the function price is the name of the item of food or drink and is of type character string. The value returned by the function is the price of an item of food or drink and is assigned to a floating point variable cost.

```
char    food[80];
float   cost;
```

Figure 7.6 illustrates that the argument **food** is passed by reference to the parameter **item[]**.The cost of the item of food is returned to the calling function as a floating-point numeric literal.

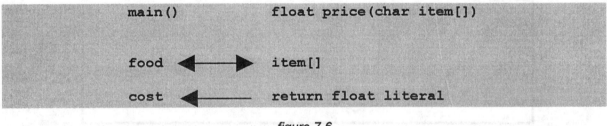

figure 7.6

Test data - *food* bacon, black pudding, eggs, chocolate, water

Notice that *water* is not listed in the menu, therefore, will return a value of zero and cause the main function to terminate.

Desk Check of function price

item	price(item)
bacon	2.00
black pudding	0.95
eggs	1.50
chocolate	0.95
water	0.00

```
/* c7_dpp\ex_10.c */

#include <stdio.h>
#include <string.h>

float price(char item[])
/* function to return the price of an item of food at Ben's Breakfast Bar;
if an item cannot be matched the price is returned as zero */

{
    if      (strcmp(item, "eggs") == 0)
            return 1.50;
    else if (strcmp(item, "bacon") == 0)
            return 2.00;
    else if (strcmp(item, "sausages") == 0)
            return 1.75;
    else if (strcmp(item, "black pudding") == 0 ||
             strcmp(item, "chocolate") == 0)
            return 0.95;
    else if (strcmp(item, "tomatoes") == 0 || strcmp(item, "cerial") == 0)
            return 1.00;
    else if (strcmp(item, "beans") == 0)
            return 0.50;
    else if (strcmp(item, "toast") == 0 || strcmp(item, "tea") == 0 ||
             strcmp(item, "coffee") == 0)
            return 0.75;
    else
            return 0.0;
}

main()
{
    char    food[80];
    float   cost;

    printf("input an item of food from the following menu\n");
    printf("\neggs      bacon     sausages    black pudding");
    printf("\nbeans     cerial    toast       tomatoes");
    printf("\ntea       coffee    chocolate\n\n");

    do
    {
        printf("? ");
        gets(food);
        cost = price(food);
        if (cost > 0.0) printf("£%-4.2f\n", cost);
    }
    while (cost > 0.0);
}
```

Results from program ex_10.c being run

```
input an item of food from the following menu

eggs       bacon      sausages    black pudding
beans      cerial     toast       tomatoes
tea        coffee     chocolate

? bacon
£2.00
? black pudding
£0.95
? eggs
£1.50
? chocolate
£0.95
? water
```

7.7 Summary

☐   A function should be written as a self-contained unit that represents a single programmed activity.

☐   A general form of function definition is:

return-type   function-name (formal-parameter list)
{
    declarations
    statements
}

☐   When calling a function the list of constants or variables after the function name is known as the *actual parameter list*.

☐   The number of actual parameters MUST be the same as the number of corresponding formal parameters.

☐   The order of the actual parameters and the formal parameters MUST be the same.

☐   The data types of the corresponding actual and formal parameters should be the same.

☐   Type conversion occurs automatically when either the actual and formal parameters do not have the same type or the function type does not match the return type.

☐   The names of the actual and formal parameters can be the same or different.

☐   Having executed a function the computer returns to the next executable statement after the function call.

☐   The computer will return to the calling function by either executing a return statement or reaching the physical end of the function.

☐   The return statement is used to assign a value to the function.

☐   A function may contain parameters and local constants, types and variables.

☐   Constants and variables, including actual parameters, that are declared as global declarations at the beginning of a program can be used anywhere within the program, including all the functions in the program.

☐   The storage classes auto, static, extern and register can be assigned to variables.

☐   Variables may have block scope or file scope.

☐   All C programs must begin execution with the main function.

☐   There is no prototype for main declared by the compiler, therefore, it is permissible to use **main()** or **void main(void)**, implying no return value and no parameters.

7.8 Questions - *answers begin on page 475*

1. Determine the output from the following program.

```
#include <stdio.h>

int alpha = 122;

main()
{
   int alpha = 97;
   {
     int alpha = 98;
     {
             int alpha = 99;
             putchar(alpha);
     }
     putchar(alpha);
   }
   putchar(alpha);
}
```

2. What are the values of x when the following program is executed?

```
#include <stdio.h>
int x = 68;

void display(void)
{
   static int character = 100;
           int x;
   x = putchar(character);
   character = character + 10;
}

main()
{
   display();
   display();
   display();
}
```

3. (a) What is the resultant type of the parameter in the segment of code?

```
void function(float) { }

function(int);
```

(b) What is the resultant return type in the segment of code?

```
double function(int)
{
   return int
}
```

4. Which of the statements are true or false? Give reasons for you answer.

(a) A variable declared as having register storage class can also be treated as an external variable?
(b) An external variable has storage allocated for every declaration of the variable in every source file that it is found?
(c) All variables in a block have an auto storage class?
(d) All variables are assumed to be static unless otherwise specified?
(e) A function may take on any of the four storage classes that are applicable to variables?

5. If the following variables are global:

```
int A,B,C;
char X,Y,Z;
```

State the errors, if any, in the following function calls and function declarations.

	function call	function declaration
(a).	alpha	void alpha(d,e,f)
(b).	beta(A,B,C)	void (beta)
(c).	delta(18'*')	int delta(int C, char Z)
(d).	gamma(X,Y)	void gamma(int i,j,k)

6. Trace through the following function and determine the value of *result* after each of the following calls.

```
result=test('a'); result=test('B'); result=test('c');

typedef enum {false, true} boolean;

boolean function test(char letter)
{
   if (letter >='A' && letter <='Z')
     return true;
   else
     return false;
}
```

7. Write and test functions to calculate and return the diameter, the circumference and the area of a circle. using the radius as the input parameter. Note: diameter = 2*radius; circumference = 2*pi*radius; and area = pi*radius*radius where pi=3.14159.

8. Write and test a function to convert an octal digit (base 8) to a description of the digit, for example 0 zero, 1 one, 2 two ... 7 seven, where the input parameter is an octal digit. Return a boolean value of true or false indicating whether the digit was in error. Exit the test program if the digit is in error.

9. Write and test a function to analyse whether a character is a vowel or not. The input parameter is a letter of the alphabet, and the function returns a Boolean variable indicating success if a letter was a vowel. Exit the test program if the letter is not a vowel.

[10]. (a) Write and test a function to input the time of day in 12-hour clock format, and whether it is am or pm, and return the time in a 24-hour clock format.

(b) Write and test a function to input two clock times in a 24-hour clock format and return the difference between the times. Cater for the fact that it does not matter the order in which the two times appear as parameters in the formal parameter list.

Note: in both parts of this question assume that the data is input in the correct format and range.

Chapter 8
Macros and Mathematics

The purpose of this chapter is to extend the reader's knowledge of the C language by including information on pre-processing directives that will enhance the programmer's repertoire of skills. It may seem incongruous to include a description of the ANSI C mathematics library in a chapter primarily focused on macros. However, such an important library must be mentioned somewhere in the book, and mathematical functions can be used effectively in parameterized macros. By the end of this chapter the reader should have a knowledge of the following topics.

- [ ] The C Preprocessor
- [ ] Simple macro definitions
- [ ] Using a macro in preference to a constant
- [ ] Parameterized macros
- [ ] Using parameterized macros in preference to functions
- [ ] Pre-defined macros
- [ ] The operators # and ##
- [ ] Conditional compilation
- [ ] Mathematics library

8.1 The C Preprocessor

An unusual feature of C is the preprocessing phase that precedes the actual compilation of a program. In chapter 3 it was stated that prior to the compilation of a C program, a preprocessor is automatically invoked by the system to preprocess every source file before compilation takes place. During preprocessing, the C program source text is modified according to the preprocessing directives that are embedded in the program. Every line in a C program that begins with the hash character # will contain a directive to the preprocessor.

Up to this point the only preprocessing directive that has been extensively used is #include, to permit the inclusion of header files into a program. For example it has been customary to use *#include<stdio.h>* when wanting to use ANSI input and output routines such as *printf, scanf, gets, puts, getchar* and *putchar*.

The major part of this chapter will explain the purpose of a further two categories of directive, the *macro definition* and *conditional compilation*.

8.2 Simple macros

A simple macro has the format

```
#define   identifier  replacement list
```

where replacement list is any sequence of C tokens - it may include identifiers, reserved words, operators and all other symbols that can appear in C programs. The preprocessor, when it encounters a macro definition, records the fact that the identifier represents the replacement list and wherever the identifier appears later in the program the preprocessor substitutes the replacement list. For example in the definitions

```
#define FALSE  0
#define TRUE   1
```

any occurrence of FALSE in a program would be replaced by the literal 0, and any occurrence of TRUE by the literal 1.

If the macro replacement is to take effect globally then the #define directive should be placed near the beginning of a program.

A **#define** may be used in preference to a **const** declaration, for example

```
const  float  pi = 3.14159;
const  char   magic[] = "abracadabra";
```

could be replaced by

```
#define  pi     3.14159
#define  magic  "abracadabra"
```

where a separate macro definition MUST be used for every constant that is required.

Warning ! When using #define do not terminate the replacement list with a semi- colon, and do not use the assignment = symbol to assign an identifier to a literal.

Although #define can also be used to specify constants in a program, it is quite a different approach to using const. The #define preprocessor directive offers the following advantages over const.

☐ #define is not subject to the same scope rules as variables,

☐ and it allows constants to be used in any constant expression.

However, there are advantages of using const compared with #define.

☐ A set of read-only values of any type may be defined in a program.

☐ Any attempt to change a const value in a program will be flagged as an error by the compiler.

☐ Values defined as const are subject to the same scope rules as variables.

8.3 Parameterized macros

An alternative format for a macro will allow parameters to be included in the identifier:

```
#define   identifier(p1, p2 ... pn) replacement list
```

where p1, p2 .. pn are the macro's formal parameters.

Figure 8.1 illustrates an extract from the TopSpeed C library reference manual for *putchar*. Notice that *putchar* is described as a macro and not a function since it is equivalent to *putc(ch, stdout)*. In the <stdio.h> header file *putchar* is defined as a parameterized macro by

```
#define putchar(c) fputc((c), stdout)
```

Note - the TopSpeed C library reference manual also describes *getchar* (not illustrated here) as a macro and not a function since it is equivalent to *getc(stdin)*. In the <stdio.h> header file *getchar* is defined as a simple macro by

```
#define getchar() fgetc(stdin)
```

The conditional operator was introduced in chapter 5. To recapitulate, the conditional expression

```
expression_1 ? expression_2: expression_3
```

is evaluated such that if expression_1 is non-zero (true) then expression_2 is the value of the conditional expression, otherwise if expression_1 is zero (false) then expression_3 is the value of the conditional expression.

The parameterized macro expression

```
#define smallest(X,Y) ((X)<(Y) ? (X):(Y))
```

implies that if X<Y is true the value of X is returned, otherwise if X<Y is false the value of Y is returned.

int putchar (int ch); A

Header file   stdio.h

. . .

The routine putchar puts a character ch on stdout. The routine is
equivalent to putc (ch, stdout). See putc.

Note: putchar is identical to fputchar but is a macro, not a function.

Return value
The macro returns the character written as an integer value. A return
value of EOF may indicate an error or end of file condition. To
determine which is the case, use ferror or feof.

Example   . . .

figure 8.1

Using parameterized macros and conditional expressions it is possible to define a whole range of functions
as the following examples demonstrate.

```
#define to_upper(c) ('a'<= (c) && (c) <='z' ? (c) - 32 : (c))
```

In this macro expression if the parameter (c) is a lower case letter then the expression (c) - 32 will be
evaluated, giving the upper case equivalent of the letter. If the letter is already in upper case then it remains
as (c).

```
#define digit(x) ('0'<=(x) && (x)<='9' ? TRUE : FALSE)
```

this macro can be used to validate a character being a decimal digit.

```
#define letter(L) ('A'<=to_upper(L) && to_upper(L) <= 'Z' ? TRUE : FALSE)
```

and this to validate a character as being either in the range A-Z or a-z. Notice that it is permissible to
include in a macro previously defined macros such as TRUE, FALSE and to_upper(L).

The example program that follows illustrates the uses of the macros that have been defined in this section.

```
/* c8_dpp\ex_01.c program to demonstrate the use of macros */

#include <stdio.h>
#define TRUE   1
#define FALSE 0
#define smallest(X,Y) ((X)<(Y) ? (X):(Y))
#define to_upper(c) ('a'<=(c) && (c)<='z' ? (c)-32:(c))
#define digit(x) ('0'<=(x) && (x)<='9' ? TRUE:FALSE)
#define letter(L) ('A'<=to_upper(L) && to_upper(L)<='Z' ? TRUE:FALSE)

int     first, second;
char    letter;
int     character;

main()
{
        printf("input a pair of integers ");
        scanf("%d%d", &first,&second); getchar();
        printf("smallest number is %d\n", smallest(first, second));

        printf("input a single alphabetic character ");
        scanf("%c", &letter); getchar();
        printf("upper case letter is %c\n", to_upper(letter));

        printf("input a single character ");
        scanf("%c", &character);
        if digit(character)
           printf("digit\n");
        else if letter(character)
           printf("letter\n");
        else
           printf("cannot classify\n");

}
```

Results from program ex_01.c being run

```
input a pair of integers 25 3
smallest number is 3
input a single alphabetic character q
upper case letter is Q
input a single character %
cannot classify
```

Using a parameterized macro instead of a function call has the following advantages.

☐ The program code may run slightly faster.

☐ A macro can be used with parameters of any type, provided the context of the parameters is consistent with the rest of the program.

The disadvantages of using a macro instead of a function are:

☐ Because the replacement list is inserted in-line with the program code, the compiled code will often be larger.

☐ Macros cannot be passed as parameters in a function call.

☐ A macro may evaluate its parameters more than once.

Finally the scope of a macro normally covers the entire program from the definition of the macro to the end of the program. The scope can be confined by using the statement **#undef identifier** at the place in the program where the macro is not to be used any further.

8.4 Pre-defined macros

A number of predefined macros may be used without giving definitions for them. These macros must not be undefined or redefined. The names of the macros are:

__**FILE**__ supplies the current source file name as a string literal

__**LINE**__ supplies the current source code file line number as a decimal integer

__**DATE**__ supplies the compilation date in the form of a string literal having the format Mmm dd yyyy

__**TIME**__ supplies the compilation time in the form of a string literal having the format hh:mm:ss

__**STDC**__ supplies the integer constant 1 if the compiler conforms to the ANSI standard

Note - pre-defined macros use a **double** underscore __ before and after each identifier as part of the identifier.

The following program illustrates several of these pre-defined macros.

```
/* c8_dpp\ex_02.c program to demonstrate the use of pre-defined macros */

#include <stdio.h>

main()
{
        printf("%s\n", __FILE__);
        printf("%d\n", __LINE__);
        printf("%s\n", __DATE__);
        printf("%s\n", __TIME__);
}
```

Results from program ex_02.c being run

```
ex_02.c
8
Dec 05 1994
16:27:56
```

8.5 Operators # and

The next example program serves to introduce the # **operator**, and to illustrate that a parameterized macro can be used as a template for code that is used many times in a program.

The # **operator** converts a macro parameter into a string literal, for example in the definition:

```
#define   printer(x)   printf(#x "=%d\n", x)
```

#x will be replaced by the string literal for x. The statement printer(A) would display A = 3, if the value of A was 3.

Notice in the following macro definition:

```
#define   input(y)   (printf("input " #y " "), scanf("%d",&y))
```

that it is possible to include more than one statement in a replacement list, provided the statements are separated by the comma operator.

There also exists a ## **operator** used to *paste* symbols together. For example

```
#define   var(i) Y##i
```

when used in

```
float var(0), var(1), var(2)
```

would produce

```
float Y0, Y1, Y2
```

```
/*
c8_dpp\ex_03.c
program to demonstrate the use of the # operator
*/

#include <stdio.h>

#define printer(x) printf(#x "=%d\n", x)
#define input(y) (printf("input " #y " "), scanf("%d",&y))
```

```
int a,b;

main()
{
    input(a);
    input(b);
    printer(a+b);
    printer(a-b);
    printer(a*b);
    if (a != 0) printer(b/a);
}
```

Results from program ex_03.c being run

```
input a 15
input b 24
a+b=39
a-b=-9
a*b=360
b/a=1
```

8.6 Conditional compilation

There is a group of preprocessor directives that can be used to stipulate which segments of code are to be compiled. The directives are:

```
#if, #ifdef, #ifndef, #elif, #else, #endif
```

The practice of commenting-out source code, that might contain comments, when testing a program cannot be achieved in C, since nested comments are not allowed. However, by using the preprocessor directives **#if .. #end**, it is possible to delimit a segment of program that should not be compiled.

```
#define FALSE 0
#if FALSE
   /* lines of code to temporarily omit */
#endif
```

Since the expression after **#if** is (0) all the statements up to **#endif** will be ignored by the compiler. If the macro definition was re-written as #define FALSE 1 then the expression after **#if** would be true and the statements after the expression would be compiled.

The **#if** and **#elif** directive can be combined with the **defined** operator to test whether a macro has been defined. For example in writing

```
#if defined MSDOS
...
#endif
```

it is possible to execute the statements between **#if** and **#endif** provided MSDOS has been defined as a macro earlier in the program by the statement

```
#define MSDOS
```

Notice from this simple macro that it is legal for the replacement list to be empty!

The ability to test whether a particular operating system is present in the production of code is an extremely useful feature in attempting to write portable code. It is possible to write

```
#if defined MSDOS
...
#elif defined UNIX
...
#elif defined ULTRIX
...
#endif
```

where the appropriate code will be executed if one of the macros has been previously defined in the program or included file.

External variables are declared outside the body of a function and can be shared by several functions in different files.

If the function **main()**, stored in file *main.c*, contained the code:

```
#define MAIN
#include <definition.h>
int flag; /* global variable */
.
.
```

then the declaration of the integer variable *flag* would not require to be declared as an external variable in this function. This would be ensured if the header file <definition.h> contained the statement:

```
#if !defined MAIN
   extern int flag;
#endif
```

In the file *main.c*, **MAIN** has been defined, therefore, the declaration of flag as an external integer is not required. However, in other files that include the header file <definition.h> the identifier flag will be declared as an external integer variable.

Note - the directives **#ifdef** and **#ifndef** are superfluous since they are equivalent to the statements **#if defined** and **#if !defined** respectively.

Note also that **#else** provides for a default if the condition associated with **#if** is false in the statement

```
#if
...
#else
...
#endif
```

8.7 Mathematics library

A library reference manual is normally supplied with a C compiler. Each library function is described in detail in this manual, with at least one page being devoted to each function. Figure 8.2 illustrates an extract from the Jensen & Partners TopSpeed C Library Reference manual that contains a description for the entry **double log(double x)**.

---

double log(double x);   A

Header file	math.h
See also	log10, exp, matherr, pow
Portability	ANSI
Multi-thread	None.

The function log returns the natural logarithm of its double precision floating point argument x.

Return value

The function returns the logarithm result. If x<=0, the function prints a DOMAIN error to stderr, returns -HUGE_VAL and sets errno to ERANGE.

Error handling can be altered by assigning a new handler to the matherr variable.

Example

```
#include <stdio.h>
#include <math.h>

main()
{
    double result;
    double x=2.718;

    result=log(x);
    printf("Log of %g is %.2g\n", x, result);
    return(0);
}
```

---

figure 8.2

A library function is normally described under the following headings.

The name of the function.
The name of the header file associated with the function.
A see also list of related or alternate functions.
A comment on the portability of the statement, for example ANSI standard, UNIX/DOS/OS2, etc.
Multi-thread (pseudo-concurrent) capabilities of the function.
A summary of the function.
A return value of the function and how to detect errors from it.
An example of how to use the function.

The ANSI standard specifies a wide range of mathematical functions, which take double parameters and return double results except where otherwise specified. All the functions have their conventional meanings. The following functions are defined within the **math.h** header file.

Trigonometric - note angle x is in radians

double cos(double x)   returns the cosine of x
double sin(double x)   returns the sine of x
double tan(double x)   returns the tangent of x

Hyperbolic - note angle x is in radians

double tanh(double x)   returns the hyperbolic tangent of x
double sinh(double x)   returns the hyperbolic sine of x
double cosh(double x)   returns the hyperbolic cosine of x

Inverse trigonometric

double acos(double x)   returns the arc cosine of x, which must be in the range -1 .. +1
double asin(double x)   returns the arc sine of x, which must be in the range -1 .. +1
double atan(double x)   returns the arc tangent of x
double atan2(double x, double y)   returns the arc tangent of y/x

Power, exponential, logarithmic, etc

double log(double x)   returns the natural logarithm of x
double log10(double x)   returns the base 10 logarithm of x
double exp(double x)   returns the exponential result of x
double pow(double x, double y)   raises x to the power of y
double sqrt(double x)   returns the square root of x, where x >= 0

Absolute values and rounding

double fabs(double x)   returns the absolute value of x
double ceil(double x)   rounds x towards infinity, to the nearest integer, and returns this value

double floor(double x)   rounds x towards zero , to the nearest integer, and returns this value

Division and remainder

double modf(double x, double *intptr)   breaks x into integer and fractional parts, where the integer part is stored at *intptr*, and returns the fractional part

Warning! the reader should make reference to the chapter on pointers before using modf.

double fmod(double x, double y)   returns the floating point remainder of x/y - if y is 0 the function returns 0

Miscellaneous

double frexp(double val, int *exptr)   breaks *val* into a mantissa in the range 0.5 .. 1.0 and an exponent - the function returns the mantissa the exponent is stored at *exptr*

Warning! the reader should make reference to the chapter on pointers before using frexp.

double ldexp(double x, int exp)   returns the value of x * 2^{exp}

There are other mathematical functions, defined in the header **stdlib.h**, a selection of which follow.

int abs(int num)   returns the absolute value of the integer num
long labs(ling num)   returns the absolute value of the long integer num

div_t div(int num, int den)   returns a structure of type div_t containing quotient (int quot) and remainder (int rem) having divided *num* by *den*
ldiv_t ldiv(long num, long den)   returns a structure of type ldiv_t containing the quotient (long quot) and remainder (long rem) having divided *num* by *den*

Warning! the reader should make reference to the chapter on structures and arrays before using div and ldiv.

int rand(void)   returns pseudo-random number in the range 0 - RAND_MAX
void srand(unsigned seed)   sets the start point at the value seed for the pseudo-random generator

Example - The following program prints the tangent of angles between 0 degrees and 20 degrees in steps of 1 degree. The **tan** function requires an argument that represents an angle in radians, therefore, within the parameterized macro it has been possible to convert the angle from degrees to radians.

```
/*
c8_dpp\ex_04.c program to display a table of tangents
*/

#include <stdio.h>
#include <math.h>

#define pi 3.14159
#define tangent(x)  (float)tan(x*pi/180.0)

main()
{
        int   angle;

        printf("angle\ttangent(angle)\n");
        for (angle = 0; angle <= 20; angle++)
            printf("%d\t%6.4f\n", angle, tangent(angle));
}
```

Results from program ex_04.c being run

angle	tangent(angle)
0	0.0000
1	0.0175
2	0.0349
3	0.0524
4	0.0699
5	0.0875
6	0.1051
7	0.1228
8	0.1405
9	0.1584
10	0.1763
11	0.1944
12	0.2126
13	0.2309
14	0.2493
15	0.2679
16	0.2867
17	0.3057
18	0.3249
19	0.3443
20	0.3640

Example - In the final example in this chapter a macro is defined to calculate the logarithm of a number of any valid base. This macro is used in writing a program to find the logarithms of the numbers from 2 to 10 in steps of 0.5 to the bases 2 to 10 in steps of 2. The output is in the form of a table displaying the numbers down the page and bases across the page.

```
/*
c8_dpp\ex_05.c
program to display a table of logarithms
*/

#include <stdio.h>
#include <math.h>

#define logarithm(b,n) (log(n) / log(b))   /* (b)ase (n)umber */

main()
{
        double  number;
        int     base;

        printf("number                    bases\n");
        printf("               2      4      6      8      10\n");

        number = 2.0;
        while (number <=10.0)
        {
            printf("%6.1f", number);
            for (base=2; base<=10; base=base+2)
                printf("%8.4f", logarithm(base, number));
            printf("\n");
            number=number+0.5;
        }
}
```

Results from program ex_05.c being run

number		bases			
	2	4	6	8	10
2.0	1.0000	0.5000	0.3869	0.3333	0.3010
2.5	1.3219	0.6610	0.5114	0.4406	0.3979
3.0	1.5850	0.7925	0.6131	0.5283	0.4771
3.5	1.8074	0.9037	0.6992	0.6025	0.5441
4.0	2.0000	1.0000	0.7737	0.6667	0.6021
4.5	2.1619	1.0850	0.8394	0.7233	0.6532.
5.0	2.3219	1.1610	0.8982	0.7740	0.6990
5.5	2.4594	1.2297	0.9514	0.8198	0.7404

6.0	2.5850	1.2925	1.0000	0.8617	0.7782
6.5	2.7004	1.3502	1.0447	0.9901	0.8129
7.0	2.8074	1.4037	1.0860	0.9358	0.8451
7.5	2.9069	1.4534	1.1245	0.9690	0.8751
8.0	3.0000	1.5000	1.1606	1.0000	0.9031
8.5	3.0875	1.5437	1.1944	1.0292	0.9294
9.0	3.1699	1.5850	1.2263	1.0566	0.9542
9.5	3.2479	1.6240	1.2565	1.0826	0.9777
10.0	3.3219	1.6610	1.2851	1.1073	1.0000

8.8 Summary

☐ Simple macros may be introduced into a program as an alternative to constants.

☐ Parameterized macros can be used in place of explicitly coded functions.

☐ A set of five macros are predefined and must not be redefined or undefined.

☐ The scope of a macro covers its point of declaration (#define) through to either the end of the program file or the declaration of the end of the macro (#undef).

☐ It is possible to replace a preprocessing token parameter with a string literal token by using the operator #.

☐ If, in the replacement list, a parameter is immediately preceded or followed by ## processing token, the parameter is replaced by the corresponding argument's preprocessing token sequence.

☐ The preprocessor can be used to selectively include/ exclude line of input source from further processing by the compiler, by using a #if directive.

☐ Both <math.h> and <stdlib.h> contain a range of useful mathematical functions which may be included in parenthesised macros or used in the same manner as other functions.

8.9 Questions - *answers begin on page 478*

Write and test parameterized macros as answers to questions 1-3 inclusive.

1. Test characters for being hexadecimal digits. Exit the test program on a digit in error.

2. Test whether the second number in a set of three numbers represents a maximum value.

3. Calculate and display the area of a triangle given the lengths of two sides a,b and the included angle C^o - the formula for the area of the triangle is 0.5*a*b*sin(C).

4 Re-write your answer to question 7 in the previous chapter (section 7.8), to replace all functions and input and output statements by parameterized macros.

[5]. Display a graph of the function exp(-x)*sin(2*pi*x) for x in the range 0..3.5^c in steps of 0.05^c. Scale the function up by a factor of 40, and plot the ordinate of the function from an imaginary vertical axis 40 units from the left-hand edge of the screen. What happens to the graph after a short period of time?

Chapter 9

One-dimensional arrays

Up to now little importance has been attached to the organisation of data in the memory of a computer. All variables have been associated with only discrete items of data. This chapter introduces the array, which is the commonest of the data structures and is available in most high-level languages, and uses methods for accessing data that can lead to simple and more effective programming solutions. By the end of the chapter the reader should have an understanding of the following topics.

- [ ] Concept of a one-dimensional array.

- [ ] The declaration of an array.

- [ ] Input and output of data stored in an array.

- [ ] Arrays of characters.

- [ ] String processing.

9.1 One-dimensional array

Consider for a moment how you would store, say, five integer values. The obvious answer would be to create five variable names:

```
int number_1, number_2, number_3, number_4, number_5;
```

and assign a value to each consecutive variable.

number_1 = 54;
number_2 = 26;
number_3 = 99;
number_4 = -25;
number_5 = 13;

If the same approach was adopted to store, say, fifty integer values then the amount of coding would become tedious to perform. Clearly there must be a better way of storing data of the same type, so that the amount of coding can be reduced to a minimum.

Well there is, and the answer is to use an *array*. Arrays come in various dimensions, however, within the scope of this chapter only one dimensional arrays will be considered.

A picture of a one-dimensional array, containing five storage cells is illustrated in figure 9.1. It is important to remember the following points.

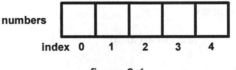

figure 9.1

- ☐ The contents of the array MUST be of the same data type. In other words an array can contain all integers, or all reals or all characters, or all strings, but not a mixture of each type.

- ☐ Each item in the array is stored in a separate cell. If an array contained five integers, then each integer would occupy a single cell.

- ☐ Each cell has a unique location value assigned to it showing its position within the array. This location value is known as either a subscript or an index and starts at value 0 (zero).

- ☐ The array is given only ONE name, irrespective of the number of items it contains.

- ☐ Before an array can be used it MUST be declared like any other variable. The array depicted in figure 9.1 might be declared as **int numbers[5]**; this states that the name of the variable is *numbers*. It is an array containing five cells, having subscripts numbered 0 through to 4 respectively. The contents of the array is of type integer.

- ☐ Access to an item of data within a cell is by using the name of the array followed by the position, subscript or index number, contained within square brackets.

To store the number 54 at cell position 0 in the array is possible by using the statement *numbers[0]=54*; similarly to store number 26 at cell position 1 use *numbers[1]=26*, etc.

9.2 Input and output of data

Figure 9.2 illustrates that the array called *numbers* contains five integers. These numbers can be stored in the array by either initialisation at the time of declaring the array or by direct assignment.

```
numbers    54   26   99   -25   13
index      0    1    2    3     4
```

figure 9.2

The array can be initialised with data by declaring:

```
int numbers[5] = {54,26,99,-25,13};
```

The declaration of the maximum number of cells in the array can be omitted if initialisation is present, therefore,

```
int numbers[] = {54,26,99,-25,13};
```

is also possible.

Alternatively the data may be directly assigned to each cell as follows.

```
numbers[0]=54;
numbers[1]=26;
numbers[2]=99;
numbers[3]=-25;
numbers[4]=13;
```

The contents of the array can be displayed on a screen by using *printf* statements. For example:

```
printf("%d\n", numbers[0]);
printf("%d\n", numbers[1]);
printf("%d\n", numbers[2]);
printf("%d\n", numbers[3]);
printf("%d\n", numbers[4]);
```

would display the contents of the array on five lines of a screen.

These statements have been incorporated into the following program so that the array *numbers* can be created and its contents displayed.

```
/*
c9_dpp\ex_01.c
program to assign numbers directly to the cells of an array
and display the contents of the cells
*/

#include <stdio.h>

main()
{
        int numbers[5] = {54,26,99,-25,13};

        printf("contents of array\n\n");
        printf("cell 0 %d\n", numbers[0]);
        printf("cell 1 %d\n", numbers[1]);
        printf("cell 2 %d\n", numbers[2]);
        printf("cell 3 %d\n", numbers[3]);
        printf("cell 4 %d\n", numbers[4]);
}
```

Results from program ex_01.c being run

```
contents of array

cell 0   54
cell 1   26
cell 2   99
cell 3   -25
cell 4   13
```

The original idea of introducing an array to store the integers, was to reduce the amount of coding required to assign the numbers to the store and output the numbers from the store. The previous example hardly inspires confidence that the original idea can be implemented! All it proves is that the same name, *numbers* , using different subscripts, 0 through 4, can be used in place of five different names. The program was introduced only to show the reader that it is possible to access explicitly any cell in the array.

To reduce the amount of coding it is necessary to replace the explicit use of the subscript or index by a control variable identifier. Instead of explicitly coding numbers[0], numbers[1], numbers[2], numbers[3] and numbers[4] it is far easier to use numbers[index], and embed this statement in a *for* loop changing the value of index from 0 to 4. For example numbers can be input from a keyboard and stored in the array using:

```
for (index=0; index < 5; index++)
   scanf("%d", &numbers[index]);
```

and the contents of each cell of the array can be displayed on a screen using

```
for (index=0; index < 5; index++)
   printf("%d", numbers[index]);
```

This idea of using a control variable identifier, in this case *index*, to control access to the contents of the array is demonstrated in the next program.

```
/*
c9_dpp\ex_02.c
program to input numbers into a one-dimensional array
and display the contents of the array
*/

#include <stdio.h>

main()
{
        int numbers[5];
        int index;

        /* input numbers into the array */
        printf("input five integers, one per line\n\n");
        for (index = 0; index < 5; index++)
        {
            printf("cell %d ", index);
            scanf("%d", &numbers[index]);
        }
        printf("\n\n");

        /* output numbers from the array */
        printf("contents of array\n\n");
        for (index = 0; index < 5; index++)
            printf("cell %d\t%d\n", index, numbers[index]);
}
```

Results from program ex_02.c being run

```
input five integers, one per line

cell 0 54
cell 1 26
cell 2 99
cell 3 -25
cell 4 13
```

171

```
contents of array

cell 0    54
cell 1    26
cell 2    99
cell 3    -25
cell 4    13
```

The use of a *for* statement to control the index to an array is not confined to input and output, but can be used to compare data between cells. In this next program five numbers are stored in an array, and the contents of the array is then inspected to find the largest number.

The for loop controls the index such that it is possible to gain access to consecutive items of data and compare each item with the largest number found so far.

```
largest = numbers[0];
for (index = 1; index < size; index++)
    if (numbers[index] > largest) largest = numbers[index];
```

The variable *largest* is assigned the first value in the array. The control variable identifier is then set to access the remaining cells in the array. If a number in one of these cells is greater than the current value of the variable *largest* then *largest* is assigned this value.

```c
/*
c9_dpp\ex_03.c
program to input numbers into a one-dimensional array and find
and display the largest number in the array
*/

#include <stdio.h>
#define size 5

main()
{
        int numbers[size];
        int largest;
        int index;

        /* input numbers into the array */
        printf("input five integers, one per line\n\n");
        for (index = 0; index < size; index++)
        {
            printf("cell %d ", index);
            scanf("%d", &numbers[index]);
        }
```

```
        /* calculate and output the largest number in the array */
        largest = numbers[0];
        for (index = 1; index < size; index++)
            if (numbers[index] > largest) largest = numbers[index];

        printf("largest number in array is %d\n", largest);
}
```

results from program ex_03.c being run

```
input five integers, one per line

cell 0 54
cell 1 26
cell 2 99
cell 3 -25
cell 4 13
largest number in array is 99
```

9.3 Array of characters

A variable of *string* data type is represented as an array of characters where the lower bound for the array index starts at 0 and the end of a string is automatically marked by the inclusion of a *null* character. For this reason the declaration of the size of the array that holds a string must always be one cell larger than the number of characters in the string.

Figure 9.3 illustrates an array that contains ten characters. In the program that follows, despite the data being defined as a variable of type *string*, it is possible to access each cell of this array to display the contents of the array, as the following program demonstrates.

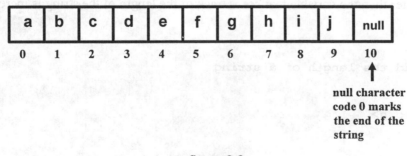

null character
code 0 marks
the end of the
string

figure 9.3

173

```
/*
c9_dpp\ex_04.c
program to demonstrate that a string is an array of characters
*/

#include <stdio.h>

main()
{
    char    characters[11];
    int     index;

    /* input a string */
    printf("input ten characters\n");
    gets(characters);

    /* output the contents of the string one character at a time */
    for (index = 0; index < 10; index++)
        printf("%c",characters[index]);
}
```

Results from program ex_04.c being run

```
input ten characters
abcdefghij
abcdefghij
```

The next program is written to find the length of a string. The program is written with the knowledge that a string is terminated by a *null* character. Therefore, starting at the beginning of the string (index = 0), each consecutive cell of the array is examined until a *null* character is discovered. If the contents of a cell is not a *null* character then the variable that keeps track of the length of the string is increased by 1.

```
/*
c9_dpp\ex_05.c
program to find the length of a string
*/

#include <stdio.h>

main()
{
    const   char null = 0;
            char data[255];
            int  length = 0;
```

174

```
       printf("input a line of text\n"); gets(data);

       while (data[length] != null) length++;

       printf("length of text is %d characters\n", length);
}
```

Results from program ex_05.c being run

```
input a line of text
How many characters in this string?
length of text is 35 characters
```

In the next example a line of text is input from a keyboard. Each character of the line of text is examined, if a lower case character is found it is converted into an upper case character, otherwise the character remains unchanged. The contents of the line of text is then displayed on the screen.

```
/*
c9_dpp\ex_06.c
program to change every alphabetic character in a string to upper case
*/

#include <stdio.h>
#define to_upper(c) ('a'<=(c) && (c)<='z' ? (c)-32:(c))

main()
{
       const char  null = 0;
            char   text[255];
            int    index;

       printf("input a line of text\n");
       gets(text);

       for (index = 0; text[index] != null; index++)
            text[index] = to_upper(text[index]);

       printf("capitalized text\n%s", text);
}
```

175

Results from program ex_06.c being run

```
input a line of text
This is a test of the procedure Capitalize .. and it works!
capitalized text
THIS IS A TEST OF THE PROCEDURE CAPITALIZE .. AND IT WORKS!
```

9.4 Arrays as parameters

In the previous section it was discovered that a character string is represented as an array of characters. In chapter 7 it was stated that a character string could be used as a parameter in the formal parameter list of a function. The corresponding argument in the actual parameter list was passed to the formal parameter by reference and not as a local copy of the argument being assigned to the formal parameter of the function.

A natural conclusion to reach, is that all arrays, and not just character strings, can be used as parameters in functions, with the corresponding array argument being passed to the formal parameter by reference.

Since array parameters are passed by reference any change to the contents of the formal array parameter must result in a change to the contents of the actual array parameter since both parameter and argument are represented by the same array. The exception to this statement is when the formal array parameter is defined as a constant.

9.5 Worked examples

Problem - In rolling a die (singular of dice) one of the six faces will appear uppermost. If the die was rolled many thousands of times each of the six faces should have an equal probability of appearing uppermost, provided the die was not biased (loaded!). Write a program that counts the number of times each of the six faces appears uppermost when rolled many number of times. At the end of the trial display the number of times each of the six faces of the die appeared uppermost.

Screen Layout

```
12345678901234567890123456789012345678901234567890123456789012345678901234567890
input number of trials (0 to exit) 6000
number of spots 1        2        3        4        5        6
frequency       1072     988      1011     987      983      959
```

The solution to this problem relies on the fact that an array is declared that contains the frequency of occurrences of the spots. An array containing seven cells is declared with indices 0..6. Cells 1..6 are used to store the frequency of occurrence of each face of the die. The first cell (0) is not used. Figure 9.4 illustrates the contents of the cells after 6000 trials (rolling the die 6000 times).

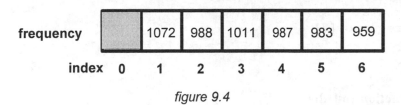

figure 9.4

Algorithm for the function roll_die

for every trial
    calculate a random number in the range 1 to 6 to represent the number of spots
    increase the frequency by 1 for calculated number of spots

To calculate a random number the ANSI function *rand*, described in the previous chapter, is used to generate a random number in the range *0 .. RAND_MAX*. This value can then be converted into a random number in the range 1 .. 6 by using the expression *(rand() % 6 + 1)* in a simple macro *die_value*.

If *die_value* is used as a subscript to the array *frequency*, then the statement *frequency[die_value]++* will increase the contents of the cell *die_value* by 1.

Data Dictionary for the function roll_die - The formal parameter list for this function contains two items, the name of the array used to store the frequency of occurrences of the spots and the number of times the die is to be rolled (trials). The function does not return a value, since the argument for the array parameter will change its values since it is passed by reference. The function contains a local variable used to count the number of trials.

```
void      roll_die(long int die[], long int trials)
long int  roll;
```

Algorithm for the function main

input the number of trials
while number of trials is positive do
    initialise the frequency of occurrences to zero
    roll the die for the number of trials
    display the frequency of occurrences of the spots
    input the number of trials

Data Dictionary for the function main - The arguments to be passed to the function *roll_die* are the array *frequency* and the number of *trials*. The main function also contains a local variable used to count the number of spots.

```
      int    spots;
long  int    trials;
long  int    frequency[7];
```

Test data - 10

Desk Check of function roll_die

die_value	die[die_value]	trials	roll	(roll<=trials)?
		10	1	true
3	1		2	true
5	1		3	true
2	1		4	true
3	2		5	true
1	1		6	true
3	3		7	true
4	1		8	true
2	2		9	true
6	1		10	true
3	4		11	false

```
/*
c9_dpp\ex_07.c
program to simulate throwing a die for different numbers of trials and
record the frequency that each side of the die (spots) appears in each
trial
*/

#include <stdio.h>
#include <stdlib.h>
#define die_value (rand() % 6 + 1)

void roll_die(long int die[], long int trials)
/* function to update the frequency of occurrences of the spots 1..6 ap-
pearing on a die over a set number of trials */

{
    long int roll;

    for (roll=1; roll <= trials; roll++)
        die[die_value]++;
}
```

```
main()
{
        int     spots;
    long int    trials;
    long int    frequency[7];

    printf("input number of trials (0 to exit) ");
    scanf("%ld", &trials);

    while (trials > 0)
    {
       for (spots=1; spots<=6; spots++)
          frequence[spots] = 0;

       roll_die(frequency, trials);

       printf("\nnumber of spots\t1      2       3       4       5        6\n");
       printf("frequency\t");
       for (spots=1; spots<=6; spots++)
          printf("%-7ld", frequency[spots]);

       printf("\n\ninput number of trials (0 to exit) ");
       scanf("%ld", &trials);
    }
}
```

Results from program ex_07.c being run

```
input number of trials (0 to exit) 6000
number of spots    1        2        3       4        5        6
                   1072     988      1011    987      983      959
input number of trials (0 to exit) 0
```

emordnilap ?

Problem - Write a program to test a word for being a palindrome, that is a word spelt the same backwards as forwards. The method used to test the word is to inspect the characters at either end of the word, if these are the same then the next two characters at either end of the word are compared. The comparisons continue until there is no match between the characters, or there are no further comparisons possible. The movement of the indices is shown in figure 9.5.

179

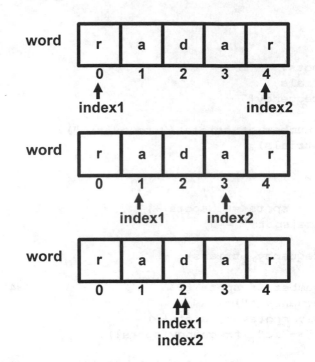

figure 9.5

Algorithm for the function is_palindrome

initialise the first index to point to the first letter in the word
initialise the second index to point to the last letter in the word
initialise a boolean flag to true indicating that the letters being pointed at match (even if they don't)

while the first index is not larger than the second index and the letters pointed at match do
    if the letters being pointed at are the same
        increase the position of the first index by 1
        decrease the position of the second index by 1
    else
        set the boolean flag to false indicating that the letters being pointed at do not match

return the value of the boolean flag

In order to initialise the second index to point to the last letter in the word, it will be necessary to know the length of the word. This is the same algorithm that was given earlier in the chapter to find the length of a string.

Data Dictionary for the function is_palindrome - The formal parameter list for this function is the array used to store the word to be analysed. The function returns an enumerated boolean value true if the word is a palindrome, otherwise it returns the value false.

It is necessary to declare local integer variables for the two indices and the length of the word. A boolean flag to indicate whether the word is a palindrome or not, must also be declared. In addition the ASCII value for a null character can be represented as a constant.

```
boolean is_palindrome(const char word[])
const    char      null   = 0;
         int       length = 0;
         int       index_1, index_2;
         boolean   characters_match;
```

Algorithm for the function main

input a single word
if word is palindrome
    display word is a palindrome
else
    display the word is NOT a palindrome

```
┌─────────────────────────────────────────────────────────────────┐
│                       Screen Layout                               │
├─────────────────────────────────────────────────────────────────┤
│12345678901234567890123456789012345678901234567890123456789012345678901234567890│
│input a single word radar                                          │
│radar is a palindrome                                              │
│input a single word mouse                                          │
│mouse is NOT a palindrome                                          │
└─────────────────────────────────────────────────────────────────┘
```

Test data - *radar*

Desk Check of the function is_palindrome

index_1	0	1	2	3
length	5			
index_2	4	3	2	1
characters_match	true			
(index_1 <= index_2 && characters_match)?	true	true	true	false
word[index_1]	r	a	d	
word[index_2]	r	a	d	
(word[index_1] == word[index_2])?	true	true	true	
is_palindrome(word)				true

```
/*
c9_dpp\ex_08.c
program to input a word and test whether it is a palindrome
*/

#include <stdio.h>
#define to_upper(c) ('a'<=(c) && (c) <= 'z' ? (c) - 32 : (c))

typedef enum{false, true} boolean;

boolean is_palindrome(char word[])
/* function returns true if word is a palindrome otherwise returns false */
{
      const   char      null    = 0;
              int       length = 0;
              int       index_1, index_2;
              boolean   characters_match;

      index_1 = 0;
      while (word[length] != null) length++;
      index_2 = length - 1;
      characters_match = true;

      while (index_1 <= index_2 && characters_match)
          if (to_upper(word[index_1]) == to_upper(word[index_2]))
          {
              index_1++;
              index_2--;
          }
          else
              characters_match = false;

      return characters_match;
}

main()
{
      char      word[255];

      printf("input a single word "); scanf("%s", word);

      if (is_palindrome(word))
          printf("%s is a palindrome\n", word);
      else
          printf("%s is NOT a palindrome\n", word);

}
```

Results from program ex_08.c being run twice

```
input a single word radar
radar is a palindrome
input a single word mouse
mouse is NOT a palindrome
```

A a E e I i O o U u

vowels?

Problem - Write a program to input a sentence and inspect each character. Keep a count of the numbers of different vowels that appear in the sentence and display these values when the end of the sentence is reached. The solution to this problem is similar to that of the dice. An array is used to keep a count of the frequency of occurrences of vowels in a sentence, rather than spots on a die. The array illustrated in figure 9.6 indicates the frequency of occurrences of vowels in a sentence. Notice that it is more meaningful to use enumerated constants as subscripts rather than the integers 0..4 that they represent.

frequency	0	5	2	2	1
index	A=0	E=1	I=2	O=3	U=4

figure 9.6

```
Screen Layout

12345678901234567890123456789012345678901234567890123456789 0
input a sentence - terminate with a full stop
Count the vowels in this sentence.
vowels   A  E  I  O  U
         0  5  2  2  1
```

Algorithm for the function vowel_analysis

convert character to upper case letter
switch letter
'A'   increase A-frequency by 1
'E'   increase E-frequency by 1
'I'   increase I-frequency by 1
'O'   increase O-frequency by 1
'U'   increase U-frequency by 1

Note - the letter cannot be used directly as a subscript to the array, therefore, a switch statement is used as a means of selecting the correct cell to increase in the array.

Data Dictionary for the function vowel_analysis - The formal parameter list for this function contains two items, the integer array for keeping a count on the number of vowels in a sentence and a letter from the sentence to be analysed.

```
void vowel_analysis(int vowel_count[], char letter)
```

Algorithm for the function main

This algorithm assumes that the sentence is stored in the input buffer. Each character from the buffer is then examined until the terminating full stop is located.

input character
while character is not a full stop do
    analyse character
    input next character
display the contents of the array for storing the vowel count

Data Dictionary for the function main - The arguments to be passed to the function vowel_analysis are the integer array for keeping a count of the number of vowels and the current character to be analysed. The contents of the array can be initialised to zero at its point of declaration. There is a local variable of type vowel used as a subscript to the array and a constant representing the terminating full stop at the end of a sentence.

```
const   char    full_stop = '.';
        int     frequency[5] = {0};
        char    character;
        vowel   letter;
```

Test data - *Count the vowels in this sentence.*

Desk check of function vowel_analysis

letter	index	vowel_count[index]
C		
o	O	1
u	U	1
n		
t		
space		
t		
h		
e	E	1
space		
v		
o	O	2
w		

letter index vowel-count[index]

e	E	2
l		
space		
i	I	1
n		
space		
t		
h		
i	I	2
s		
space		
s		
e	E	3
n		
t		
e	E	4
n		
c		
e	E	5
.		

```
/*
c9_dpp\ex_09.c program to count the number of vowels in a sentence
*/

#include <stdio.h>
#define to_upper(c) ('a'<=(c) && (c)<='z' ? (c)-32 : (c))

typedef enum {A,E,I,O,U} vowel;

void vowel_analysis(int vowel_count[], char letter)
/* function to analyse a character and update the vowel frequency counter
*/
{
    letter = to_upper(letter);

    switch(letter)
    {
    case 'A': vowel_count[A]++; break;
    case 'E': vowel_count[E]++; break;
    case 'I': vowel_count[I]++; break;
    case 'O': vowel_count[O]++; break;
    case 'U': vowel_count[U]++;
    }
}
```

```
main()
{
      const   char    full_stop = '.';
              int     frequency[5] = {0};
              char    character;
              vowel   letter;

      printf("input a sentence - terminate with a full stop\n");
      character = getchar();

      /* update vowel count */
      while (character != full_stop)
      {
         vowel_analysis(frequency, character);
         character = getchar();
      }

      /* output contents of vowel count */
      printf("\n\nvowels\t\tA   E   I   O   U   \nfrequency\t");
      for (letter = A; letter <= U; letter++)
          printf("%-4d", frequency[letter]);
}
```

Results from program ex_09.c being run

```
input a sentence - terminate with a full stop
Count the vowels in this sentence.


vowels          A  E  I  O  U
                0  5  2  2  1
```

9.6 Summary

☐ A one-dimensional array is a data structure that can be used to store data of the same type.

☐ An array is subdivided into cells, with each cell having a unique subscript or index value, the first cell has an index of 0 (zero).

☐ The maximum number of cells that an array contains is declared in a program and remains constant. For this reason an array is known as a static data structure.

☐ Access to any item of data in the array is through the name of the array, followed by the position of the data in the array, that is the subscript or index value of the cell that contains the data.

☐ A loop control variable in a *for* statement is a useful way of representing the subscript or index of an array. By varying the value of the loop control variable it is possible to access any cell within the array.

☐ A variable of string data type is represented as an array of characters. The initial subscript is taken to be zero. The string is terminated by a null character.

☐ The contents of a variable of string data type can be accessed as individual characters stored from cell 0 in a one-dimensional array.

☐ Array parameters are passed by reference, therefore, any changes to the parameter will result in corresponding changes to the argument.

☐ Because array parameters are passed by reference there is no extra memory space needed for making a local copy of the array.

9.7 Questions - *answers begin on page 479*

1. Re-write the following programs found in this chapter, so they contain the functions listed.

(a) ex_02.c   **void input_data(int array[], int N)**
                   void display_data(int array[], int N)

where the function input_data will allow keyboard input of N integers stored in the array and the function display_data will output to a screen the N integers stored in the array.

(b) ex_03.c   **int largest(int array[], int N)**

where the function largest will return the largest integer from the array containing N integers.

(c) ex_05.c   **int length(char array[])**

where the function length will return the number of characters stored in the character string array. The terminating null character is not to be included in the length of the string.

(d) ex_06.c   **void capitalize(char array[])**

where the function capitalize will convert any lower-case letters in the array to upper-case letters.

2. Write a program to store the alphabet as characters in an array. The program should display:

(a). The entire alphabet.
(b). The first six characters of the alphabet.
(c). The last ten characters of the alphabet.
(d). The tenth character of the alphabet.

[3]. Write a program to input ten integers in numerical order into a one-dimensional array X; copy the numbers from array X to another one-dimensional array Y such that array Y contains the numbers in descending order. Output the contents of array Y.

4. The monthly sunshine record for a holiday resort follows.

month	JAN	FEB	MAR	APR	MAY	JUN	JUL	AUG	SEP	OCT	NOV	DEC
hours of sunshine	100	90	120	150	210	250	300	310	280	230	160	120

Write a program to perform the following:

    (a) store the hours of sunshine in a one-dimensional array; and the names of the months in another one-dimensional array. Note the names of the months are themselves strings, which are represented by one-dimensional arrays. Therefore, the declaration becomes **char months[12][4]**.
    (b) calculate and display the average hours of sunshine over the year;
    (c) calculate and display the names of the months with the highest and lowest number of hours of sunshine.

Structure your answer such that the two arrays are global and there are three functions with the following prototypes:

float average(void);
int highest(void);
int lowest(void);

All output is performed in the main function.

[5]. Code and test the following functions.

    (a) **void delete(char string[], int I, int N)** - changes the value of the string by deleting N characters starting at the Ith character of the string.
    (b) **void insert(char string_1[], char string_2[], int I)** - changes the value of string_2 by inserting string_1 at the Ith position of string_2.
    (c) **void substring(char string[], int I, int N)** - modifies the string by creating a substring which is the N characters starting at the Ith position.
    (d) **void concat(char string_1[], char string_2[])** - modifies string_1 by the concatenation (joining together) of the string_1 and string_2.
    (e) **int position(char string_1[], char string_2[])** - scans through the string_2 to find the first occurrence of the substring string_1 within string_2. The value returned is the index within string_2 of the first character of the matched substring.

Chapter 10
Structures and arrays

In the previous chapter one-dimensional arrays were introduced for the storage of data of one type only. This chapter continues the theme of arrays by showing how a mixture of data types may be stored in an array under the umbrella of a new type known as a structure. The chapter also covers the use of two-dimensional arrays and the concept of arrays beyond two dimensions. By the end of the chapter the reader should have an understanding of the following topics.

- ☐ The format and organisation of structures.

- ☐ An array of structures.

- ☐ Input and output of data stored as a structure.

- ☐ Searching structures in an array.

- ☐ Two-dimensional arrays.

- ☐ The concept of multi-dimensional arrays.

10.1 Structures

It was stated in the previous chapter that the contents of all the cells in an array MUST be of the same data type. In other words an array can contain all integers, or all reals, or all characters, but not a mixture of each type.

This statement is perfectly true, however, it does not preclude a mixture of data types from being stored in a cell of an array, provided that the types come under the umbrella of a structure.

A structure is a collection of one or more members, which may be of different data types, grouped together under a single name. In other high-level languages a structure would be known as a record, and the collection of members as fields.

Figure 10.1 illustrates how a date can be divided into the members *day, month and year*, where each member is of type integer.

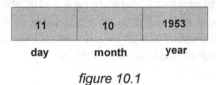

figure 10.1

If a structure is to be used to represent the variable *birthday*, then it might be coded as follows.

```
struct {
        int day;
        int month;
        int year;
      } birthday;
```

Individual members in this structure are accessed by the variable name birthday, followed by the required component.

```
birthday.day, birthday.month, birthday.year
```

An alternative approach is to give the structure a name or tag:

```
struct date_of_birth {
                      int day;
                      int month;
                      int year;
                     };
```

and use the tag in declaring the variable *birthday*.

```
struct date_of_birth birthday;
```

It is also possible to combine both definitions, so that the structure is given a tag and a variable is declared as having this structure.

```
struct date_of_birth {
                     int day;
                     int month;
                     int year;
                     } birthday;
```

Structure variables can be initialised at the point of declaration. In the previous example *birthday* can be initialised as follows:

```
struct date_of_birth {
                     int day;
                     int month;
                     int year;
                     } birthday = {11, 10, 1953};
```

Alternatively the members of a structure can be initialised by assignment.

```
  birthday.day = 11; birthday.month = 10; birthday.year = 1953
```

If two variables have the same structure then it is possible to assign the contents of one variable to another. For example if two variables are defined as:

```
struct date_of_birth Fred = {18, 3, 1948};
struct date_of_birth Sue;
```

then the assignment **Sue = Fred** is legal and implies that Sue's age is the same as Fred's age.

An alternative means of dealing with structures is to define the structure as a type. This essentially gives a type name (not a tag) to a structure. For example,

```
typedef struct   {
                  int  day;
                  int  month;
                  int  year;
                  } date_of_birth;
```

Thus a variable *birthday*, of type *date_of_birth*, may then be declared as:

```
              date_of_birth birthday;
```

For the author this is a preferred method of declaring structured types since it is more in-line with other high-level languages. This method will be used in the remainder of the book when declaring structure types.

Example - The first program example illustrates how a structure type *date_of_birth* is declared and used to store the fields *day, month* and *year* of a birthday. The contents of this structure is then displayed on a screen.

```
/*
c10_dpp\ex_01.c
program to create a structure and display the contents
*/

#include <stdio.h>

main()
{
    typedef struct {
                    int day;
                    int month;
                    int year;
                 } date_of_birth;

    date_of_birth birthday;

    printf("input a date of birth as DD MM 19YY ");
    scanf("%d%d%d", &birthday.day, &birthday.month, &birthday.year);

    printf("day %d\n",   birthday.day);
    printf("month %d\n", birthday.month);
    printf("year %d\n",  birthday.year);
}
```

Results from program ex_01.c being run

```
input a date of birth as DD MM 19YY 11 10 1953
day 11
month 10
year 1953
```

Example - The previous program can be extended to store more than one structure. The variable name *birthday* needs to be redefined as an array that will store records of type *date_of_birth*:

```
date_of_birth  birthdays[5];
```

Each record that is input at the keyboard can then be stored into consecutive locations of this five cell array, as depicted in figure 10.2. When all five records have been stored the contents of the array is then displayed on a screen.

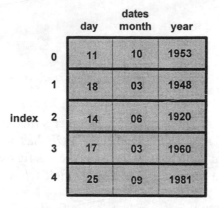

figure 10.2

```
/*
c10_dpp\ex_02.c
program to create an array of records and display the contents
*/

#include <stdio.h>

main()
{
    typedef struct {
                    int day;
                    int month;
                    int year;
                  } date_of_birth;

    date_of_birth birthdays[5] = {{11,10,1953},
                                 {18, 3,1948},
                                 {14, 6,1920},
                                 {17, 3,1960},
                                 {25, 9,1981}};
    int index;

    for (index=0; index < 5; index++)
        printf("%-3d%-3d%4d\n", birthdays[index].day,
                                birthdays[index].month,
                                birthdays[index].year);

}
```

Results from program ex_02.c being run

```
11 10 1953
18 3  1948
14 6  1920
17 3  1960
25 9  1981
```

It is possible for a member of a structure to also be another structure. For instance in figure 10.3 the structure has two fields *name* and *DOB*. However, *DOB* has a data type *date_of_birth*, where *date_of_birth* had previously been defined as a structure type. As figure 10.3 illustrates, a single member *DOB* of a structure, can itself be a structure containing the fields *day, month* and *year*.

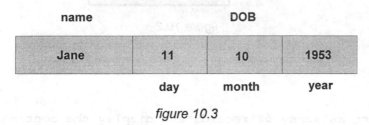

figure 10.3

Example - The next program is merely an extension of the previous program. Instead of storing records containing dates of birth in an array it stores the names of people and their corresponding dates of birth in an array. Figure 10.4 illustrates the storage of the new records in the array.

index	name	day	month	year
0	Jane	11	10	1953
1	Fred	18	03	1948
2	Henry	14	06	1920
3	Patrick	17	03	1960
4	Susan	25	09	1981

figure 10.4

```
/*
c10_dpp\ex_03.c
program to create an array of records and display the contents
*/

#include <stdio.h>

main()
{
    typedef struct {
                    int    day;
                    int    month;
                    int    year;
                } date_of_birth;

    typedef struct {
                    char               name[80];
                    date_of_birth      birth_date;
                } names_dates;

    names_dates birthdays[5] =  {{"Jane",11,10,1953},
                                 {"Fred",18,3,1948},
                                 {"Henry",14,6,1920},
                                 {"Patrick",17,3,1960},
                                 {"Susan",25,9,1981}};
    int index;

    for (index=0; index < 5; index++)
        printf("%s\t%-3d%-3d%4d\n", birthdays[index].name,
                                    birthdays[index].birth_date.day,
                                    birthdays[index].birth_date.month,
                                    birthdays[index].birth_date.year);
}
```

Results from program ex_03.c being run

```
Jane      11 10 1953
Fred      18 3  1948
Henry     14 6  1920
Patrick   17 3  1960
Susan     25 9  1981
```

Example - The final program in this section is an extension of the program to create an array of names and dates of birth. Having input the data and stored it in an array, the user is invited to type the name of a person, the array is searched for that name, and if a match is found the date of birth for that person is displayed. Notice in this example that the array is passed as an argument in a function call.

```
/*
c10_dpp\ex_04.c
program to create an array of records and given the name
of a person search the array for their date of birth
*/

#include <stdio.h>
#include <string.h>
#define size 5

typedef struct {
                int     day;
                int     month;
                int     year;
             } date_of_birth;

typedef struct {
                char            name[80];
                date_of_birth   birth_date;
             } names_dates;


char whose_birthday[80];

int   search(names_dates birthdays[])
/* function to search the array and return the value of the index
when a match for the name is found, otherwise it returns the size
of the array */
{
     int index = 0;

     while (index < size)
        if (strcmp(whose_birthday, birthdays[index].name) != 0)
           index++;
        else
           return index;

     return index;
}

main()
{
     names_dates birthdays[size] =   {{"Jane",11,10,1953},
                                      {"Fred",18,3,1948},
                                      {"Henry",14,6,1920},
                                      {"Patrick",17,3,1960},
                                      {"Susan",25,9,1981}};
```

```
    int index;

    printf("name? "); gets(whose_birthday);
    index = search(birthdays);
    if (index == size)
        printf("name not found\n");
    else
        printf("birthday %-3d%-3d%4d\n", birthdays[index].birth_date.day,
                                          birthdays[index].birth_date.month,
                                          birthdays[index].birth_date.year);
}
```

Results from program ex_04.c being run four times

```
name? Henry
birthday  14   6   1920
name? George
name not found
name? Patrick
birthday  17   3   1960
name? Jane
birthday 11 10 1953
```

10.2 Two-dimensional arrays

An array is not confined to one dimension (one subscript or index), but can be extended to two-dimensions and beyond, in order to provide a flexible data structure for the solution to a problem. A two-dimensional array is a repetition of a one-dimensional array. The structure can be thought of as a matrix or grid structure. In figure 10.5 the two-dimensional array named matrix is composed from three one-dimensional arrays.

	0	1	2	3	4	5
0	16	21	8	3	-7	9
1	-3	11	0	5	9	7
2	13	7	-64	19	14	2

figure 10.5

The declaration of the two-dimensional array in figure 10.5 is given as:

```
int matrix[3][6];
```

Access to any element in the two-dimensional array is through a row subscript, followed by a column subscript. For example matrix[0][5] = 9; matrix[2][0] = 13; matrix[1][2] = 0, etc.

The contents of the two dimensional array can be initialised in a similar way to one-dimensional arrays:

```
int matrix[3][6] = {{16,21,8,3,-7,9},
                    {-3,11,0,5,9,7},
                    {13,7,-64,19,14,2}};
```

where the first row of initialisation corresponds to the first row of the array, the second row of initialisation corresponds to the second row of the array, and so on. If a row of initialisation values does not contain enough values then the remaining elements are set to zero. If there are not enough rows of initialisation values then the remaining rows are set to zero.

The contents of a two-dimensional array can be accessed and displayed, using a double loop, as follows.

```
for (row=0; row < 3; row++)
{
   for (column=0; column < 6; column++)
     printf("%d\t", matrix[row][column]);

   printf("\n");
}
```

The following desk check of this code indicates how the row and column loop variables are used to gain access to the cells of the two-dimensional array.

row	column	(row<3)?	(column<6)?	matrix[row][column]
0	0	true	true	16
0	1	true	true	21
0	2	true	true	8
0	3	true	true	3
0	4	true	true	-7
0	5	true	true	9
0	6	true	false	
1	0	true	true	-3
1	1	true	true	11
1	2	true	true	0
1	3	true	true	5
1	4	true	true	9
1	5	true	true	7
1	6	true	false	
2	0	true	true	13
2	1	true	true	7

row	column	(row<3)?	(column<6)?	matrix[row][column]
2	2	true	true	-64
2	3	true	true	19
2	4	true	true	14
2	5	true	true	2
2	6	true	false	
3		false		

The following program stores the numbers found in the array depicted in figure 10.5 and sums and displays the numbers in each column and the numbers in each row.

```
/*
c10_dpp\ex_05.c
program to store numbers in a two-dimensional array,
display the contents of the array and calculate and
display the sum of each row and the sum of each column
*/

#include <stdio.h>

main()
{
        int matrix[3][6] = {{16,21,8,3,-7,9},
                             {-3,11,0,5,9,7},
                             {13,7,-64,19,14,2}};

        int row, column;
        int row_sum, column_sum;

        /* display contents of array */
        for (row=0; row < 3; row++)
        {
            for (column=0; column < 6; column++)
                printf("%6d", matrix[row][column]);
            printf("\n");
        }

        printf("\n");

        /* sum and display numbers in each row */
        for (row=0; row < 3; row++)
        {
            row_sum = 0;
            for (column=0; column < 6; column++)
                row_sum = row_sum + matrix[row][column];

            printf("sum of row %d is %d\n", row, row_sum);
        }
```

```
        printf("\n");

        /* sum and display numbers in each column */
        for (column=0; column < 6; column++)
        {
              column_sum = 0;
              for (row=0; row < 3; row++)
                    column_sum = column_sum + matrix[row][column];

              printf("sum of column %d is %d\n", column, column_sum);
        }
}
```

Results from program ex_05.c being run

```
    16      21      8       3      -7       9
    -3      11      0       5       9       7
    13       7    -64      19      14       2

sum of row 0 is 50
sum of row 1 is 29
sum of row 2 is -9

sum of column 0 is 26
sum of column 1 is 39
sum of column 2 is -56
sum of column 3 is 27
sum of column 4 is 16
sum of column 5 is 18
```

10.3 Worked examples

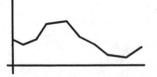

ANNUAL RAINFALL

Problem - The annual rainfall is recorded on a monthly basis over four regions, North, South, East and West of an island. Design and write a program to store the data in a two-dimensional array and calculate the average rainfall for each region over the year and the driest month taking the average rainfall for the four regions. The following table is an indication of the data involved.

Months	Jan	Feb	Mar	Apr	May	Jun	Jul	Aug	Sep	Oct	Nov	Dec
North	14	13	11	9	5	3	1	1	4	8	9	12
South	17	18	15	13	11	9	7	8	9	10	13	15
East	9	8	6	4	2	1	0	1	3	7	9	10
West	12	11	9	6	4	2	1	3	5	8	10	13

```
                          Screen Layout

12345678901234567890123456789012345678901234567890123456789 0
                    rainfall
region        total      average
North          90          7
South         145         12
East           60          5
West           84          7

Jan Feb Mar Apr May Jun Jul Aug Sep Oct Nov Dec
13  12  10  8   5   3   2   3   5   8   10  12

driest month is Jul
```

It is evident from the screen layout that the names of the four regions and the names of the months need to be displayed. These can be displayed as string literals or as the respective contents of two two-dimensional arrays. The latter approach will lead to succinct programming.

The first two-dimensional array to store the names of the months has twelve rows and four columns. If a three character abbreviation is used for each month then four columns will be needed for the three letters plus the null terminator. The second two-dimensional array to store the names of the regions has four rows and six columns. The longest string has five characters, plus the null terminator. Both arrays are shown in figure 10.6

```
row      column              row      column
         0123                         012345

0        Jan                 0        North
1        Feb                 1        South
2        Mar                 2        East
3        Apr                 3        West
4        May
5        Jun                 char regions[4][6]
6        Jul
7        Aug
8        Sep
9        Oct
10       Nov
11       Dec

char months[12][4]
```

figure 10.6

201

To display the contents of either array it is not necessary to use a column subscript. For example to display the abbreviation for the month of March *printf("%s", months[2])* is all that is required. Similarly to display the region South *printf("%s", regions[1])* is sufficient.

The solution to the problem divides into three parts:

(i)   initialise the three two-dimensional arrays with the rainfall data, months and regions respectively;
(ii) calculate and display the average rainfall for each region;
(iii) calculate and display by month the average rainfall in all regions and conclude which month is the driest.

Part (i) can be declared and initialised as data local to the main function. Parts (ii) and (iii) can be coded as two separate functions named *average_rainfall* and *monthly_rainfall* respectively. The contents of the three arrays will be passed as arguments to the functions *average_rainfall* and *monthly_rainfall*.

Algorithm for the function average_rainfall

display the headings for total and average rainfall table

for each region
    display the name of region
    initialise total rainfall to zero

    for each month
        increase total rainfall by the rainfall for the month

    calculate and display average annual rainfall for the region

Data Dictionary for the function average_rainfall - The formal parameter list for this function contains two items, an array with rainfall data and an array with regions. The function does not return a value. There is a requirement to declare local variables to control the *for* loops for the regions and the months, and local variables to store the total rainfall and the average rainfall over the twelve months.

```
void average_rainfall(int rainfall[][12], char regions[][6])
int  region, month;
int  total_by_region, average_by_region;
```

Notice that in passing a two-dimensional array as an argument that it is necessary to state the number of columns in the respective formal parameter array. It would also be quite acceptable to state the number of rows, therefore, void average_rainfall(**int rainfall[4][12], char regions[4][6]**) would also compile without errors.

Test data - see earlier data on rainfall per region per month. This data will be stored in a two-dimensional array with rows representing regions and columns representing months.

Desk Check of the function average_rainfall - excludes screen output

region	0	0	0	0	0	0	0	0	0	0	0	0
month	0	1	2	3	4	5	6	7	8	9	10	11
rainfall[region][month]	14	13	11	9	5	3	1	1	4	8	9	12
total_by_region	14	27	38	47	52	55	56	57	61	69	78	90
average_by_region												7

region	1	1	1	1	1	1	1	1	1	1	1	1
month	0	1	2	3	4	5	6	7	8	9	10	11
rainfall[region][month]	17	18	15	13	11	9	7	8	9	10	13	15
total_rainfall	17	35	50	63	74	83	90	98	107	117	130	145
average_rainfall												12

region	2	2	2	2	2	2	2	2	2	2	2	2
month	0	1	2	3	4	5	6	7	8	9	10	11
rainfall[region][month]	9	8	6	4	2	1	0	1	3	7	9	10
total_rainfall	9	17	23	27	29	30	30	31	34	41	50	60
average_rainfall												5

region	3	3	3	3	3	3	3	3	3	3	3	3
month	0	1	2	3	4	5	6	7	8	9	10	11
rainfall[region][month]	12	11	9	6	4	2	1	3	5	8	10	13
total_rainfall	12	23	32	38	42	44	45	48	53	61	71	84
average_rainfall												7

Algorithm for the function monthly_rainfall

for each month
*   display the name of the month*

initialise amount of rain to a large value
for each month
*   initialise total rainfall to zero*
*   for each region*
*   increase total rainfall by rainfall for region for that month*
*   calculate average rainfall over the four regions for that month*

*   display average rainfall*

*   if average rainfall < amount of rain*
*   set amount of rain to average rainfall*
*   set driest month to month*

display driest month

Data Dictionary for the function monthly_rainfall - The formal parameter list for this function contains two items, an array with rainfall data and an array of months. The function does not return a value. There is a requirement to declare local integer variables for the indices region, month and the driest month; totals for the amount of rain and the total rainfall and the average rainfall over all the regions per month.

```
void monthly_rainfall(int rainfall[][12], char months[][4])
int   region, month;
int   driest_month;
int   amount_of_rain, total_rainfall;
int   average_by_month;
```

Test data - see earlier data on rainfall per region per month. This data will be stored in a two-dimensional array with rows representing regions and columns representing months.

Desk Check of the function monthly_rainfall - excludes screen output and gives a sample for January, July and December only.

average_rainfall	32767				13	
month	0					
region	0	1	2	3		
rainfall[region][month]	14	17	9	12		
total_rainfall	14	31	40	52		
average				13		
(average < average_rainfall)?				true		
driest_month					0	

.

average_rainfall	3				2	
month	6					
region	0	1	2	3		
rainfall[region][month]	1	7	0	1		
total_rainfall	1	8	8	9		
average				2		
(average < average_rainfall)?				true		
driest_month					6	

.

average_rainfall	10				12	
month	11					
region	0	1	2	3		
rainfall[region][month]	12	15	10	13		
total_rainfall	12	27	37	50		
average				12		
(average < average_rainfall)?				false		
driest_month					6	

```
/*
c10_dpp\ex_06.c
program to store in a two-dimensional array the rainfall in each of four
regions per month, taken over the period of a year; calculate the
average rainfall for each region over the year and the wettest month
taking the total rainfall for the four regions
*/

#include <stdio.h>
#include <limits.h>

void average_rainfall(int rainfall[][12], char regions[][6])
/* function to calculate and display the total and average
annual rainfall over four regions */
{
        int region, month;
        int total_by_region, average_by_region;

        /* print heading */
        printf("        \t\t        rainfall\n");
        printf("region\t\ttotal\t\taverage\n");

        /* calculate the average rainfall for each region */
        for (region=0; region < 4; region++)
        {
             printf("%s\t\t", regions[region]);
             total_by_region = 0;

             for (month=0; month < 12; month++)
                  total_by_region = total_by_region + rainfall[region][month];

             average_by_region = total_by_region / 12;
             printf("%d\t\t%d\n", total_by_region, average_by_region);
        }
}

void monthly_rainfall(int rainfall[][12], char months[][4])
/* function to calculate and display the average rainfall per month
for all of the regions and the driest month on the island */
{
        int region, month;
        int driest_month;
        int amount_of_rain, total_rainfall;
        int average_by_month;
```

```
        printf("\n\n");
        /* display the names of the months */
        for (month=0; month < 12; month++)
            printf("%s ", months[month]);
        printf("\n");

        /* calculate the driest month taking the total rainfall in all regions
        */
        amount_of_rain = INT_MAX;
        for (month=0; month < 12; month++)
        {
            total_rainfall = 0;
            for (region=0; region < 4; region++)
                total_rainfall = total_rainfall + rainfall[region][month];
            average_by_month = total_rainfall / 4;
            printf("%-4d", average_by_month);

            if (average_by_month < amount_of_rain)
            {
                amount_of_rain = average_by_month;
                driest_month = month;
            }
        }

        printf("\n\ndriest month is %s\n", months[driest_month]);
}

main()
{
    int rainfall[4][12] = {{14,13,11,9,5,3,1,1,4,8,9,12},
                           {17,18,15,13,11,9,7,8,9,10,13,15},
                           {9,8,6,4,2,1,0,1,3,7,9,10},
                           {12,11,9,6,4,2,1,3,5,8,10,13}};

    char months[12][4] = {"Jan","Feb","Mar","Apr","May","Jun",
                          "Jul","Aug","Sep","Oct","Nov","Dec"};

    char regions[4][6] = {"North","South","East","West"};

    average_rainfall(rainfall, regions);
    monthly_rainfall(rainfall, months);
}
```

Results from program ex_06.c being run

```
                          rainfall
region              total              average
North               90                 7
South               145                12
East                60                 5
West                84                 7

Jan Feb Mar Apr May Jun Jul Aug Sep Oct Nov Dec
13  12  10  8   5   3   2   3   5   8   10  12

driest month is Jul
```

Problem - The results of students taking four examinations are stored as records containing the following fields:

(i)   a unique student number in the range 100..999;
(ii)   the name of the student which may have duplicates in other records;
(iii)   the percentage marks in the four examinations.

Design and write a program that stores the records in an array, such that the contents of the array may be searched on student number or name. If a match is found for either the number or the name then display the contents of the appropriate record together with the average mark attained over the four examinations.

Since the student number is unique, only one record may exist for a given number. However, this is not the case for a student name. There may be several students with the same name, in which case if a match for the name is found the search must continue for further possible matches, displaying the required information after each match.

The structure of a record can be defined as

```
typedef struct    {
                  int  number;
                  char name[80];
                  int  marks[4];
                  } record;
```

with the array containing the records being declared as:

```
record students[number_of_students];
```

The arrays that are used in the solution to this problem are illustrated in figure 10.7. Notice in this illustration that the array *students* contains ten records. The *name* of the student is a character string and also requires to be represented as a separate array of characters. The four *marks* are also stored in another separate array of integers.

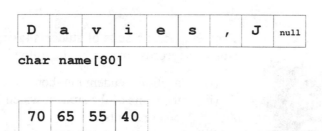

```
100  Rankin,W    45 55 65 75
150  Jones,D     60 80 90 75
250  Smith,P     90 80 45 60
300  Davies,J    70 65 55 40
400  Smith,P     40 50 60 55
450  Adams,C     25 40 35 40
455  Collins,Z   55 87 43 20
501  Evans,M     65 75 70 95
525  Jones,D     45 80 75 55
550  Owens,H     45 55 65 70
```

record students[number_of_students]

D	a	v	i	e	s	,	J	null

char name[80]

70	65	55	40

int marks[4]

figure 10.7

Since it is necessary to give the user of the program a choice as to whether to search the students array on *number* or *name*, it would be wise to incorporate a menu into the program that gave the user the choice. The screen layout gives a good indication as to the functionality of the program.

Notice that the user is given a choice (1) to search on the student number, or (2) to search on the student name, or (3) to finish using the program.

If the request is (1) the user is then asked for the student number. If a match is found between the number and a record stored in the array then the matched record is displayed and the average for the examination marks calculated and displayed. If the student number does not exist the user is prompted to choose from the menu again.

If the request is (2) then the user is asked for the name of the student. If the name is repeated in the array of records, a record is displayed for each occurrence of the name, and the average is calculated and displayed as before. If the name does not exist the system re-prompts the user with the menu.

```
                         Screen Layout

12345678901234567890123456789012345678901234567890

1 - search on number
2 - search on name
3 - finish

? 1
input student number 300

300 Davies,J    70  65  55  40   average 57

1 - search on number
2 - search on name
3 - finish

? 2
input student name Jones,D

150 Jones,D     60  80  90  75   average 76
525 Jones,D     45  80  75  55   average 63

1 - search on number
2 - search on name
3 - finish

? 3
```

In the development of this program it will be necessary to design and code functions to do the following.

A function to search the students array for the student number, if found return the value of the index, else return the size of the array. Clearly since the subscripting of an array starts at zero, the last entry in the array will appear at the subscript given by the number of records stored - 1, therefore, returning the size of the array will indicate that the student number cannot be found. The function prototype might be coded as:

```
    int search_number(record array[], int student_number);
```

A function to search the students array for a student name, if found return the value of the index, else return the size of the array. This function would work well if there were no duplicate names in the array. As it is currently described it will always return the index of the first occurrence of a name and not the successive indices. One solution is to introduce a second formal parameter that marks the position in the array at which searching must take place. By changing the value of this parameter it will be possible to step through the array every time a match is found. The function prototype might be coded as:

```
    int search_name(record array[], char student_name[], int start_at);
```

209

A function to display the contents of a record will require a parameter that indicates the position of the record, *at_index*, in the students array. The function prototype might be coded as:

```
void display_record(record array[], int at_index);
```

A function to calculate and return the average mark for a student will require a parameter that indicates the position of the record, at_index, in the student array. The function prototype might be coded as:

```
int average_mark(record array[], int at_index);
```

Algorithm for the function search_number - upon inspection of the records in the array, illustrated in figure 10.7, it is clear that the records have been entered into the array in student number sequence. This fact will be kept in mind when developing the following algorithm. If a student number is less than the number it is being compared with, then it cannot exist in the array. If the student number is greater than the number it is being compared with, then the record may exist later in the array. Of course, it goes without saying, that if the student number is equal to the number being compared then a match exists.

initialise array index to zero (subscript of the first cell)
initialise a boolean flag found to false

while array index is less than the number of students and the number is not found do
    if student number is equal to the number in the record in the array
        set boolean flag found to true
    else if student number is less than the number in the record in the array
        set array index to the number of students
    else
        increase the array index by 1 to point at the next record in the array

return the value of the array index

Data Dictionary for function search_number - The function contains two formal parameters the students record *array* and the integer *student_number*. The function returns the integer value of an index. There are two local variables, an integer *index* used as a subscript to the array and a boolean variable denoting whether a number has been *found*.

```
int       search_number(record array[], int student_number)
int       index;
boolean   found;
```

Test data - student_number *400*

The following desk checks assume that global constants *number_of_students* and *number_of_marks* have been defined that represent the ten records and four marks respectively.

Desk check for function search_number - using the data listed in figure 10.7.

number_of_students	10				
student_number	400				
index	0	1	2	3	4
found	false				true
(index < number_of_students && !found)?	true	true	true	true	true	false
array[index].number	100	150	250	300	400
(student_number == array[index].number)?	false	false	false	false	true
(student_number < array[index].number}?	false	false	false	false

Algorithm for the function search_name

initialise a boolean flag found to false
initialise array index to start at position

while array index is less than the number of students and the number is not found do
　　if student name is equal to the name in the record in the array
　　　　set boolean flag found to true
　　else
　　　　increase array index by 1 to point at the next record in the array

return the value of array index

Data Dictionary for the function search_name - The function contains three formal parameters the students record *array*, the *student_name* character string and the value of the index, *start_at*, for starting the search. The function returns the integer value of an index. There are two local variables, an integer *index* used as a subscript to the array and a boolean variable denoting whether a number has been *found*.

```
int       search_name(record array[], char student_name[], int start_at)
int       index;
boolean   found;
```

Test data - *student_name*　　Smith,P　　*start_at*　0, 3

Desk check of function search_name - using the data listed in figure 10.7 and checked twice with *start_at* 0 and 3.

number_of_students	10			
student_name	Smith,P			
index	0	1	2	
found	false			true
(index < number_of_students && !found)?	true	true	true	false
array[index].name	Rankin,W	Jones,D	Smith,P	
(student_name equals array[index].name)?	false	false	true	

211

number_of_students	10		
student_name	Smith,P		
index	3	4	
found	false		true
(index < number_of_students && !found)?	true	true	false
array[index].name	Davies,J	Smith,P	
(student_name equals array[index].name)?	false	true	

Algorithm for the function display_record

display the student number
display the student name
for each mark
   display mark

Data Dictionary for the function display_record - the function contains two formal parameters, the student record array and the array index, *at_index*, of the record to be displayed. The function does not return a value. The function contains one local variable, an integer index used as a subscript to the array of marks.

```
void display_record(record array[], int at_index)
int  index;
```

Test data - *at_index* 3

Desk Check of function display_record - using the data listed in figure 10.7

at_index	3					
number_of_marks	4					
array[at_index].number	300					
array[at_index].name	Davies,J					
index		0	1	2	3	4
(index < number_of_marks)?		true	true	true	true	false
array[at_index].marks[index]		70	65	55	40	

Algorithm for the function average_mark

initialise total of marks to zero
for every mark
   increase total of marks by corresponding mark in array of marks for corresponding record

return the average of the total of marks

Data Dictionary for the function average_mark - the function contains two formal parameters, the student record array and the array index, *at_index*, of the student record whose marks are to be averaged.

The function returns the average of the marks for the selected record. The function contains two local variables, one to keep a running total of the marks and the other as an integer index used as a subscript to the array of marks.

```
int average_mark(record array[], int at_index)
int total;
int index;
```

Test data - *at_index* 1

Desk Check of function average_mark - using the data listed in figure 10.7

number_of_marks	4				
at_index	1				
index	0	1	2	3	4
(index < number_of_marks)?	true	true	true	true	false
array[at_index].marks[index]	60	80	90	75	
total	60	140	230	305	
total / number_of_marks					76

Algorithm for the function main

initialise boolean flag for more data to true
do
   display menu
   input menu code

   switch menu code
   '1':   *input student number*
           set index to value returned by function search_number
           if index not equal to the number of students
               call function to display_record
               display value returned by function average_mark
   '2':   *input student name*
           initialise start_at index to zero
           while start-at index less than number of students do
               set index to the value returned by the function search_name
               if index not equal to the number of students
                   call function to display_record
                   display value returned by function average_mark
               set start_at to value of index + 1
   '3':   *set boolean flag for more to false*
  default: *display error message*

while more data

Data Dictionary for the function main - The array used to store student records can be initialised at its point of declaration. The function contains local variables to represent a *student_number*, a *student_name*, a *menu_code*, two integer indices *index* and *start_at* to gain access to the array and an enumerated boolean variable to signify more data.

```
record      students[number-of_students];
char        menu_code;
int         student_number;
char        student_name;
int         index;
int         start_at;
boolean     more;
```

```
/*
c10_dpp\ex_07.c

program to create an array of records that contains the following data

- student number (unique 3 digit number)
- student name (may contain duplicates)
- percentage marks in four final examinations

from the program it is possible to perform the following

- search the array on student number
- search the array on student name

and if the record is found then

- display the contents of a chosen record
- calculate and display the average mark for any student

*/

#include <stdio.h>
#include <string.h>

#define number_of_students 10
#define number_of_marks 4

typedef struct {
                int    number;
                char   name[80];
                int    marks[4];
            } record;

typedef enum{false, true} boolean;
```

```
int search_number(record array[], int student_number)
/* function to search the array for the student_number,
if found return the value of the index, else return the
size of the array */

{
     int      index = 0;
     boolean found = false;

     while (index < number_of_students && !found)
         if      (student_number == array[index].number)
                found = true;
         else if (student_number < array[index].number)
                index = number_of_students;
         else
                index++;

     return index;
}

int search_name(record array[], char student_name[], int start_at)
/* function to search the array for the student_name from the index
value start_at in the array, if found return the value of the index,
else return the size of the array */

{
     int      index;
     boolean found = false;

     index = start_at;
     while (index < number_of_students && !found)
        if (strcmp(student_name, array[index].name) == 0)
           found = true;
        else
           index++;
     return index;
}

void display_record(record array[], int at_index)
/* function to display the contents of a record in the array
at_index position */

{
     int index;

     printf("\n%-4d%s\t", array[at_index].number, array[at_index].name);
     for (index=0; index < number_of_marks; index++)
         printf("%-4d", array[at_index].marks[index]);
}
```

```
int average_mark(record array[], int at_index)
/* function to calculate and return the average mark for a
student whose record is located at_index in the array */


{
    int total = 0;
    int index;

    for (index=0; index < number_of_marks; index++)
        total = total + array[at_index].marks[index];

    return total / number_of_marks;
}

main()
{
    record students[number_of_students] = {{100,"Rankin,W",  45,55,65,75},
                                            {150,"Jones,D",   60,80,90,75},
                                            {250,"Smith,P",   90,80,45,60},
                                            {300,"Davies,J",  70,65,55,40},
                                            {400,"Smith,P",   40,50,60,55},
                                            {450,"Adams,C",   25,40,35,40},
                                            {455,"Collins,Z",55,87,43,20},
                                            {501,"Evans,M",   65,75,70,95},
                                            {525,"Jones,D",   45,80,75,55},
                                            {550,"Owens,H",   45,55,65,70}};

    char    menu_code;
    int     student_number;
    char    student_name[80];
    int     index;
    int     start_at;
    boolean more = true;

    do
    {
        printf("\n\n");
        printf("1 - search on number\n");
        printf("2 - search on name\n");
        printf("3 - finish\n\n");
        printf("? ");
        menu_code = getchar();
        getchar(); /* clear keyboard buffer */
```

```
        switch (menu_code)
        {
        case '1' : printf("input student number ");
                   scanf("%d", &student_number); getchar();
                   index = search_number(students, student_number);
                   if (index != number_of_students)
                   {
                       display_record(students, index);
                       printf("average %d\n", average_mark(students, index));
                   }
                   break;

        case '2' : printf("input student name ");
                   gets(student_name);
                   start_at = 0;
                   while (start_at < number_of_students)
                   {
                     index = search_name(students, student_name, start_at);
                     if (index != number_of_students)
                     {
                         display_record(students, index);
                         printf("\taverage %d\n", average_mark(students, index));
                     }
                     start_at = index+1;
                   }
                   break;

        case '3' : more = false;
                   break;

        default  : printf("error in menu code try again\b\n");
        }
    }
    while (more);
}
```

Results from program ex_07.c being run

```
1 - search on numbers
2 - search on name
3 - finish

? 1
input student number 300

300 Davies,J  70  65  55  40    average 57
```

```
1 - search on numbers
2 - search on name
3 - finish

? 2
input student name Jones,D

150 Jones,D    60  80  90  75    average 76

525 Jones,D    45  80  75  55    average 63

1 - search on numbers
2 - search on name
3 - finish

? 3
```

10.4 Beyond two dimensions

It is possible to create an array with more than two dimensions. A three-dimensional array is a repetition of two-dimensional arrays, a four-dimensional array is a repetition of three-dimensional arrays , and so on.

Figure 10.8 illustrates a three-dimensional array which consists of **two**, two-dimensional arrays; each two-dimensional array consists of **three**, one-dimensional arrays; each one-dimensional array contains **two** cells. Hence, the dimensions of the three-dimensional array are described as **[2][3][2]**, and since these arrays contain integers a declaration for the complete structure might be **int three_D [2][3][2]**.

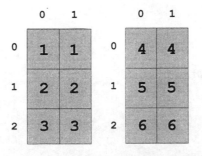

```
three_D [2][3][2]
is a repetition of
two-dimensional arrays
```

figure 10.8

In the program that follows, the three-dimensional array illustrated in figure 10.8, has been initialised at the point of declaration and the contents of the array displayed.

```
/*
c10_dpp\ex_08.c
program to demonstrate the initialisation and access
to a three dimensional array
*/

#include <stdio.h>

main()
{
    int three_D[2][3][2] = {{{1,1},{2,2},{3,3}},{{4,4},{5,5},{6,6}}};

    int i,j,k;

    for (i=0; i<2; i++)
    {
        for (j=0; j<3; j++)
        {
            for (k=0; k<2; k++)
                printf("%2d", three_D[i][j][k]);
            printf("\n");
        }
        printf("\n");
    }
}
```

Results from program ex_08.c being run

```
 1 1
 2 2
 3 3

 4 4
 5 5
 6 6
```

10.5 Summary

☐   A structure is a collection of one or more members, which may be of different types, grouped together under a single name.

☐   A variable may be declared as having a specific structure.

□   A structure may be given a tag or name, that can be used to declare a variable of the same structure type.

□   The previous two methods can be combined to give a structure a tag and declare a variable as having a specific structure.

□   Structure variables may be initialised at the point of declaration.

□   Individual members of a structure can be accessed by qualifying each member with the name of the corresponding structure variable.

□   If two variables have the same structure it is possible to assign the contents of one variable to another.

□   An array may contain mixed data types within the umbrella of a structure.

□   An array can have more than one dimension.

□   An N-dimensional array can be thought of as a repetition of (N-1)-dimensional arrays.

□   Arrays of any dimension may be initialised at the point of declaration.

10.6 Questions - *answers begin on page 483*

1. Write a program to store the names of foods and their prices, as displayed at Ben's Breakfast Bar (section 2.1), as records in an array. Extend the program to:

(a). Repeatedly input the name of an item of food and display the price. Quit from the iterative process when the name of the food does not exist.
(b). Input an amount of money and display all the individual items of food that cost the same or less than the amount of money.

2. Write a program to input and store in an array, the ten records illustrated in figure 10.9, that contain the names of towns/ cities and their corresponding telephone area codes for Scotland. Include a procedure to search for the name of the town/ city when given the area code. Display the result of the search. Exit the program on the input of an illegal area code.

Aberdeen	01224
Ayr	01292
Dundee	01382
Edinburgh	0131
Falkirk	01324
Fort William	01397
Glasgow	0141
Inverness	01463
Perth	01738
Stirling	01786

figure 10.9

[3]. Write a program to store two twenty digit integers as characters of a string and perform the operations of addition and subtraction on the two integers. Output the answer as a string of digits.

[4]. A selection of towns/ cities in three counties in the England have populations to the nearest 100 as shown in figure 10.10.

county	town/ city	population
Wiltshire	Salisbury	37,000
	Swindon	170,000
	Marlborough	7,000
Oxfordshire	Oxford	115,800
	Banbury	38,600
	Witney	17,500
Dorset	Poole	137,000
	Dorchester	14,500
	Weymouth	49,400

figure 10.10

Initialise the following arrays.

(a) A one-dimensional array containing the names of the counties.
(b) A two-dimensional array containing records of the names of the towns/ cities and their respective populations, where each row represents a different county, in the order given in the first array.

Using the arrays from (a) and (b) write procedures to input the name of a county and the name of a town/ city, and perform a serial search on the one-dimensional array to match the county and obtain a row subscript, then perform a serial search on the two-dimensional array, to match the town/ city, and obtain a column subscript. Using the row and column subscripts, access the two-dimensional array and display the value for the population of the chosen town/ city.

Write further code to input the name of a county and output the total population for the towns/cities listed in the county. Re-express this figure as a percentage of the population of all the towns/ cities defined in the array.

[5]. From the saying "thirty days hath September, April, June and November, and all the rest have thirty-one, except for February that has twenty-eight days clear and twenty-nine in a Leap Year", write a program to:

(a). store the names and number of days in each month as records in an array;

(b). display a calendar for any year remaining in the twentieth century (1995 .. 2099), printing the year and the names of the months; the value for the date is to be printed under the name of the day.

6. Design and write a program to enable the user to construct a crossword similar to that illustrated in figure 10.11. The user will be required to input the starting and finishing co-ordinates of a word and the word string. The computer will store the letters of the word either across or down the 15x15 array, depending upon the values of the co-ordinates. Display the contents of the array after each word has been stored.

columns

	1	2	3	4	5	6	7	8	9	10	11	12	13	14	15
1	J	U	I	C	E										
2	A				L	A	U	N	C	H					
3	M	O	D	E	M			A							
4								U							
5								G							
6								H							
7								T							
8								Y							
9															
10															
11															
12															
13															
14															
15															

rows

figure 10.11

Chapter 11
Pointers

Before progressing with any further developments in C, it is vital to introduce the topic of pointers that underpins the remainder of the work found in this text. The use of pointers is put into context with subjects the reader is already familiar with, such as formal parameters in functions, arrays and strings. By the end of this chapter the reader should have a knowledge of the following topics.

- ☐ The definition of a pointer.

- ☐ The use of pointers in a formal parameter list.

- ☐ Accessing arrays through pointers.

- ☐ Dynamic arrays.

- ☐ Pointers to functions.

11.1 Pointers

A declaration such as **int X = -163;** implies that X is an identifier of a location in memory for storing a datum of type integer, in this case the value -163. This information is depicted in figure 11.1

figure 11.1

A pointer is an identifier that does not store a scalar data value, but stores an address of where to find the data in memory. This address literally points to where the data is stored. When a pointer variable is declared, the declaration only allocates storage space for the pointer and does not allocate storage space for the information being pointed at by the pointer.

In the following example **P** has been declared as a pointer to an address containing an integer as **int *P**. Pointers are allocated memory from the system heap (a storage area for dynamically allocated variables) by the function **malloc**, and de-allocated memory, so that it is returned to the system heap, by the function **free**. Figure 11.2 illustrates typical operations for the allocation, use and deallocation of a pointer to memory.

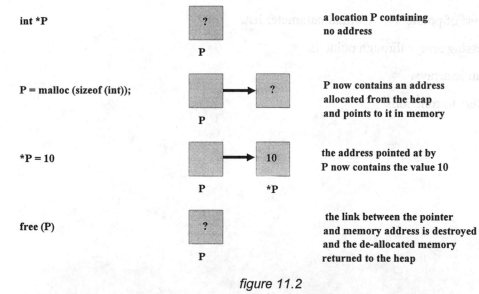

figure 11.2

The function *malloc* allocates a block of bytes and returns a pointer to the block. The size of the bytes allocated is dependent upon the data being pointed at. The **sizeof** operator returns the amount of storage space required for a value of the specified type. Hence the statement **P = malloc (sizeof(int))** will assign to **P** the address of the area of memory allocated from the heap to store an integer. The **indirection operator** * allows the programmer to identify the value of the integer that is being pointed at by **P**, therefore, the result of the assignment ***P = 10** is to store the value 10 at the area of memory pointed at by P. Finally statement **free(P)** returns the block of memory that **P** originally pointed at to the heap.

Other pointers can be assigned to existing pointers as illustrated in figure 11.3. This implies that they both point at the same address. For example given the declaration of a pointer

int *Q; and P=malloc(sizeof (int)); then Q =P;

implies that both **P** and **Q** point at the same address.

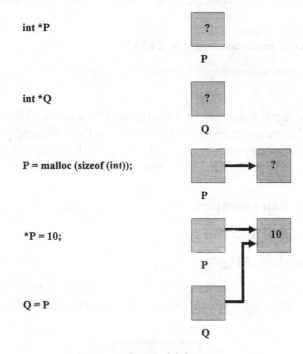

figure 11.3

The program that follows demonstrates the facts that have been presented in this section.

```
/*
c11_dpp\ex_01.c
program to demonstrate the creation of a pointer to an integer,
and the re-assignment of another pointer to the same area of memory
*/

#include <stdio.h>
#include <stdlib.h>

main()
{

      int *P, *Q;   /* declare two pointers */
```

225

```
    P = malloc(sizeof(int));
    printf("input a single integer "); scanf("%d",P);
    Q = P;
    printf("value of the integer being pointed at is %d\n", *Q);
    free(P);
}
```

Results from program ex_01.c being run

```
input a single integer 12345
value of integer being pointed at is 12345
```

Note - when using *scanf* to input a number or a character, the address of the variable is required. But variable **P** is a pointer and hence an address, so scanf("%d", **&P**) would imply input the contents of the address of **P**, which itself is another address and not the value of the integer. Therefore scanf("%d", **P**) is used correctly in the program. Note also that ***Q** is the value of the integer that is being pointed at by **Q**.

11.2 Address and indirection operators

It is understood that a declaration of the form:

```
        int largest = INT_MAX;
```

implies that the identifier *largest* contains, or stores, the value of INT_MAX which happens to be 32767 on a 16-bit computer. Pictorially *largest* might be seen as a box containing the value 32767, as shown in figure 11.4.

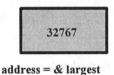

address = & largest

figure 11.4

This box represents an area of computer memory used for storing the integer *largest*. The address of this area of memory is denoted by **&largest**, where **&** is the *address operator* .

The declaration:

```
        int *IntPointer;
```

implies that the variable *IntPointer* contains an address of a variable of type integer. The asterisk * in front of *IntPointer* instructs the compiler that *IntPointer* is a pointer and not a variable of type integer.

Although the value of a pointer variable may change during the execution of a program, the variable must always point to data of the same type. In this example data of type integer.

The statement **IntPointer = &largest;** assigns the address of *largest* to *IntPointer*, causing *IntPointer* to point at the variable *largest*, as depicted in figure 11.5.

An *indirection operator* * allows the programmer to identify the value of the integer that is being pointed at by IntPointer, therefore, the result of this assignment implies that *IntPointer = largest.

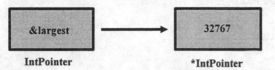

&largest   32767

IntPointer   *IntPointer

IntPointer = &largest /* an address in computer memory */

IntPointer = largest / value contained in memory at the address &largest */

figure 11.5

11.3 Parameters

In chapter 7 it was stated that some arguments in an actual parameter list are passed by value (by content), implying that a local copy of the value passed, is used by the function and not the original. In other high-level languages an argument can be passed by variable (by reference), implying that the value of the argument can be changed by the function and its new value accessed outside of the function.

Up to this point in the text, passing an argument by reference, has only been possible if the argument was an array.

Reference parameters, other than arrays, are possible in C. The formal parameters in a function are declared as pointers, and the actual parameters (arguments) used in the function call are treated as addresses of the variables and not the variables themselves.

For example, a function used to separate the whole part of a real number from its decimal fraction may be coded as:

```
void split(float local_number, int *whole_number, float *fractional_part)
{
   *whole_number = local_number;
   *fractional_part = local_number - (int) local_number;
}
```

and called by **split(number, &whole, &fraction);** where *number, whole and fraction* are declared in the main function as **float number; int whole; float fraction;**

Figure 11.6 illustrates that *number* is passed to the function *split* as a local copy, and that any changes to *local_number* in the function *split* do not alter *number* in the main function. The addresses &*whole* and &*fraction* are passed to the pointers *whole_number* and *fractional_part*. Any reference to *whole_number* and *fractional_part* in the function *split* must change the contents of *whole* and *fraction* in the main function.

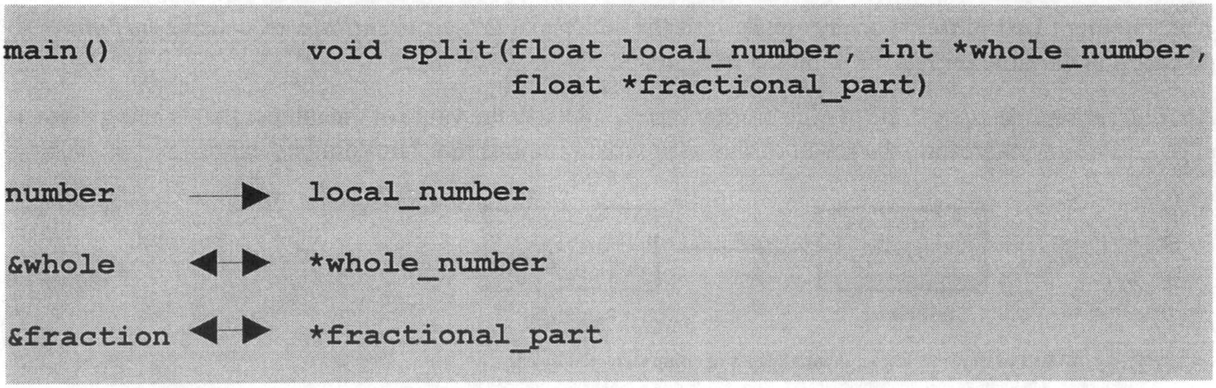

```
main()              void split(float local_number, int *whole_number,
                               float *fractional_part)


number    ━━━━▶   local_number

&whole    ◀━━▶   *whole_number

&fraction ◀━━▶   *fractional_part
```

figure 11.6

The following program illustrates the points raised in this section.

```c
/*
c11_dpp\ex_02.c
program to demonstrate the use of pointers in a formal parameter list
*/

#include <stdio.h>

void split(float local_number, int *whole_number, float *fractional_part)
{
        *whole_number = local_number;
        *fractional_part = local_number - (int) local_number;
}

main()
{
        float number = 3.14159;
        float fraction;
        int    whole;

        split(number, &whole, &fraction);

        printf("whole %d\tfraction %f\n", whole, fraction);
}
```

Results from program ex_02.c being run

```
whole 3 fraction 0.141590
```

11.4 Arrays

In chapters 9 and 10 subscripts or indices were used to access elements in an array. However, it is also possible to use pointers to access the contents of an array. In the following code a pointer *ptr* has been declared and is made to point at the first cell of the array named table. This has been illustrated in figure 11.7.

```
int  table[6] = {16,21,8,3,-7,9};
int *ptr;
ptr = &table[0]; /*  the pointer, which is an address, is assigned the
                     address of the first cell in the array  */
```

It is worth noting that when an array is declared, the name of the array is actually a pointer to the first element in the array. Therefore, by writing the array name **table** (a pointer) it is the same as writing **&table[0]** (a pointer to the first clement). The declaration of int table[6]; implies that *(table+0) = 16. Similarly *(table+1) = 21, *(table+2) = 8, etc. But table[0] = 16, table[1] = 21, table[2] = 8, etc. Therefore, *(table+i) is the same as table[i].

Warning! Do not attempt to modify, using pointer arithmetic, the name of an array. This value is a constant pointer and not a pointer variable.

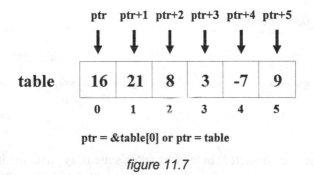

ptr = &table[0] or ptr = table

figure 11.7

It is possible to access the first cell through the pointer **ptr**, thus: printf("%d", *ptr); would display 16, the contents of cell 0. In order to allow the pointer **ptr** to traverse the addresses of the cells of the array, it is possible to perform arithmetic on a pointer. An integer can be added to a pointer to get it to point to another address, for example **ptr = ptr + 1** (or **ptr++**) causes the pointer to point to the second cell in the array table.

The contents of the one-dimensional array table can be displayed using the following segment of code.

```
for (ptr=table; ptr < table+6; ptr++)
  printf("%-4d", *ptr);
```

Two pointers can be subtracted as follows.

```
int *ptr1, *ptr2;
ptr1=&table[5];
ptr2=&table[0];
```

then **ptr1 - ptr2** represents the difference in the addresses of **&table[5]** and **&table[0]** which is 5.

The program that follows illustrates how the array can be accessed and its contents displayed.

```
/*
c11_dpp\ex_03.c
program to demonstrate access to an array using pointers
*/

#include <stdio.h>

main()
{
    int table[6] = {16,21,8,3,-7,9};
    int *ptr;

    for (ptr = table; ptr < table+6; ptr++)
        printf("%-4d", *ptr);
}
```

Results from program ex_03.c being run

```
16   21   8    3    -7   9
```

11.5 Strings

A string is stored as successive characters in the computer's memory, with the last character of the string being the string terminator (a null character). The beginning of the string is represented as a pointer to the first character of the string. For example:

```
char *magic = "abracadabra";
```

then magic is assigned as a pointer to the first character of "abracadabra", as depicted in figure 11.8.

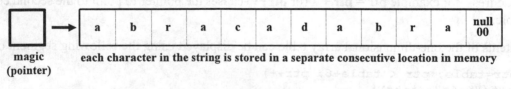

magic
(pointer)   each character in the string is stored in a separate consecutive location in memory

figure 11.8

The following program illustrates a method of displaying the string array on the screen.

230

```
/*
c11_dpp\ex_04.c
program to demonstrate the use of a pointer to access a character string
*/

#include <stdio.h>

main()
{
    const char null = 0;
        char *magic = "abracadabra";
        char *ptr;

    for (ptr = magic; *ptr != null; ptr++)
        printf("%c", *ptr);
}
```

Results from program ex_04.c being run

```
abracadabra
```

If the string was declared as a one-dimensional array and initialised as follows

```
char magic[ ] = "abracadabra";
```

then the same code can be used to display the contents of *magic* on the screen. Despite the same code being used to access the string there are differences in the manner in which the string and name of the string can be used. In the array declaration of the string the contents of the string can be modified, however, in the pointer version no attempt should be made to modify the string. In the array declaration *magic* is the name of an array and it cannot point to a different array, by contrast the pointer variable can be changed in the program so that it contains a different address and hence points to a different string!

11.6 Dynamic arrays

When a pointer variable is declared, the declaration only allocates storage space for the pointer and does not allocate storage space for the information being pointed at by the pointer. For example when a pointer variable to a string is declared as **char *string;** only the address of the pointer variable is allocated. Memory space needs to be allocated to store the characters in the string.

The function **malloc** found in the header file <stdlib.h> allocates memory, it requires one argument which represents the number of bytes requested, and returns a pointer to the first byte. For example:

```
char *string;
string = malloc(256);
```

allocates 256 bytes to the character string array and points to the first character in this string array.

231

The storage space is allocated from an area of memory known as the heap. The size of the heap is finite, and clearly too many requests for storage space from the heap will exhaust the amount of memory available for allocation. For this reason whenever allocated memory space is no longer required it should be returned to the heap by using the function **free**. In this example the 256 bytes of storage needed to accommodate the characters of string would be returned to the heap by the statement **free(string)**.

The following program indicates how memory space is allocated to a character array being pointed at by *string*. A value for the string array is input using *get(string)*. A further area of memory is allocated to a second array of characters pointed at by *copy*. The amount of memory allocated to the character array *copy* is determined by the length of string. Note the ANSI function **strlen** returns the length of a string. The string array is then copied into the *copy* array and the contents of this new array is output. The storage space allocated to *string* and *copy* is then returned to the heap using the function *free*.

```
/*
c11_dpp\ex_05.c
program to demonstrate the creation of a dynamic character array
*/

#include <stdio.h>
#include <stdlib.h>
#include <string.h>


char *string, *copy;

main()
{
        string = malloc(256);
        printf("input string ");
        gets(string);
        copy = malloc(strlen(string) + 1);
        strcpy(copy, string);
        printf("string input was ");
        puts(copy);
        free(copy);
        free(string);
}
```

Results from program ex_05.c being run

```
input string Peace on Earth? Maybe one day!
string input was Peace on Earth? Maybe one day!
```

Space allocation for arrays other than strings is achieved through the function **calloc**, also found in header <stdlib.h>. This function requires two parameters, the first represents the size of the array, and the second represents the size of the data held in each cell of the array.

If a one-dimensional array pointed at by table, is to store integers it could be declared as:

```
int *table;
```

However, if the number of integers that table will hold is not known in advance, memory allocation for the array can be postponed until the size of the array is known. During program execution if the size of the array is found to be n, say, then memory can be allocated by using:

```
table = calloc( n, sizeof(int));
```

The format of *malloc* and *calloc* given in the library reference manual are:

```
void *malloc(size_t size),
    and
void *calloc(size_t nmemb, size_t size)
```

respectively. Notice the use of void * for the return type in both functions. In ANSI C, void * is a **generic pointer type**, used when the type being pointed to is not known. Note also that the type **size_t** is implementation dependent, some compilers will use *unsigned int*, as in the case of TopSpeed C, and others will use *unsigned long int*. The amount of storage space to be allocated will depend upon the type of data being stored in the array. The value of **size** can be either a constant, for example 256, an expression (strlen(string) + 1) or the size of the data type being stored (sizeof(int)). Note that **sizeof** is an operator in C that returns the number of bytes that a data type needs for storage. The generic pointer returned, is automatically converted to the required type when the assignment is performed.

The format of **free** is described in the library reference manual as:

```
void free(void *ptr);
```

where the pointer (ptr) is described as a generic pointer type, therefore, a pointer of any type may appear as an actual parameter. For example:

```
free(table); /* table points to data of type int */
free(string); /* string points to data of type char */
```

These features are illustrated in the next program to create a dynamic array.

```
/*
c11_dpp\ex_06.c
program to dynamically declare the size of an integer array
*/

#include <stdio.h>
#include <stdlib.h>

main()
{
    int *table; /* pointer to the array name table */
    int *ptr;   /* pointer used in place of subscript */
    int size;   /* size of the table declared at run-time */

    printf("input the number of cells in the table ");
    scanf("%d", &size);

    table = calloc(size, sizeof(int)); /* allocate memory space */

    /* input numbers into table */
    printf("input numbers into array\n\n");
    for (ptr=table; ptr<table+size; ptr++)
        scanf("%d", ptr);

    /* display the contents of the table */
    printf("\n\ncontents of table\n");
    for (ptr=table; ptr<table+size; ptr++)
        printf("%-3d", *ptr);

    free(table);
}
```

Results from program ex_06.c being run

```
input the number of cells in the table 6
input numbers into array
21 13 -7 0 18 101

contents of table
21 13 -7 0  18 101
```

11.7 Pointers to functions

The following example uses Simpson's rule, which provides a method of finding the area between a plotted function y=f(x), the x-axis and the limits x=a, x=b. An approximation to the area becomes $1/3h(Y_0+4Y_1+Y_2)$.

If the area under the plotted function is divided into strips, illustrated in figure 11.9, and Simpson's rule is applied to each strip between the limits x=a and x=b, then clearly the more strips there are, the more accurate the estimation of the area will be. Also the more strips there are, the smaller h will become.

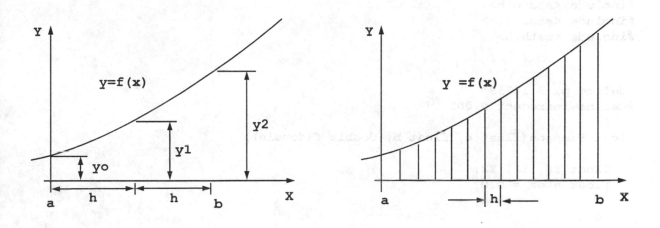

figure 11.9

In C it is possible to pass a pointer to a function as an argument in an actual parameter list. For example, if the function *Simpson* uses Simpson's rule to calculate the area under a curve between the limits x=a and x=b for any curve passed to the function, the formal parameter list would be defined as:

```
float Simpson(float a, float b, double (*f)(double))
```

where **a** and **b** are the upper and lower limits of integration and **(*f)** indicates that **f** is a pointer to a function that requires an argument of type double and returns a value that is of type double. The notation can be simplified, by replacing **(*f)(double)** with **f(double)**. The function Simpson can be called using a variety of mathematical functions that represent different curves, for example:

        Simpson(0, pi/2, sin);
        Simpson(0,1, exp);
        Simpson(0,9,sqrt);

where the functions sin, exp and sqrt are all described in the header file <math.h> as follows:

        double sin(double x);
        double exp(double x);
        double sqrt(double x);

The final program in the chapter uses Simpson's rule to perform the integrations mentioned in this section.

235

```
/*
c11_dpp\ex_07.c
program to illustrate the use of a pointer to a function
*/

#include <stdio.h>
#include <stdlib.h>
#include <math.h>



#define pi 3.14159
#define increment 0.001

float Simpson(float a, float b, double f(double))
{
    float Y0, Y1, Y2;
    float area = 0.0;

    do
    {
        Y0 = f(a);
        Y1 = f(a+increment);
        Y2 = f(a+2*increment);
        area = area + (increment / 3) * (Y0+4*Y1+Y2);
        a = a + 2*increment;
    } while (a < b);
    return area;
}

main()
{
    printf("integral of sin(x) 0<=x<=pi/2 %f\n", Simpson(0,pi/2,sin));
    printf("integral of exp(x) 0<=x<=1 %f\n", Simpson(0,1,exp));
    printf("integral of sqrt(x) 0<=x<=9 %f\n", Simpson(0,9,sqrt));
}
```

Results from program ex_07.c being run

```
integral of sin(x) 0<=x<=pi/2 1.001187
integral of exp(x) 0<=x<=1 1.723699
integral of sqrt(x) 0<=x<=9 18.004187
```

11.8 Summary

- ☐ A pointer is an identifier that stores an address of an item of data.

- ☐ The declaration of a pointer variable only allocates storage space for the pointer and does not allocate storage space for the information being pointed at by the pointer.

- ☐ Storage allocation is through the functions **malloc** and **calloc** found in <stdlib.h>.

- ☐ Storage allocation is taken from the system heap. Storage space is re-allocated back to the heap upon execution of the function **free** also found in <stdlib.h>.

- ☐ The indirection operator * is used to specify the contents of the memory being pointed at by the pointer variable.

- ☐ The address operator & is used to specify the memory address of a variable.

- ☐ Actual parameters (arguments) may be passed by reference to a function provided the arguments are specified as addresses, and the corresponding formal parameters as pointers.

- ☐ The name of an array is a pointer to the first cell of the array. As a consequence array parameters are always passed by reference.

- ☐ A pointer may be initialised to the address of the first cell of an array. The pointer may have arithmetic performed upon it to enable access to be gained to other cells within the array.

- ☐ A character string is an array of characters with a null character appended to the end of the string. The name of the string is a pointer to the first cell of the array.

- ☐ Memory allocation to arrays is through the function calloc. However, malloc may also be used for string arrays.

- ☐ A pointer to a function may be passed as an argument.

11.9 Questions - *answers begin on page 486*

1. Declare three pointers to the types int, float and char. Allocate memory from the heap to store values that are input of type int, float and char respectively. Display the contents of the addresses being pointed at by the three pointers. De-allocate memory back to the heap.

[2]. Re-write the program *ex_06.c* found in *chapter 9* on *one-dimensional arrays*, to encompass a function with the following prototype.

```
char *to_upper(char *array);
```

where the function *to_upper* converts any lower-case letters found in the array and returns a pointer to a string containing upper-case characters. The advantage of this function is that the contents of the original array need not be changed.

3. A carpenter has a supply of various lengths of wood. The carpenter wants to cut from them as many 5 metre lengths as possible and where a 5 metre length cannot be cut the carpenter will cut 2 metre lengths.

Write a program to input a length of wood and calculate and output the number of 5 metre, and 2 metre lengths and the amount of wasted wood. Repeat the program for different lengths of wood being input and keep a running total of the number of 5 metre and 2 metre pieces and the cumulative length of wasted wood. At the end of the data, output the total number of 5 metre, 2 metre pieces and cumulative length of wasted wood.

A suitable function to calculate the number of pieces of wood that can be cut to a set size from a length of wood might have the following prototype.

```
void calculate(float *length, float size, int *pieces);
```

where the parameter *length* is reduced according to the number of *pieces* cut to *size*. This implies that the reference value of length, after the function call, will give the length of wasted wood.

[4]. The letters of the alphabet A through Z can be represented in Morse code. Each letter is represented by a combination of up to four dots (.) and/or dashes (-). For example

```
A=".-   ", B="-...", C="-.-.", D="-.. " through Z="--.."
```

In these groups of characters spaces have been deliberately introduced to fill the code up to the maximum of four characters. However, the space does not represent part of the code. The codes for the letters A through Z can be represented as the following character string.

```
char *MorseData =  ".-   -...-.-.  .    ..-.--. ......  .----.- .-..-- "
                   "-.   --- .-- --.-.-. ... -  .. ...-.-- -..--.----..";
```

Write a program to input a message string and using the character string MorseData, convert the message into Morse code and display the result.

[5]. Create a function that will display a graphical output on a screen for the trigonometric functions sine(x) and cosine(x), where the range of values of x, in degrees, and the name of the trigonometric function are formal parameters.

Chapter 12
Program development

This chapter may be considered as a milestone within the book. In one chapter it brings together the majority of programming topics that have been previously explained. As the size and complexity of programs increases, it is necessary to introduce a technique of dividing a programming solution into several parts, where each part is dedicated to a particular activity, which will ultimately be coded into functions that together form a C program. The need for machine-testing individual functions, followed by integrative testing of the completed program is explained. Finally an alternative approach to constructing a program from the individual functions stored in separate files is examined. By the end of the chapter the reader should have a knowledge of the following topics.

☐   The use of pseudo-code as a means of expressing a program design in English.

☐   Refining the pseudo-code into self-contained units that will ultimately be developed into functions.

☐   Documenting the development of each function.

☐   Testing the design of each function for logical errors.

☐   Coding and machine-testing each function as a self-contained unit.

☐   Constructing a program from the pre-tested functions.

☐   Integrative testing of the complete program.

☐   The use of a program header file.

☐   The *make* facility.

12.1 Specification

Problem - A number of competitors take part in skiing time-trials over a down-hill course. The number of competitors is known in advance, together with the names of the competitors and the world regions they represent. There are competitors from each of four world regions - Canada, Europe, Scandinavia and the United States of America. Only one competitor at a time is allowed down the course, therefore, it is possible to record the time to complete the course for each competitor.

A computerised system is required that will allow for the input of the number of entrants to the trials and the name, world region and time to complete the course for each competitor.

After the details of a competitor have been input, the system must display information about the current fastest competitor, before further input is possible.

At the end of the trials, the system must report for each world region, on the number of entrants competing, the mean time (average) to complete the race, the fastest time to complete the course and the name of the competitor with the fastest time.

Screen layout - Figures 12.1 through to 12.4 illustrate the input and output required. Figure 12.1 is a prompt to the user to enter the number of competitors in the trials.

Screen Layout
12345678901234567890123456789012345678901234567890123456789012345678901234567890
number of entrants? 6

figure 12.1

This is followed by a request to enter the name of a specific competitor, the world region they represent and the time taken to complete the course, as illustrated in figure 12.2. Notice that a menu is output with a choice from four world regions. The user is expected to only input the first letter of the appropriate world region.

Screen Layout

```
12345678901234567890123456789012345678901234567890123456789012345678901234567890
competitor number 1
name? Erickson

[C]anada
[E]urope
[S]candinavia
[U]nited States of America

world region? S
time to complete? 20.20
```

figure 12.2

The third screen depicted in figure 12.3 illustrates the information that is to be displayed after a competitor has completed the course.

Screen Layout

```
12345678901234567890123456789012345678901234567890123456789012345678901234567890

CURRENT FASTEST  -> time: 19.90  name: Grant  region: United States
```

figure 12.3

The fourth and final screen illustrates the information that is displayed after all the competitors have completed the timed trials. Notice that the number of entrants, average time, fastest time and the name of the fastest competitor must be computed for each of the four world regions.

```
┌─────────────────────────────────────────────────────────────────────────────┐
│                              Screen Layout                                    │
├─────────────────────────────────────────────────────────────────────────────┤
│12345678901234567890123456789012345678901234567890123456789012345678901234567890│
│S K I N G      C H A M P I O N S H I P      R E S U L T S                      │
│                                                                               │
│world               number of          average fastest name                   │
│region              entrants           time    time                           │
│                                                                               │
│Canada                     1           20.25   20.25   Ferguson                │
│Europe                     2           21.85   19.95   Wundt                   │
│Scandinavia                1           20.20   20.20   Erickson                │
│United States              2           19.95   19.90   Grant                   │
└─────────────────────────────────────────────────────────────────────────────┘
```

figure 12.4

12.2 Data structures

From figure 12.4 it may be evident to the reader that the information required for each world region might be represented as a structure. Figure 12.5 illustrates such a structure. Notice that no field has been set aside for the world region. The reason for this will be obvious shortly. A field has been included to represent the total times for all competitors representing a particular region. With the information on the number of competitors and the total times the mean time can be calculated. After the fastest time has been computed the fields that represent the fastest time and the name of the fastest competitor are updated.

number of competitors	total times	mean	fastest time	name of fastest competitor
2	43.70	21.85	19.95	Wundt

figure 12.5

The representation of this structure in C is

```
typedef struct {
                int     number-of_competitors;
                float   total_times;
                float   mean;
                float   fastest_time;
                float   name_of_fastest[80];
            } statistics;
```

which is a record structure of type statistics.

region	number of competitors	total times	mean	fastest time	name of fastest competitor
CAN	1	20.25	20.25	20.25	Ferguson
EUR	2	43.70	21.85	19.95	Wundt
SCA	1	20.20	20.20	20.20	Erickson
USA	2	39.90	19.95	19.90	Grant

figure 12.6

Since there are four world regions it would make sense to have four separate records, each stored in a separate cell of a one-dimensional array as illustrated in figure 12.6.

Notice that the subscripts to this array have been given names that represent each of the four world regions. The array is subscripted from 0..3 in the normal way, and the values CAN, EUR, SCA and USA are merely labels that represent the values 0..3 when declared as constants of the enumerated type world_region.

```
typedef enum {CAN, EUR, SCA, USA} world_region;
```

Therefore, CAN, EUR, SCA and USA may be used as subscripts in place of the values 0,1,2,3 respectively.

12.3 Algorithm design using step-wise refinement

At this stage in the development of the program no attempt should be made to use a computer to write C code. Algorithm design is essentially a paper-and-pencil exercise away from the computer. It is a time of problem solving and expressing a solution in a notation known as pseudo-code.

The solution to the problem is best viewed as layers of abstraction, starting at the highest possible layer that gives an overview of how to solve the problem. Each line of this top layer has been numbered to enable easy identification of each stage of the solution. The indentation of the pseudo-code implies the range for the respective loop or branch of a selection statement.

> *1. initialisation of the fields in the array*
> *2. input number of entrants*
>
> *3. for every entrant*
> *4.   input data for entrant*
> *5.   modify appropriate fields in the array*
> *6.   output information on the current fastest competitor*
>
> *7. output final results*

This is the first level in the solution to the problem. The next stage is to take each statement and refine it down to a lower level. Hence the technique of algorithmic design is known as *successive decomposition* or *step-wise refinement*.

1. initialisation of the fields in the array
1.1   for every region
1.2   set number of competitors to zero
1.3   set total times to zero
1.4   set fastest time to a large value

Note - variables that are directly assigned values such as the mean and the name of the fastest competitor do not require to be initialised. However, variables that require to be updated must be initialised to a known value. Since the fastest time will be compared with the time to complete the course this value must be set to a high value that is out of range of all other times. Any time compared with this value must by definition be less, and therefore, a faster time.

2. input number of entrants
2.1   do
2.2   input number of entrants
2.3   while entrants not valid

Note - the validity of all data input to a computer must be tested, otherwise, correct calculations cannot be made. The design of this algorithm suggests that the computer must continue to loop until valid data has been input.

3. for every entrant

This statement cannot be refined further since it will ultimately be coded as a *for* loop in C.

4. input data for entrant
4.1   display competitor number
4.2   input name of competitor
4.3   display menu of world regions
4.4   do
4.5   set error to false
4.6   input code for world region
4.7   switch (world region)
4.8   C: set region label to CAN
4.9   E: set region label to EUR
4.10   S: set region label to SCA
4.11   U: set region label to USA
4.12   default: set error to true
4.13   while error
4.14   do
4.15   input time to complete course
4.16   while time not valid

5. modify appropriate fields in the array
5.1   increase number of competitors for a given region
5.2   increase total times for all competitors in region
5.3   if number of competitors in a region is not zero
5.4   calculate mean time to complete for a given region
5.5   if time to complete is less than the fastest time for given region
5.6   update fastest time to complete for a given region
5.7   update name of competitor with the fastest time for a given region

6. output information on the current fastest competitor
6.1   display fastest time for a given region
6.2   display the name of the competitor with the fastest time
6.3   display the name of the region for the fastest competitor

In order to display the fastest time for a given region it will be necessary to find the region with the fastest time. This is not so much a refinement of 6.1, but recognising that in the design it will be necessary to produce pseudo-code for this requirement. This will be described later under *(8) find region with fastest time*.

Similarly in displaying the name of a region it will be necessary to convert an enumerated constant CAN, EUR, SCA, USA to a string literal that describes the region. For example CAN will be displayed as Canada, EUR as Europe, etc. There is a necessity to produce further pseudo-code for this requirement. This will be described later under *(9) name of region*.

7. output final results
7.1   display headings
7.2   for every region
7.3   display name of region
7.4   display number of competitors
7.5   if number of competitors not zero
7.6   display mean time for region
7.7   display fastest time for region
7.8   display name of competitor in region with fastest time

8. find region with fastest time
8.1   initialise region with fastest time to CAN
8.2   set fastest time to fastest time for region CAN
8.3   for every region after CAN
8.4   if fastest time for region is less than fastest time
8.5   set fastest time to regions fastest time
8.6   set fastest region to region

9. *name of region*
9.1   *switch (region)*
9.2   *CAN : set name of region to Canada;*
9.3   *EUR : set name of region to Europe;*
9.4   *SCA : set name of region to Scandinavia*
9.5   *USA : set name of region to United States*

The statements represented by the numbers 1 through to 9, with the exception of statement 3, form the basis of eight separate functions. The next stage in the development of the program is to map the pseudo-code defined in this section into suitable functions.

12.4 Function development

For the development of each function the stages that are normally followed in developing a program will be used. From the algorithms represented by pseudo-code in the previous section, a data dictionary, test data, a desk check of the design and finally the coded function will be documented.

Algorithm for the function initialise

1. initialisation of the fields in the array
1.1 for every region
1.2   set number of competitors to zero
1.3   set total times to zero
1.4   set fastest time to a large value

Data dictionary - The formal parameter list for this function contains one parameter, the one-dimensional array of records. Since this parameter is an array, and therefore a pointer to the first element, a local copy of the array is NOT made. The contents of the original array in the actual parameter list will be referenced and updated. The function does not return a value directly but by reference through the formal parameter. Since the contents of the array for each region needs to be initialised it is necessary to declare a local auto variable *region* of enumerated type world_region.

```
void            initialise(statistics counters[])
world_region    region;
```

Test data - None since this function requires no input only the assignment of values.

Desk Check

region	CAN	EUR	SCA	USA
number of competitors	0	0	0	0
total times	0.0	0.0	0.0	0.0
fastest time	3.4E+38	3.4E+38	3.4E+38	3.4E+38

Note - in the desk check the names *number of competitors*, *total times* and *fastest time* refer to the variables *counters[region].number_of_competitors*, *counters[region].total_times* and *counters[region].fastest_time* respectively.

```
void initialise(statistics counters[])
/* function to intialise fields in the array counters */
{
        world_region region;

        for (region=CAN; region<=USA; region++)
        {
            counters[region].number_of_competitors = 0;
            counters[region].total_times           = 0.0;
            counters[region].fastest_time          = FLT_MAX;
        }
}
```

Algorithm for the function number_of_entrants

2. input number of entrants
2.1   do
2.2   input number of entrants
2.3   while entrants not valid

Data dictionary - the formal parameter in this function is a pointer to the number of entrants. This is to allow the value to be accessed by reference, otherwise it would have to be returned as the value of the function.

Note - it is easier to input a number as a string, then use the ANSI library function **atoi** to convert the string to an integer value. If the input string *entrants_string* cannot be interpreted as a number the function **atoi** returns 0. Therefore, the function *number_of_entrants* will continue to be executed until a positive integer has been input.

```
void    number_of_entrants(int *entrants)
char    entrants_string[80];
```

Test data - *entrants_string*   abc   3.4E+38   -13   6

Desk check

entrants_string	*abc*	*3.4E+38*	*-13*	*6*
(entrants not valid)?	true	true	true	false
*entrants	0	0	0	6

```
void number_of_entrants(int *entrants)
/* function to return as a parameter the number of entrants in the race */

{
    char  entrants_string[80];
    do
    {
        printf("number of entrants? ");
        gets(entrants_string);
        *entrants = atoi(entrants_string);
    }
    while (*entrants <= 0);
}
```

Algorithm for the function input_data

4. input data for entrant
4.1   display competitor number
4.2   input name of competitor
4.3   display menu of world regions
4.4   do
4.5   set error to false
4.6   input code for world region
4.7   switch (world region)
4.8   C: set region label to CAN
4.9   E: set region label to EUR
4.10   S: set region label to SCA
4.11   U: set region label to USA
4.12   default: set error to true
4.13   while error
4.14   do
4.15   input time to complete course
4.16   while time not valid

Data dictionary - The function contains four formal parameters. The first is a competitor number, used in a prompt to enter the details of a particular competitor. The second is a character array used to store the name of a competitor and is a pointer to the first cell of the array, therefore, the data will be accessed by reference. The third and fourth parameters are both pointers to the name of a world region and the time to complete the course.

The function also contains three local variables. A single character *region*, converted to upper case, and corresponding to a menu code for a world region. A boolean variable *error* used to trap illegal menu codes. If the code is correct then a pointer to *region_name* is assigned the corresponding enumerated constant. In requesting the time to complete the race a string *time_string* is input and not a real number. The ANSI library function **atof** converts a string to a floating-point value. If the string cannot be interpreted as a number, the function **atof** returns 0. Therefore, the function input_data will continue to prompt for a number until a positive real number is input.

```
void        input_data( int              competitor_number,
                        char             name_of_competitor[],
                        world_region     *region_name,
                        float            *race_time)
boolean    error;
char       time_string[80];
char       region;
```

Test data

competitor_number	1	
name_of_competitor	Erickson	
region	x	s
time_string	-12	20.20

Desk check - *does not include any output*

competitor_number	1			
name_of_competitor	Erickson			
error	false	true	false	
region	x X		s S	
region_name			SCA	
(error)?		true	false	
time_string			-12	20.20
race_time			0	20.20
*(*race_time<=0.0)?*			true	false

```
void input_data(int              competitor_number,
                char             name_of_competitor[],
                world_region     *region_name,
                float            *race_time)
/* function to input the name, world region and time to complete
for a competitor
*/

{
    boolean error;
    char    time_string[80];
    char    region;

    printf("competitor number %d\n", competitor_number);
    printf("name? "); gets(name_of_competitor);
    printf("\n[C]anada");
    printf("\n[E]urope");
    printf("\n[S]candinavia");
    printf("\n[U]nited States of America\n\n");
```

```
    do
    {
        error = false;
        printf("world region? "); region = getchar(); getchar();
        region = to_upper(region);

        switch (region)
        {
        case 'C': *region_name = CAN; break;
        case 'E': *region_name = EUR; break;
        case 'S': *region_name = SCA; break;
        case 'U': *region_name = USA; break;
        default : error = true;
        }
    }
    while (error);

    do
    {
        printf("time to complete? ");
        gets(time_string);
        *race_time = (float) atof(time_string);
    }
    while (*race_time <= 0.0);
}
```

Algorithm for the function update-counters

5. *modify appropriate fields in the array*
5.1   *increase number of competitors for a given region*
5.2   *increase total times for all competitors in region*
5.3   *if number of competitors in a region is not zero*
5.4   *calculate mean time to complete for a given region*
5.5   *if time to complete is less than the fastest time for given region*
5.6   *update fastest time to complete for given region*
5.7   *update name of competitor with the fastest time for given region*

Data dictionary - the function contains four formal parameters. In changing the values of the array of records for a particular region it is necessary to pass a parameter for the region, the time recorded for the current time trial, the name of the current competitor and the array to be updated. There are no local variables required.

```
void update_counters(world_region  region,
                     float          race_time,
                     char           name_of_competitor[],
                     statistics     counters[])
```

Test data - *region* SCA *race_time* 20.20 *name_of_competitor* Erickson

Desk check

region	SCA	
race_time	20.20	
number_of_competitors	0	1
total_times	0.0	20.20
(number_of_competitors not zero) ?	true	
mean		20.20
(race_time less than fastest-time)?	true	
fastest_time	3.4E+38	20.20
name_of_fastest		Erickson

```
void update_counters(world_region  region,
                     float          race_time,
                     char           name_of_competitor[],
                     statistics     counters[])
/* function to increase the number of competitors in a world region,
increase the total time for competitors in the same world region and
update the name of the fastest competitor for that region
*/

{
    /* increase number of competitors in a given region*/
    counters[region].number_of_competitors++;

    /* increase total times for all competitors in that region */
    counters[region].total_times += race_time;

    /* calculate mean time to complete for a given region */
    if (counters[region].number_of_competitors != 0)
        counters[region].mean = counters[region].total_times /
                                counters[region].number_of_competitors;

    /* calculate fastest time to complete and update name of fastest
    competitor in that region */
    if (race_time < counters[region].fastest_time)
    {
        counters[region].fastest_time = race_time;
        strcpy(counters[region].name_of_fastest, name_of_competitor);
    }
}
```

Upon the inspection of this function it would appear that a new item of coding has been introduced:

```
counters[region].total_times += race_time;
```

Since this is meant to increase the total time by the race_time, a statement of the form

```
counters[region].total_times = counters[region].total_times + race_time;
```

is what might have been expected! C has a shorthand notation for this type of assignment where += is known as a **compound assignment**. The advantage of such an operator is that counters[region].total_times is only evaluated once in the first expression compared with twice in the second expression. Similar compound statements exist for other binary additive and multiplicative operators -=, *=, /=, %=.

Algorithm for the function display_current_fastest

6. output information on the current fastest competitor
6.1   display fastest time for a give region
6.2   display the name of the competitor with the fastest time
6.3   display the name of the region for the fastest competitor

Data dictionary - The function has two formal parameters, the array of records and the region with the current fastest time. The function does not return a value.

```
void display_current_fastest(statistics counters[], world_region region)
```

Test data

region	EUR
fastest_time	19.95
name_of_fastest	Wundt

Desk check - *output only*

CURRENT FASTEST -> time: 19.95 name: Wundt region: Europe

```
void display_current_fastest(statistics counters[], world_region region)
/* function to display the details of the current fastest competitor */

{
        printf("\n\nCURRENT FASTEST  -> ");
        printf("time: %-6.2f ", counters[region].fastest_time);
        printf("name: %s  region: %s", counters[region].name_of_fastest,
                                    name_of_region(region));
        printf("\n\n");
}
```

Note this function assumes the existence of a function **name_of_region(region)** that returns the name of a region as a string literal.

The value of the region that is passed to this function as a parameter must be the region with the fastest time. Therefore, it is assumed that another function exists **current_fastest(counters)**, that returns the region with the fastest time.

Algorithm for the function display_results

7. output final results
7.1   display headings
7.2   for every region
7.3   display name of region
7.4   display number of competitors
7.5   if number of competitors not zero
7.6   display mean time for region
7.7   display fastest time for region
7.8   display name of competitor in region with fastest time

Data dictionary - The function has just one formal parameter, the array of records. The function does not return a value. There is one local auto variable *region* of type world_region.

```
void          display_results(statistics counters[])
world_region  region;
```

Test data

region	CAN	EUR	SCA	USA
number_of_competitors	1	2	1	2
mean	20.25	21.85	20.20	19.95
fastest_time	20.25	19.95	20.20	19.90
name_of_fastest	Ferguson	Wundt	Erickson	Grant

Desk check - *output only*

SKIING CHAMPIONSHIP RESULTS

world region	number of entrants	average time	fastest time	name
Canada	1	20.25	20.25	Ferguson
Europe	2	21.85	19.95	Wundt
Scandinavia	1	20.20	20.20	Erickson
United States	2	19.95	19.90	Grant

```
void display_results(statistics counters[])
/* function to display the results for each region */

{
        world_region region;

        printf("S K I I N G    C H A M P I O N S H I P    R E S U L T S\n\n");
        printf("world\t\tnumber of\taverage\tfastest\tname\n");
        printf("region\t\tentrants\ttime\ttime\t\n\n");

        for (region=CAN; region<=USA; region++)
        {
            printf("%s",name_of_region(region));
            printf("\t\t%-3d",counters[region].number_of_competitors);
            if (counters[region].number_of_competitors != 0)
            {
                printf("\t%6.2f", counters[region].mean);
                printf("\t%6.2f", counters[region].fastest_time);
                printf("\t%s", counters[region].name_of_fastest);
            }
            printf("\n");
        }
}
```

Algorithm for the function current_fastest

8. find region with fastest time
8.1   initialise region with fastest time to CAN
8.2   set fastest time to fastest time for region CAN
8.3   for every region after CAN
8.4   if fastest time for region is less than fastest time
8.5   set fastest time to regions fastest time
8.6   set fastest region to region

Data dictionary - This function will return the name of the region with the fastest time, therefore the function is designated as returning data of type world_region. There is only one formal parameter and this is the array of records. Local auto variables are declared for the *fastest_time, region* and *fastest_region*. The fastest_time represents the fastest time over all the regions, and the fastest_region is the name of the region that contains the fastest time.

```
world_region      current_fastest(statistics counters[])
float             fastest_time;
world_region      region, fastest_region;
```

Test data - the contents of the array counters is described as follows for each region

region	CAN	EUR	SCA	USA
fastest_time	20.25	19.95	20.20	19.90

Desk check

	CAN	EUR	SCA	USA
region				
fastest time for region		19.95	20.20	19.90
(fastest time for region < fastest_time)?		true	false	true
fastest_region	CAN	EUR		USA
fastest_time	20.25	19.95		19.90

```
world_region current_fastest(statistics counters[])
/* function to return the region of the competitor with the current
fastest time */

{
        float           fastest_time;
        world_region    region, fastest_region;

        fastest_region = CAN;
        fastest_time   = counters[CAN].fastest_time;

        for (region=EUR; region<=USA; region++)
            if (counters[region].fastest_time < fastest_time)
            {
                fastest_time = counters[region].fastest_time;
                fastest_region = region;
            }

        return fastest_region;
}
```

Algorithm for the function name_of_region

9. name of region
9.1   switch (region)
9.2   CAN : set name of region to Canada;
9.3   EUR : set name of region to Europe;
9.4   SCA : set name of region to Scandinavia;
9.5   USA : set name of region to United States

Data dictionary - The function has one formal parameter *region* of the enumerated type *world_region*. The function returns a character string that represents the string literal for the name of the region. The value returned is a pointer to the array that represents the character string. There are no local parameters.

```
char *name_of_region(world_region region)
```

Test data - *region* SCA

Desk check
region	SCA
name_of_region(region)	Scandinavia

```
char *name_of_region(world_region region)
/* function to return the name of a world region as a string*/

{
        switch (region)
        {
        case CAN : return "Canada        ";
        case EUR : return "Europe        ";
        case SCA : return "Scandinavia   ";
        case USA : return "United States ";
        }
}
```

12.5 Testing functions

Up to this point the development of the functions has been a pencil-and-paper exercise. The next stage in the development of the program is to compile and test each function separately. Remember at the beginning of chapter 7, it was stated that "..a function can be thought of as a building block..a complete program is built from many different building blocks or functions, each having been tested before being used as part of the whole program".

In this section a small selection of the functions will be tested, and it is left as an exercise at the end of the chapter for the reader to test all the functions.

Before a function can be tested it must be encapsulated in a program known as a test harness. There are eight functions to test, which implies writing eight test harnesses. Each test harness must describe the data types that were explained earlier in the chapter. To recapitulate these data types are coded as:

```
typedef enum{false, true} boolean;
typedef enum{CAN,EUR,SCA,USA} world_region;
typedef struct {
                int    number_of_competitors;
                float  total_times;
                float  mean;
                float  fastest_time;
                char   name_of_fastest[80];
            } statistics;
```

To avoid having to write this code into every test harness it is possible for the code to be stored in a header file. For the purpose of this exercise the file will be named "a:\c12_dpp\types.h". To include the code in the test harnesses is simply a matter of coding the statement

                    #include "a:\c12_dpp\types.h"

The first test harness is used to test the function **initialise**.

```
/*
c12_dpp\test_1.c
*/

#include <stdio.h>
#include <float.h>
#include "a:\c12_dpp\types.h"

void initialise(statistics counters[])
/* function to intialise fields in the array counters */
{
        world_region region;

        for (region=CAN; region<=USA; region++)
        {
                counters[region].number_of_competitors = 0;
                counters[region].total_times           = 0.0;
                counters[region].fastest_time          = FLT_MAX;
        }
}

main()
{
        statistics    results[4];
        world_region region;

        initialise(results);
```

```
        for (region=CAN; region<=USA; region++)
        {
            printf("region %d\n", region);
            printf("number of competitors %d\n",
                    results[region].number_of_competitors);
            printf("total times %f\n", results[region].total_times);
            printf("fastest time %f\n\n", results[region].fastest_time);
        }
}
```

Results from program test_1.c being run

```
region 0
number of competitors 0
total times 0.000000
fastest time 3.402823e+38

region 1
number of competitors 0
total times 0.000000
fastest time 3.402823e+38

region 2
number of competitors 0
total times 0.000000
fastest time 3.402823e+38

region 3
number of competitors 0
total times 0.000000
fastest time 3.402823e+38
```

Notice that the region has been displayed as an integer representing the subscripts 0..3 to the array of records. This is quite natural since the enumerated constants CAN..USA are only labels that represent the values 0..3.

From the results it would appear that the function initialise does assign the required values to the chosen fields. Remember that the remaining fields in the array have not been initialised so care must be exercised when attempting to display the values of these other fields in future tests!

As a further example of the use of a test harness the function **update_counters** will be tested. In this example it has been necessary to assign data to the array, before the function can be thoroughly tested.

```
/*
c12_dpp\test_4.c
*/

#include <stdio.h>
#include <string.h>
#include "a:\c12_dpp\types.h"

void update_counters(world_region region,
                     float         race_time,
                     char          name_of_competitor[],
                     statistics    counters[])
/* function to increase the number of competitors in a world region,
increase the total time for competitors in the same world region and
update the name of the fastest competitor for that region
*/

{
        /* increase number of competitors in a given region */
        counters[region].number_of_competitors++;

        /* increase total times for all competitors in that region to complete */
        counters[region].total_times += race_time;

        /* calculate mean time to complete for a given region */
        if (counters[region].number_of_competitors != 0)
            counters[region].mean = counters[region].total_times /
                                    counters[region].number_of_competitors;

        /* calculate fastest time to complete and update name of fastest
        competitor in that region */
        if (race_time < counters[region].fastest_time)
        {
                counters[region].fastest_time = race_time;
                strcpy(counters[region].name_of_fastest, name_of_competitor);
        }
}

main()
{
        statistics results[4] = {{0,0.0,  0.0,   3.4E+38,""},
                                 {1,23.75,23.75,23.75,  "Edwards"},
                                 {1,20.20,20.20,20.20,  "Erickson"},
                                 {1,21.50,21.50,21.50,  "Grant"}};

        world_region region;

        update_counters(EUR, 19.95, "Wundt", results);
        update_counters(USA, 20.00, "Williams", results);
```

```
        for (region=CAN; region<=USA; region++)
        {
              printf("region %d\n", region);
              printf("competitors %d\n", results[region].number_of_competitors);
              printf("total times %f\n", results[region].total_times);

              if (results[region].number_of_competitors != 0)
                 printf("mean          %f\n", results[region].mean);

              printf("fastest       %f\n", results[region].fastest_time);

              if (results[region].number_of_competitors != 0)
                 printf("name          %s\n", results[region].name_of_fastest);

              printf("\n");
        }
}
```

Results from program test_4.c being run

```
region 0
competitors 0
total times 0.000000
fastest       3.400000e+38

region 1
competitors 2
total times 43.700001
mean          21.850000
fastest       19.950001
name          Wundt

region 2
competitors 1
total times 20.200001
mean          20.200001
fastest       20.200001
name          Erickson

region 3
competitors 2
total times 41.500000
mean          20.750000
fastest       20.000000
name          Williams
```

Upon checking the results it appears that the function update_counters does function correctly.

12.6 The main function

The main function has not yet been coded. This function calls the previously developed functions in the correct sequence for processing the data. The design of the main function resembles the first-level pseudo-code developed earlier in the chapter.

Algorithm for the function main

1. *initialisation of the fields in the array*
2. *input number of entrants*

3. *for every entrant*
4. *input data for entrant*
5. *modify appropriate fields in the array*
6. *output information on the current fastest competitor*

7. *output final results*

Data dictionary - To identify the variables that are local to the main function is a matter of inspecting the formal parameter lists of every function that is being called and make a list of the actual parameters that will need to be declared. The final list of local declarations follows together with the coding of the main function. Notice that the function *current_fastest* is used as an actual parameter in the function *display_current_fastest* since the function returns a value for the fastest region. The testing of this function is postponed until after the complete program has been built using all the previously developed functions.

```
main()
{
      int            competitor_number;
      int            entrants; /* number of entrants in competition */
      char           name_of_competitor[80];
      world_region   region;
      float          race_time;
      statistics     counters[4];

      initialise(counters);
      number_of_entrants(&entrants);

      for (competitor_number=1; competitor_number <= entrants;
            competitor_number++)
      {
            input_data(competitor_number, name_of_competitor,
                        &region, &race_time);
            update_counters(region, race_time, name_of_competitor, counters);
            display_current_fastest(counters, current_fastest(counters));
      }

      display_results(counters);
}
```

12.7 The complete program

After function testing has been successfully completed the program can be built from the functions. At this point it would be wise to build the program by cutting and pasting the functions from their test harnesses using an editor. This will help to minimise any transcription errors. Notice in building the program the order has been to include header files, function prototypes, the main function and the supporting functions. Function prototypes have been included to resolve any forward references to functions. Hence the order the functions appear in the source file will make no difference at the compilation stage.

```
/*
c12_dpp\ex_01.c
program to input the name, global region, and times of competitors
in a cross-country skiing race and calculate the following information:
(i)    number of competitors from each world region
(ii)   time of the fastest competitor from each world region
(iii)  mean time for all competitors from each world region
(iv)   the name of the fastest competitor from each world region
(v)    the current fastest competitor
*/

#include <stdio.h>
#include <string.h>
#include <stdlib.h>
#include <float.h>
#include "a:\c12_dpp\types.h"

#define to_upper(c)  ('a' <= (c) && (c) <= 'z' ? (c) - 32 : (c));

/* function prototypes */

void initialise(statistics counters[]);
void number_of_entrants(int *entrants);

void input_data(int             competitor_number,
                char            name_of_competitor[],
                world_region    *region_name,
                float           *race_time);

void update_counters(world_region region,
                float           race_time,
                char            name_of_competitor[],
                statistics      counters[]);

void display_current_fastest(statistics counters[], world_region region);
void display_results(statistics counters[]);
world_region current_fastest(statistics counters[]);
char *name_of_region(world_region region);
```

```
main()
{
      int            competitor_number;
      int            entrants; /* number of entrants in competition */
      char           name_of_competitor[80];
      world_region   region;
      float          race_time;
      statistics     counters[4];

      initialise(counters);
      number_of_entrants(&entrants);

      for (competitor_number=1; competitor_number <= entrants;
           competitor_number++)
      {
          input_data(competitor_number, name_of_competitor,
                     &region, &race_time);
          update_counters(region, race_time, name_of_competitor, counters);
          display_current_fastest(counters, current_fastest(counters));
      }
      display_results(counters);
}

void initialise(statistics counters[])
/* function to intialise fields in the array counters */
{
        world_region region;

        for (region=CAN; region<=USA; region++)
        {
            counters[region].number_of_competitors = 0;
            counters[region].total_times            = 0.0;
            counters[region].fastest_time            = FLT_MAX;
        }
}

void number_of_entrants(int *entrants)
/* function to return as a parameter the number of entrants in the race */
{
      char  entrants_string[80];

      do
      {
          printf("number of entrants? ");
          gets(entrants_string);
          *entrants = atoi(entrants_string);
      }
      while (*entrants <= 0);
}
```

263

```
void input_data(int         competitor_number,
                char        name_of_competitor[],
                world_region *region_name,
                float       *race_time)
/* function to input the name, world region and time to complete
for a competitor
*/

{
    boolean error;
    char    time_string[80];
    char    region;

    printf("competitor number %d\n", competitor_number);
    printf("name? "); gets(name_of_competitor);
    printf("\n[C]anada");
    printf("\n[E]urope");
    printf("\n[S]candinavia");
    printf("\n[U]nited States of America\n\n");

    do
    {
        error = false;
        printf("world region? "); region = getchar(); getchar();
        region = to_upper(region);

        switch (region)
        {
        case 'C' : *region_name = CAN; break;
        case 'E' : *region_name = EUR; break;
        case 'S' : *region_name = SCA; break;
        case 'U' : *region_name = USA; break;
        default : error = true;
        }
    }
    while (error);

    do
    {
        printf("time to complete? ");
        gets(time_string);
        *race_time = (float) atof(time_string);
    }
    while (*race_time <= 0.0);
}
```

```
void update_counters(world_region region,
                     float         race_time,
                     char          name_of_competitor[],
                     statistics    counters[])
/* function to increase the number of competitors in a world region,
increase the total time for competitors in the same world region and
update the name of the fastest competitor for that region */

{
        /* increase number of competitors in a given region*/
        counters[region].number_of_competitors++;

        /* increase total times for all competitors in that region to
           complete */
        counters[region].total_times += race_time;

        /* calculate mean time to complete for a given region */
        if (counters[region].number_of_competitors != 0)
            counters[region].mean = counters[region].total_times /
                                    counters[region].number_of_competitors;

        /* calculate fastest time to complete and update name of fastest
        competitor in that region */
        if (race_time < counters[region].fastest_time)
        {
                counters[region].fastest_time = race_time;
                strcpy(counters[region].name_of_fastest, name_of_competitor);
        }
}


void display_current_fastest(statistics counters[], world_region region)
/* function to display the details of the current fastest competitor */

{
        printf("\n\nCURRENT FASTEST  -> ");
        printf("time: %-6.2f ", counters[region].fastest_time);
        printf("name: %s   region: %s", counters[region].name_of_fastest,
                                    name_of_region(region));
        printf("\n\n");
}


void display_results(statistics counters[])
/*  function to display the results for each region */

{
        world_region region;

        printf("S K I I N G    C H A M P I O N S H I P    R E S U L T S\n\n");
        printf("world\t\tnumber of\taverage\tfastest\tname\n");
```

```
            printf("region\t\tentrants\ttime\ttime\t\n\n");

            for (region=CAN; region<=USA; region++)
            {
                printf("%s",name_of_region(region));
                printf("\t\t%-3d",counters[region].number_of_competitors);
                if (counters[region].number_of_competitors != 0)
                {
                    printf("\t%6.2f", counters[region].mean);
                    printf("\t%6.2f", counters[region].fastest_time);
                    printf("\t%s", counters[region].name_of_fastest);
                }
                printf("\n");
            }
}

world_region current_fastest(statistics counters[])
/* function to return the region of the competitor with the current
fastest time */
{
        float           fastest_time;
        world_region    region, fastest_region;

        fastest_region = CAN;
        fastest_time   = counters[CAN].fastest_time;

        for (region=EUR; region<=USA; region++)
            if (counters[region].fastest_time < fastest_time)
            {
                fastest_time = counters[region].fastest_time;
                fastest_region = region;
            }

        return fastest_region;
}

char *name_of_region(world_region region)
/* function to return the name of a world region as a string*/

{
        switch (region)
        {
        case CAN : return "Canada        ";
        case EUR : return "Europe        ";
        case SCA : return "Scandinavia   ";
        case USA : return "United States ";
        }
}
```

12.8 Integrative testing

Although the individual functions, apart from the main function, have been compiled and tested separately, there is a need to test the complete program. This final phase of testing should ensure that the complete program meets the requirements described in the specification at the beginning of the chapter.

After the program has been constructed it is compiled and linked in the usual manner and provided there are no errors, run with the following test data.

entrants	competitor_number	name_of_competitor	region	race_time
6				
	1	Erickson	S	20.20
	2	Edwards	E	23.75
	3	Grant	U	19.90
	4	Ferguson	C	20.25
	5	Wundt	E	19.95
	6	Williams	U	20.00

Partial results from program ex_01.c being run

```
number of entrants? 6

competitor number 1
name? Erickson

[C]anada
[E]urope
[S]candinavia
[U]nited States of America

world region? S
time to complete? 20.20


CURRENT FASTEST -> time: 20.20   name: Erickson   region: Scandinavia


competitor number 2
name? Edwards

[C]anada
[E]urope
[S]candinavia
[U]nited States of America

world region? E
time to complete? 23.75
```

```
CURRENT FASTEST -> time: 20.20  name: Erickson  region: Scandinavia

competitor number 3

                    .
                    .
                    .
                    .
                    .

CURRENT FASTEST -> time: 19.90  name: Grant  region: United States


S K I N G   C H A M P I O N S H I P    R E S U L T S

world           number of          average fastest name
region          entrants           time    time

Canada               1             20.25   20.25   Ferguson
Europe               2             21.85   19.95   Wundt
Scandinavia          1             20.20   20.20   Erickson
United States        2             19.95   19.90   Grant
```

12.9 An alternative approach

This alternative approach to building the program begins with the header file. It is normal practice to put the following information in a header file so that it can be included in all program files.

constant definitions
type declarations
structure declarations
external declarations
function declarations
macros

A new header file for the same problem, named a:\c12_dpp\header.h, has been constructed that contains type declarations, function declarations and a parameterized macro. Notice from the type declarations that in the interest of portability of programs that *raw* C data types have not been used. For example in this header file under the type declarations the *raw* C data types char, int, float and void have been replaced by CHAR, INT, FLOAT and VOID respectively. The reason for the change, is that if the program was ported to a computer with a different representation of say int or float, the only lines in the header file that would need to be be changed would be the declaration of int and float, and not every reference to int and float in the program files.

Since functions within program files may use functions, such as *current_fastest* and *name_of_region* it is necessary to list the prototypes of the functions in the function declaration section of the header file to overcome any forward references.

```
/* c12_dpp\header.h */

/* type declarations */

typedef enum{false, true} boolean;
typedef enum{CAN,EUR,SCA,USA} world_region;

typedef char  CHAR;
typedef int   INT;
typedef float FLOAT;
typedef void  VOID;

typedef struct {
                INT   number_of_competitors;
                FLOAT total_times;
                FLOAT mean;
                FLOAT fastest_time;
                CHAR  name_of_fastest[80];
            } statistics;

/* function declarations */

VOID initialise(statistics counters[]);
VOID number_of_entrants(INT *entrants);

VOID input_data(INT            competitor_number,
                CHAR           name_of_competitor[],
                world_region   *region_name,
                FLOAT          *race_time);

VOID update_counters(world_region region,
                     FLOAT          race_time,
                     CHAR           name_of_competitor[],
                     statistics     counters[]);

VOID display_current_fastest(statistics counters[], world_region region);
VOID display_results(statistics counters[]);
world_region current_fastest(statistics counters[]);
CHAR *name_of_region(world_region region);

/* macros */

#define to_upper(c) ('a' <= (c) && (c) <= 'z' ? (c) - 32 : (c));
```

The following changes are made to the functions developed and coded in section 12.4.

The header file "a:\c12_dpp\types.h" is replaced by the new header file "a:\c12_dpp\header.h".

All raw C data types are replaced by the corresponding types CHAR, INT, FLOAT and VOID.

Each function is stored in a separate .c file.

For example the function *initialise* has been modified as described and stored in a file named **_initial.c** and is listed below.

```
/*
c12_dpp\_initial.c
*/

#include <stdio.h>
#include <float.h>
#include "a:\c12_dpp\header.h"

VOID initialise(statistics counters[])
/* function to intialise fields in the array counters */
{
        world_region region;

        for (region=CAN; region<=USA; region++)
        {
            counters[region].number_of_competitors = 0;
            counters[region].total_times           = 0.0;
            counters[region].fastest_time          = FLT_MAX;
        }
}
```

Using this alternative approach the program has been re-developed from a total of nine function files including the main function. In the original development of the program, each function file, with the exception of the main function, was separately compiled and tested. Therefore the alternative approach offers little hardship in the creation of nine separate function files, since this is only a matter of editing each test harness.

The obvious disadvantage of this approach is seen when changes are made to either the header file or function files. All the files dependent upon the changes will need to be re-compiled again! But not to worry, help is at hand in the form of the **make** facility.

Make is a UNIX tool (see appendix C) which is now widely available for MSDOS and is included with most C compilers. The make facility requires a *make file*, which contains commands to show what files are to be compiled and linked. For example, the *make file* used in this example is named *ex_02.PR* and is specific to TopSpeed C in an MSDOS environment and contains the following information.

```
#system auto exe
#model small
#compile
        a:\c12_dpp\_initial,
        a:\c12_dpp\_entrant,
        a:\c12_dpp\_data,
        a:\c12_dpp\_count,
        a:\c12_dpp\_fastest,
        a:\c12_dpp\_region,
        a:\c12_dpp\_current,
        a:\c12_dpp\_results,
        a:\c12_dpp\_main
#link ex_02
```

The first command **#system auto exe** indicates the target operating system and file type for this *make file*. The *auto* indicates that the target operating system is the same as the development operating system, in this case MSDOS. The *exe* indicates that an executable file is being built.

The second command **#model small** indicates the memory model to use.

The third command **#compile** causes each nominated source file to be compiled. In this example each filename represents the nine function files, including the main function.

Finally the **#link** command links together all the files listed into the nominated executable file *ex_02.exe*.

When the *make* command is invoked, every function file contained in the *make* file will be automatically compiled. If compilation was successful the files would be linked to form an executable run time file. However, if changes were made to any of the files or the header file, then when invoking the *make* facility for a second time only those files that were dependent upon the changes would be automatically re-compiled.

The program can be run by specifying the name of the *.exe* file after the MSDOS prompt, or alternatively run from within the TopSpeed C environment.

The *makefile* for the same program, developed in a UNIX environment, is given in appendix C - section C.4.

12.10 Modular programming

Writing a program as a collection of modules (functions and groups of functions), rather than a single unit, offers the following advantages.

A large program can be designed as a collection of smaller modules. This has the advantage that each module can be designed, coded and tested independently of the remaining modules. A clear interface between the modules can be established through the function prototypes.

Members of a programming team can be assigned individual modules to develop, hence the allocation of work in project management can be improved.

271

Program modification is easier, since a programmer can change the details of the implementation of the functions, without affecting the rest of the program, provided the function prototypes remains the same.

Separate compilation of modules is possible, hence changes to modules do not result in the entire program having to be re- compiled.

Programmers can develop libraries of re-usable code. This not only saves time in the development of a system, but contributes towards the reliability of the system, since the modules have already undergone testing for other programs.

12.11 Summary

☐ Write a rough outline of how to solve the problem. This will be very brief and the first attempt at solving the problem. No detailed coding is expected at this stage. From this outline it is possible to state the initial functions that can be used in the program.

☐ For each function derive an outline of the code required, and refine this code further until you reach a point when the code will form a 1-1 correspondence with statements in C.

☐ Invent simple test data and predict the corresponding results. Use this test data to trace through design of the function and produce a table of values for the intended variables. At the end of this desk check compare the values of the intended variables with the anticipated results. The results of the desk check and the anticipated results should agree, if not there is probably a logical error in the design of the program.

☐ Document the purpose and nature of all identifiers in each function.

☐ Code each function and embed it into a test harness program so that it can be independently compiled and tested.

☐ Copy, using an editor, the procedures from the test harnesses into the final program. This way the number of transcription errors that can occur in the functions is drastically reduced.

☐ Compile and if necessary edit and recompile the program in order to remove any errors, including syntax errors.

☐ Test the program using the same test data that was used for the desk check. Ensure that the results are consistent with those expected. Apply more stringent tests on the program using data that, where possible, will test the program to its limits.

☐ Use a header file that encompasses all the constants, types, structures, external declarations, prototypes and macros that are required by all the functions in a program.

☐ As an aid to portability never use raw C data types in a program.

☐ A program may be stored in a single file or alternatively built from individual function files and header files. This latter approach is a preferred method of program development since it reaps the benefits of modular programming.

12.12 Questions - *answers begin on page 488*

[1]. Define and implement test harnesses for the following functions found in the text.

(a) *number_of_entrants*
(b) *input_data*
(c) *current_fastest*
(d) *name_of_region*
(e) *display_current_fastest*
(f) *display_results*

2. The lengths of four sides of a quadrilateral and one internal angle are input to a computer. Design and write a computer program to categorise the shape of the quadrilateral as a square, rhombus, rectangle, parallelogram or irregular quadrilateral.

The rules for determining the shape of the quadrilateral are given in the following table.

name	all sides equal?	opposite sides equal?	right angle?
square	true	true	true
rectangle	false	true	true
rhombus	true	true	false
parallelogram	false	true	false

The basic design for this program might be as follows.

do
    input angle and lengths of four sides
    analyse and display name of shape
while more data

Implement the program as one file containing the following function prototypes.

void input_data(int *angle, float *side1, float *side2, float *side3, float *side4);
/* function to input one angle and the length of four sides */
char *analyse_shape(int angle, float sideA, float sideB, float sideC, float sideD);
/* function to return the name of the quadrilateral */
boolean more_data(void);
/* function to return true if more data is required otherwise return false */

[3]. A teacher records the names of pupils and the distance they live from school. The distance from school falls into one of the following four categories.

distance to school	category
0 to less than 1 mile	A
1 to less than 5 miles	B
5 to less than 10 miles	C
10 miles or further	D

For a class of pupils, the data input to the computer will be, the number of pupils in the class followed by the name and distance each pupil lives from the school. From this data the name of each pupil and the distance category are stored in separate records in a one-dimensional array. When data input is complete, the computer will output the names and number of pupils in each of the four categories.

A first level design might appear as follows.

input class size
allocate storage space for each pupil record in an array
while number of pupils processed is not equal to the class size
    input name and distance to school of pupil
    insert pupil name and distance category record into the next free cell in the array
    increase the number of pupils processed by 1
output the names of pupils and number of pupils in each of the categories

Implement the program as one file containing the following function prototypes.

void class_size(int *size);
/* function to input the class size */
void name_distance(char pupil[], float *distance);
/* function to input the name and distance to school of a pupil */
void update(record names[], char pupil[], float distance);
/* function to insert the name and category into a record and store in the next free cell in an array */
void display_results(record names[], int size);
/* function to display the contents of the array names, listing the names of the pupils by category together with the number of pupils in each category */

4. A computerised minefield is divided into a 10x10 matrix as illustrated in figure 12.7. Write a game program to generate the random position of the mines in the field. The number of mines is also a random number in the range 1..10 inclusive. Invite a player to input pairs of co-ordinates of a path through the minefield. The computer generates the starting position in the South, and the only legal move a player can make is to any adjacent position in the matrix. The object of the game is to trace a path through the field , without stepping on a mine, and to finish at the Northern perimeter of the matrix. Only at the end of the game should the computer reveal the positions of the mines.

In order to generate a different number of mines and a different starting position each time the game is played you are recommended to generate a new seed value for the random number generator. If a value for elapsed time is used as the seed in the function *srand*, then a new starting point will be possible in the random number generator. From the header file <time.h> it is possible to obtain elapsed time in seconds by using the function **time(&tt)**, where **tt** is of type **time_t**. A call to *srand((unsigned)tt)* will cause a new starting position to be chosen when using the random number generator *rand()*.

```
                        NORTH
            0 1 2 3 4 5 6 7 8 9
          0
          1
          2
          3
          4
          5
          6
          7
          8
          9 ^
          input coordinates of next step 8 0
```

```
                        NORTH
            0 1 2 3 4 5 6 7 8 9
          0
          1
          2 M
          3 ^
          4 ^
          5     ^
          6 M ^
          7   ^
          8 ^
          9 ^
```

figure 12.7 The start and finish of a game

The first level of design of this program might be as follows.

initialise the matrix by generating a number of mines, their positions and the starting position
display the matrix without showing the positions of the mines
do

    do

        input co-ordinates of next adjacent step
    while illegal move

    search for mine in current position and plot current position

    if area mined
        display the matrix with the positions of the mines
    else
        display the matrix showing the route taken so far

while no mine found or not reached the Northern perimeter
if no mine found display the matrix showing the safe route

Implement the program as one file containing the following function prototypes.

```
void initialise(int *last_row, int *last_column);
/* function to plant the mines in the minefield */
boolean mine(int row, int column);
/* return true if a mine is found at the co-ordinates [row,column] */
void display(boolean reveal);
/* function to display the path taken across the minefield, and the positions of the mines if reveal is
true */
```

[5]. Write a program to play noughts and crosses against the computer. Use a two-dimensional array to store the noughts and crosses. Let the computer be the cross and the position of play by the computer is created using a random number generator. Display the board on the screen and the final result of the game as illustrated in figure 12.8.

```
X|   |
---------
  |   |
---------
  |   |

input position of play 2 2

X|   |
---------
  | O |
---------
  |   |

X|   |
---------
  | O |
---------
  |   |X

input position of play 1 2

X| O |
---------
  | O |
---------
  |   |X

X| O |
---------
  | O |X
---------
  |   |X

input position of play 3 2

X| O |
---------
  | O |X
---------
  | O |X

you win - smarty pants!!
```

figure 12.8 A game of noughts and crosses

For the reader who has not played noughts and crosses before, the rules are as follows.

Each player takes a turn in selecting a square on the board in which to place either a cross or a nought. The object of the game is to prevent your opponent from completing any horizontal, vertical or diagonal line of crosses or noughts which will result in a winning line. If after several moves it is not possible for either competitor to make a winning line then there is a stale mate.

However in this simulation, the computer will not deliberately attempt to block the opponent's line of noughts since the computer is only to be programmed to place a cross in any free space, generated at random, on the board. Use the method of generating random numbers suggested in the previous question.

In this simulation, only when every square on the board has been filled without a successful line of noughts or crosses being generated, will the game result in a stale mate.

Store each of the following function prototypes, including the main function, in separate files and implement the program using the MAKE facility.

```
void display(void);
/* display the contents of the board on a screen */
void initialise(void);
/* fill the noughts and crosses board with spaces, and generate a new seed for the random number gen-
erator */
void play(player who);
/* function to allow a player to make a particular move, where player is an enumerated type containing
the constants computer and you respectively */
boolean check_position(int row, int column);
/* check to see if the position given by the co-ordinates [row,column] on the board is free */
boolean check_winner(player who)
/* check to see if the current player has won */
```

You will also need to create a new header file that includes type declarations, an external declaration of the noughts and crosses board as a two-dimensional array, function prototypes and any macros.

The first level of design of this program might be as follows.

do
    initialise the board
    set number of moves to zero
    do
        set computer to current player
        play the move
        display the move
        increase the number of moves by 1
        check for winner
            if computer wins display message that computer has won
            if no winner and the number of moves is less than 9
                set person (computer user) to current player
                play the move
                display the move
                increase the number of moves by 1
                check for winner
                if person wins display message that user has won
    while no winner and number of moves is less than 9

        if no winner and number of moves is equal to 9 display stale mate
        request for another game
while another game requested

Chapter 13
Recursion, sorting and searching

This chapter is divided into three topics, with the first topic on recursion also finding its way into the second and third topics on sorting and searching respectively.

Functions have been used by calling them from within another function. By now this method of access to such units of code should be familiar to the reader. The calling of one function from within another function is quite acceptable. But what if the function being called is the same function that is doing the calling? The function is in effect calling itself. The technique is known as recursion.

Methods used to organise information must provide for a means of sorting information using a defined key or keys, and a means of searching through the information efficiently using a particular key, such that the access time to information is fast. Within the chapter both non-recursive and recursive methods for sorting and searching for data are examined. By the end of the chapter the reader should have an understanding of the following topics.

☐ A definition of recursion and its implications.

☐ The use of recursive functions.

☐ The development of the algorithms for a selection sort and an insertion sort.

☐ The recursive quick sort algorithm.

☐ A method of searching for information in an array that contains data that has been sorted.

☐ The recursive binary search algorithm.

13.1 Recursion

It would be tempting to offer a simple definition of recursion as a function that called itself. However, this would be incomplete, since there is no mention of how the called function gets closer to the solution or how to stop the function repeatedly calling itself.

Recursion can be regarded as a technique for performing routine R, by performing a similar routine R_i. The routine R_i is exactly the same in nature as the original routine R, however, it represents a solution to a smaller problem than R.

Thus routine R recursively calls routine R_1; routine R_1 recursively calls routine R_2; routine R_{n-1} recursively calls routine R_n. Where R_n is a solution to a smaller problem than R_{n-1}; R_2 is a solution to a smaller problem than R_1; R_1 is a solution to a smaller problem than R. Eventually the recursive calls must lead to a solution R_n, which cannot allow for further recursive calls, since a terminating criterion has been reached.

With these facts in mind, the reader should always address the following three questions before constructing a recursive solution.

How can you define the solution in terms of a smaller solution of the same type?

How is the size of the solution being diminished at each recursive call?

What instance or level of the solution, can serve as the degenerate case, and does the manner in which the solution size is diminished ensure that this degenerate case will always be reached?

In this section three worked examples will be fully explained with the aid of diagrams. The reader is advised to spend some time on this section in order to understand the technique of recursion.

The following program contains a function to output the value of variable *level* , in the range from 1 to 5 inclusive. Rather than constructing a loop, the value of *level* is updated and output in the function, the function is then called again recursively to repeat updating *level* and to output the value of *level*. The function is recursively called until *level* becomes equal to 5.

```c
/* c13_dpp\ex_01.c program to demonstrate recursive calls and returns */

#include <stdio.h>

void output(int level)
{
    level++;
    printf("recursive call to level %d\n", level);
    if (level < 5)
        output(level); /* recursive call made here */
    else
        return;

    printf("returning through level %d\n", level);
}
```

```
main()
{
    output(0);
}
```

Results from program ex_01.c being run

```
recursive call to level 1
recursive call to level 2
recursive call to level 3
recursive call to level 4
recursive call to level 5
returning through level 4
returning through level 3
returning through level 2
returning through level 1
```

In the context of this solution, consider the three questions about constructing recursive algorithms given earlier. A smaller solution has been defined since only one value of level is output by the function and not all five values. Since level is being increased by 1, after each recursive call, the size of the solution is being diminished since level will eventually become equal to 5. The degenerate case is when level is equal to 5. No further recursion is then possible, and all values in the range 1..5 have been output.

In figure 13.1 on the next page, a recursive call produces another instance or level of the function, depicted by the code being superimposed upon the calling code.

The remaining code after *output(level)*, is not shown in the recursive calls to levels 1,2,3 and 4, since this is not yet executed.

Level 5 serves as the degenerate case in which level=5. No further recursion is possible and the code:

```
if (level < 5)
    output(level); /* recursive call made here */
else
    return;
```

will cause *return* to be executed. The computer must return through each level or instance of the code, before the program can finish. Since the computer is returning to the function that invoked the call, the next statement after the call, *output(level)*, will be executed. However, *output(level)*, was in one branch of a selection, therefore, the next statement to be executed will be after the selection statement. For this reason all the code that had been executed is now blacked-out, since it will not be used as the computer returns back through the levels, or instances, of the function. Notice also, that within each level the value of level has remained the same as it was when the level was originally invoked. Hence, in returning through the levels, the parameter *level* is output as 4,3,2 and 1 respectively.

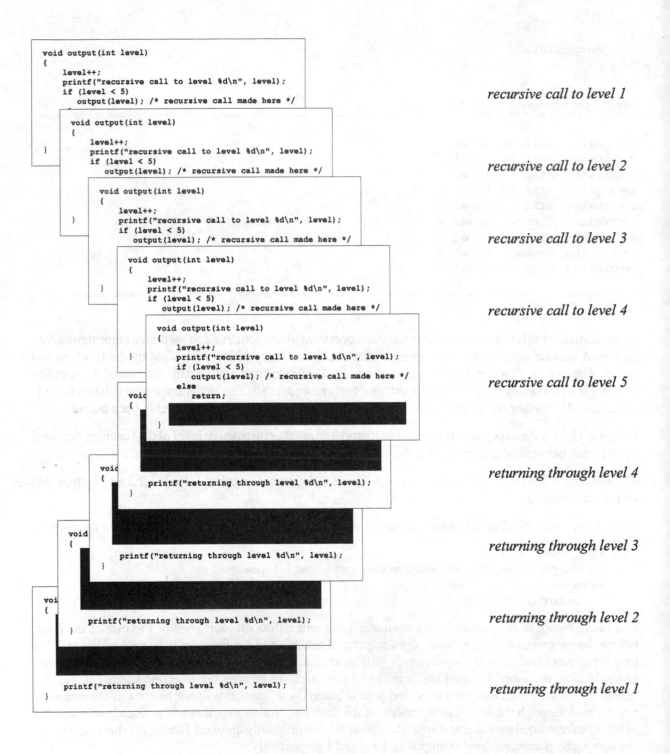

figure 13.1 recursive calls to function output

The second program in this section illustrates how a function can be called recursively to output the contents of a string backwards.

```
/* c13_dpp\ex_02.c program to print a string backwards */

#include <stdio.h>

char alphabet[]="abcdefghijklmnopqrstuvwxyz";

void write_backwards(char alpha_string[], int index)
{
        if (index >= 0)
        {
            putchar(alpha_string[index]);
            write_backwards(alpha_string, index-1);
        }
}

main()
{
        write_backwards(alphabet, 25);
}
```

Results from program ex_02.c being run

```
zyxwvutsrqponmlkjihgfedcba
```

There are two observations to make from the program and figure 13.2.

The identifier *index* is set at the last cell of the array and the contents, z, output; *index* is then reduced by 1 and a recursive call to *write_backwards* outputs y, *index* is then reduced by 1 and *write_backwards* is recursively called again. The output of characters continues until the *index* is less than zero. The recursive call *write_backwards(alpha, index-1)* is the last executable statement of the function *write_backwards*, and although the computer must return through each instance of function *write_backwards*, no further output is possible.

```
void write_backwards(char alpha_string[], int index)
{
    if (index >= 0)
    {
      putchar(alpha_string[index]);
      write_backwards(alpha_string, index-1);
    }
}
```

```
void write_backwards(char alpha_string[], int index)
{
    if (index >= 0)
    {
       putchar(alpha_string[index]);
       write_backwards(alpha_string, index-1);
    }
}
```

z

y
.
.
.
.
.
.
.

```
void write_backwards(char alpha_string[], int index)
{
    if (index >= 0)
    {
       putchar(alpha_string[index]);
       write_backwards(alpha_string, index-1);
    }
}
```

a

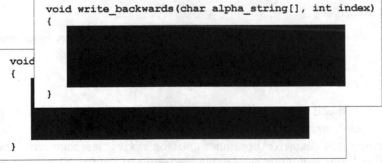

figure 13.2 recursive calls to function write_backwards

The last program in this section illustrates how a function can be called recursively to calculate the factorial value of a number.

Factorial n, written as n!, is defined as: n*(n-1)*(n-2) .. 3*2*1. Hence 5! = 5*4*3*2*1 = 120.

```
/* c13_dpp\ex_03.c program to calculate the factorial of a number */

#include <stdio.h>

long int factorial(int n)
{
      if (n==0)
          return 1;
      else
          return n * factorial(n-1);
}

main()
{
      int n;

      for (;;)
      {
          printf("input a number - 0 to exit ");
          scanf("%d", &n);

          if (n<=0) break;

          printf("%d!\t%10ld\n", n, factorial(n));
      }
}
```

Results from program ex_03.c being run

```
input a number - 0 to exit 3
3!           6
input a number - 0 to exit 4
4!          24
input a number - 0 to exit 5
5!         120
input a number - 0 to exit 6
6!         720
input a number - 0 to exit 0
```

In this example the value of the factorial of a number cannot be calculated until the function has recursively reached factorial(0). Upon returning to the next instance of factorial(1), the value 1*factorial(0) can then be calculated. Returning to the instance of factorial(2), the value 2*factorial(1) can then be calculated. Finally returning to the instance of factorial(3), the value 3*factorial(2) can be calculated.

This information is illustrated in figure 13.3.

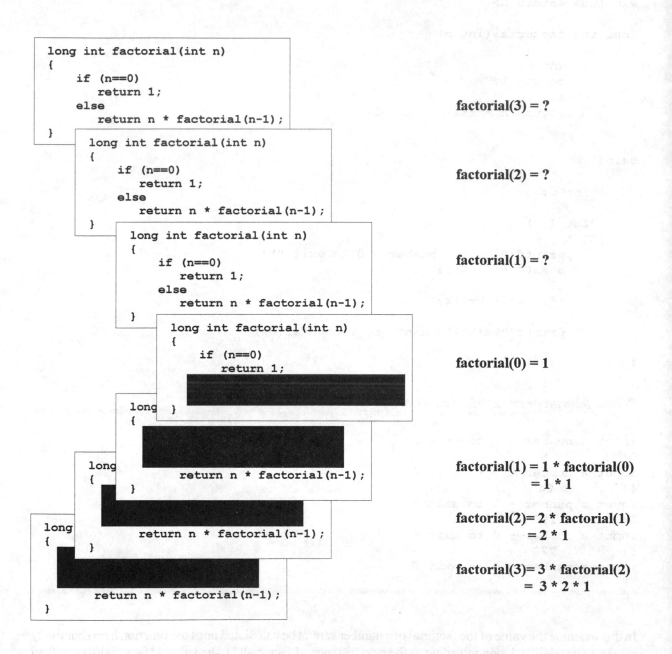

figure 13.3 recursive call to the function factorial

13.2 Selection sort

Sorting methods used in computing can be classified into two areas - internal sorting and external sorting. Internal sorting involves the storage in main memory of all the data to be sorted. However, when the amount of data is too large to be stored and sorted in the main memory, it is stored on an external secondary storage medium, such as tape or disk, and successive parts of the data are sorted in the main memory. Such a technique is known as external sorting. The type of sorting method that is used will depend upon at least one of the following factors.

The amount of information to be sorted. Clearly it would be very time consuming to use a relatively inefficient sorting method on a large quantity of data.

The computer configuration being used - the size of the main memory and the number of tape/ disc units.

The nature of the application and the urgency of the results.

In this section two internal methods for sorting numbers held in an array will be explained. The first is known as the *selection* sort.

figure 13.4 an illustration of a selection sort

Figure 13.4 illustrates the movement of integers in a one-dimensional array, when a selection sort is used to place the integers into ascending order (lowest value to highest value). The contents of the cells from 0 to 4 are inspected for the largest number (18), and when found swapped with the number in cell 4. The contents of the cells from 0 to 3 are inspected for the largest number (15), and when found swapped with the number in cell 3. The contents of the cells from 0 to 2 are inspected for the largest number (13), and when found swapped with the number in cell 2. The contents of the cells from 0 to 1 are inspected for the largest number (8), and when found swapped with the number in cell 1. When there is only the contents of cell 0 to inspect the numbers are assumed to have been sorted into ascending order.

To generalise, if N represents the number of integers to be sorted, stored in the cells of an array from 0 to N-1, the largest number in 0 to N-1 cells is found, and swapped with the number in cell N-1. The process is repeated, with N being decreased by 1 each time, until N=0.

This method of sorting numbers can be developed into two functions. The first function will return the position of the largest element in any sized array.

```
int position_of_largest(int numbers[], int limit)
/* function to return the position of the largest number
in the array numbers with bounds 0..limit */
{
        int largest = numbers[0];
        int index;
        int index_of_largest = 0;

        for (index=1; index<=limit; index++)
            if (numbers[index] > largest)
            {
                largest = numbers[index];
                index_of_largest = index;
            }

        return index_of_largest;
}
```

The second function calls the first function to find the largest number in the n-element array. This number is then swapped with the number at the end of the array. The process is repeated for n-1 elements, then n-2 elements until eventually n is reduced to zero.

```
void selection_sort(int numbers[], int size)
/* function to sort an array of integers into ascending order */
{
        int index, position, temp_store;

        for (index=size-1; index > 0; index--)
        {
            /* find the position of the largest number in the array bounds */
            position = position_of_largest(numbers, index);

            /* swap numbers */
            temp_store = numbers[index];
            numbers[index] = numbers[position];
            numbers[position] = temp_store;
        }
}
```

Using the data from figure 13.4, the reader is advised to desk check the two functions, to gain a better understanding of the selection sort algorithm.

The following program initialises an array with those numbers depicted in figure 13.4, sorts the numbers into ascending order in the array, and displays the contents of the sorted array.

```
/* c13_dpp\ex_04.c program to demonstrate a selection sort */

#include <stdio.h>

int position_of_largest(int numbers[], int limit)
/* function to return the position of the largest number
in the array numbers with bounds 0..limit */
{
        int largest = numbers[0];
        int index;
        int index_of_largest = 0;

        for (index=1; index<=limit; index++)
            if (numbers[index] > largest)
            {
                largest = numbers[index];
                index_of_largest = index;
            }

        return index_of_largest;
}

void selection_sort(int numbers[], int size)
/* function to sort an array of integers into ascending order */
{
        int index, position, temp_store;

        for (index=size-1; index > 0; index--)
        {
            position = position_of_largest(numbers, index);
            temp_store = numbers[index];
            numbers[index] = numbers[position];
            numbers[position] = temp_store;
        }
}

main()
{
        int numbers[5] = {18,7,15,8,13};
        int index;

        selection_sort(numbers, 5);

        for (index=0; index<5; index++)
            printf("%d\t", numbers[index]);
}
```

Results from program ex_04.c being run

```
7    8    13   15   18
```

13.3 Insertion sort

The second sorting method known as the insertion sort follows. Figures 13.5 and 13.6 illustrate how integer numbers stored in a one-dimensional array are ordered within the array, using this method.

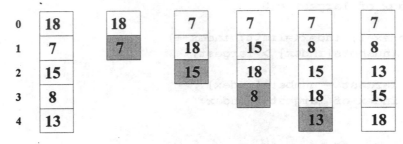

figure 13.5 an illustration of an insertion sort

The second number (7) in the array, is compared with the first (18) and ordered into ascending sequence (7,18). The next number (15) in the array, is then inserted into the correct position (7,15,18) in relation to the previously ordered numbers. The next number (8) in the array, is inserted into the correct position (7,8,15,18) in relation to the previously ordered numbers. Finally, the last number (13) in the array, is inserted into the correct position (7,8,13,15,18) in relation to the previously ordered numbers. Since this was the last number in the array, the numbers are now stored in ascending order.

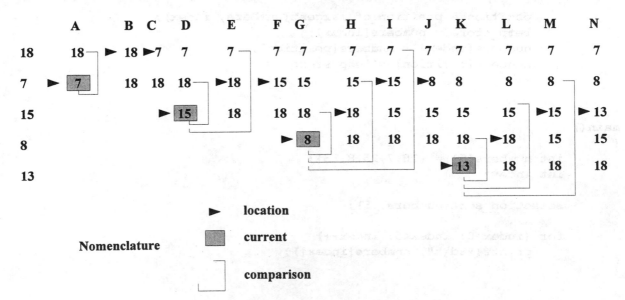

figure 13.6 movement of numbers in an insertion sort

The following *insertion_sort* function can replace the selection_sort function given in the previous program without any loss of functionality to the program. The function *position_of_largest* is no longer required.

```
void insertion_sort(int numbers[], int size)
/* function to sort an array of integers into ascending order */
{
    int current, location, index;

    for (index=1; index <= size-1; index++)
    {
        current=numbers[index];
        location=index;
        while (location > 0 && numbers[location-1] > current)
        {
            numbers[location] = numbers[location-1];
            location--;
        }
        numbers[location] = current;
    }
}
```

Figure 13.7 illustrates a desk check of the insertion sort algorithm. The reader is recommended to trace through the insertion sort algorithm in order to gain a better understanding of the technique.

Desk Check of algorithm for Insertion Sort in conjunction with figure 13.6

column in fig 13.6	index	current	location	numbers [location-1]	numbers [location]	numbers [location-1] > current ?
A	1	7	1	18	7	true
B			0		18	
C			0		7	
D	2	15	2	18	15	true
E			1	7	18	false
F			1		15	
G	3	8	3	18	8	true
H			2	15	18	true
I			1	7	15	false
J			1		8	
K	4	13	4	18	13	true
L			3	15	18	true
M			2	8	15	false
N			2		13	

figure 13.7 desk check of the insertion sort algorithm

13.4 Quick sort algorithm

In this method an array is divided into two partitions. The dividing point is chosen to be the mid-point position in the array. Starting at the lowest position in the array (within the first partition) a comparison is made between a datum at this position and the datum at the mid-point position. If the datum is less than the datum at the mid-point position a comparison is made with the next datum in the partition. Comparisons continue until a datum is found to be larger or equal in size to the datum at the mid-point position. Starting at the highest position in the array (within the second partition) the process is repeated until a datum is found that is smaller or equal in size to the datum at the mid-point position. The data in each partition that prevented further comparisons from being made is then swapped over. Further comparisons and swapping of data will continue until each datum in each partition has been compared. All keys above the mid-point or pivot will be less than the pivot key and all keys below the pivot will be greater than the pivot key. The contents of the partitions are not yet ordered, so the method is then applied to each partition recursively until the sub partitions contain only one item of data. Figure 13.8 illustrates the ordering of the keys about the pivot point before the technique is applied to the sub-partitions recursively. Figure 13.9 also illustrates the recursive nature of the quick sort algorithm.

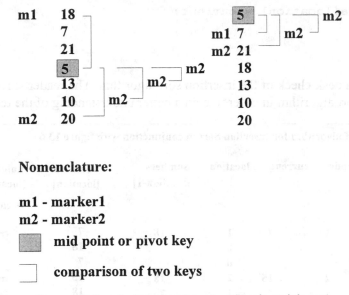

Nomenclature:

m1 - marker1

m2 - marker2

◼ **mid point or pivot key**

▢ **comparison of two keys**

figure 13.8 ordering about a pivot key in quick sort

The program that follows figure 13.9 contains a function *quick_sort* derived from the explanation given at the beginning of this section.

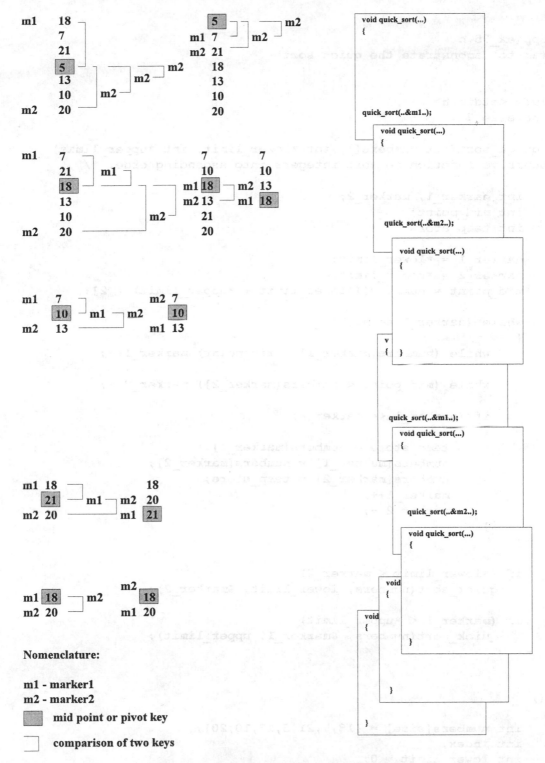

Nomenclature:

m1 - marker1
m2 - marker2

▨   mid point or pivot key

▢   comparison of two keys

figure 13.9 recursive nature of quick sort

```
/*
c13_dpp\ex_05.c
program to demonstrate the quick sort
*/

#include <stdio.h>
#define size 7

void quick_sort(int numbers[], int *lower_limit, int *upper_limit)
/* recursive function to sort integers into ascending order */
{
        int marker_1, marker_2;
        int mid_point;
        int temp_store;

        marker_1 = *lower_limit;
        marker_2 = *upper_limit;
        mid_point = numbers[(*lower_limit + *upper_limit) / 2];

        while (marker_1 <= marker_2)
        {
            while (numbers[marker_1] < mid_point) marker_1++;

            while (mid_point < numbers[marker_2]) marker_2--;

            if (marker_1 <= marker_2)
            {
                temp_store = numbers[marker_1];
                numbers[marker_1] = numbers[marker_2];
                numbers[marker_2] = temp_store;
                marker_1++;
                marker_2--;
            }
        }

        if (*lower_limit < marker_2)
           quick_sort(numbers, lower_limit, &marker_2);

        if (marker_1 < *upper_limit)
           quick_sort(numbers, &marker_1, upper_limit);

}

main()
{
        int numbers[size] = {18,7,21,5,13,10,20};
        int index;
        int lower_limit = 0;
        int upper_limit = size-1;
```

```
        quick_sort(numbers, &lower_limit, &upper_limit);

        for (index=0; index < size; index++)
            printf("%d\t", numbers[index]);
}
```

Results from program ex_05.c being run

```
    5    7   10   13   18   20   21
```

The ANSI C library contains a function associated with the header file <stdlib.h> for sorting an array of data using the quick sort algorithm. The prototype for the function is:

```
void qsort(const void *base, size_t num, size_t width,
           int (*compare) (const void *e1, const void *e2));
```

where   *base*   is the array being sorted;
        num   is the number of elements in the array;
        width   represents the number of bytes required to store an element;
        compare   is a pointer to a user supplied function that compares array elements
                     (e.g. e1 and e2) and returns an integer value indicating their relationship:

$$\text{if } e1 < e2, \text{ return } < 0$$
$$\text{if } e1 = e2, \text{ return } = 0$$
$$\text{if } e1 > e2, \text{ return } > 0$$

The array is ordered by increasing value. Reversing the sense of less than and greater than in *compare* will cause the array to be ordered by decreasing value. Notice that the parameters for the function *compare* are of a *generic pointer type*, used since the type being pointed at is not known.

The original array is overwritten with the sorted array.

The following program illustrates how to use the library function **qsort**, and replaces the quick_sort function developed in the previous example.

```
/* c13_dpp\ex_06.c program to demonstrate the quick sort */

#include <stdio.h>
#include <stdlib.h>
#define size 7

int compare(const void *n1, const void *n2);
```

```
main()
{
        int numbers[size] = {18,7,21,5,13,10,20};
        int index;

        qsort(numbers, size, sizeof(int), compare);

        for (index=0; index < size; index++)
            printf("%d\t", numbers[index]);
}

int compare(const void *n1, const void *n2)
{
        return *((int *)n1) - *((int *)n2);
}
```

13.5 Sequential search

The concept of searching for information is not new to the reader. In chapter 10 a function was developed for searching for a student number *search_number*, knowing that the number in the array appeared in ascending sequence. This algorithm can be adapted to cater for searching for strings that are ordered in an array. When the information held in an array is sorted into search key order then it is not always necessary to search through an entire array before discovering that the information is not present.

Consider for a moment the following information held in the array depicted in figure 13.10. Alphabetically Adams is before Davies, Davies is before Evans, Evans is before Farthing, etc.

0	Adams	18 Milestone Road
1	Davies	72 Sherwood Avenue
2	Evans	433 Lake Street
3	Farthing	10 Almond Avenue
4	Fielding	21 Turnpike Boulevard
5	Hewitt	30 Chester Street
6	Jones	336 Cornwallis Road
7	Mowbray	45 Brookside Avenue
8	Peters	113 Flemming Avenue
9	Quayle	212 Wiltshire Boulevard
10	Rankin	732 High Road

figure 13.10 an array of records

If a search was to be made on the contents of the array for the key Ellis then the following comparisons, illustrated in figure 13.11, would be necessary before it was discovered that Ellis was not in the array. Ellis is alphabetically greater than both Adams and Davies so may be found further on in the array. Ellis is alphabetically less than Evans, therefore, an entry for Ellis cannot exist in the array since the names are ordered into alphabetical sequence. By sorting the contents of the array into alphabetical order on the name of each person only three key comparisons were necessary before discovering that Ellis did not exist in the array. If the array had not been sorted by name then every name in the array would have been compared before it was discovered that the name did not exist in the array.

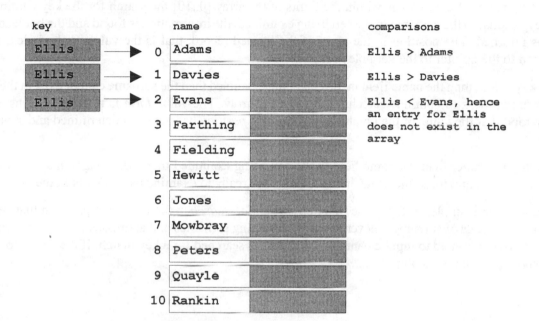

figure 13.11 a sequential search on an array of records

Assuming that the records are stored into consecutive array locations from 0 through to 10, the following algorithm is used in searching for a surname in the array.

```
boolean sequential_search(names_addresses table[],
                    int size, char key[], int *position)
/* function to search the records of an ordered array for a key */
{
    int      index=0;

    while (index < size)
    {
        if (strcmp(key, table[index].name) == 0)
        {
            *position = index;
            return true;
        }
    }
```

```
        else if (strcmp(key, table[index].name) < 0)
            return false;
        else
            index++;
    }
    return false;
}
```

The *index* used to access each cell of the array is initialised to 0, the first cell position of the array.

While the value of the *index* is within the limits of the array [0..10] the search for the key continues. If the key is equal to the surname in the cell being examined, the information is found and the boolean value *true* is returned. The position in the array of the located record, that is the value of the index, is also assigned to the pointer to the variable *position*.

If the key is less than the name field in the cell being examined then the surname cannot exist in the array, and it is pointless to continue searching through the array. The value *false* is returned as long as it is understood that the value of the pointer to the variable *position* has not been determined and should not be used.

If the key is greater than the name field in the cell being examined then the surname may exist further down the array, and the value of the index is increased ready to examine the contents of the next cell.

This algorithm is implemented as the function *sequential_search* in the following program that stores in alphabetical order of surname, eleven records containing surnames and addresses in a one-dimensional array. A user is invited to input a name and the array is searched for a key match. If the key is found the corresponding address is output.

```
/*
c13_dpp\ex_07.c
program to create an array of records and given the name
of a person search the array for their address
*/

#include <stdio.h>
#include <string.h>

typedef enum {false, true} boolean;

typedef struct {
                char    name[20];
                char    address[40];
            }   names_addresses;
```

```
boolean sequential_search(names_addresses table[],
                          int size, char key[], int *position)
/* function to search the records of an ordered array for a key */
{
    int     index=0;

    while (index < size)
    {
        if (strcmp(key, table[index].name) == 0)
        {
            *position = index;
            return true;
        }
        else if (strcmp(key, table[index].name) < 0)
            return false;
        else
            index++;
    }
    return false;
}

main()
{
    #define number_of_entries 11

    names_addresses table[number_of_entries] =
    {{"Adams",    "18 Milestone Road"},
     {"Davies",   "72 Sherwood Avenue"},
     {"Evans",    "433 Lake Street"},
     {"Farthing", "10 Almond Avenue"},
     {"Fielding", "21 Turnpike Boulevard"},
     {"Hewitt",   "30 Chester Street"},
     {"Jones",    "336 Corwallis Road"},
     {"Mowbray",  "45 Brookside Avenue"},
     {"Peters",   "113 Flemming Avenue"},
     {"Quayle",   "212 Wiltshire Boulevard"},
     {"Rankin",   "732 High Road"}};


    int index;
    char name_key[20];

    printf("name? "); gets(name_key);

    if (sequential_search(table, number_of_entries, name_key, &index))
        printf("address %s\n", table[index].address);
    else
        printf("name not found\n");
}
```

```
name? Quayle
212 Wiltshire Boulevard
name? Ellis
name not found
name? Fielding
21 Turnpike Boulevard
```

13.6 Binary search algorithm

This method requires that the keys are sorted prior to the search and that the information is stored in an array. From figure 13.12 the array is divided into two parts by the mid-point. The mid-point is calculated as (first+last)/2 and in this example assigned to the variable *location*. The key *Quayle* is compared with the key at *location* and since *Quayle > Hewitt*, *Quayle* may be found in the lower sub-array within the bounds (location+1 .. last). The process is repeated with a new mid-point being calculated as (location+1+last)/2 and assigned to the variable *location*. The key *Quayle* is compared with the key at the *location* and since *Quayle > Peters*, *Quayle* may be found in the lower sub-array within the bounds (location+1 .. last). The process is repeated again with a new mid-point being calculated. Note when a sub-list contains an even number of keys the mid-point may be taken to be the next lowest key from the centre. A match for the key *Quayle* exists at *location* =9. If the value for *first* had exceeded the value for *last* then no match can be found for the key. Notice that only three comparisons are necessary compared with ten comparisons if a serial or sequential search had been performed.

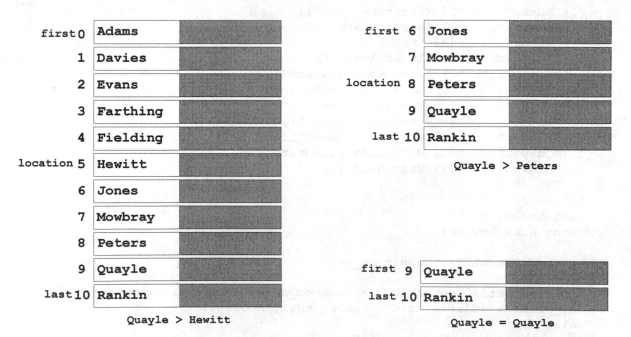

figure 13.12 a binary search for a surname in an array

A binary search can be succinctly implemented using recursion. The search involves calculating a mid-point from the lowest and highest indices of an array and if the key is in the lower-half of the sub-array repeating the process within the bounds (first .. location-1). However, if the key is in the upper-half of the sub-array repeating the process within the bounds (location+1 .. last). Recursion continues until the bounds of the sub-array cross-over (first > last), or a match for the key is found. Figure 13.13 illustrates the recursive calls to the function *binary_search*. The function *binary_search* has the following prototype

```
boolean binary_search(names_addresses table[], char key[],
                int first, int last, int *location);
```

where *table* is the array to be searched, *key* is a string to be matched with the keys in the array, *first*, *last* and *location* are as described. The following program uses the binary search to locate the address of a person given the surname as key. The results are similar to those found in the previous section, only the method of searching for a key is different.

```
/*
c13_dpp\ex_08.c
program to create an array of records and given the name
of a person binary search the array for their address
*/

#include <stdio.h>
#include <string.h>

typedef enum {false, true} boolean;

typedef struct {
            char    name[20];
            char    address[40];
        } names_addresses;

boolean binary_search(names_addresses table[], char key[],
                int first, int last, int *location)
/* function to binary search the records of an ordered array for a key */
{
    if (first > last)
        return false;
    else
    {
        *location = (first+last) / 2;
        if (strcmp(key, table[*location].name)==0)
            return true;
        else if (strcmp(key, table[*location].name) < 0)
            return binary_search(table, key, first, *location-1, location);
        else
            return binary_search(table, key, *location+1, last, location);
    }
}
```

```
main()
{
    #define number_of_entries 11

    names_addresses table[number_of_entries] =
    {{"Adams",    "18 Milestone Road"},
     {"Davies",   "72 Sherwood Avenue"},
     {"Evans",    "433 Lake Street"},
     {"Farthing", "10 Almond Avenue"},
     {"Fielding", "21 Turnpike Boulevard"},
     {"Hewitt",   "30 Chester Street"},
     {"Jones",    "336 Corwallis Road"},
     {"Mowbray",  "45 Brookside Avenue"},
     {"Peters",   "113 Flemming Avenue"},
     {"Quayle",   "212 Wiltshire Boulevard"},
     {"Rankin",   "732 High Road"}};

    int first = 0;
    int last  = number_of_entries-1;
    int location;
    char name_key[20];

    printf("name? "); gets(name_key);

    if (binary_search(table, name_key, first, last, &location))
        printf("address %s\n", table[location].address);
    else
        printf("name not found\n");
}
```

The ANSI C library contains a function in the header file <stdlib.h> for searching an array of data using the binary search algorithm. The prototype for the function is:

```
void *bsearch(const void *key, const void *base, size_t num, size_t width,
              int (*compare) (const void *e1, const void *e2));
```

where *key*   is a pointer to the element being sought;
       base   is a pointer to the base of the array to be searched;
       num   is the number of elements in the array;
       width   represents the number of bytes required to store an element;
       compare   is a pointer to a user supplied function that compares array elements
                   (e.g. e1 and e2) and returns an integer value indicating their relationship:
                   if e1 < e2, return < 0
                   if e1 = e2, return = 0
                   if e1 > e2, return > 0

The function returns a pointer to the first matching element if found, otherwise the value NULL is returned.

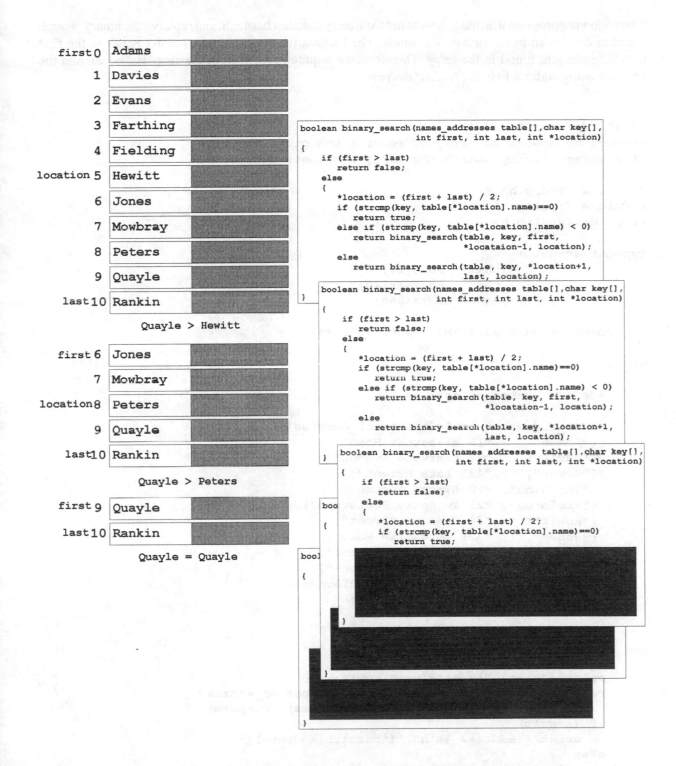

figure 13.13 recursive calls to function binary_search

The following program illustrates how to use the library function **bsearch**, and replaces the binary_search function developed in the previous example. The bsearch function returns a pointer *result* to the first matching element found in the array. Therefore, the required record from the array is **result*, and the corresponding address field is *(*result).address*.

```
/* c13_dpp\ex_09.c
program to create an array of records and given the name
of a person binary search the array for their address */

#include <stdio.h>
#include <string.h>
#include <stdlib.h>

typedef struct {
                char    name[20];
                char    address[40];
            }  names_addresses;

int compare(const void *n1, const void *n2);

main()
{
    #define number_of_entries 11

    names_addresses table[number_of_entries] =
    {{"Adams",     "18 Milestone Road"},
     {"Davies",    "72 Sherwood Avenue"},
     {"Evans",     "433 Lake Street"},
     {"Farthing",  "10 Almond Avenue"},
     {"Fielding",  "21 Turnpike Boulevard"},
     {"Hewitt",    "30 Chester Street"},
     {"Jones",     "336 Corwallis Road"},
     {"Mowbray",   "45 Brookside Avenue"},
     {"Peters",    "113 Flemming Avenue"},
     {"Quayle",    "212 Wiltshire Boulevard"},
     {"Rankin",    "732 High Road"}};

    names_addresses *result;
    char            name_key[20];

    printf("name? "); gets(name_key);
    result = bsearch(name_key, table, number_of_entries,
                    sizeof(names_addresses), compare);
    if (result)
       printf("address %s\n", (*result).address);
    else
       printf("name not found\n");
}
```

```
int compare(const void *n1, const void *n2)
{
    return strcmp(  (*(names_addresses *)n1).name,
                    (*(names_addresses *)n2).name );
}
```

13.7 Summary

- [] A recursive routine will repeatedly call itself until a criterion for terminating is satisfied.

- [] The computer must return through each instance of the recursive routine that has been invoked.

- [] Each instance of a recursive routine represents a smaller solution to a problem, where all the instances represent the complete solution to the problem.

- [] In the selection sort the largest item of data is located and transferred to the end of the structure holding the data. The area over which the structure is examined is reduced by one storage unit, and the largest item of data is located and transferred to the end of the structure. These operations continue until the size of the structure is reduced to one storage unit. The contents of the original structure has then been ordered.

- [] In the insertion sort the contents of the first and second storage units are examined and ordered. This operation is extended to the first, second and third storage units and the data is ordered. The process continues extending the number of storage units to be examined by one. At every examination the contents of the storage units is ordered. After all the storage units have been examined the data will have been ordered.

- [] In the quick sort algorithm an array is divided into two partitions by a pivot key. Keys in each partition are compared for an ordered sequence with the pivot key. When an ordered sequence in each partition is no longer possible the offending keys are swapped. Further comparisons and swapping of keys continues until each key in each partition has been compared. All the keys above and below the pivot key will then be ordered, however, the partitions themselves are not yet ordered. The algorithm is then applied to each partition recursively until the sub partitions contain only one item of data.

- [] Searching for data held in key order in an array is made more efficient when the data is ordered. If the value of the key is greater than the item being inspected then the key may be found further on in the array. However, if the value of the key is less than the item being inspected then the key cannot exist in the array and the search must be abandoned.

- [] The binary search algorithm relies upon the fact that the contents of the array must be ordered. The technique repeatedly divides an array into smaller arrays that are likely to contain the key, until either a key match is possible or the array cannot be subdivided further.

13.8 Questions - *answers begin on page 491*

1. Write recursive functions to:

(a) sum a one-dimensional array containing positive integers only;

(b) raise a number to a power, for example $X^n = X * X^{n-1}$ where n > 0;

(c) generate the first fifteen numbers in a Fibonacci series where the nth element is the sum of the (n-2) and (n-1) elements for n > 2, for example 1 1 2 3 5 8 13 21 ...

To test each function embed it into a separate program.

2. The median of a set of numbers is that number which has the same number of values above and below it. For example, in the set [1,3,9,18,7,5,4] the median is 5 since three numbers are larger [7,9,18] and three numbers are smaller [1,3,4] than 5. Write a program to compute the median of a set of non-zero integers input to the computer in any order

   (a) for an odd number of values;
   (b) for an even number of values.

Note: clearly for an odd number of values the median will be the central value of the ordered set of numbers. An even number of values will not have one central value, but two central values. The median is taken to be the average of the two central values.

[3]. Write a program to store positive integers in a one-dimensional array, such that the numbers are not in any predefined order. Compare adjacent numbers in the array, and swap the numbers such that the first number of the pair is always smaller than the second number of the pair. Repeat the process for all the adjacent numbers in the array.

Repeat the process described in the previous paragraph until all the numbers are sorted into ascending order, that is no swapping of pairs of numbers was necessary. This algorithm is known as a *bubble* sort.

[4]. Implement the *selection_sort* as a recursive function, and modify the program *c13_dpp\ex_04.c* to test your answer.

[5]. Write a program to create an array of up to 100 unsorted records having the following format.

```
typedef struct   {
                int  number;
                char name[20]
           } student_id;
```

where *number* is a unique student number that corresponds with the *name* of a student.

Sort the array on the key number using **qsort**.

Given a *number* search the array using **bsearch** for the *name* of the student and display this name if it is found.

Chapter 14
Files

In the previous chapters input was confined to entering data through a keyboard and output to displaying information on a screen. When there is a requirement to permanently store data there is a need to create files. Data can be written to or read from files held on magnetic and optical media. This chapter covers the use of text and binary files and the methods of accessing the information held on the files. By the end of the chapter the reader should have an understanding of the following topics.

- [ ] The concept of a data stream.

- [ ] The redirection of input and output from files held on a storage medium, to replace keyboard input and screen output.

- [ ] The use of library routines that permit file processing.

- [ ] The creation and manipulation of data held on both text and binary files.

- [ ] Merging of data stored on two files.

- [ ] Direct access to records held on a binary file.

14.1 Streams

The term stream is used to define any input source or output destination for data. The only streams that have been used in the previous chapters are from keyboard input and screen output. However, it is possible to define further streams that use other devices, such as a printer or a disk unit.

A stream is represented by a file pointer which is a value of type FILE *, and in ANSI C there are three standard streams whose file pointers have the following names:

stdin   standard input from a keyboard;
stdout   standard output to a screen;
stderr   standard output of error messages to a screen.

The standard input and output streams can be regarded as files. The functions *scanf* and *printf* that relate to keyboard input and screen output have equivalent functions for respective input and output from files held on other devices. The format of these new functions is:

fscanf(FILE *stream, const char *format, [arguments] ...); and
fprintf(FILE *stream, const char *format, ...);

However, since *stdin* and *stdout* are file pointers it is possible to substitute scanf and printf with fscanf and fprintf respectively, and retain input from the keyboard and output to the screen as if scanf and printf were being used.

The following program reads numbers input at the keyboard (stdin), displays on the screen (stdout) a running total for the numbers and calculates and displays the average of the numbers.

```
/*
c14_dpp\ex_01.c
program to demonstrate input and output from the standard streams
stdin and stdout
*/

#include <stdio.h>

main()
{
    int    integer;
    int    sum = 0;
    int    counter = 0;
    float mean;

    fscanf(stdin, "%d", &integer);
    while (integer != 0)
    {
        sum += integer;
        fprintf(stdout, "sum of integers so far .. %d\n", sum);
        counter++;
        fscanf(stdin, "%d", &integer);
    }
```

```
        mean = (float) sum / counter;
        fprintf(stdout, "mean value of integers is %6.1f\n", mean);
}
```

Results from program ex_01.c being run

```
8
sum of integers so far .. 8
4
sum of integers so far .. 12
2
sum of integers so far .. 14
9
sum of integers so far .. 23
2
sum of integers so far .. 25
0
mean value of integers is    5.0
```

14.2 Redirection

The use of a keyboard as a source and a screen as a destination, can be modified by redirecting the standard input and output. In both MSDOS and UNIX it is possible to redirect standard input and standard output to other devices. For example in MSDOS data can be input and output to a disk unit. If the source of data is to come from a disk-based file named **a:\numbers.txt**, and the output is to be written to a file called **a:\results.txt** then redirection is possible by modifying the command line statement used for running the program. The command line to redirect input and output for a program named **ex_02** would be defined as:

```
  C> ex_02 <a:\numbers.txt >a:\results.txt
```

where C is the MSDOS prompt. [Note - UNIX has a similar redirection technique - see appendix C]

The following program is similar to the previous example. The functions fscanf and fprintf have been substituted by scanf and printf, respectively, and the program is run using the command line given above.

```
/*
c14_dpp\ex_02.c
program to demonstrate redirection for input and output
*/

#include <stdio.h>

main()
{
        int     integer;
        int     sum = 0;
```

309

```
    int    counter = 0;
    float mean;

    scanf("%d", &integer);
    while (integer != 0)
    {
        sum += integer;
        printf("sum of integers so far .. %d\n", sum);
        counter++;
        scanf("%d", &integer);
    }
    mean = (float) sum / counter;
    printf("mean value of integers is %6.1f\n", mean);
}
```

The contents of the text file **numbers.txt**, created using an editor, and stored on disk drive (a) was:

```
    8  4  2  9  2  0
```

and after the command

```
ex_02 <a:\numbers.txt >a:\results.txt
```

and the program had been executed, the contents of the text file **results.txt**, stored on disk drive (a) was:

```
sum of integers so far .. 8
sum of integers so far .. 12
sum of integers so far .. 14
sum of integers so far .. 23
sum of integers so far .. 25
mean value of integers is 5.0
```

14.3 Opening and closing files

In using standard input and output streams as files it was not necessary to open or close the streams, since this is performed automatically by the system. However, when the programmer defines new streams it is necessary to open a file before it can be used. Similarly when a file is no longer required, or the mode of access is to change, then it should be closed.

A file can be opened using the function **fopen**, whose prototype declaration in the **<stdio.h>** library is described as:

```
        FILE *fopen(const char *path, const char *type);
```

where the function opens the file specified by path, and associates a stream with that file. The character string type specifies the access mode for the file, and can be any of the following.

"r"	Read only - file must exist
"w"	Write only - file need not exist
"a"	Write only from the end of the file - file need not exist
"r+", and "w+"	Read and write starting at the beginning of the file
"a+"	Read and append.

In addition to these values the characters 't' or 'b' may be added after the first character of mode to specify text or binary files respectively.

The function *fopen* returns a pointer to the open stream. If the stream could not be successfully opened a NULL pointer is returned.

There are three ways in which the name of a file can be input into a program.

(i) The name can be implicitly contained in the fopen statement, for example:

```
FILE *text;
text = fopen("a:text.txt", "r");
```

where **a:text.txt** implies that a file with the name **text.txt** may exist in the directory of the disk held on drive (a).

(ii) The name of the file can be input at run-time, prior to the file being opened, for example:

```
FILE *text;
char *filename;
{
   filename = malloc(30);
   printf("input the path and name of the file ");
   gets(filename);
   text = fopen(filename, "r");
   .
   .
```

(iii) The names of files can be passed as arguments in a command line when giving the command to run a program. For example if a program file called *prog.exe* had been created that required the names of the data files *file1.txt, file2.txt* and *file3.txt* to be passed to the main program as parameters, the command line would be input as:

```
   prog    file1.txt    file2.txt    file3.txt
```

To accommodate these program parameters the function main must contain the parameters **argc** and **argv**, as follows:

```
   main (int argc, char *argv[])
```

where **argc** is the number of command line parameters including the name of the program, in this example argc is 4; **argv[]** is an array of pointers to the command line parameters, in this example argv[0] points to prog, argv[1] points to file1.txt, argv[2] points to file2.txt, argv[3] points to file3.txt and argv[4] is a null pointer.

During run-time if a program attempted to open a file that did not exist the program would be suspended. To overcome this problem it is possible to check whether the number of command line arguments is correct and whether the files exist if they are to be read. The following segment of code will check whether the correct number of parameters in the command line

```
prog    file1.txt    file2.txt    file3.txt
```

are present.

```
main ( int argc, char *argv[])
{
   FILE *filename1, *filename2, *filename3;
   if (argc != 4)
   {
      fprintf(stderr, "ERROR - command line arguments\a\n");
      exit(errno);
   }
   .
   .
```

The next segment of code can be used to check whether a file can be opened for reading.

```
   filename1 = fopen(argv[1], "r");
   if (filename1 == NULL)
   {
      fprintf(stderr, "ERROR - file %s cannot be opened\a\n", argv[1]);
      exit(errno);
   }
   .
   fclose(filename1); fclose(filename2); fclose(filename3);
   .
}
```

Warning! When defining a path for a particular file be careful of the use of backslash. The compiler will treat \ in a string literal as the beginning of an escape character. For example in the statement fopen("a:\book\text.txt, "w"); the compiler would treat \b and \t as escape characters and return a null pointer. When a backslash is required use \\, hence the statement is changed to fopen("a:\\book\\text.txt, "w").

See also appendix C - C.6 File manipulation - before running any programs under UNIX from this chapter since the path names will need to be changed.

In these segments of code the function **exit**, defined in the header file **<stdlib.h>**, causes a program to terminate; *errno* is a global variable, defined in the header **<errno.h>**, and can be set by library functions. The value of *errno* indicates the type of error that has occurred. A value of zero implies no error.

A file is closed by using the **fclose** function. In the previous segment of code *fclose(filename1)*, *fclose(filename2)*, and *fclose(filename3)* close the streams *filename1*, *filename2* and *filename3*, respectively.

14.4 Text files

A text file is a collection of ASCII characters, written in lines, with a specific end of line marker, and an end of file marker. Text files can be created using an editor, in the same way as programs are created. Alternatively, a text file can be created from within a program, by writing information to a file that has been opened in the appropriate mode.

The following library functions, found in the header file **<stdio.h>** are used to create text files.

int fputc(int c, FILE *stream) ; writes a character c to stream, if an error occurs it returns a negative integer constant EOF, otherwise it returns the ASCII code for the character.

int fputs(const char *s, FILE *stream); writes the string s to stream; note fputs does not write a new line character unless one is present in s; if an error occurs it returns a negative integer constant EOF, otherwise it returns a non-negative integer.

int fprintf(FILE *stream, const char *format, ...) ; writes a variable number of data items to an output stream, using a format string to control the appearance of the output; if an error occurs it returns a negative value, otherwise it returns the number of characters that were written

The following functions, found in the header file **<stdio.h>** are used to read from text files.

int fgetc(FILE *stream) ; reads a character from stream; if the end of the input file is reached or an error occurs it returns a negative integer constant EOF, otherwise it returns the ASCII code for the character that was read.

char *fgets(char *s, int n, FILE *stream) ; reads from stream into the array that s points to, stopping at the first new line character or when n-1 characters have been read. The new line character, if read, is stored in the array. If the end of the input file is reached or an error occurs the function returns a null pointer, otherwise a pointer to the string read is returned.

int fscanf(FILE *stream, const char *format, ...) ; reads any number of data items from stream, using format to indicate the layout of input. If the end of the file is reached or an error occurs the function returns a negative integer constant EOF, otherwise the function returns the number of items of data read.

int ferror(FILE *stream); tests a stream's error flag - the function returns a non-zero value for an error, otherwise it returns zero.

In order to explicitly test whether the end of file has been reached there is an end of file function **feof** which has the format: **int feof(FILE *stream);** and returns a non-zero value if the end of stream has been reached.

Figure 14.1 illustrates what happens when a text file is opened with the name *data* and the file read line by line. In opening the file for reading, a *file position* indicator points to the first line of the file to be read. At this stage the function *feof(data)* returns a value of zero since the end of the file has not been encountered. The *price* and *name* of the appliance are read using the functions *fscanf(data, "%f", &price)* and *fgets(appliance, string_length, data)* respectively. The file position indicator is then automatically moved to the next line and provided the end of the data file has not been encountered the next line can be read. The process of reading from the file continues while the end of the data file is not encountered.

	text file - data	feof(data)?	fscanf(data,"%f",&price); fgets(appliance,string_length,data);
file position →	395.95 television 550.00 music centre 149.95 freezer	0 (false)	price = 395.95 appliance = television
file position →	395.95 television 550.00 music centre 149.95 freezer	0 (false)	price = 550.00 appliance = music centre
file position →	395.95 television 550.00 music centre 149.95 freezer	0 (false)	price = 149.95 appliance = freezer
file position →	395.95 television 550.00 music centre 149.95 freezer	not 0 (true)	

figure 14.1 reading lines in a text file

Worked Examples

Problem A text file contains the following lines of data that relate to the insured values of several domestic appliances. For example, a television is insured for £395.95, a music centre is insured for £550.00, desk-top computer is insured for £995.95, etc. Note - there is no *new line* character after the last line in the file.

395.95 television
550.00 music centre
995.95 desk-top computer
199.95 microwave oven
299.99 washing machine
149.95 freezer

The first program demonstrates how to open the file, and read and display the contents line by line. The sequence of operations can be expressed in pseudo-code as:

open file for reading
while not end of file
    read price
    read name of appliance
    display price and name of appliance
close file

Notice in the program, if the file cannot be opened, this fact is reported and the program is abandoned.

```
/*
c14_dpp\ex_03.c
program to read a file and display the contents on a screen
*/
#include <stdlib.h>
#include <stdio.h>
#include <errno.h>
#define filename "a:\\c14_dpp\\data.txt"
#define read "r"
#define string_length 20
main()
{
     FILE *data;
     float price;
     char  appliance[string_length];

     /* attempt to open file */
     data = fopen(filename, read);
     if (data == NULL)
     {
        printf("%s cannot be opened\n", filename);
        exit(errno);
     }

     /* read and display every line in the file */
     while (! feof(data))
     {
        fscanf(data, "%f", &price);
        fgets(appliance, string_length, data);
        printf("%6.2f\t%s", price, appliance);
     }

     /* close data file */
     fclose(data);
}
```

Results displayed on a screen from program ex_03.c being run

```
395.95 television
550.00 music centre
995.95 desk-top computer
199.95 microwave oven
299.99 washing machine
149.95 freezer
```

Problem When using files, output does not necessarily need to be directed to a screen, it can be directed to another text file. In the next example the contents of the file used in the previous program is modified such that the price of each appliance is increased by the rate of inflation, and the new price together with the name of the appliance is written to a text file.

The sequence of operations can be expressed in pseudo-code as:

open input file for reading
open output file for writing
while not end of input file
    read price
    read name of appliance
    increase price by rate of inflation
    write price and name of appliance to output file
close input file
close output file

```
/*
c14_dpp\ex_04.c
program to read a file and update its contents and write
the new values to another file
*/
#include <stdlib.h>
#include <stdio.h>
#include <errno.h>
#define input_file  "a:\\c14_dpp\\data.txt"
#define output_file "a:\\c14_dpp\\new_data.txt"
#define read "r"
#define write "w"
#define string_length 20

main()
{
    float inflation = 0.025; /* rate of inflation at 2.5% */
    FILE   *data;
    FILE   *new_data;
    float price;
    char  appliance[string_length];

    /* attempt to open files */
    data = fopen(input_file, read);
    new_data = fopen(output_file, write);
```

```
        if (data == NULL || new_data == NULL)
        {
            printf("file cannot be opened\n");
            exit(errno);
        }

        /* read and update every line in the file
           and write the new values to another file */

        while (! feof(data))
        {
            fscanf(data, "%f", &price);
            fgets(appliance, string_length, data);
            price = price + (price * inflation);
            fprintf(new_data, "%7.2f\t%s", price, appliance);
        }

        /* close data files */
        fclose(data);
        fclose(new_data);
}
```

Results written to the file new_data.txt from program ex_04.c being run

```
 405.85 television
 563.75 music centre
1020.85 desk-top computer
 204.95 microwave oven
 307.49 washing machine
 153.70 freezer
```

Directing output to a file is fine until you want to view the contents of the file. In these circumstances it is not always convenient to direct the output to a screen, since the output scrolls off the screen when the file contains a considerable number of lines. Printed output on paper, of the contents of the file, is usually more acceptable. It is possible to direct output that normally appears on a screen, to a text file stored on a magnetic/ optical disk. The contents of the text file can, at the users request, be printed on paper.

For example if a text file had been created using the name **a:\report.txt** then to obtain a print-out of the report in a PC-based environment, the following commands should be given from MSDOS.

```
C:PRINT a:\report.txt.
```

Provided a printer is connected on-line, the contents of the report will be output to the printer.

See appendix C - section C.6 File manipulation - for printing under UNIX

Problem The text file illustrated in figure 14.2 has been created using an editor, and stored under the name **books.txt**.

Each line in the file contains the quantity in stock, the price of the book and the title of a book. For example there is one copy of *Art in Athens* priced £8.95.

Note - there is no *new line* character after the last line in the file.

```
1 8.95 Art in Athens
2 3.75 Birds of Prey
1 7.50 Eagles in the USA
3 5.20 Gone with the Wind
2 3.75 Hate, Lust and Love
3 5.95 Maths for Adults
3 3.75 Modern Farming
3 5.20 Raiders of Planet X
1 8.95 Splitting the Atom
1 3.75 The Invisible Man
2 3.75 The Otter
4 5.95 The Tempest
2 5.95 The Trojan Wars
2 3.75 Under the Seas
2 7.50 Vampire Bats
```

figure 14.2 contents of the books.txt file

A report is to be printed on the contents of this file. The design of a report is made considerably easier if the reader adopts the habit of planning the layout of the report on a report layout sheet, similar to the one shown in figure 14.3. If such a document cannot be obtained then paper pre-ruled into squares with numbered columns can be used. Such a document is an aid towards coding the format strings in the output statements of a program. Notice from the design of the document that when the stock level falls to one item the report indicates that the stock should be replenished. Notice also that totals are calculated for the number of books and value of all the books in stock and printed at the end of the report.

```
                    Report Layout
┌─────────────────────────────────────────────────────────────┐
│123456789012345678901234567890123456789012345678901234567890   │
│          STOCK REPORT ON BOOKS                                │
│quantity    price            title                             │
│       1    8.95 *REORDER* Art in Athens                       │
│       2    3.75           Birds of Prey                       │
│                                                               │
│                                                               │
│number of books in stock 3                                     │
│value of books in stock £ 16.45                                │
└─────────────────────────────────────────────────────────────┘
```

figure 14.3 the layout of the report on books

The algorithm to read the file containing the details of the books and create a new report file is expressed in the following pseudo-code.

open input file for reading
open output file for writing
write headings to the output file

while not end of input file
    read quantity and price of book from input file
    read title of book from input file
    write quantity and price of book to output file

    if quantity <= re-order level then
        write "REORDER" to output file
    else
        write blank spaces to output file

    write title of book to output file
    increase total quantity of books by quantity
    increase total price of books by price

write total quantity of books to output file
write total price of books to output file
close input file
close output file

```
/*
c14_dpp\ex_05.c
program to read a file containing a stock list of books and
write the contents of the file, showing which books to reorder,
and the total number of books together with the total value
of the stock, to another file
*/
#include <stdlib.h>
#include <stdio.h>
#include <errno.h>
#define input_file  "a:\\c14_dpp\\books.txt"
#define output_file "a:\\c14_dpp\\report.txt"
#define read "r"
#define write "w"
#define string_length 25

main()
{
     const int re_order_level = 1;
```

```
            FILE   *books;
            FILE   *report;
            int    quantity;
            float price;
            char   title[string_length];
            int    total_quantity = 0;
            float total_price = 0.0;

    /* attempt to open files */
    books = fopen(input_file, read);
    report = fopen(output_file, write);

    if (books == NULL || report == NULL)
    {
       printf("file cannot be opened\n");
       exit(errno);
    }

    fprintf(report, "                    STOCK REPORT ON BOOKS\n\n");
    fprintf(report, "quantity price                 title\n\n");

    while (! feof(books))
    {
       fscanf(books, "%d%f", &quantity, &price);
       fgets(title, string_length, books);

       fprintf(report, "%8d%6.2f", quantity, price);

       if (quantity <= re_order_level)
          fprintf(report, " *REORDER* ");
       else
          fprintf(report, "            ");

       fprintf(report, "%s", title);

       total_quantity += quantity;
       total_price = total_price + (price * quantity);
    }

    fprintf(report, "\n\nnumber of books in stock %3d\n", total_quantity);
    fprintf(report, "value of books in stock £%7.2f\n", total_price);

    /* close data files */
    fclose(books);
    fclose(report);
}
```

320

Results written to the file report.txt from program ex_05.c being run

```
            STOCK REPORT ON BOOKS

quantity price              title

       1  8.95 *REORDER*    Art in Athens
       2  3.75              Birds of Prey
       1  7.50 *REORDER*    Eagles in the USA
       3  5.20              Gone with the Wind
       2  3.75              Hate, Lust and Love
       3  5.95              Maths for Adults
       3  3.75              Modern Farming
       3  5.20              Raiders of Planet X
       1  8.95 *REORDER*    Splitting the Atom
       1  3.75 *REORDER*    The Invisible Man
       2  3.75              The Otter
       4  5.95              The Tempest
       2  5.95              The Trojan Wars
       2  3.75              Under the Seas
       2  7.50              Vampire Bats

number of books in stock   32
value of books in stock £ 170.15
```

Problem In the final example in this section the poem *I watched a blackbird* by Thomas Hardy 1840-1928 has been created using an editor and stored on disk under the filename **Hardy.txt**. A listing of the poem is given here.

THOMAS
HARDY
1840-1928

> *I watched a blackbird on a budding sycamore*
> *One Easter Day, when sap was stirring twigs to the core;*
> *I saw his tongue, and crocus-coloured bill*
> *Parting and closing as he turned his trill;*
> *Then he flew down, seized on a stem of hay,*
> *And upped to where his building scheme was under way,*
> *As if so sure a nest were never shaped on spray.*

A program is to read the text file, and process each line such that:

(i) The number of letters in each word is analysed, and a frequency count is recorded for word size; for example frequency[1] is the number of one-letter words, frequency[2] is the number of two-letter words, frequency[3] is the number of three-letter words, and so on.

(ii) Each line of text is written to a second file, and the frequency of word lengths in the line are written on the next line of the file as depicted in figure 14.4. For example, in the first line of the poem there are 3 one-letter words, 1 two-letter word, 2 seven-letter words, 1 eight-letter word and 1 nine-letter word.

```
                            Report Layout

123456789012345678901234567890123456789012345678901234567890123456789

I watched a blackbird on a budding sycamore

letters in word   1  2  3  4  5  6  7  8  9  10  11  12  13  14  15
word frequency     3  1  0  0  0  0  2  1  1   0   0   0   0   0   0

One easter day, when sap was stirring twigs to the core;

letters in word   1  2  3  4  5  6  7  8  9  10  11  12  13  14  15
word frequency     0  1  5  2  1  1  0  1  0   0   0   0   0   0   0

I saw his tongue, and crocus-coloured bill

letters in word   1  2  3  4  5  6  7  8  9  10  11  12  13  14  15
word frequency     1  0  3  1  0  2  0  1  0   0   0   0   0   0   0
```

figure 14.4 layout for the word analysis

The pseudo-code design of the program follows.

1   open input file for reading
2   open output file for writing
3   while not end of input file
4   process line of text
5   write information to output file
6   close input file
7   close output file

4   process line of text
4.1   initialise frequency count of words
4.2   read line from input file
4.3   analyse words in line

4.1   *initialise frequency count of words*
4.1.1 *for number of letters in word from 1 to 15*
4.1.2   *set frequency of words to zero*

4.3   *analyse words in line*
4.3.1 *obtain first character in line*
4.3.2 *while not end of line and not end of string*
4.3.3   *if character not a word delimiter then*
4.3.4   *increase letter count by 1*
4.3.5   *else*
4.3.6   *increase frequency of n-lettered word by 1*
4.3.7   *initialise letter counter to zero*
4.3.8   *obtain next character in line*

5   *write information to output file*
5.1   *write line of poem to output file*
5.2   *write "letters in word" to output file*
5.3   *for number of letters in word from 1 to 15*
5.4   *write number of letters in word to output file*
5.5   *write "word frequency" to output file*
5.6   *for number of letters in word from 1 to 15*
5.7   *write word frequency to output file*
5.8   *write blank lines to output file*

```
/*
c14_dpp\ex_06.c
program to analyse the size of words in a passage of text
*/
#include <stdlib.h>
#include <stdio.h>
#include <errno.h>
#define max_length 80
#define max_char 15
#define null 0
#define space 32
#define hyphen 45
#define comma 44
#define period 46
#define colon 58
#define semi_colon 59
#define carriage_return 13
#define line_feed 10

#define read "r"
#define write "w"
```

```
#define input_file "a:\\c14_dpp\\Hardy.txt"
#define output_file "a:\\c14_dpp\\results.txt"

void initialise(int frequency[])
/* function to initialise the frequency count of each word to zero */


{
    int counter;

    for (counter=1; counter <= max_char; counter++)
        frequency[counter] = 0;
}



FILE *open_file(char filename[], char mode[])
/* function to open a file in a specific mode and return
the name of the file if it can be opened, otherwise
return NULL
*/
{
    FILE *file;


    file = fopen(filename, mode);
    if (file == NULL)
    {
        printf("%s cannot be opened\n", filename);
        exit(errno);
    }
    else
        return file;
}

void analysis(char line[], int frequency[])
/* function to calculate the size of each word in one line of text;
the frequencies of word length are stored in an array called frequency */


{
    int  index = 0;
    int  counter = 0;
    char character;

    character = line[index];
    while (index <= max_length && character != null)
    {
        if (character != space && character != hyphen &&
            character != comma && character != period &&
            character != colon && character != semi_colon &&
```

```
            character != carriage_return && character != line_feed)
            counter++;
        else
        {
                frequency[counter]++;
                counter = 0;
        }
        index++;
        character = line[index];
    }
}

void write_info(FILE *filename, char line[], int frequency[])
/* function to copy a line to the output file (filename),
and write the frequency of word sizes on the next lines of
the output file
*/

{
    int counter;

    fprintf(filename, "%s", line);
    fprintf(filename, "\nletters in word ");

    for (counter=1; counter <= max_char; counter++)
        fprintf(filename, "%3d", counter);

    fprintf(filename, "\nword frequency   ");

    for (counter=1; counter <= max_char; counter++)
        fprintf(filename, "%3d", frequency[counter]);

    fprintf(filename, "\n\n");
}

void process_line(FILE *file, char line[], int frequency[])
/* function to read a line from the input file and return the line
as a string of characters
*/

{
    initialise(frequency);
    fgets(line, max_length, file);
    analysis(line, frequency);
}
```

```
main()
{
    FILE *text, *output;
    int  frequency[max_char+1];
    char line[max_length+1];

    text   = open_file(input_file, read);
    output = open_file(output_file, write);

    while (! feof(text))
    {
        process_line(text, line, frequency);
        write_info(output, line, frequency);
    }

    fclose(text);
    fclose(output);
}
```

Results from running program ex_06.c are stored on the file results.txt as shown here

```
I watched a blackbird on a budding sycamore

letters in word   1  2  3  4  5  6  7  8  9 10 11 12 13 14 15
word frequency    3  1  0  0  0  0  2  1  1  0  0  0  0  0  0

One easter day, when sap was stirring twigs to the core;

letters in word   1  2  3  4  5  6  7  8  9 10 11 12 13 14 15
word frequency    0  1  5  2  1  1  0  1  0  0  0  0  0  0  0

I saw his tongue, and crocus-coloured bill

letters in word   1  2  3  4  5  6  7  8  9 10 11 12 13 14 15
word frequency    1  0  3  1  0  2  0  1  0  0  0  0  0  0  0

parting and closing as he turned his trill;

letters in word   1  2  3  4  5  6  7  8  9 10 11 12 13 14 15
word frequency    0  2  2  0  1  1  2  0  0  0  0  0  0  0  0

Then he flew down, seized on a stem of hay,

letters in word   1  2  3  4  5  6  7  8  9 10 11 12 13 14 15
word frequency    1  3  1  4  0  1  0  0  0  0  0  0  0  0  0
```

And upped to where his building scheme was under way,

letters in word	1	2	3	4	5	6	7	8	9	10	11	12	13	14	15
word frequency	0	1	4	0	3	1	0	1	0	0	0	0	0	0	0

As if so sure a nest were never shaped on spray.

letters in word	1	2	3	4	5	6	7	8	9	10	11	12	13	14	15
word frequency	1	4	0	3	2	1	0	0	0	0	0	0	0	0	0

14.5 Binary files

A binary file consists of a sequence of arbitrary bytes that are not in a human-readable form. Such files can only be created by a specific program, they cannot, unlike a text file, be created using an editor.

There are two functions associated with input and output of binary files, **fread** and **fwrite**, respectively. The format of fread is:

size_t fread(void *buffer, size_t size, size_t nritems, FILE *stream);

where the function *fread* reads a specified number of data elements from a stream;

buffer points to the block in which the data will be stored; *size* specifies the size (in bytes) of each element being read; *nritems* specifies the number of items to be read; and *stream* specifies the stream from which the data will be read.

The function *fread* returns the number of complete items read. If this value is less than *nritems*, use *feof* or *ferror* to determine whether the end of file was reached or whether another error occurred.

The *fwrite* function has a similar format to fread:

int fwrite(const void *buffer, size_t size, size_t num, FILE *st);

where the *fwrite* writes up to *num* blocks, each of *size* bytes, from *buffer* to the stream *st*. The stream pointer, if there is one, is incremented by the number of bytes written. However, if an error occurs, the position of the stream pointer or the state of a partially written item are undefined.

The function returns the number of complete items actually written. If an error or end of file condition occurs, this number will be less than *num*. Again the functions *ferror* or *feof* should be used to determine which condition caused *fwrite* to terminate. If either *num* or *size* is zero, the return value will be zero and no bytes are written.

Worked Examples

Problem A binary file is to contain information about members of a swimming club. Each record of the file contains information on the name, sex, age and competition results for each member and can be represented by the following structure.

```
typedef struct   {
                    char name[20];
                    char sex;
                    int  age;
                    int  results[3];
                  } record;
```

Typical records in the file **members.bin** might contain the following data.

```
Jones      M 17 1 2 3
Evans      F 15 1 0 1
```

The entry for competition results shows the placing (1) first, (2) second, (3) third and (0) not placed or absent from the competition for a member over the previous three swimming competitions.

The following algorithm is designed to create a binary file of data.

1   open members file for writing
2   fill an output buffer (array) with records
3   write the contents of the buffer (array) to the members file
4   display the contents of the buffer (array)
5   close members file

2   fill an output buffer (array) with records
2.1   do
2.2   create a record and store in the next consecutive location of the buffer (array)
2.3   while more records to create
2.4   return the size of the buffer (array)

2.2   create a record
2.2.1 input name, sex and age of swimmer
2.2.2 input the last three competition results for the swimmer

4   display contents of buffer (array)
4.1   for every entry in the buffer (array)
4.2   display name, sex and age of swimmer
4.3   display the last three results of the swimmer

```
/* c14_dpp\ex_07.c program to produce a binary file */
#include <stdlib.h>
#include <stdio.h>
#include <errno.h>
#define members_file "a:\\c14_dpp\\members.bin"
#define buffer_size 100
#define write_bin "wb"

typedef struct {
                char name[20];
                char sex;
                int  age;
                int  results[3];
            } record;

FILE *open_file(char filename[], char mode[])
/* function to open a file in a specific mode and return
the name of the file if it can be opened, otherwise
return NULL
*/
{
    FILE *file;

    file = fopen(filename, mode);
    if (file == NULL)
    {
        printf("%s cannot be opened\n", filename);
        exit(errno);
    }
    else
        return file;
}

record create_record(void)
/* function to supply the data fields of a single record */
{
        record swimmer;

        printf("name? "); gets(swimmer.name);
        printf("sex? ");   swimmer.sex = getchar();
        printf("age? ");   scanf("%d", &swimmer.age);
        printf("results? ");
        scanf("%d%d%d", &swimmer.results[0],
                        &swimmer.results[1],
                        &swimmer.results[2]);
        getchar();
        return swimmer;
}
```

```
void fill_buffer(record buffer[], int *size)
/* function to fill the output buffer with records */
{
     int   index = 0;
     char more_data;

     do
     {
        buffer[index] = create_record();
        index++;
        printf("more data Y[es] or N[o]? ");
        more_data=toupper(getchar()); getchar();
     }
     while (more_data == 'Y');
     *size = index;
}


void display_buffer(record buffer[], int size)
/* function to display the contents of a file buffer */
{
     int index;

     for (index=0; index < size; index++)
        printf("%s\t%c %3d %2d%2d%2d\n",
               buffer[index].name, buffer[index].sex, buffer[index].age,
               buffer[index].results[0],
               buffer[index].results[1],
               buffer[index].results[2]);
}

main()
{
     FILE    *members;
     record buffer[buffer_size];
     int     size;

     members = open_file(members_file, write_bin);
     fill_buffer(buffer, &size);
     fwrite(buffer, sizeof(record), size, members);
     display_buffer(buffer, size);
     fclose(members);
}
```

Contents of file members.bin, created from program ex_07.c being run

```
Jones     M 17 1 2 3
Holmes    M 18 1 1 1
Evans     F 15 1 0 1
Peters    F 14 1 1 0
Nichols   M 18 1 2 2
Adams     F 15 1 1 2
Betts     M 17 3 0 1
Jenkins   M 16 1 0 1
Patel     F 15 2 0 1
Morgan    F 15 1 0 3
Phelps    M 17 1 2 1
Smith     F 16 1 1 3
```

Problem The binary file of members that has been created can be used to create two new files of swimmers. A file of male swimmers in the age range (16 < age <= 18) and a file of female swimmers in the age range (14 < age <= 16). The files will contain the names of the eligible members and the total number of points scored by each member over the previous three competitions.

A points system is used to signify how well a swimmer did in the last three competitions. Three points are awarded for first place, two points for second place and one point for third place. No points are awarded for not being placed or being absent from a competition. For example, a member with two first places and one second place would be awarded eight points.

The algorithm used to split the file on the criteria given is:

open members file for reading
open males file for writing
open females file for writing

read entire contents of members file into a buffer (array)

for each record in the buffer (array)
    initialise the points to zero
    calculate the points based on the competition results
    if swimmer is male and aged between 16 and 18 then
        copy name and points to male record buffer
        write contents of male record buffer to male file
    else if swimmer is female and aged between 14 and 16 then
        copy name and points to female record buffer
        write contents of female record buffer to female file

```
        close members file
        close male file
        close female file

        open male file for reading
        open female file for reading

        display contents of male file
        display contents of female file

        close male file
        close female file
```

```c
/*
c14_dpp\ex_08.c
program to read a binary file and create two new binary files
*/
#include <stdlib.h>
#include <stdio.h>
#include <string.h>
#include <errno.h>
#define members_file "a:\\c14_dpp\\members.bin"
#define male_file    "a:\\c14_dpp\\males.bin"
#define female_file  "a:\\c14_dpp\\females.bin"
#define buffer_size 100
#define write_bin "wb"
#define read_bin "rb"

typedef struct {
                char name[20];
                char sex;
                int  age;
                int  results[3];
        } record;

typedef struct {
                char name[20];
                int  points;
        } team_record;

FILE *open_file(char filename[], char mode[])
/* function to open a file in a specific mode and return
the name of the file if it can be opened, otherwise
return NULL
*/
{
    FILE *file;
```

```
      file = fopen(filename, mode);
      if (file == NULL)
      {
         printf("%s cannot be opened\n", filename);
         exit(errno);
      }
      else
         return file;
}

void display_file(FILE *name)
/* function to display the contents of a binary file */
{
      team_record buffer[1];

      fread(buffer, sizeof(team_record), 1, name);
      while (! feof(name))
      {
         printf("%3d %s\n", buffer[0].points, buffer[0].name);
         fread(buffer, sizeof(team_record), 1, name);
      }
      printf("\n");
}

main()
{
      FILE         *members, *males, *females;
      record       buffer[buffer_size];
      team_record male_buffer[1];
      team_record female_buffer[1];
      int          size;
      int          index, competition;
      int          points;

      members = open_file(members_file, read_bin);
      males   = open_file(male_file, write_bin);
      females = open_file(female_file, write_bin);

      size = fread(buffer, sizeof(record), buffer_size, members);

      for (index=0; index < size; index++)
      {
         points=0;

         for (competition=0; competition < 3; competition++)
            if (buffer[index].results[competition] > 0)
               points = points + 4 - buffer[index].results[competition];
```

```
        if (buffer[index].sex == 'M' &&
            buffer[index].age > 16 && buffer[index].age <=18)
        {
            strcpy(male_buffer[0].name, buffer[index].name);
            male_buffer[0].points = points;
            fwrite(male_buffer, sizeof(team_record), 1, males);
        }
        else if (buffer[index].sex == 'F' &&
                 buffer[index].age > 14 && buffer[index].age <= 16)
        {
            strcpy(female_buffer[0].name, buffer[index].name);
            female_buffer[0].points = points;
            fwrite(female_buffer, sizeof(team_record), 1, females);
        }
    }
    fclose(members);
    fclose(males);
    fclose(females);

    males = open_file(male_file, read_bin);
    females = open_file(female_file, read_bin);

    display_file(males);
    display_file(females);

    fclose(males);
    fclose(females);
}
```

Results from program ex_08.c being run

```
6 Jones
9 Holmes
7 Nichols
4 Betts
8 Phelps

6 Evans
8 Adams
5 Patel
4 Morgan
7 Smith
```

Problem Having successfully split the members file into two separate files, it is required to read each file and produce a list of the three best male swimmers and the three best female swimmers, based upon the highest number of points scored over the previous three competitions.

The following algorithm reads the contents of the **males.bin** file into an array, sorts the contents of the array into descending order using points as a key, and displays the first three records in the array. This process is repeated for the **females.bin** file.

open males file for input
read the entire contents of the males file into a buffer
sort the contents of the buffer into descending order on points scored
if size of buffer >= 3 then
    display top-three swimmers from the buffer
close males file

```
/* c14_dpp\ex_09.c program to read a binary files sort them on points
scored and display the first three records in each file */

#include <stdio.h>
#include <stdlib.h>
#include <errno.h>
#define male_file    "a:\\c14_dpp\\males.bin"
#define female_file  "a:\\c14_dpp\\females.bin"
#define buffer_size 100
#define read_bin "rb"

typedef struct {
               char name[20];
               int  points;
            } team_record;

FILE *open_file(char filename[], char mode[])
/* function to open a file in a specific mode and return
the name of the file if it can be opened, otherwise
return NULL
*/
{
    FILE *file;

    file = fopen(filename, mode);
    if (file == NULL)
    {
        printf("%s cannot be opened\n", filename);
        exit(errno);
```

```
    }
    else
        return file;
}

void top_three(team_record buffer[])
/* function to display the first three records from an array */
{
    int index;

    for (index=0; index < 3; index++)
        printf("%2d %s\n", buffer[index].points, buffer[index].name);

    printf("\n\n");
}

int compare(const void *n1, const void *n2)
{
    return (*(team_record *)n2).points - (*(team_record *)n1).points;
}

main()
{
    FILE          *males, *females;
    team_record buffer[buffer_size];
    int           size;

    males   = open_file(male_file, read_bin);
    females = open_file(female_file, read_bin);

    size = fread(buffer, sizeof(team_record), buffer_size, males);
    qsort(buffer, size, sizeof(team_record), compare);
    if (size >= 3)
    {
        printf("male swimming team\n");
        top_three(buffer);
    }

    size = fread(buffer, sizeof(team_record), buffer_size, females);
    qsort(buffer, size, sizeof(team_record), compare);
    if (size >= 3)
    {
        printf("female swimming team\n");
        top_three(buffer);
    }

    fclose(males);
    fclose(females);
}
```

Results from program ex_09.c being run

```
male swimming team
9 Holmes
8 Phelps
7 Nichols

female swimming team
8 Adams
7 Smith
6 Evans
```

14.6 Merging files

If two binary files contain records that are already sorted on a key, then it is possible to create a third file using the contents of the original two files such that the information held on the third file is also sorted on the same key.

The technique of merging two binary files involves the interleaving of the records to form a new binary file. The algorithm for merging the two files relies upon the fact that both files are already sorted on a key.

The keys of the two files to be merged are compared, if the keys are in ascending order, the record with the lower key value is written to the new file. The file that supplied the record is then read again and processing continues until the end of both files is encountered.

In the following algorithm to merge two files, it is necessary to compare the key of *file_a* with the key of *file_b*. However, when the end of either file is reached it is necessary to set the key field, of the file that has ended, to a higher value than all the other keys in the two files. The purpose of this practice is to force the remainder of the records in the remaining file to be copied to *file_c*. The first character in the key field is substituted with ~ (ASCII code 126), thus setting the key to *high_key*.

The action of reading a record must be followed by testing for the end of the file, and if this condition is true, then setting the key field to a *high_key*.

open file_a and file_b for reading (the two files to be merged)
open file_c for writing (the file that eventually contains the records from file_a and file_b)
read file_a, at end of file set key of file_a to high_key
read file_b, at end of file set key of file_b to high_key
while not end of both files
    if key file_a < key file_b then
        write file_a record to file_c
        read file_a, at end of file set key of file_a to high_key
    else
        write file_b record to file_c
        read file_b, at end of file set key of file_b to high_key
close all files

The reader is recommended to desk check this algorithm. Use the data displayed after program ex_08.c was run, but first manually sort the data for each file on the key surname.

In the next program the binary data files **males.bin** and **females.bin** are both sorted using the surname as the key. The files are then merged using the two-way merging algorithm and the contents of the new file containing the merged data is then displayed on the screen.

```c
/* c14_dpp\ex_10.c
program to sort two binary files into alphabetical sequence
merge the files into one and display the contents of the new file */

#include <stdio.h>
#include <errno.h>
#include <stdlib.h>
#include <string.h>
#define male_file     "a:\\c14_dpp\\males.bin"
#define female_file   "a:\\c14_dpp\\females.bin"
#define merged_file   "a:\\c14_dpp\\merged.bin"
#define buffer_size 100
#define read_bin "rb"
#define write_bin "wb"
#define tilde "~"   /* high value */

typedef struct {
                char name[20];
                int  points;
            } team_record;

FILE *open_file(char filename[], char mode[])
/* function to open a file in a specific mode and return
the name of the file if it can be opened, otherwise
return NULL
*/
{
    FILE *file;

    file = fopen(filename, mode);
    if (file == NULL)
    {
        printf("%s cannot be opened\n", filename);
        exit(errno);
    }
    else
        return file;
}

void write_records(team_record buffer[], int size, FILE *name)
/* function to copy the contents of the buffer to a binary file */
```

```
{
     fwrite(buffer, sizeof(team_record), size, name);
}

void merge_files(FILE *file_1, FILE *file_2, FILE *file_3)
/* function to perform a two-way merge to produce a third file */
{
     const char  high_value[1] = tilde;
     team_record buffer_1[1], buffer_2[1], buffer_3[1];

     fread(buffer_1, sizeof(team_record), 1, file_1);
     if (feof(file_1)) strcpy(buffer_1[0].name, high_value);
     fread(buffer_2, sizeof(team_record), 1, file_2);
     if (feof(file_2)) strcpy(buffer_2[0].name, high_value);

     while (! feof(file_1) || ! feof(file_2))
     {
         if (strcmp(buffer_1[0].name, buffer_2[0].name) < 0)
         {
             strcpy(buffer_3[0].name, buffer_1[0].name);
             buffer_3[0].points = buffer_1[0].points;
             fwrite(buffer_3, sizeof(team_record), 1, file_3);
             fread(buffer_1, sizeof(team_record), 1, file_1);
             if (feof(file_1)) strcpy(buffer_1[0].name, high_value);
         }
         else
         {
             strcpy(buffer_3[0].name, buffer_2[0].name);
             buffer_3[0].points = buffer_2[0].points;
             fwrite(buffer_3, sizeof(team_record), 1, file_3);
             fread(buffer_2, sizeof(team_record), 1, file_2);
             if (feof(file_2)) strcpy(buffer_2[0].name, high_value);
         }
     }
}


void display_file(FILE *name)
/* function to display the contents of a binary file */
{
     team_record buffer[1];

     fread(buffer, sizeof(team_record), 1, name);
     while (! feof(name))
     {
         printf("%3d %s\n", buffer[0].points, buffer[0].name);
         fread(buffer, sizeof(team_record), 1, name);
     }
     printf("\n");
}
```

```
int compare(const void *n1, const void *n2)
{
    return strcmp((*(team_record *)n1).name, (*(team_record *)n2).name);
}


main()
{
    FILE        *males, *females, *merged;
    team_record buffer[buffer_size];
    int         size;

    males   = open_file(male_file, read_bin);
    females = open_file(female_file, read_bin);

    /* read files independently into buffer, sort records and write
       records back to files */

    size = fread(buffer, sizeof(team_record), buffer_size, males);
    qsort(buffer, size, sizeof(team_record), compare);
    fclose(males);
    males = open_file(male_file, write_bin);
    write_records(buffer, size, males);
    fclose(males);

    size = fread(buffer, sizeof(team_record), buffer_size, females);
    qsort(buffer, size, sizeof(team_record), compare);
    fclose(females);
    females = open_file(female_file, write_bin);
    write_records(buffer, size, females);
    fclose(females);

    /* open files male and female files for reading and merged
       file for writing */

    males   = open_file(male_file, read_bin);
    females = open_file(female_file, read_bin);
    merged  = open_file(merged_file, write_bin);

    /* perform a two-way merge on the male and female files
       writing the result to the merged file */

    merge_files(males, females, merged);

    fclose(males);
    fclose(females);
    fclose(merged);
```

```
    /* open merged file for reading so that its contents
       can be displayed */


    merged = open_file(merged_file, read_bin);

    display_file(merged);

    fclose(merged);
}
```

Results from program ex_10.c being run

```
8 Adams
4 Betts
6 Evans
9 Holmes
6 Jones
4 Morgan
7 Nichols
5 Patel
8 Phelps
7 Smith
```

14.7 Direct access

The organisation of text and binary files means that it is necessary to read each record in a file until the required record is located. With a *direct access* file it is possible to go directly to the record that is required without having to search through the records in the file.

The function **fseek** moves the file pointer associated with the specified stream. The pointer is moved to a location that is offset bytes from the specified origin. The next operation on the stream will take place at the new location.

The format of fseek is **int fseek(FILE *stream, long offset, int origin);**

where **stream** specifies the file name; **offset** the number of bytes to move from the origin, and **origin** specifies the reference location for the move. Origin must be one of the following values:

SEEK_SET   beginning of the file;
SEEK_CUR   current file position;
SEEK_END   end of file.

Problem In the final example of the chapter data from both a text file and a direct access file are processed. A compact disk player enables the user to select the tracks on a compact disk in random order. This idea can be incorporated into a program to demonstrate the use of a direct access file in allowing a user to select any track at random and the artist's name, title of the song/ tune and the length of playing time to be displayed on a screen.

Each line in the text file is ordered by track number, starting at track 1, followed by track 2, etc. A sample of the data held on the file follows implying that *Simply Red* is at track 1, *Robert Palmer* at track 2, etc.

```
3.23 Simply Red        If you don't know me by now
4.48 Robert Palmer     Mercy mercy me I want you
4.09 Paul Young        Wherever I leave my hat
3.35 Tina Turner       Let's stay together
  .      .                 .
  .      .                 .
```

The algorithm for the program is:

1 open music text file for reading
2 open CD binary file for writing
3 transfer data from the music text file to the CD binary file
4 close music text file
5 close CD binary file
6 open CD binary file for reading
7 read CD binary file by direct access and display information
8 close CD binary file

3   transfer data from music text file to the CD binary file
3.1   while not end of music text file
3.2   read line of music text file into buffer
3.3   copy contents of buffer to CD binary file
3.4   increase line count by 1
3.5   return number of lines read from music text file

7   read CD binary file by direct access and display information
7.1   input track required
7.2   while track number in range of CD file
7.3   seek track on CD file
7.4   read record into buffer
7.5   display information from track
7.6   input track required

```
/*
c14_dpp\ex_11.c
program to demonstrate direct access to a binary file
*/
#include <stdlib.h>
#include <stdio.h>
#include <errno.h>
#define music_file "a:\\c14_dpp\\music.txt"
#define cd_file    "a:\\c14_dpp\\cd.bin"

#define read "r"
#define read_bin "rb"
#define write_bin "wb"

typedef struct {
                float duration;
                char  artist_title[60];
            } information;

FILE *data;            /* text file */
FILE *compact_disk;    /* random access file */

FILE *open_file(char filename[], char mode[])
/* function to open file in a specific mode and return
the name of the file if it can be opened otherwise return NULL
*/
{
    FILE *file;

    file = fopen(filename, mode);
    if (file == NULL)
    {
        printf("%s cannot be opened\n", filename);
        exit(errno);
    }
    else
        return file;
}


int transfer(FILE *file_1, FILE *file_2)
/* function to read a text file, transfer the information to a
   binary file and return the number of lines read */
{
    information buffer[1];
    int         lines = 0;

    while (! feof(file_1))
    {
```

343

```
        /* read a single line from the text file */
        fscanf(file_1, "%f", &buffer[0].duration);
        fgets(buffer[0].artist_title, 60, file_1);

        /* transfer this line to the binary file */
        fwrite(buffer, sizeof(information), 1, file_2);
        lines++;
    }
    return lines;
}


void track_selector(FILE *name, long int max_track)
/* function to select the information stored on a particular track */
{
    int         track;
    information buffer[1];

    printf("track? "); scanf("%d", &track);
    while (track > 0 && track <= max_track)
    {
        fseek(name, (long int) (track-1) * sizeof(information), SEEK_SET);
        fread(buffer, sizeof(information), 1, name);
        printf("duration:    %5.2f minutes\n", buffer[0].duration);
        printf("artist/title: %s\n", buffer[0].artist_title);
        printf("track? "); scanf("%d", &track);
    }
}



main()
{
    int tracks;

    data         = open_file(music_file, read);
    compact_disk = open_file(cd_file, write_bin);

    tracks = transfer(data, compact_disk);
    fclose(compact_disk);

    compact_disk = open_file(cd_file, read_bin);
    track_selector(compact_disk, tracks);

    fclose(data);
    fclose(compact_disk);
}
```

Results from program ex_11.c being run

```
track? 10
duration:        4.51 minutes
artist/title: Kenny Thomas        Thinking about your love

track? 5
duration:        4.14 minutes
artist/title: Lisa Stansfield     Change

track? 3
duration:        4.09
artist/title: Paul Young          Wherever I lay my hat

track? 0
```

14.8 Summary

☐   All input and output in C is from streams. A stream can be regarded as a file, however, it is not confined to disk or tape files, but extends to other devices such as keyboard, screen and printer.

☐   Input and output can be redirected using command line parameters.

☐   A file can be opened for reading as long as it exists. However, a file opened for writing need not already exist. If it does the original file will be overwritten. A file can also be opened in an append mode, in which case data can be inserted at the end of a file.

☐   The name of a file can be input into a program implicitly at the time of writing the program; as a text string at run-time; or as a parameter in a command line at run-time.

☐   A text file is a collection of ASCII characters separated into lines by *new line* characters. A text file can be created using either an editor or a program.

☐   When creating a text file it is important to know whether the last line in the file is terminated with a *new line* character. If a *new line* exists then the last line containing text will be processed twice unless the technique of reading ahead is adopted. This technique involves reading a line, then testing for the end of the file. The coding in the program c14_dpp\ex_03.c would be modified to using the read ahead technique if a *new line* had been present after the last line in the file.

```
fscanf(data,"%f",&price);fgets(appliance,string_length,data);
while (! feof(data))
{
    printf("%6.2f\t%s",price, appliance);
    fscanf(data,"%f",&price);fgets(appliance,string_length,data);
}
```

□ The <stdio.h> header file lists the following functions for processing text files:

> for output - **fputc**, **fputs** and **fprintf**;
> for input - **fgetc**, **fgets** and **fscanf**;
> for detecting the end of the file - **feof**;
> for detecting an error - **ferror**.

□ Binary files cannot be created using an editor, but are a product of a specific program. Information is read or written to binary files in blocks of data using the functions **fread** and **fwrite** respectively.

□ Direct access files are normally binary files. The position of any record in the file can be specified relative to either the beginning of the file (SEEK_SET), current file position (SEEK_CUR) or end of file (SEEK_END). The file position is then located using **fseek**.

14.9 Questions - *answers begin on page 494*

[1]. Create a text file *food.txt* containing the input data required for the "Ben's Breakfast Bar" program (c7_dpp\ex_10.c) described in chapter 7, section 7.6. Using redirection, re-run this program so that data is read from the text file that you have created and the output is directed to a second text file of your choice. List the contents of both files.

2. Using an editor create a file *booze.txt* that contains the details of items of stock in a bar. Each line in the file contains the data: *stock quantity*, *unit price* and *description*; for example a line of text might contain: **3 15.00 Brandy** which represents 3 bottles of Brandy at £15.00 per bottle.

Write a program to read each line from the text file *booze.txt* and create a report *stock.txt* similar to that illustrated in figure 14.5, where the value of the stock is the product of the respective quantity and price.

```
                          Report Layout

12345678901234567890123456789012345678901234567890
          BAR STOCK REPORT

QUANTITY PRICE    VALUE DESCRIPTION

3          15.00  45.00 Brandy
5          10.50  52.50 Gin
5          12.00  60.00 Rum
10          9.50  95.00 Vodka
8          12.20  97.60 Whiskey

TOTAL         £  350.10
```

figure 14.5 report on bar stock

[3]. A text file *viewers.txt* contains the following three fields per line.

    category of programme
    estimated size of viewing audience (millions)
    name of a television programme

where the category of programme is coded using a single character as follows:

    D - drama
    L - light entertainment
    M - music
    S - science fiction

A typical record from the file might contain the following data:

```
D 5.25 NYPD Blue
```

and indicates that the television programme NYPD Blue was watched by 5.25 million viewers, and falls in the category of drama.

Using an editor create the text file with programmes of your own choice such that the contents of this file is ordered on the category code as the key. This will group all the drama programmes together, all the light entertainment programmes together, etc.

Write a program to input a category code and generate a report on the screen similar to that shown in figure 14.6. This report lists the names of all the programs in the chosen category, together with the audience viewing figures and finally the total number of viewers who watched programmes in that category.

```
                        Report Layout

12345678901234567890123456789012345678901234567890123456789 0

 CATEGORY - DRAMA

audience           programme
millions

 5.25              NYPD Blue
 7.45              Murder She Wrote
 7.50              L.A.Law

20.20   total audience
```

figure 14.6 report on audience viewing figures

4. A multiple-choice questionnaire allows participants one of four possible answers per question. For example:

Question: *How many times a day do you brush your teeth?*

Answer: *(a) never*
    (b) once
    (c) twice
    (d) more than twice

In a survey it is possible to record a participant's answers as a string of letters, for example, the string

baaabdcbbbbbdddddaaaaacccdccccccccbbbb

may represent answers to forty different questions from a survey.

The string of data can at present be stored in forty bytes of storage (+ one byte for the terminating null character). If such information is to be stored for many hundreds of thousands of participants then storage capacity of the order of Megabytes will be required.

To save on storage space the strings can be compressed by introducing a new coding regime. For example there is much repetition in this string

aaa
bbbbb
dddddd
.
.

If a character is repeated more than three times then it may be encoded using a special symbol that indicates repetition @ followed by the number of characters being repeated, followed by the character being repeated.

aaa could be represented by @3a but this does nothing to improve storage space;
bbbbb could be represented by @5b giving a saving of two bytes;
dddddd could be represented by @6d giving a saving of three bytes.

Using this technique the example string can be compressed into:

baaabdc@5b@6d@5acccd@9c@4b

saving a total of fourteen bytes.

Create a text file *data.txt* containing lines of strings similar to the one shown in the example. The maximum string length should be restricted to 80 characters.

Write a program to read each line in the text file, encode each line using the technique described, and write the new encoded strings to both the screen and another text file *new_data.txt*. This program should maintain totals for the number of characters processed in *data.txt* and the number of characters written to the file *new_data.txt*. Using these figures compute and display the percentage compression gained.

Extend the program to read each line in the file *new_data.txt*, decode the information and display it on the screen.

[5](a). Write a program to create a binary file *account.bin* that contains records about a person's transactions for a credit card account. A format for a record is given as:

    date of transaction - format MmmDD
    amount of transaction - maximum value 9999.99
    credit or debit C or D
    description of the transaction - maximum 80 characters

A typical transaction record might contain the following information

`Dec18 75.50 D Good Food Restaurant`

The file should, at the time of creation, be ordered on the date of the transaction.

(b). Write a second program to read the file *account.bin* and create a text file *statemnt.txt* containing a monthly credit card statement similar to the one shown in figure 14.7. Assume for the purpose of this exercise that the name and address of the account, account number and date of issue are literals coded in the program and not variables.

```
┌─────────────────────────────────────────────────────────────┐
│                      Report Layout                            │
├─────────────────────────────────────────────────────────────┤
│12345678901234567890123456789012345678901234567890            │
│              CREDIT CARD ACCOUNT                              │
│                                                              │
│Mr.Henry J.Smithers          5115 0042 2345 6000             │
│Hatton Gardens                                                │
│Liverpool                    31/12/94                         │
│                                                              │
├─────────────────────────────────────────────────────────────┤
│Dec01   550.00       balance outstanding                     │
│Dec10   250.00       XYZ Supermarket                         │
│Dec13   150.00       Toy Fair                                │
│Dec18    75.50       Good Food Restaurant                    │
│Dec21   250.00CR     payment received                        │
│Dec24   350.00       Speedy Travel Co                        │
│                                                              │
│       £1125.50      new balance                             │
└─────────────────────────────────────────────────────────────┘
```

figure 14.7 monthly credit card statement

6. An alphabetic key is used to access a record position in a direct access file. The size of the file is limited to just twenty records. The alphabetic key must first be transformed into a number in the range 0..19, using a hashing algorithm, before access to the file is possible.

For example, the name **George** can be transformed into a number by summing the corresponding ASCII code for each letter and finding the remainder after dividing the sum by 20 (the maximum number of records in the file).

G=71; **e**=101; **o**=111; **r**=114; **g**=103; **e**=101

The alphabetic key George is transformed into the numeric key:

(71+101+111+114+103+101) modulus 20
= 601 modulus 20
= 1

The name George has generated a record position 1, therefore information relating to the key George may be stored at this record position in a direct access file. However, using the same hashing algorithm, there may be other names that also generate the same record position as George. This is known as a collision.

(a). Write a program to input and store ten names together with the annual birth date for the corresponding person in a direct access file. Generate the record positions using the hashing algorithm described. If a name causes a collision then use different names until the collision is avoided. When ten names and birth dates have been stored display the positions and contents of these records. For example part of this listing might contain the following information:

```
record      person      birthdate
position

0           Hazel       23 September
1           George      18 February
2           Jane        11 October
3
.
.
```

(b). Either adapt part (a) or write a second program to input a name, convert the name into a record position using the same hashing algorithm. Access a record in the direct access file using the record position generated, compare the name key with the name stored in the record and if this is the same then display the birth date of the person.

Chapter 15
Lists and trees

In chapter 11 the reader was introduced to the concept of a pointer and the creation of dynamic arrays. Within this chapter the subject of dynamic data structures is taken further through the discussion of linked lists and binary trees. By the end of the chapter the reader should have a knowledge of the following topics.

- [ ] The creation of a linked list.

- [ ] Displaying the contents of a linked list.

- [ ] Searching a linked list and the insertion and deletion of nodes in the list.

- [ ] First In First Out (FIFO) queues.

- [ ] Last In First Out (LIFO) stacks.

- [ ] The construction of a binary tree.

- [ ] The different techniques for traversing a binary tree.

- [ ] Binary tree maintenance.

15.1 Linked lists

In chapter 11 it was stated that a pointer is an identifier that does not store a scalar data value, but stores an address of where to find the data in memory. This address literally points to where the data is stored. A self-referential structure is a structure containing a field with a pointer to the same structure. For example, figure 15.1 illustrates a record containing two fields, the first will store a string of characters *word[80]* and the second is a pointer *link* to data of type *struct record*. If this structure is defined to be a *node*, then the pointer is in effect pointing to data contained within another node.

```
struct record {
                  char word[80];
                  struct record *link;
           };
typedef struct record node;
```

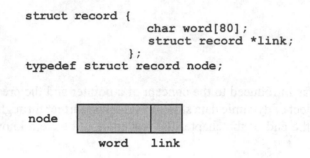

figure 15.1 A description of a node

When a pointer variable is declared, the declaration only allocates storage space for the pointer and does not allocate storage space for the information being pointed at by the pointer. If a pointer *ptr_to_first* is declared as:

```
node *ptr_to_first;
```

then it will be necessary to allocate memory space to store the data being pointed at, by using the function *malloc*. The statement

```
ptr_to_first = malloc(sizeof(node));
```

allocates enough memory to store data in a node. However, the node does not contain any data at this stage. But the node is a record containing two fields, therefore, to store data into these fields it will be necessary to use the dot (.) notation, by qualifying the variable name with the name of the field. The *word* and *link* fields can both be accessed by ***ptr_to_first.word** and ***ptr_to_first.link** respectively. C uses an operator -> which is a combination of the indirection operator (*) and the dot(.) notation, and as a result access to the word and link fields can be through **ptr_to_first->word** and **ptr_to_first->link** respectively. Data can be assigned to the fields by the following statements.

```
strcpy(ptr_to_first->word, "apple");
ptr_to_first->link = NULL;
```

The resulting structure would be a single node containing the word *apple* and the NULL pointer. A NULL pointer is used to indicate that a pointer variable does not currently point to data of a particular type.

In the first program in this chapter a linked list is built containing the three nodes illustrated in figure 15.2. In this example it has been necessary to declare two further pointers, *ptr_to_second* and *ptr_to_third* that respectively point to the second and third nodes in the linked list. Notice that as a means of linking the first node with the second it is necessary to allocate memory space for the second node by **ptr_to_first ->link = malloc(sizeof(node))**. The second node can then be pointed at by **ptr_to_second = ptr_to_first ->link**. The word field in this second node is then assigned the value *banana*, and the link in this second node is used to allocate memory space for the third node. The variable **ptr_to_third** is then made to point at the third node by **ptr_to_third = ptr_to_second->link**. The third node is assigned value *date* and the link in this node is set to NULL indicating the end of the linked list and depicted as / in figure 15.2. The contents of the list can be displayed by printing the contents of the word field for the three nodes that are respectively **ptr_to_first->word, ptr_to_second->word** and **ptr_to_third->word**.

```
/*
c15_dpp\ex_01.c
program to create and display a linked list containing three nodes
*/

#include <stdio.h>
#include <stdlib.h>
#include <string.h>

struct record {
                char            word[80];
                struct record *link;
            };

typedef struct record node;

main()
{
    node *ptr_to_first, *ptr_to_second, *ptr_to_third;

    ptr_to_first = malloc(sizeof(node));
    strcpy(ptr_to_first->word, "apple");
    ptr_to_first->link = malloc(sizeof(node));
    ptr_to_second = ptr_to_first->link;
    strcpy(ptr_to_second->word, "banana");
    ptr_to_second->link = malloc(sizeof(node));
    ptr_to_third = ptr_to_second->link;
    strcpy(ptr_to_third->word, "date");
    ptr_to_third->link = NULL;
    printf("%s\n", ptr_to_first->word);
    printf("%s\n", ptr_to_second->word);
    printf("%s\n", ptr_to_third->word);
}
```

Results from program ex_01.c being run

```
apple
banana
date
```

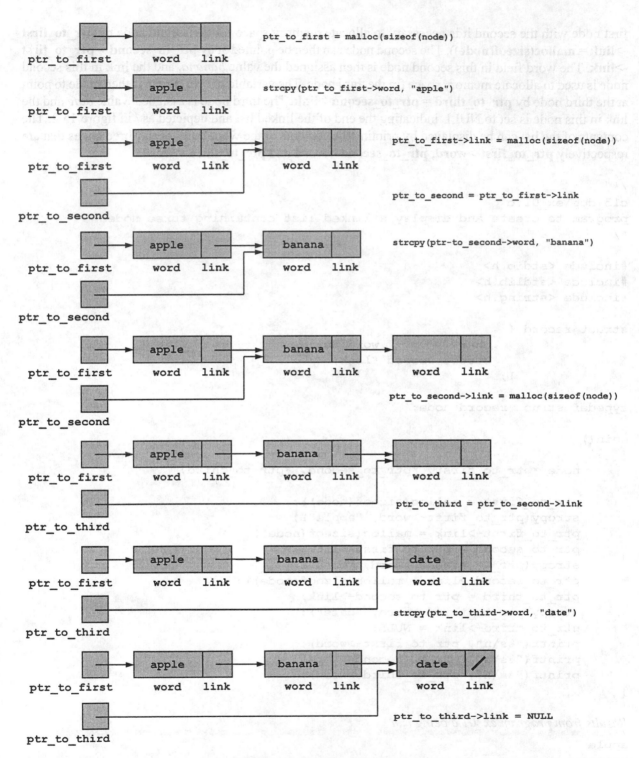

figure 15.2 Building a linked list

The second program in this section illustrates how to create and display a linked list of any size. The linked list can be created using two functions, the first *create_list* allows the user to input words into the list and manipulates the pointer to the next node. The second function *create_node* allocates space for a new node and stores a word together with a NULL pointer in the node. The process of building nodes is illustrated in figure 15.3 and should be studied in conjunction with the code in procedures create_list and create_node found in the program c15_dpp\ex_02.c. Initially the pointer *head* is assigned the value NULL and passed as a parameter to the function create_list. Upon entering create_list the user is invited to type a word at the keyboard and provided it is not the terminating character both the head of the list and the word are passed as parameters to the function create_node. The function create_node stores the word in a node and assigns the link as NULL and returns a pointer to the newly created node. Upon returning to create_list the pointer head is assigned the value returned by create_node, resulting in the head pointing to the first node in the linked list. Another pointer *last* is also assigned to point to the first node in the list.

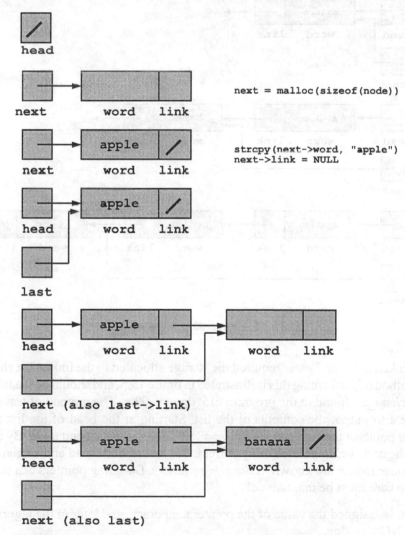

figure 15.3 Building a linked list of any size

The user inputs a second word, and provided it is not the terminating symbol, the function create_node is called again this time passing a pointer *last_link* to the next node to be created and the word to be inserted into the new node. Upon returning from create_node *last->link* is updated to point at the second node and *last* is then assigned to point at the second node. The process continues until the user inputs the terminating symbol.

Figure 15.4 illustrates how to traverse a linked list in order to display its contents on a screen. The technique requires writing the contents of *current->word*, then replacing the value of the pointer *current* by *current->link* which is a pointer to the next node in the list. When the value of current is NULL the end of the list will have been reached. This figure should be studied in conjunction with the function *list_out* found in program c15_dpp\ex_02.c.

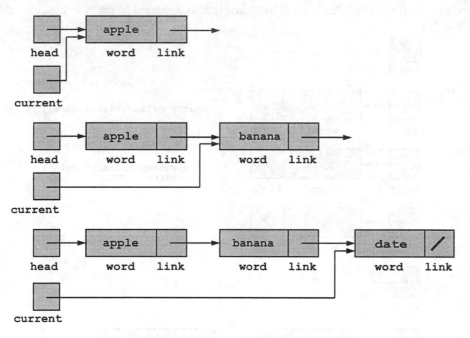

figure 15.4 traversing a linked list

Finally when the linked list is no longer required the storage allocated to the linked list should be returned to the heap. The method of performing this is illustrated in figure 15.5, and should be studied in conjunction with the function *clean_up* found in the program c15_dpp\ex_02.c. The method of traversing the linked list is similar to that to output the contents of the list. Starting at the head of the list two pointers are introduced, *current* points at the first node and *temporary* points at the second node. By de-allocating the storage space for the node being pointed at by current, this leaves both head and current with nothing to point at and as a consequence are known as *dangling* pointers. Dangling pointers can lead to some error prone situations, so care must be maintained!

The pointer current is assigned the value of the pointer temporary, and later in the algorithm, the pointer head is assigned a NULL value.

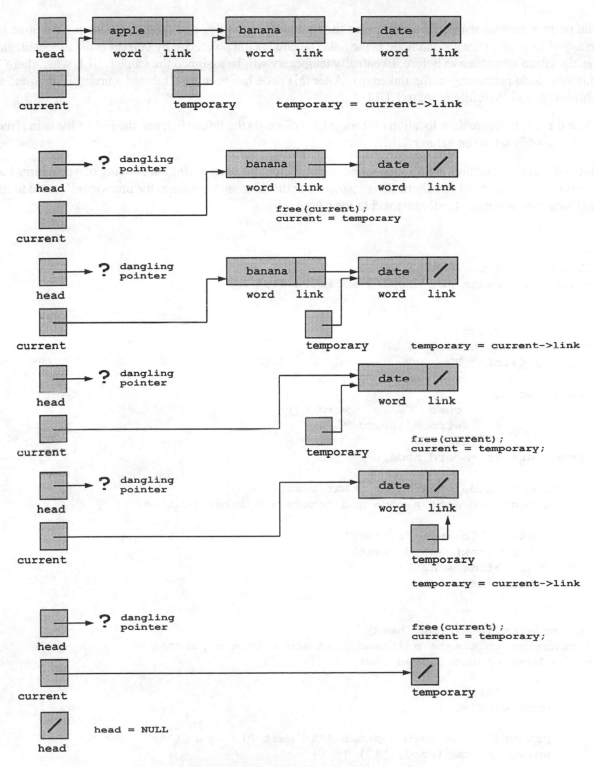

figure 15.5 de-allocation of storage space

The pointer current is in effect pointing at the first node in the list, and the pointer temporary must be arranged to point at the second node in the list. The node being pointed at by current is de-allocated, and the algorithm continues as before. Eventually temporary will be assigned the value NULL when there is only one node remaining in the linked list. After this node has been de-allocated, current is assigned to temporary, and therefore is set to NULL.

Since there is no more de-allocation of storage to perform on the linked list, and the linked list is in effect empty, head is set at the value NULL.

Note - dynamic structures are only allocated memory from the heap during the running of a program. The function *clean_up* is not strictly necessary since after the program terminates the memory allocated to the data structure is automatically restored to the heap.

```
/*
c15_dpp\ex_02.c
program to create and display a linked list
*/

#include <stdio.h>
#include <stdlib.h>
#include <string.h>

struct record {
                char            word[80];
                struct record *link;
            };
typedef struct record node;

node *create_node(node *next, char text[])
/* function to create a node and return a pointer to it */
{
        next=malloc(sizeof(node));
        strcpy(next->word, text);
        next->link = NULL;
        return next;
}


node *create_list(node *head)
/* function to create a linked list and return a pointer
to the head of the linked list */
{
        node *last;
        char word[80];

        printf("input word - enter ! to exit "); scanf("%s", word);
        while (strcmp(word, "!") != 0)
        {
            if (head == NULL)
```

```
            {
                head = create_node(head, word);
                last = head;
            }
            else
            {
                last->link = create_node(last->link, word);
                last = last->link;
            }
            printf("input word - enter ! to exit "); scanf("%s", word);
        }
        return head;
}

void list_out(node *head)
/* function to display the contents of a linked list */
{
        node *current;

        current = head;
        printf("\n\n");
        if (current == NULL)
            printf("list empty\n");
        else
        {
            while (current != NULL)
            {
                printf("%s\n", current->word);
                current = current->link;
            }
        }
}

node *clean_up(node *head)
/* function to deallocate storage space for nodes and
return memory back to the heap */
{
        node *current, *temporary;

        current = head;
        while (current != NULL)
        {
                temporary = current->link;
                free(current);
                current = temporary;
        }
        head = NULL;
        return head;
}
```

```
main()
{
      node *head = NULL;

      head = create_list(head);
      list_out(head);
      head = clean_up(head);
      list_out(head);
}
```

Results from program ex_02.c being run

```
input word - enter ! to exit apple
input word - enter ! to exit banana
input word - enter ! to exit date
input word - enter ! to exit fig
input word - enter ! to exit lemon
input word - enter ! to exit orange
input word - enter ! to exit !

apple
banana
date
fig
lemon
orange


list empty
```

15.2 Insertion and deletion

In order to maintain a linked list it will be necessary to insert new nodes into the list and delete redundant nodes from the list. The method of insertion and deletion of nodes is straightforward, but relies on the list having first been searched for the position to insert a new node or the position of removal of an existing node. The prototype for the function *search* is given as:

```
node *search(node *head, char key[], boolean *found);
```

The function *search* relies upon the fact that the contents of the list **must be ordered** on a particular key. In the examples given so far the names of the fruits have been input in alphabetical sequence. When searching for a node that already exists in order to delete it, if the node is found the function returns a pointer to the previous node, unless the node is at the head of the list, in which case the function returns a NULL value.

1. The key is located as the first node in the ordered list

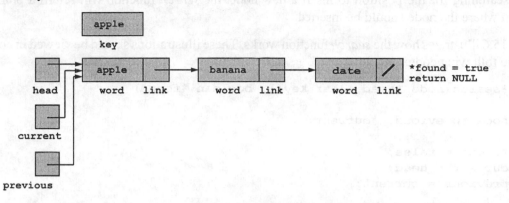

2. The key is located in any position after the first node in the ordered list

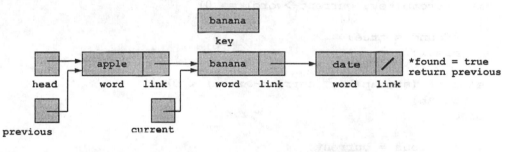

3. The key does not lie within the range of values

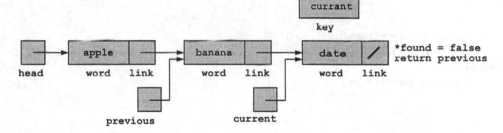

4. The search for the key has reached the end of the list without success

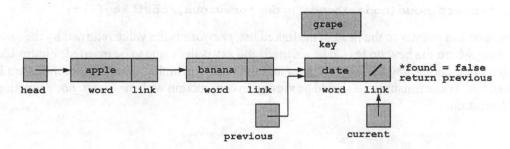

figure 15.6 search function mechanism

When searching for the position to insert a new node, the *search* function will return a pointer to the position where the node should be inserted.

Figure 15.6 illustrates how the *search* function works. These illustrations should be viewed in conjunction with the following code.

```
node *search(node *head, char key[], boolean *found)
{
    node *previous, *current;

    *found = false;
    current = head;
    previous = current;

    while (current != NULL)
    {
        if (strcmp(key, current->word) == 0)
        {
            *found = true;
            break;
        }
        else if (strcmp(key, current->word) < 0)
            break;
        else
        {
            previous = current;
            current = current->link;
        }
    }
    if (current == head)
        return NULL;
    else
        return previous;
}
```

The prototype for the function *insert_node* is:

```
node *insert_node(node *head, node *previous, char key[]);
```

where *head* is a pointer to the head of the linked list, *previous* is the value returned by the *search* function indicating where the new node is to be inserted, and *key* is the value to be inserted. Figure 15.7 illustrates how the node containing the word *almond* and the node containing the word *artichoke* are inserted into a linked list. These illustrations should be viewed in conjunction with the *insert_node* function given after the illustration.

1. Insertion of a new node at the head of the list having first searched for the key and returned null

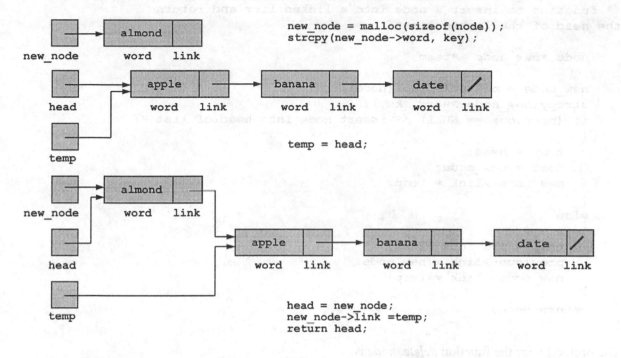

```
new_node = malloc(sizeof(node));
strcpy(new_node->word, key);
```

```
temp = head;
```

```
head = new_node;
new_node->link =temp;
return head;
```

2. Insertion of a new node into a list other than at the head having first searched for the key and returned previous

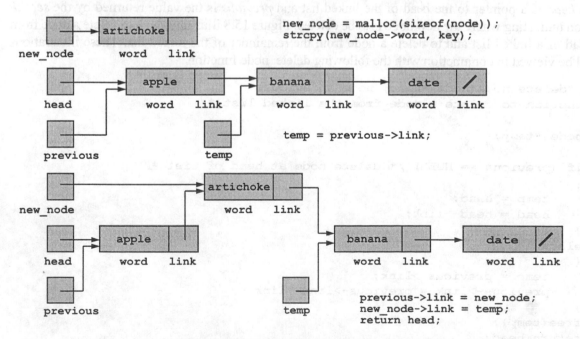

```
new_node = malloc(sizeof(node));
strcpy(new_node->word, key);
```

```
temp = previous->link;
```

```
previous->link = new_node;
new_node->link = temp;
return head;
```

figure 15.7 insertion of a node into a linked list

363

```
node *insert_node(node *head, node *previous, char key[])
/* function to insert a node into a linked list and return
the head of the linked list*/
{
    node *new_node, *temp;

    new_node = malloc(sizeof(node));
    strcpy(new_node->word, key);
    if (previous == NULL) /* insert node into head of list */
    {
        temp = head;
        head = new_node;
        new_node->link = temp;
    }
    else
    {
        temp = previous->link;
        previous->link = new_node;
        new_node->link = temp;
    }
    return head;
}
```

The prototype for the function *delete_node* is:

```
node *delete_node(node *head, node *previous);
```

where *head* is a pointer to the head of the linked list and *previous* is the value returned by the *search* function indicating where the new node is to be deleted. Figure 15.8 illustrates how to delete a node from the head of a linked list and to delete a node from the remainder of the linked list. These illustrations should be viewed in conjunction with the following delete_node function.

```
node *delete_node(node *head, node *previous)
/* function to delete a node from the linked list */
{
    node *temp;

    if (previous == NULL) /* delete node at head of list */
    {
        temp = head;
        head = head->link;
    }
    else
    {
        temp = previous->link;
        previous->link = previous->link->link;
    }
    free(temp);
    return head;
}
```

1. Deletion of a node at the head of the list having first searched for the key

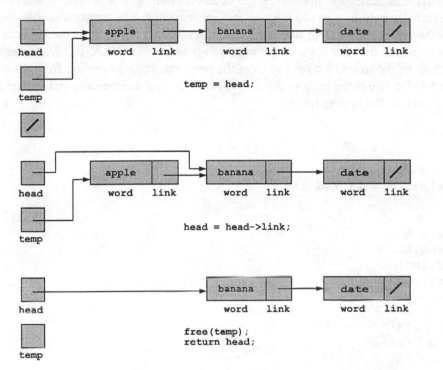

```
temp = head;
```

```
head = head->link;
```

```
free(temp);
return head;
```

2. Deletion of a node from a list other than at the head having first searched for the key

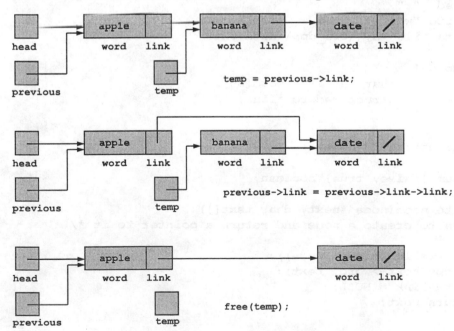

```
temp = previous->link;
```

```
previous->link = previous->link->link;
```

```
free(temp);
```

figure 15.8 the deletion of a node from a linked list

365

The following program is devised to maintain a linked list containing words. The words to be stored in the linked list are initially held in a text file in alphabetical sequence. The function *create_list* used in an earlier section has been modified so that words are read from the text file and not the keyboard. Once the linked list has been created the user is given the opportunity to insert new words, delete existing words, examine the contents of the linked list or quit from the program. Prior to exiting from the program the contents of the linked list is written back to the original text file and the memory space used to build the list is de-allocated back to the system heap.

```c
/*
c15_dpp\ex_03.c
program to maintain a linked list
*/

#include <stdio.h>
#include <errno.h>
#include <stdlib.h>
#include <string.h>
#include <ctype.h>

#define insert  'I'
#define delete  'D'
#define examine 'E'
#define quit    'Q'

#define read  "r"
#define write "w"
#define data_file "a:\\c15_dpp\\data.txt"

struct record {
                char          word[80];
                struct record *link;
              };

typedef struct record node;

typedef enum {false, true} boolean;

node *create_node(node *next, char text[])
/* function to create a node and return a pointer to it */
{
        next=malloc(sizeof(node));
        strcpy(next->word, text);
        next->link = NULL;
        return next;
}
```

```
node *create_list(node *head, char filename[])
/* function to create a linked list from the contents of
a text file and return a pointer to the head of the linked list */
{
        node *last;
        char word[80];
        FILE *file;


        file = fopen(filename, read);
        if (file == NULL)
        {
            printf("%s cannot be opened\n", filename);
            exit(errno);
        }

        fscanf(file, "%s", word);
        while (! feof(file))
        {
            if (head == NULL)
            {
                head = create_node(head, word);
                last = head;
            }
            else
            {
                last->link = create_node(last->link, word);
                last = last->link;
            }
            fscanf(file, "%s", word);
        }
        fclose(file);
        return head;
}

node *search(node *head, char key[], boolean *found)
/* function to search an ordered linked list for a word,
    if found return the pointer to the previous node unless
    the node is at the head of the list in which case return NULL
    else return the pointer to the position where the node
    should be inserted/ deleted */
{
    node *previous, *current;

    *found = false;
    current = head;
    previous = current;
```

```
        while (current != NULL)
        {
            if (strcmp(key, current->word) == 0)
            {
                *found = true;
                break;
            }
            else if (strcmp(key, current->word) < 0)
                break;
            else
            {
                previous = current;
                current = current->link;
            }
        }
        if (current == head)
            return NULL;
        else
            return previous;
}


node *insert_node(node *head, node *previous, char key[])
/* function to insert a node into a linked list and return
the head of the linked list*/
{
    node *new_node, *temp;

    new_node = malloc(sizeof(node));
    strcpy(new_node->word, key);

    if (previous == NULL) /* insert node into head of list */
    {
        temp = head;
        head = new_node;
        new_node->link = temp;
    }
    else
    {
        temp = previous->link;
        previous->link = new_node;
        new_node->link = temp;
    }

    return head;
}
```

```
node *delete_node(node *head, node *previous)
/* function to delete a node from the linked list */
{
    node *temp;

    if (previous == NULL) /* delete node at head of list */
    {
        temp = head;
        head = head->link;
    }
    else
    {
        temp = previous->link;
        previous->link = previous->link->link;
    }

    free(temp);
    return head;
}


void list_out(node *head)
/* function to display the contents of a linked list */
{
        node *current;

        current = head;
        printf("\n\n");
        if (current == NULL)
            printf("list empty\n");
        else
        {
            while (current != NULL)
            {
                printf("%s\n", current->word);
                current = current->link;
            }
        }
}

void save_list(node *head, char filename[])
/* function to transfer the contents of the linked list
to a text file */
{
        FILE *file;
        node *current;

        file = fopen(filename, write);
        if (file == NULL)
```

```
        {
            printf("%s cannot be opened\n", filename);
            exit(errno);
        }

    current = head;
    while (current != NULL)
    {
        fprintf(file, "%s\n", current->word);
        current = current->link;
    }

    fclose(file);
}



node *clean_up(node *head)
/* function to deallocate storage space for nodes and
return memory back to the heap */
{
    node *current, *temporary;

    current = head;
    while (current != NULL)
    {
        temporary = current->link;
        free(current);
        current = temporary;
    }
    head = NULL;
    return head;
}

char menu(void)
{
    char reply;

    printf("\ndo you want to: \n");
    printf("[I]nsert a new entry \n");
    printf("[D]elete an existing entry \n");
    printf("[E]xamine the list \n");
    printf("[Q]uit \n");
    printf("input I, D, E or Q ");
    reply = getchar(); getchar();
    reply = toupper(reply);
    return reply;
}
```

```
main()
{
      node      *head = NULL;
      node      *previous;
      char      key[80];
      boolean found;


      head = create_list(head, data_file);

      for (;;)
      {
          switch (menu())
          {
          case insert:  printf("input word "); gets(key);
                        previous = search(head, key, &found);
                        if (! found)
                            head = insert_node(head, previous, key);
                        else
                            printf("\n\nERROR WORD EXISTS\n\n");
                        break;

          case delete:  printf("input word "); gets(key);
                        previous = search(head, key, &found);
                        if (found)
                            head = delete_node(head, previous);
                        else
                            printf("\n\nERROR WORD NOT FOUND\n\n");
                        break;

          case examine: list_out(head); break;

          case quit:    save_list(head, data_file);
                        clean_up(head); exit(errno);

          default:      printf("\n\nERROR - MENU CODE\n\n");
          };
      };
}
```

Results from program ex_03.c being run

```
do you want to:
[I]nsert a new entry
[D]elete an existing entry
[E]xamine the list
[Q]uit
input I, D, E or Q E

apple
banana
date

do you want to:
[I]nsert a new entry
[D]elete an existing entry
[E]xamine the list
[Q]uit
input I, D, E or Q I
input word almond

do you want to:
[I]nsert a new entry
[D]elete an existing entry
[E]xamine the list
[Q]uit
input I, D, E or Q E

almond
apple
banana
date

do you want to:
[I]nsert a new entry
[D]elete an existing entry
[E]xamine the list
[Q]uit
input I, D, E or Q D
input word date


do you want to:
[I]nsert a new entry
[D]elete an existing entry
[E]xamine the list
[Q]uit
input I, D, E or Q E
```

```
almond
apple
banana

do you want to:
[I]nsert a new entry
[D]elete an existing entry
[E]xamine the list
[Q]uit
input I, D, E or Q D
input word date

ERROR WORD NOT FOUND

do you want to:
[I]nsert a new entry
[D]elete an existing entry
[E]xamine the list
[Q]uit
input I, D, E or Q I
input word apple

ERROR WORD EXISTS

do you want to:
[I]nsert a new entry
[D]elete an existing entry
[E]xamine the list
[Q]uit
input I, D, E or Q Q
```

15.3 Queues

Queues are a familiar aspect of everyday life. People queue in orderly lines to wait for buses, or to wait to be served in a bank. There are many examples in computing of the use of queues. In a real-time system queues of processes wait to use a processor or queues of jobs wait to use a resource such as a printer. The general concept of a queue is a line of objects that has a front and a rear. The first object in the queue is said to be at the front of the queue, whereas the last object in the queue is said to be at the rear of the queue. In a First in First Out (FIFO) queue, an object can only join the queue at the rear and leave at the front.

Queues can be built out of linked lists. To allow a node to join a FIFO queue requires a new node *temporary* to be introduced. This node will contain the details of the last member to join the queue. The function *insert_node* to insert a new node into the rear of a FIFO queue relies upon the existence of two further functions - *queue_empty* will return a boolean value indicating whether the queue is empty or not, and *find_rear* will return a pointer to the last node in the FIFO queue. The code required to insert a new node at the rear of the queue follows figure 15.9 and should be read in conjunction with this figure.

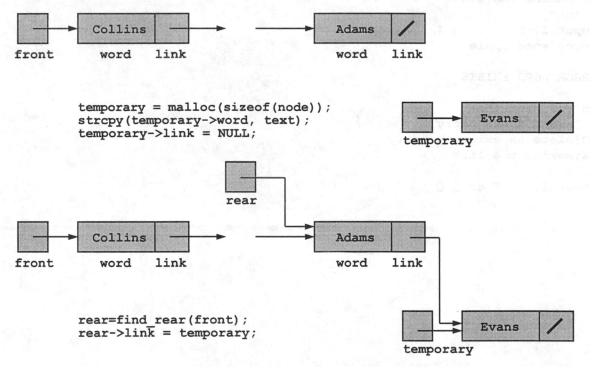

figure 15.9 insert into the rear of a FIFO queue

374

```
node *insert_node(node *front, char text[])
/* function to insert a node into the rear of the queue
and return a pointer to the front node */
{
    node *rear, *temporary;

    temporary = malloc(sizeof(node));
    strcpy(temporary->word, text);
    temporary->link = NULL;

    if (! queue_empty(front))
    {
        rear = find_rear(front);
        rear->link = temporary;
        return front;
    }
    else
        return temporary;
}
```

Members of a FIFO queue can only leave from the front. Figure 15.10 illustrates how a node can be removed from the front of a queue. This figure should be viewed in conjunction with the code remove_node that follows the figure. The function remove_node also relies upon the existence of the function queue_empty.

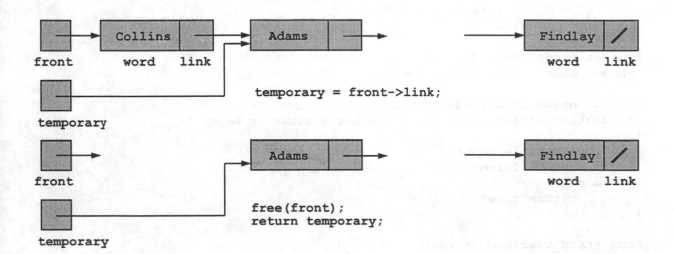

figure 15.10 removal from the front of a FIFO queue

```c
node *remove_node(node *front)
/* function to remove a node from the front of the queue
and return a pointer for the new front */
{
    node *temporary;

    if (! queue_empty(front))
    {
        temporary = front->link;
        free(front);
        return temporary;
    }
    else
        return NULL;
}
```

The following program illustrates how to insert and remove nodes from a FIFO queue.

```c
/* c15_dpp\ex_04.c
program to insert and remove nodes from a FIFO queue
*/

#include <stdio.h>
#include <stdlib.h>
#include <string.h>

struct record {
                char            word[80];
                struct record *link;
              };

typedef struct record node;
typedef enum {false, true} boolean;

boolean queue_empty(node *front)
/* function to test and return whether a queue is empty */
{
    if (front != NULL)
        return false;
    else
        return true;
}

node *find_rear(node *front)
/* function to find and return the position of the rear of the queue */
{
    node *rear = NULL;
```

```
        while (front != NULL)
        {
            rear  = front;
            front = front->link;
        }
        return rear;
}

node *remove_node(node *front)
/* function to remove a node from the front of the queue
and return a pointer for the new front */
{
        node *temporary;

        if (! queue_empty(front))
        {
            temporary = front->link;
            free(front);
            return temporary;
        }
        else
            return NULL;
}

node *insert_node(node *front, char text[])
/* function to insert a node into the rear of the queue
and return a pointer to the front node */
{
        node *rear, *temporary;

        temporary = malloc(sizeof(node));
        strcpy(temporary->word, text);
        temporary->link = NULL;

        if (! queue_empty(front))
        {
            rear = find_rear(front);
            rear->link = temporary;
            return front;
        }
        else
            return temporary;
}

void list_out(node *front)
/* function to display the contents of a linked list */
{
        node *current;
```

```
            current = front;
            printf("\n\n");
            if (current == NULL)
                printf("list empty\n");
            else
            {
                while (current != NULL)
                {
                    printf("%s\n", current->word);
                    current = current->link;
                }
            }
    }

main()
{
        node *queue = NULL;

        queue = insert_node(queue, "apple");
        list_out(queue);
        queue = insert_node(queue, "banana");
        list_out(queue);
        queue = insert_node(queue, "grape");
        list_out(queue);
        queue = remove_node(queue);
        list_out(queue);
        queue = remove_node(queue);
        queue = remove_node(queue);
        list_out(queue);
}
```

Results from program ex_04.c being run

```
apple

apple
banana

apple
banana
grape

banana
grape

list empty
```

15.4 Stacks

A stack is a queue in which members of the queue can join and leave at one end only. The queue is known as a LIFO queue - Last in First Out. The entry/ exit point of the stack is known as the stack top and the position of this stack top is controlled by a stack pointer. An item that joins the queue is said to be pushed on to the stack. An item that leaves the queue is said to be popped from the stack. The methods used for pushing and popping items from a stack are illustrated in figures 15.11 and 15.12 respectively, and should be viewed in conjunction with the code that follows each figure.

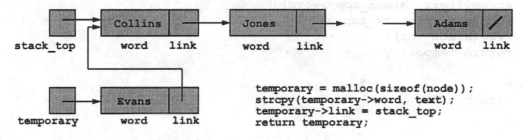

```
temporary = malloc(sizeof(node));
strcpy(temporary->word, text);
temporary->link = stack_top;
return temporary;
```

figure 15.11 pushing an item on a stack

```
node *push(node *stack_top, char text[])
/* function to insert a node into the top of the stack
and return a pointer to the new stack top */
{
    node *temporary;

    temporary = malloc(sizeof(node));
    strcpy(temporary->word, text);
    temporary->link = stack_top;
    return temporary;
}
```

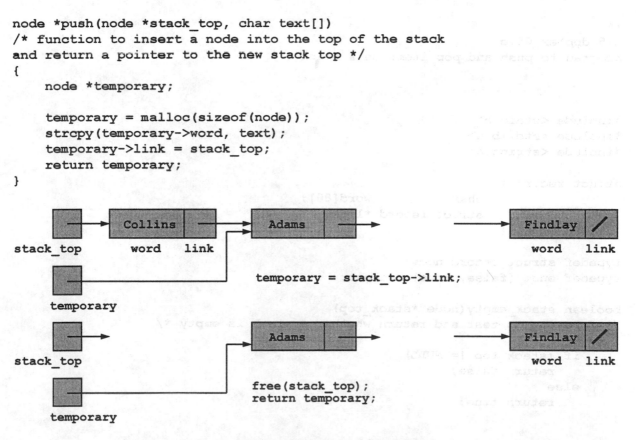

```
temporary = stack_top->link;
```

```
free(stack_top);
return temporary;
```

figure 15.12 popping an item from a stack

```
node *pop(node *stack_top, char text[])
/* function to remove a node from the top of a stack
and return a pointer for the new stack top; text contains
the contents of the top of the stack prior to removal */
{
    node *temporary;

    if (! stack_empty(stack_top))
    {
        strcpy(text, stack_top->word);
        temporary = stack_top->link;
        free(stack_top);
        return temporary;
    }
    else
        return NULL;
}
```

The next program illustrates the use of push and pop to insert and remove words from a stack.

```
/*
c15_dpp\ex_05.c
program to push and pop items on a stack
*/


#include <stdio.h>
#include <stdlib.h>
#include <string.h>

struct record {
                char            word[80];
                struct record *link;
            };

typedef struct record node;
typedef enum {false, true} boolean;

boolean stack_empty(node *stack_top)
/* function to test and return whether a stack is empty */
{
    if (stack_top != NULL)
        return false;
    else
        return true;
}
```

```
node *pop(node *stack_top, char text[])
/* function to remove a node from the top of a stack
and return a pointer for the new stack top; text contains
the contents of the top of the stack prior to removal */
{
    node *temporary;

    if (! stack_empty(stack_top))
    {
        strcpy(text, stack_top->word);
        temporary = stack_top->link;
        free(stack_top);
        return temporary;
    }
    else
        return NULL;
}


node *push(node *stack_top, char text[])
/* function to insert a node into the top of the stack
and return a pointer to the new stack top */
{
    node *temporary;

    temporary = malloc(sizeof(node));
    strcpy(temporary->word, text);
    temporary->link = stack_top;
    return temporary;
}


void list_out(node *stack_top)
/* function to display the contents of a linked list */
{
    node *current;

    current = stack_top;
    printf("\n\n");
    if (current == NULL)
        printf("list empty\n");
    else
    {
        while (current != NULL)
        {
            printf("%s\n", current->word);
            current = current->link;
        }
    }
}
```

```
main()
{
        node *stack = NULL;
        char word[80];

        stack = push(stack, "apple");
        stack = push(stack, "banana");
        stack = push(stack, "grape");
        list_out(stack);
        stack = pop(stack, word);
        list_out(stack);
        stack = pop(stack, word);
        stack = pop(stack, word);
        list_out(stack);
}
```

Results from program ex_05.c being run

```
grape
banana
apple

banana
apple

list empty
```

15.5 Binary trees

The dynamic data structures described so far had nodes that contained only one pointer which were used to point to the next node in either a linked list, queue or stack. It is possible for a node to contain more than one pointer. However, in this section the reader will be introduced to nodes containing two pointers, left and right, such that the next node to be pointed at is dependent upon a condition related to the data being stored in the node. Figure 15.13 illustrates the structure of a node in a binary tree.

```
struct record {
                struct record *left;
                int          number;
                struct record *right;
               };
typedef struct record tree;
```

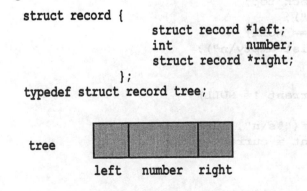

figure 15.13 the structure of a binary tree node

382

Initially in building a binary tree if the root of the tree (parent) is NULL then the tree is said to be empty. The algorithm used to insert a node into the tree can be coded as:

```
parent = malloc(sizeof(tree));
parent->left = NULL;
parent->number = number;
parent->right = NULL;
```

where in this example *number* is the value of a random number 56 to be inserted into the tree. This information is represented in figure 15.14.

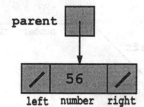

figure 15.14 inserting a node into a binary tree

If it is required to insert a second node, containing the random number 78, into the tree such that the numbers will be kept in an ordered sequence, then the reasoning would be:

if number to be inserted is *less than* number in parent node then
    branch left
else
    branch right

Therefore, if the next random number to be inserted into the binary tree is 78 a node must be attached to the right of the parent node since 78 is greater than 56. This is illustrated in figure 15.15. Note the new parent to the new node becomes **parent->right**.

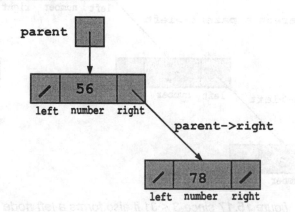

figure 15.15 inserting another node into the binary tree

If the random numbers 31, 3, 17, 67 and 99 are also to be inserted into this binary tree, the tree will grow as depicted in the set of figures 15.16 through to 15.20 inclusive.

The number 31 is compared with parent->number (56) since 31 < 56 and parent->left is NULL, the new node is built to the left of the parent node. Notice that the parent pointer to this new node is parent->left.

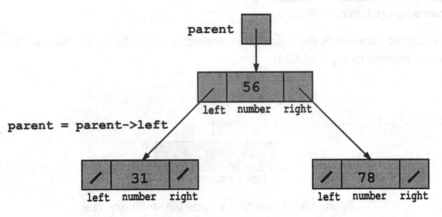

figure 15.16 since 31 < 56 it forms a left node

The number 3 is compared with parent->number (56) since 3 < 56, branch left making the new value of the parent = parent->left and make a further comparison with parent->number (31). Since 3 < 31 and parent->left is NULL, the new node is built to the left of the parent node. Notice that the parent pointer to this new node is parent->left.

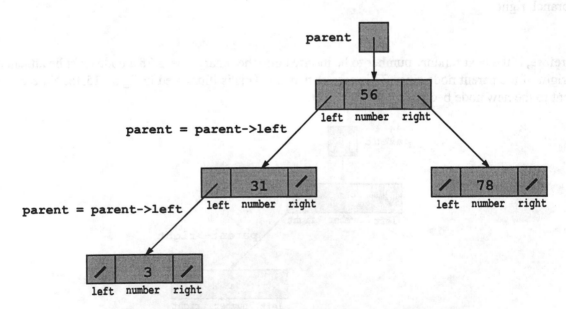

figure 15.17 since 3 < 31 it also forms a left node

The number 17 is compared with parent->number (56) since 17 < 56, branch left making the new value of the parent = parent->left and make a further comparison with parent->number (31). Since 17 < 31, branch left making the new value of parent = parent->left and make a further comparison with parent->number (3). Since 17 > 3 and parent->right is NULL, the new node is built to the right of the parent node. Notice that the parent pointer to this new node is parent->right.

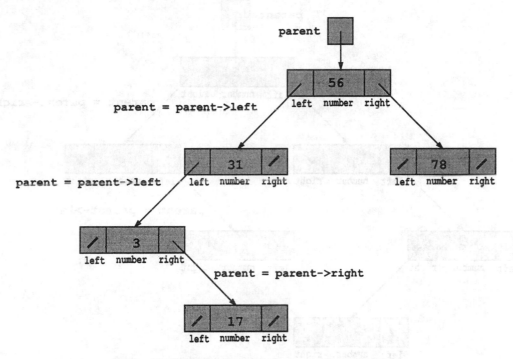

figure 15.18 since 17 > 3 insert a node to the right

385

The number 67 is compared with parent->number (56) since 67 > 56, branch right making the new value of the parent = parent->right and make a further comparison with parent->number (78). Since 67 < 78 and parent->left is NULL, the new node is built to the left of the parent node. Notice that the parent pointer to this new node is parent->left.

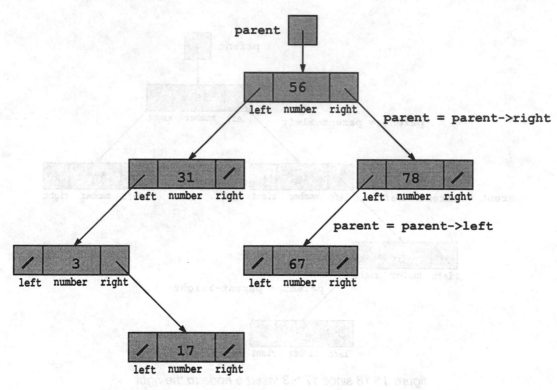

figure 15.19 since 67 < 78 insert node to the left

The number 99 is compared with parent->number (56) since 99 > 56, branch right making the new value of the parent = parent->right and make a further comparison with parent->number (78). Since 99 > 78 and parent->right is NULL, the new node is built to the right of the parent node. Notice that the parent pointer to this new node is parent->right.

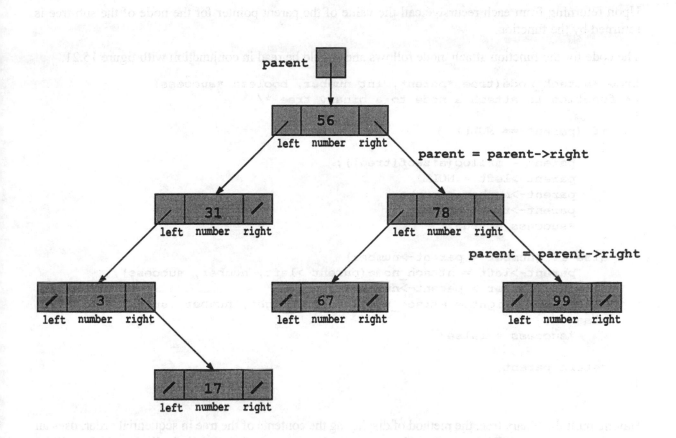

figure 15.20 since 99 > 78 insert node to right

The function used to attach a node to a tree has the following prototype:

```
tree *attach_node(tree *parent, int number, boolean *success);
```

where the root pointer (parent) is passed as a parameter, together with the number to be input into the tree. The parameter success is a reference parameter and is assigned the boolean value *true* if the number is attached to the tree, otherwise it is assigned the boolean value *false* if the number already exists in the tree. This algorithm, therefore, does not cater for duplicate entries in the same tree.

If the pointer parent (initially the root of the tree) is NULL then space for the root node is allocated from the heap and the value for the number inserted into the node. The left and right pointers are also set at NULL.

If the random number is less than that found in the root node, then the function is recursively called again but this time the parent is the value of *parent->left*. Similarly if the random number is greater than that found in the root node, then the function is recursively called again but this time the parent is the value *parent->right*.

Upon returning from each recursive call the value of the parent pointer for the node of the sub-tree is returned by the function.

The code for the function attach_node follows and should be read in conjunction with figure 15.21.

```
tree *attach_node(tree *parent, int number, boolean *success)
/* function to attach a node to a binary tree */
{
    if (parent == NULL)
    {
        parent = malloc(sizeof(tree));
        parent->left = NULL;
        parent->number = number;
        parent->right = NULL;
        *success = true;
    }
    else if (number < parent->number)
        parent->left = attach_node(parent->left, number, success);
    else if (number > parent->number)
        parent->right = attach_node(parent->right, number, success);
    else
        *success = false;

    return parent;
}
```

Having built the binary tree, the method of displaying the contents of the tree in sequential order, uses an *in-order* tree traversal. During an in-order traversal, the contents of each node is displayed after all the nodes in its left sub-tree have been visited, and before any node in its right sub-tree. The following function *display_tree* is used to display the contents of a binary tree. The reader is advised to trace through this recursive algorithm using the tree depicted in figure 15.20 to gain an understanding of why it should display the numbers in sequential order.

```
void display_tree(tree *parent)
/* function to output the contents of the tree in order */
{
    if (parent != NULL)
    {
        display_tree(parent->left);
        printf("%3d", parent->number);
        display_tree(parent->right);
    }
}
```

To digress for a moment, there are two other algorithms for traversing a binary tree - *pre-order* and *post-order* traversals. In a pre-order traversal a node is processed before the computer traverses either of the node's subtrees, however, with post-order traversal both the subtrees of a node are traversed before processing the node.

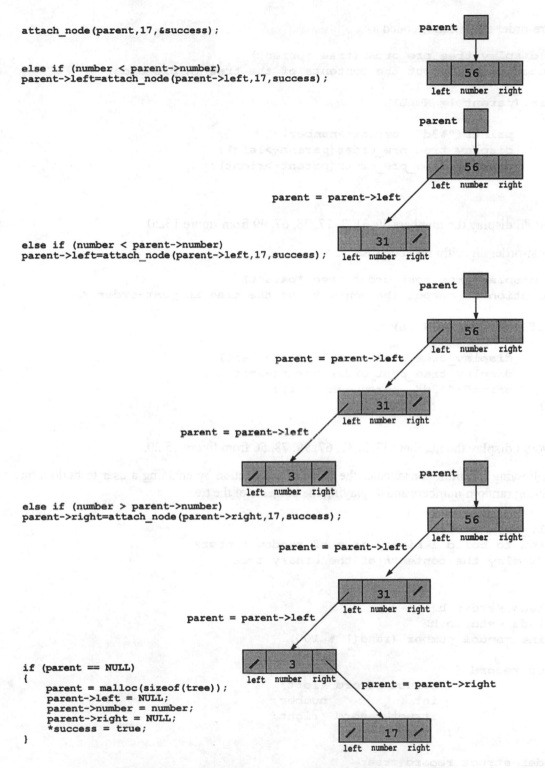

figure 15.21 insertion of a node into a binary tree

The pre-order algorithm is coded as:

```
void display_tree_pre_order(tree *parent)
/* function to output the contents of the tree in pre-order */
{
    if (parent != NULL)
    {
        printf("%3d", parent->number);
        display_tree_pre_order(parent->left);
        display_tree_pre_order(parent->right);
    }
}
```

and would display the numbers 56, 31, 3, 17, 78, 67, 99 from figure 15.20.

The post-order algorithm is coded as:

```
void display_tree_post_order(tree *parent)
/* function to output the contents of the tree in post-order */
{
    if (parent != NULL)
    {
        display_tree_post_order(parent->left);
        display_tree_post_order(parent->right);
        printf("%3d", parent->number);
    }
}
```

and would display the numbers 17, 3, 31, 67, 99, 78, 56 from figure 15.20.

The following program consolidates the work of this section by enabling a user to build a binary tree containing random numbers and displaying the contents of the tree.

```
/* c15_dpp\ex_06.c
program to build a binary tree of random numbers
and display the contents of the binary tree
*/

#include <stdio.h>
#include <stdlib.h>
#define random_number (rand() % 100)

struct record {
                struct record  *left;
                int            number;
                struct record  *right;
            };

typedef struct record tree;
typedef enum {false, true} boolean;
```

```
tree *initialise_tree(void)
/* initialise the root of the tree to NULL */
{
    return NULL;
}


tree *attach_node(tree *parent, int number, boolean *success)
/* function to attach a node to a binary tree */
{
    if (parent == NULL)
    {
        parent = malloc(sizeof(tree));
        parent->left = NULL;
        parent->number = number;
        parent->right = NULL;
        *success = true;
    }
    else if (number < parent->number)
        parent->left = attach_node(parent->left, number, success);
    else if (number > parent->number)
        parent->right = attach_node(parent->right, number, success);
    else
        *success = false;
    return parent;
}


void display_tree(tree *parent)
/* function to output the contents of the tree in order */
{
    if (parent != NULL)
    {
        display_tree(parent->left);
        printf("%3d", parent->number);
        display_tree(parent->right);
    }
}


main()
{
    tree    *parent;
    int     count, number;
    boolean success;

    parent = initialise_tree();
    for (count=1; count <= 15; count++)
    {
      do
      {
          number = random_number;
```

```
            parent = attach_node(parent, number, &success);
            if (success) printf("%3d", number);
        }
        while (! success);
    }
    printf("\n\n");
    display_tree(parent);
}
```

Results from program ex_06.c being run

```
23  89  43   2  17  99  56  66  34  19  73  59  81  91  13

 2  13  17  19  23  34  43  56  59  66  73  81  89  91  99
```

15.6 Removing nodes

When a node is to be removed from a tree it is necessary to search the tree for that node. Figure 15.22 illustrates how the number 17 is found prior to removing the node. The method of searching through the tree is similar to that depicted in figure 15.21, when it was necessary to search for the correct place to insert the new node.

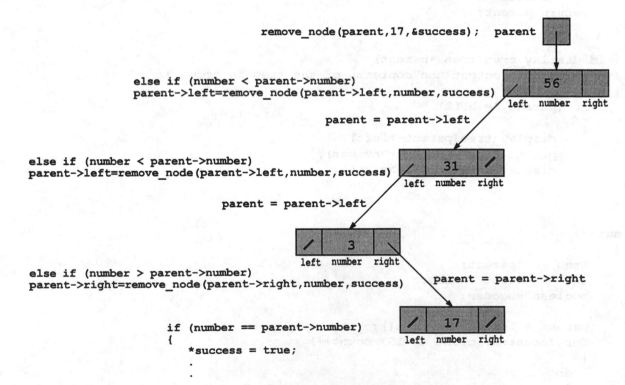

figure 15.22 a recursive search for a node

392

The removal of a node from a tree is not such a simple matter as attaching a new node to the tree. When the node to be removed has been located it might be a leaf node (no children), a node with either the left or right pointers NULL (one child) or a node with both left and right pointers pointing at two respective sub-trees (two children). Figure 15.23 through to figure 15.25 illustrates how to delete the node in each of the three cases respectively. These figures should be viewed in conjunction with the following code.

```
tree *remove_node(tree *parent, int number, boolean *success)
/* function to remove a node from a tree */
{
    tree *temp;
    int  new_number;

    if (parent != NULL)
    {
        if (number == parent->number)
        {
            *success = true;
            if (parent->left == NULL && parent->right == NULL)
            {
                temp = parent;
                free(temp) ;
                parent = NULL;
            }
            else if (parent->left == NULL)
            {
                temp = parent;
                parent = parent->right;
                free(temp) ;
            }
            else if (parent->right == NULL)
            {
                temp = parent;
                parent = parent->left;
                free(temp) ;
            }
            else
            {
                parent->right = successor(parent->right, &new_number);
                parent->number = new_number;
            }
        }
        else if (number < parent->number)
            parent->left = remove_node(parent->left, number, success);
        else
            parent->right = remove_node(parent->right, number, success);
    }
    else
```

```
      *success = false;
   return parent;
}
```

When a node is to be removed that has pointers to two children it is necessary to search the right sub-tree of this node for the left-most entry. It is this node that will replace the node to be deleted. The function successor is necessary in finding the contents of a node that is the next in sequence to the node to be removed.

```
tree *successor(tree *parent, int *number)
/* function to locate the left-most word in a sub-tree */
{
    tree *temp;

    if (parent != NULL)
    {
        if (parent->left == NULL)
        {
            *number = parent->number;
            temp = parent;
            parent = parent->right;
            free(temp);
        }
        else
            parent->left = successor(parent->left, number);
    }
    return parent;
}
```

When the left-most node is found (parent->left == NULL) the reference parameter *number* is assigned the random number stored at this node. A temporary pointer is assigned to point at this node in readiness for its removal. The value of the parent pointer is then re-assigned so that it points to whatever the pointer in the right node is pointing to. This may be another sub-tree or it may be NULL. The storage space associated with the temporary pointer is then de-allocated and thereby the node is removed from the tree.

The reference parameter number found in the formal parameter list of successor contains the number required to replace the number in the node to be deleted. Note the contents of this node is only replaced it is not physically deleted from the tree.

1. removal of the leaf node containing the number 17

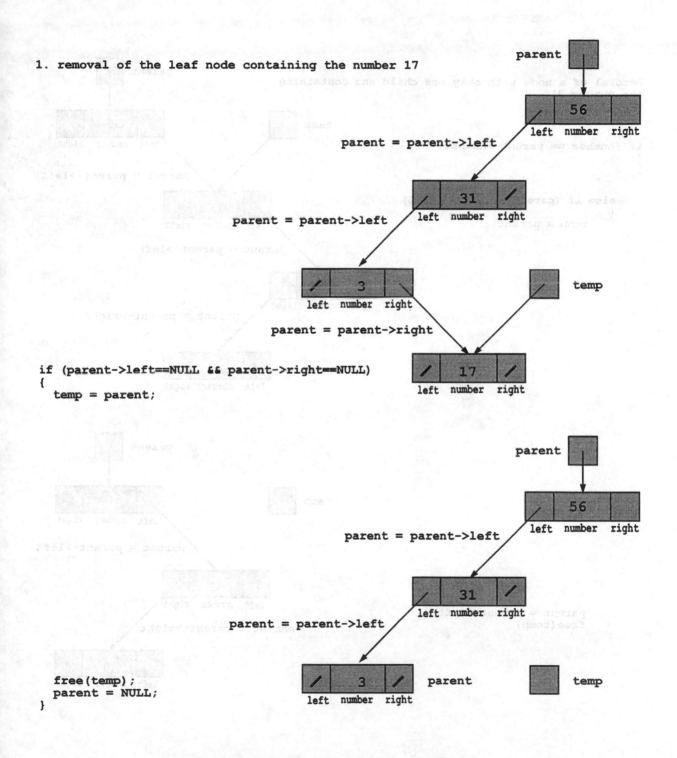

figure 15.23 removal of a leaf node (no children)

Removal of a node with only one child and containing
the number 31

```
if (number == parent->number)
{
.
.
    else if (parent->right == NULL)
    {
        temp = parent;
```

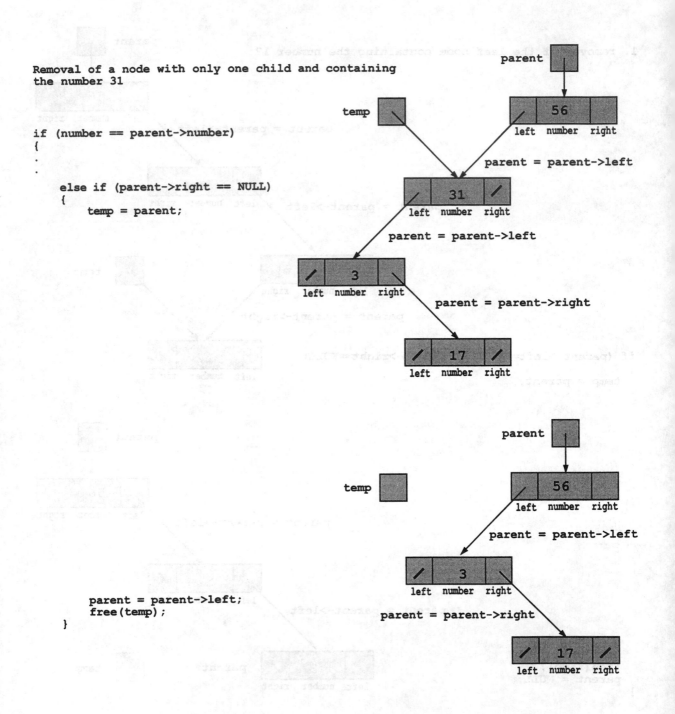

```
    parent = parent->left;
    free(temp);
}
```

figure 15.24 removal of a node with one child

Removal of a node containing two children and containing the number 56

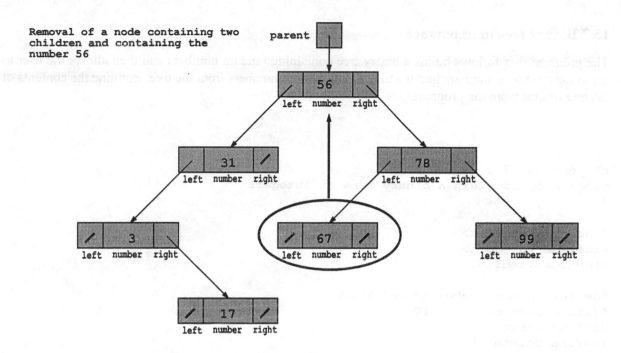

The node to be deleted must be replaced with a number that is larger than all the numbers in the left sub-tree. This element is the left-most element (67) in the right sub-tree and can be found using the function successor.

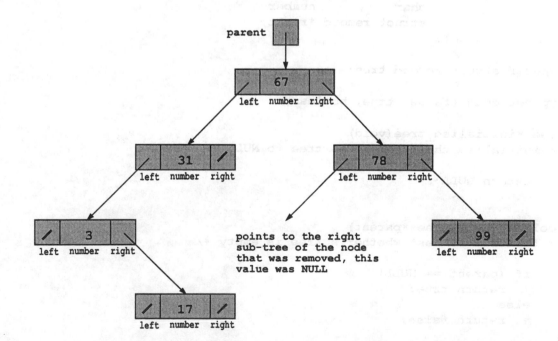

figure 15.25 removal of a node with two children

15.7 Binary tree maintenance

The program that follows builds a binary tree containing random numbers and then allows the user to insert new random numbers into the tree, delete random numbers from the tree, examine the contents of the tree or quit from the program.

```
/*
c15_dpp\ex_07.c
program to maintain a binary tree of integers
*/

#include <stdio.h>
#include <errno.h>
#include <stdlib.h>

#define random_number (rand()%100)
#define size_of_tree  10
#define insert   'I'
#define delete   'D'
#define examine 'E'
#define quit     'Q'

struct record {
                struct record *left;
                char          number;
                struct record *right;
            };

typedef struct record tree;

typedef enum {false, true} boolean;

tree *initialise_tree(void)
/* initialise the root of the tree to NULL */
{
    return NULL;
}

boolean empty(tree *parent)
/* function to test whether a tree is empty */
{
    if (parent == NULL)
        return true;
    else
        return false;
}
```

```
tree *attach_node(tree *parent, int number, boolean *success)
/* function to attach a node to a binary tree */
{
    if (parent == NULL)
    {
        parent = malloc(sizeof(tree));
        parent->left = NULL;
        parent->number = number;
        parent->right = NULL;
        *success = true;
    }
    else if (number < parent->number)
        parent->left = attach_node(parent->left, number, success);
    else if (number > parent->number)
        parent->right = attach_node(parent->right, number, success);
    else
        *success = false;

    return parent;
}

tree *build_tree(tree *parent, int size)
/* function to store random numbers in a tree */
{
    int     count;
    boolean success;

    for (count=1; count <= size; count++)
    {
        do
        {
            parent = attach_node(parent, random_number, &success);
        }
        while (! success);
    }
    return parent;
}

tree *successor(tree *parent, int *number)
/* function to locate the left-most word in a sub-tree */
{
    tree *temp;

    if (parent != NULL)
    {
        if (parent->left == NULL)
        {
            *number = parent->number;
            temp = parent;
```

```
                parent = parent->right;
                free(temp);
            }
            else
                parent->left = successor(parent->left, number);
        }
        return parent;
    }

tree *remove_node(tree *parent, int number, boolean *success)
/* function to remove a node from a tree */
{
    tree *temp;
    int  new_number;

    if (parent != NULL)
    {
        if (number == parent->number)
        {
            *success = true;
            if (parent->left == NULL && parent->right == NULL)
            {
                temp = parent;
                free(temp);
                parent = NULL;
            }
            else if (parent->left == NULL)
            {
                temp = parent;
                parent = parent->right;
                free(temp);
            }
            else if (parent->right == NULL)
            {
                temp = parent;
                parent = parent->left;
                free(temp);
            }
            else
            {
                parent->right = successor(parent->right, &new_number);
                parent->number = new_number;
            }
        }
        else if (number < parent->number)
            parent->left = remove_node(parent->left, number, success);
        else
            parent->right = remove_node(parent->right, number, success);
    }
```

400

```
        else
            *success = false;

        return parent;
}

void display_tree(tree *parent)
/* function to output the contents of the tree in order */
{
    if (parent != NULL)
    {
        display_tree(parent->left);
        printf("%3d", parent->number);
        display_tree(parent->right);
    }
}

char menu(void)
{
    char reply;

    printf("\ndo you want to: \n");
    printf("[I]nsert a random number \n");
    printf("[D]elete a number from the tree \n");
    printf("[E]xamine the tree \n");
    printf("[Q]uit \n");
    printf("input I, D, E or Q ");
    reply = getchar(); getchar();
    reply = toupper(reply);
    return reply;
}


main()
{
        tree    *parent;
        int     number;
        boolean success;

        parent = initialise_tree();
        parent = build_tree(parent, size_of_tree);

        for (;;)
        {
            switch (menu())
            {
            case insert:  do
                          {
                                number = random_number;
```

```
                        parent = attach_node(parent, number, &success);
                    }
                    while (! success);
                    printf("\ngenerated -> %d\n", number);
                    break;

        case delete:    do
                        {
                            printf("input number "); scanf("%d", &number);
                            getchar();
                            parent = remove_node(parent, number, &success);
                        }
                        while (! success && ! empty(parent));
                        break;

        case examine:   if (! empty(parent))
                        {
                            printf("\n");
                            display_tree(parent);
                            printf("\n");
                        }
                        else
                            printf("\ntree empty\n");

                        break;

        case quit:      exit(errno);

        default:        printf("\nERROR - MENU CODE\n");
        };
    };
}
```

Results from program ex_07.c being run

```
do you want to:
[I]nsert a random number
[D]elete a number from the tree
[E]xamine the tree
[Q]uit
input I, D, E or Q E

  2 13 17 19 23 34 43 56 59 66
```

```
do you want to:
[I]nsert a random number
[D]elete a number from the tree
[E]xamine the tree
[Q]uit
input I, D, E or Q I

generated->15

do you want to:
[I]nsert a random number
[D]elete a number from the tree
[E]xamine the tree
[Q]uit
input I, D, E or Q E

  2 13 15 17 19 23 34 43 56 59 66

do you want to:
[I]nsert a random number
[D]elete a number from the tree
[E]xamine the tree
[Q]uit
input I, D, E or Q D

input number 43

do you want to:
[I]nsert a random number
[D]elete a number from the tree
[E]xamine the tree
[Q]uit
input I, D, E or Q E

  2 13 15 17 19 23 34 56 59 66

do you want to:
[I]nsert a random number
[D]elete a number from the tree
[E]xamine the tree
[Q]uit
input I, D, E or Q Q
```

15.8 Summary

☐ A pointer represents an address in the memory of a computer. This address contains the data that is being pointed at.

☐ Storage space to accommodate the data must be allocated from the heap and when the storage space is no longer required should be de-allocated back to the heap.

☐ A linked list is represented as a series of records, where the first record is pointed at by a head pointer, and each record in turn points to the next record in the list, until the last record that contains a NULL pointer.

☐ If the keys representing data in a linked list are ordered, then the insertion and deletion of records in the list is made easier.

☐ A linked list can be used to represent queues.

☐ A First In First Out (FIFO) queue will have records inserted into the end of a linked list and records deleted from the head of a linked list.

☐ A Last In First Out (LIFO) queue will have records inserted (pushed) into the head of the queue and records deleted (popped) also from the head of the queue. The head of a LIFO queue is known as the stack top.

☐ A binary tree is a structure in which each node contains two pointers. If the data to be stored in the tree is less than the contents of the current node, the data is stored in the node indicated by the left-hand pointer, otherwise, the data is stored in the node indicated by the right-hand pointer.

☐ Owing to the manner in which data can be stored in a binary tree, an in order tree traversal of a tree will result in the contents of each node being accessed in sequence, therefore, the data can be accessed as if it was sorted.

15.9 Questions - *answers begin on page 500*

1. Figure 15.26 illustrates a circular linked list containing integers. Notice that the pointer at the end of the list points to the head of the list, thus allowing the traversal of the list to take a continuous or circular path. Write a program to store 10 random numbers in the range 0..99, in respective nodes of a linked list. In this question the numbers are **not** ordered in the list. Traverse the list and display the numbers stored at the nodes. Stop traversal when the first number has been displayed for the second time around.

head

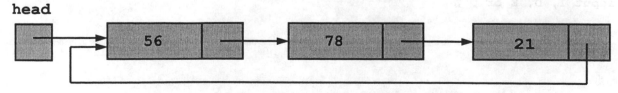

figure 15.26 a circular linked list

2. Write a program to create a linked list of non-zero random numbers stored in key disorder. Build a second linked list that contains the integers from the first linked list sorted into key order. As each integer is used from the first linked list, delete it from the first linked list. When all integers are sorted display the contents of the second linked list.

[3]. Figure 15.27 illustrates a circular double linked list structure containing a dummy node at the head of the list.

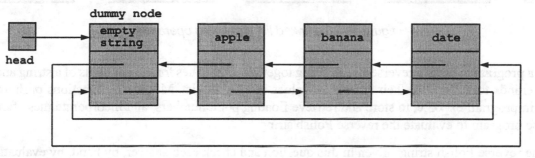

figure 15.27 a circular double-linked list

Note the dummy node contains a null or empty string, therefore all nodes to be inserted into the structure must have words alphabetically greater than the dummy node. By using the dummy node there is no special case to consider for the insertion or deletion at the head of the linked list. The dummy node is always present and should not be removed. The backward pointer in each node greatly facilitates the search function since there is no need to maintain a separate pointer that always points to the previous node.

Re-write program *c15_dpp\ex_03.c* to maintain a circular double linked list, where the structure of a record in this type of list may be declared as:

```
struct record {
        char word[80];
        struct record *link_backward;
        struct record *link;
};
```

Examine the contents of the list both in forward and backward order.

4. The following strings are examples of infix and reverse Polish strings.

infix	reverse Polish
a*b+c	ab*c+
a*(b+c/d)	abcd/+*
a*b+c/d	ab*cd/+
u+f*t	uft*+

The values of operands from these expressions are stored in a linked list similar to that illustrated in figure 15.28. The following procedure evaluate a reverse Polish string. Traverse the string from left to right and continue to push operands on a stack until an operator is encountered. For a binary operator pop two operands from the stack, evaluate the result and push the answer back on the stack. Continue traversing the reverse polish string until the end of the string, then pop the contents of the stack and display this value.

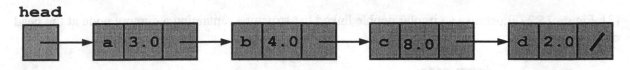

figure 15.28 a linked list for storing operands

Write a program to input a reverse Polish string together with values for the operands of a string and store the operands together with their respective values in a linked list. Modify the functions push and pop given in program ex_05.c, to store and retrieve floating point numbers, and incorporate these functions into the program to evaluate the reverse Polish string.

Use the reverse Polish strings given in this question and check each answer, by hand, by evaluating the equivalent infix expression using the same operands.

[5]. In addition to the left and right pointers a node of a binary tree may contain the following information about students' course results.

```
typedef struct {
                char id[10];      /* unique student id number */
                char name[40];    /* student name */
                char course[40];  /* the name of study course */
                int  average;     /* average % mark to date */
        } student;
```

(a) Write a program to create a binary file of records with this format.

(b) Write a second program, using *c15_dpp\ex_07.c* as a model, that will read the contents of the binary file built from running the program in (a) and store the records as nodes in a binary tree. Allow a user to:

(i)   insert a new student record into the tree;
(ii)   delete an existing student record from the tree;
(iii)   examine the contents of the tree;
(iv)   display the records of all those students on a particular course, and the mean mark of the averages for those students on the course;
(v)   search the tree on name only and display the records of all those students with the same name;
(vi)   search the tree on student_id and display the record of the corresponding student;
(vii)   quit the program, but before exiting copy the contents of the tree back to the same binary file.

Note: when a tree is written to a file it is wise to use a *pre-order* traversal of the tree so that the root node is written first. An *in-order* traversal would result in the contents of the tree being stored as an ordered sequence. Unfortunately this would cause the tree to be built as a linked list the next time the file was read.

Chapter 16
Further topics

Although the major topics of the C language have already been covered, there still remains several topics that must be dealt with to give the reader the complete picture. These topics come together as an assortment of subjects, which in themselves would not warrant a separate chapter for each topic. This chapter covers the following material.

- ☐ Access to and manipulation of binary digits.
- ☐ Variant records.
- ☐ Functions containing a variable number of arguments.
- ☐ Information hiding.

16.1 Bit manipulation

There are six operators, which operate on integer and character operands at the bit level.

There are two shift operators.

<< **left shift** - the value of a << b is the result when a is shifted left b positions. Zero bits are added at the right end to replace the bits that are shifted out.

For example, if a = 0xFABA (hexadecimal), a = 1111101010111010 (binary); then a << 5 gives a result 0101011101000000

>> **right shift** - the value of a >> b is the result when a is shifted right b positions. If a is unsigned or non-negative then zero bits are added to the left of the number. If the number is negative the result is implementation dependent. For example the JPI TopSpeed compiler propagates the sign bit.

For example, if a = 1111101010111010 then a >> 4 gives the result 1111111110101011

In addition to the shift operators there are bit operators to provide:

~complement	c = 01101110 ~c = 10010001
& and	c = 00001011 and d = 11111100 then c & d = 00001000
^ exclusive or	c ^ d = 11110111
| inclusive or	c | d = 11111111

Warning! The bit operators & and | are not equivalent to the logical operators && and ||.

The following program illustrates the six bit operators described.

```
/*
c16_dpp\ex_01.c program to illustrate bit manipulation
*/

#include <stdio.h>
#define print(x) printf(#x "= %d\n", x);

main()
{
        int i=0x00FF, j=0x000F;

        print(i);
        print(j);
        print(i << 8);      /* shift left by 8 bits */
        print(j >> 2);      /* shift right by 2 bits */
        print(~j);          /* take one's complement of j */
        print(i & j);       /* bitwise i AND j */
        print(i | j);       /* bitwise i inclusive OR j */
        print(i ^ j);       /* bitwise i exclusive OR j */
}
```

Results from program ex_01.c being run on a PC under MSDOS

```
i= 255
j= 15
i << 8= -256              [65280]
j >> 2= 3
~j= -16
i & j= 15
i | j= 255
i ^ j= 240
```

Note the figure in brackets [ ] indicates the result when the program was run on a DEC work station under UNIX.

The bit operators **&**, ^ and | can be combined with = to provide compound assignment operators **&=**, ^= and |= respectively, where the result is always stored in the first of the binary operands.

The following program illustrates how to modify bits within a number, by using the appropriate bit masks.

For example, the bit mask 0x8000 (hexadecimal) 1000000000000000 (binary) will set the sign bit of a 16-bit number when used with *or* (i |= 0x8000).

The bit mask 0x7FFF (hexadecimal) 0111111111111111 (binary) will clear the sign bit of a 16-bit number when used with *and* (j &= 0x7FFF).

Individual bits can be extracted using bit masks, and tested in an if statement where (0) false, (1) true.

A bit field (group of consecutive bits) can be modified by first clearing the field, then setting the required bits. For example

```
if j =  0x7FFF (hexadecimal)    0111111111111111 (binary)
        0xFFC7 (hexadecimal)    1111111111000111 (binary)
j &     0xFFC7                  0111111111000111 (binary)
```

has cleared bits 3, 4 and 5 (note bit 0 is the least significant bit)

Bit 4 could then be set by using the bit mask 0x0010 in conjunction with *inclusive or*:

(j & 0xFFC7 | 0x0010); /* modifying a bit field */

Finally a bit field can be retrieved by masking out unwanted bits and shifting the result. For example if bits 12, 13 and 14 are required (bit 15 is the sign bit), the bit mask 0x7000 would be used with & on the number. The result would then be shifted twelve places to the right in order to obtain the value of the bit field.

((j & 0x7000) >> 12); /* retrieving a bit field */

```
/*
c16_dpp\ex_02.c
program to illustrate access to bits
*/

#include <stdio.h>

#define print(x) printf(#x "=%d\n", x)

main()
{
        int i=0x0000, j=0xFFFF;

        print(i);
        print(j);

        print(i |= 0x8000);     /* set the sign bit */
        print(j &= 0x7FFF);     /* clear the sign bit */

        if (i & 0x8000)
        {
            printf("sign bit set ");
            print(i);
        }

        if (~j & 0x8000)
        {
            printf("sign bit is cleared ");
            print(j);
        }

        print(j & 0xFFC7 | 0x0010); /* modifying a bit field */
        print((j & 0x7000) >> 12);  /* retrieving a bit field */
}
```

Results from program ex_02.c being run on a PC under MSDOS

```
i=0
j=-1                                [65535]
i |=0x8000=-32768                   [32768]
j &=0x7FFF=32767
sign bit set i=-32768               [32768]
sign bit cleared j=32767
j & 0xFFC7 | 0x0010=32727
(j & 0x7000) >> 12=7
```

Note the figures in brackets [ ] indicate the results when the program was run on a DEC work station under UNIX.

16.2 Bit fields

An alternative method of defining and accessing bit fields is to use a structure. In the following example a six-digit date has been represented by a structure containing bit fields for day, month and year. It is possible to define the number of bits in each field. In this example five bits have been used to represent the day, giving a range from 1 .. 31; four bits to represent the month, giving a range from 1 .. 12; and seven bits to represent the year, giving a range from 0 .. 99. The total number of bits to represent a date is sixteen, or two bytes. If the fields day, month and year had each been coded as short int, the number of bytes required to store a date would have been three. Therefore, defining the number of bits in a field is a useful way in which to compress information.

```
typedef struct{
                unsigned int day    : 5;
                unsigned int month  : 4;
                unsigned int year   : 7;
            } date;
```

A field may not overlap an integer boundary. If the bit field width would cause this to happen, the field is aligned at the next integer boundary.

Bit fields must be considered as machine dependent. ANSI C permits an implementation to choose to use **long** instead of **int** when a bit field is defined with more bits than a single precision **int**.

Field members are restricted to type **int**. Arrays of fields are not allowed. Fields cannot be addressed directly by pointers and the address operator cannot be applied to a bit field member.

The following program illustrates the use of bit fields. Both a date of birth and the current date are stored in a compressed format using the bit fields described above. From this information the age of a person is calculated and displayed.

```
/*
c16_dpp\ex_03.c
program to demonstrate the use of bit fields;

the program calculates the age of a person given their date of birth and
the current date; the program is written for the twentieth century only
*/

#include <stdio.h>

typedef struct {
                unsigned int day   :5; /* least significant bits */
                unsigned int month :4;
                unsigned int year  :7; /* most significant bits */
            } date;
```

```
main()
{
    date date_of_birth, today;
    int  dd, mm, yy;
    int  age;

    printf("input all dates in the format dd mm yy\n\n");
    printf("date of birth? ");
    scanf("%d%d%d", &dd, &mm, &yy);

    date_of_birth.day   = dd;
    date_of_birth.month = mm;
    date_of_birth.year  = yy;

    printf("today's date? ");
    scanf("%d%d%d", &dd, &mm, &yy);

    today.day   = dd;
    today.month = mm;
    today.year  = yy;

    /* calculate age */
    if ((today.month > date_of_birth.month) ||
        (today.month == date_of_birth.month &&
        today.day > date_of_birth.day))
        age = today.year - date_of_birth.year;
    else
        age = today.year - date_of_birth.year - 1;

    printf("current age is %d years\n ", age);
}
```

Results from program ex_03.c being run

```
input all dates in the format dd mm yy

date of birth? 18 3 48
today's date? 5 12 94
current age is 46 years
```

16.3 Unions - variant records

When information can be represented in more than one format it is possible to define the different formats in a union. Although the compiler allocates sufficient storage to accommodate the largest member of the union, a union can only hold one of its components at a time. A union data type is similar to the structure data type in that both can contain members of different types and sizes.

From the previous example, a date was represented by two bytes of memory, with bit fields being used to store the day, month and year. In the example that follows the format can be redefined to represent an unsigned integer.

```
typedef union {
                date            today;
                unsigned int    TODAY;
            } alternative;
```

If a variable *Dday* of type *alternative* is defined, it is possible to access the date in day, month and year format:

```
Dday.today.day
Dday.today.month
Dday.today.year
```

or as an unsigned integer:

```
Dday.TODAY
```

```
/*
c16_dpp\ex_04.c
program to illustrate bit fields in structures and unions
*/

#include <stdio.h>

typedef struct  {
                unsigned int day    : 5; /* least significant bits */
                unsigned int month  : 4;
                unsigned int year   : 7; /* most significant bits */
            } date;

typedef union   {
                    date            today;
                    unsigned int TODAY;
                } alternative;

alternative Dday;
```

```
main()
{
        Dday.today.day   = 8U;  /* 01000 */
        Dday.today.month = 2U;  /* 0010 */
        Dday.today.year  = 92U; /* 1011100 */
        /* equivalent bit pattern stored in two bytes */
        /* 1011100001001000 */

        printf("%X\n", Dday.TODAY);
}
```

Results from program ex_04.c being run

```
B848
```

The next example illustrates a further use for a union. Three structures are defined, with fields to represent the area and lengths of three sides of a triangle, the area and radius of a circle and the area and lengths of the two half-axes of an ellipse.

```
typedef struct {
                float area;
                float side_a, side_b, side_c;
        } triangle;

typedef struct {
                float area;
                float radius;
        } circle;

typedef struct {
                float area;
                float axis_a, axis_b;
        } ellipse;
```

A record for each figure could be represented in a union of type shapes.

```
typedef union {
                triangle TRIANGLE;
                circle   CIRCLE;
                ellipse  ELLIPSE;
        } shapes;
```

and finally a structure can be defined that represents a single letter code for a shape T-triangle, C-circle and E-ellipse, followed by a field for the most appropriate data for the respective shape.

```
typedef struct {
                char    figure;
                shapes SHAPES;
        } figures;
```

Function prototypes can be declared that represent functions to input data for a particular shape

```
figures get_data(void);
```

calculate the area of the respective figure

```
figures calculate_area(figures data);
```

and finally print the area of the appropriate figure

```
void display_area(figures data);
```

Notice that the structure type *figures* is used in each of these prototypes to either return or receive information about a particular shape. Since shapes is declared as a union it is possible to process the appropriate shape without the need for separate functions for each shape.

```
/*
c16_dpp\ex_05.c
program to demonstrate the use of a union
*/

#include <stdio.h>
#include <math.h>
#define yes 'Y'

typedef struct {
                float area;
                float side_a, side_b, side_c;
        } triangle;

typedef struct {
                float area;
                float radius;
        } circle;

typedef struct {
                float area;
                float axis_a, axis_b;
        } ellipse;
```

```
typedef union  {
                 triangle TRIANGLE;
                 circle   CIRCLE;
                 ellipse  ELLIPSE;
            } shapes;

typedef struct {
                 char    figure;
                 shapes SHAPES;
            } figures;

char menu(void)
/* function to display a menu and return
a valid menu code */
{
     char reply;

     printf("\ninput shape\n");
     printf("[T]riangle\n");
     printf("[C]ircle\n");
     printf("[E]llipse\n");
     printf("input T, C or E ");

     do
     {
         reply = getchar(); getchar();
         reply = toupper(reply);
     } while (reply != 'T' && reply != 'C' && reply != 'E');

     return reply;
}

figures get_data(void)
/* function to input the data for a shape */
{
    figures data;
    char     code;

    code = menu();
    switch (code)
    {
    case 'T' : printf("input the lengths of the three sides ");
               scanf("%f%f%f", &data.SHAPES.TRIANGLE.side_a,
                               &data.SHAPES.TRIANGLE.side_b,
                               &data.SHAPES.TRIANGLE.side_c);
               break;
    case 'C' : printf("input the radius ");
               scanf("%f", &data.SHAPES.CIRCLE.radius);
               break;
```

416

```
     case 'E' : printf("input the lengths of the two half-axes ");
                scanf("%f%f", &data.SHAPES.ELLIPSE.axis_a,
                              &data.SHAPES.ELLIPSE.axis_b);
     }
     getchar(); /* clear input buffer */

     data.figure = code;
     return data;
}

figures calculate_area(figures data)
/* function to calculate and return the area of a figure */
{
     const float pi = 3.14159;
           float s; /* semi-perimeter of triangle */

     switch(data.figure)
     {
     case 'T': s = (data.SHAPES.TRIANGLE.side_a +
                    data.SHAPES.TRIANGLE.side_b +
                    data.SHAPES.TRIANGLE.side_c) / 2.0;

               data.SHAPES.TRIANGLE.area =
               sqrt(s*(s - data.SHAPES.TRIANGLE.side_a) *
                      (s - data.SHAPES.TRIANGLE.side_b) *
                      (s - data.SHAPES.TRIANGLE.side_c));
               break;

     case 'C': data.SHAPES.CIRCLE.area =
               pi* pow(data.SHAPES.CIRCLE.radius, 2);
               break;

     case 'E': data.SHAPES.ELLIPSE.area =
               pi * data.SHAPES.ELLIPSE.axis_a *
                    data.SHAPES.ELLIPSE.axis_b;
     }
     return data;
}

void display_area(figures data)
{
     printf("area of ");
     switch(data.figure)
     {
     case 'T': printf("triangle %8.2f\n", data.SHAPES.TRIANGLE.area);break;
     case 'C': printf("circle %8.2f\n", data.SHAPES.CIRCLE.area); break;
     case 'E': printf("ellipse %8.2f\n", data.SHAPES.ELLIPSE.area);
     }
}
```

```
main()
{
    figures data;
    char    reply;

    do
    {
        data = get_data();
        display_area(calculate_area(data));
        printf("\ncontinue? [yes/no] ");
        reply = getchar(); getchar();
        reply = toupper(reply);
    } while (reply == yes);
}
```

Results from program ex_05.c being run

```
input shape
[T]riangle
[C]ircle
[E]llipse
input T, C or E T
input the lengths of the three sides 3.0 4.0 5.0
triangle 6.00

continue? [yes/no] y

input shape
[T]riangle
[C]ircle
[E]llipse
input T, C or E C
input radius 10.0
circle 314.16

continue [yes/no] y

input shape
[T]riangle
[C]ircle
[E]llipse
input T, C or E E
input the lengths of the two half-axes 2.0 3.0
ellipse 18.85

continue [yes/no] n
```

16.4 Variadic functions

These are functions that have a variable number of arguments. Such functions are not new to the reader since both *scanf* and *printf* cater for different numbers of arguments. However, the functions created by the programmer, have up to now, only had a fixed number of arguments.

In the program that follows, a function is defined to calculate the arithmetic mean of a set of numbers. A prototype for this function may be declared as:

```
float mean(int number, ...);
```

The ellipsis ... appearing at the end of the argument list indicates that the function can take a variable number of arguments.

The header file <stdarg.h> provides a new type called *va_list* and three macros that operate on items of this type called *va_start*, *va_arg* and *va_end*.

A variable *args* needs to be declared of type **va_list**.

```
va_list args;
```

Before the variable argument list can be accessed the macro **va_start** must be called.

```
va_start(args, number);
```

where *number* is the number of arguments to follow, in the actual parameter list, of the function call.

The actual arguments can be accessed sequentially by the macro **va_arg**, for example:

```
arg = va_arg(args, int);
```

where *arg* is the value of an actual parameter and *int* represent the data type of the parameter.

Finally when all the arguments have been processed the macro **va_end** should be called.

va_end(args);

```
/*
c16_dpp\ex_06.c
demonstration of a function with a variable number of arguments
*/

#include <stdio.h>
#include <stdarg.h>

float mean(int number, ...)
/* function to return the mean for any number of parameters */
{
    va_list     args;
    int         arg;
    int         count, total = 0;
```

```
    va_start(args, number);
    for (count=0; count < number; count++)
    {
        arg = va_arg(args, int);
        total += arg;
    }
    va_end(args);
    return (float) total/number;
}

main()
{
    printf("average %4.1f\n", mean(2,10,20));
    printf("average %4.1f\n", mean(4,10,20,30,40));
    printf("average %4.1f\n", mean(10,1,2,3,4,5,6,7,8,9,10));
}
```

Results from program ex_06.c being run

```
average 15.0
average 25.0
average  5.5
```

16.5 Information hiding

In the previous chapter a stack (LIFO queue) was implemented using a linked list. This fact, together with the implementation of the functions required to initialise the stack, test it for being empty, pop and push text and display the contents of the stack were all visible to the user.

There are advantages to be gained in hiding the implementation details from view and presenting a user of a stack with only an interface of the type and functions available.

This technique can be implemented by the use of a *generic* pointer to hide the method of declaring the stack. The following file represents such an interface. Notice that all implementation details have been removed and the user is only given a definition of what is available.

```
/*
c16_dpp\ex_07.h
stack interface
*/

typedef void *stack;
typedef enum {false, true} boolean;
```

```
extern stack initialise(void);
/* function to initialise a stack */

extern boolean stack_empty(stack stack_top);
/* function to test and return whether a stack is empty */

extern stack pop(stack stack_top, char text[]);
/* function to remove text from the top of a stack
and return a pointer for the new stack top */

extern stack push(stack stack_top, char text[]);
/* function to insert text into the top of the stack
and return a pointer to the new stack top */

extern void list_out(stack stack_top);
/* function to display the contents of the stack */
```

Notice that each function is preceded by the keyword **extern**, to declare a prototype for a function that is implemented in a separate file.

This definition of a stack and its associated functions is in effect a header file and can be included in the file c16_dpp\ex_07.c that contains an implementation of the functions.

```
/*
c16_dpp\ex_07.c
implementation of the routines to manipulate a stack
*/

#include <stdio.h>
#include <stdlib.h>
#include <string.h>

#include "a:\c16_dpp\ex_07.h"

struct record {
                char            word[80];
                struct record *link;
            };

typedef struct record NODE;

stack initialise(void)
{
    return NULL;
}
```

```
boolean stack_empty(stack stack_top)
/* function to test and return whether a stack is empty */
{
     if (stack_top != NULL)
        return false;
     else
        return true;
}

stack pop(stack stack_top, char text[])
/* function to remove text from the top of a stack
and return a pointer for the new stack top */
{
     NODE *temporary, *st;

     st = stack_top;
     if (! stack_empty(stack_top))
     {
        strcpy(text, st->word);
        temporary = st->link;
        free(stack_top);
        return temporary;
     }
     else
        return NULL;
}
stack push(stack stack_top, char text[])
/* function to insert text into the top of the stack
and return a pointer to the new stack top */
{
     NODE *temporary;

     temporary = malloc(sizeof(NODE));
     strcpy(temporary->word, text);
     temporary->link = stack_top;
     return temporary;
}

void list_out(stack stack_top)
/* function to display the contents of the stack */
{
        NODE *current;

        current = stack_top;
        printf("\n\n");
        if (current == NULL)
           printf("stack empty\n");
        else
```

```
        {
            while (current != NULL)
            {
                printf("%s\n", current->word);
                current = current->link;
            }
        }
}
```

File c16_dpp\ex_07.c can be compiled and checked for syntax errors. Both the header file c16_dpp\ex_07.h and the implementation file c16_dpp\cx_07.c are stored as part of a new library of functions that operate on a data type known as a stack. The type stack is known as an *abstract* data type. This type may be imported into other programs. Data of this type are operated on only by the functions that are present in the header file.

In the final program of this chapter a variable *word_stack* is declared as an abstract data type. The stack is initialised, words are pushed on to the stack using the function push, removed from the top of the stack by the function pop, and the contents of the stack is displayed using the function list_out. Notice that by including the header file "c16_dpp\ex_07.h" the data type stack and the functions initialise, push, pop and list_out can be used without having to redefine the type *stack* or re-write the functions.

```
/*
c16_dpp\ex_08.c
program to push and pop items on a stack
*/

#include <stdio.h>
#include "a:\c16_dpp\ex_07.h"

main()
{
        stack word_stack;
        char  word[80];

        word_stack = initialise();

        /* push words on to the stack */
        word_stack = push(word_stack, "apple");
        word_stack = push(word_stack, "banana");
        word_stack = push(word_stack, "grape");

        /* display the contents of the stack */
        printf("\nstack contains"); list_out(word_stack);
```

```
        /* pop a word from the stack and display it */
        word_stack = pop(word_stack, word);
        printf("\nword popped is %s\n", word);

        /* display the contents of the stack */
        printf("\nstack contains"); list_out(word_stack);

        /* pop and display two further words from the stack */
        word_stack = pop(word_stack, word);
        printf("\nword popped is %s\n", word);
        word_stack = pop(word_stack, word);
        printf("word popped is %s\n", word);

        /* display the contents of the stack */
        printf("\nstack contains"); list_out(word_stack);
}
```

This program is compiled to check for syntax errors in the normal way, however, it must be linked to the object file c16_dpp\ex_07.c before it can be executed. The file c16_dpp\ex_08.c has dependencies on the external routines initialise, push, pop and list_out, and these must be resolved by the linker before it is possible to create a run-time file.

In chapter 12 the reader was introduced to the make facility and the need to create a make file containing a list of dependent files to compile and link together to form a run-time file. The make file ex_08.pr, required in the TopSpeed environment follows.

```
#system auto exe
#model  small

#compile "a:\c16_dpp\ex_07.c",
         "a:\c16_dpp\ex_08.c"
#link ex_08
```

When the make command is executed a run-time file is created for program ex_08.c.

Note - refer to appendix C for information on a makefile in UNIX.

Results from ex_08.pr being run

```
stack contains

grape
banana
apple

word popped is grape

stack contains
```

424

```
banana
apple

word popped is banana
word popped is apple

stack contains

stack empty
```

16.6 Summary

☐ Using the appropriate operators it is possible to shift a bit string left or right, and one's compliment a bit string.

☐ Two bit strings may have the operations of *and*, *inclusive or* and *exclusive or* applied to respective bits in the corresponding strings.

☐ Bit masks may be used to modify the contents of bit strings.

☐ It is possible to specify that fields within a structure can be composed of a set number of bits. However, this approach is essentially machine dependent.

☐ A record may be defined in many different ways, and by its very nature become a variant record. In such a case the different records can be represented as a union. Memory space is not reserved for every record in the union, but only enough space to accommodate at least the largest record.

☐ A function may be allowed to take on a variable number of arguments. In such cases there are a number of macros from the library <stdarg.h> that must be used when processing the arguments.

☐ Generic pointers may be used to hide the declaration of a data type and in effect create an abstract data type.

☐ The operations upon the abstract data type can be described as external functions in a header file.

☐ The implementation of the abstract data type and its operations can be described in a corresponding .c file.

☐ A program may include the abstract data type and its operations by the inclusion of the appropriate header file.

☐ A program that includes abstract data types and the associated operations upon that type must be linked to the external routines before a run-time file can be created. The creation of a *make* file and the execution of the *make* command allows all inter-dependent program files to be linked into one run-time file.

16.7 Questions - *answers begin on page 507*

1. *This question assumes that you are writing and testing your programs in a PC environment under MSDOS.*

The TopSpeed C library provides a function **biosequip** that reports on the hardware configuration of an IBM PC or compatible microcomputer. The prototype of this function is given as:

```
int biosequip(void);
```

and it returns an unsigned 16-bit integer, where the following bits represent information about the equipment of the computer.

Bit(s)	Meaning
0	set to 1 if the system boots from disk
1	set to 1 if a coprocessor is installed
2-3	indicates motherboard RAM size:
	00 16K
	01 32K
	10 48K
	11 64K
4-5	initial video mode
	00 unused
	01 color card 40x25 BW mode
	10 color card 80x25 BW mode
	11 monochrome card 80x25 BW mode
6-7	number of disk drives
	00 1 drive
	01 2 drives
	10 3 drives
	11 4 drives, but only if bit 0 is 1
8	set to 0 if machine does not have DMA, set to 1 otherwise
9-11	number of serial ports
12	set to 1 if a game port is attached
13	set to 1 if a serial printer is attached
14-15	number of parallel printers installed

(a) Using bit masks and shifts write a program to report on the hardware configuration of your PC.

(b) Re-write your answer to part (a) using bit fields and unions.

2. Using bit manipulation, devise functions to:

(a) Rotate either anti clockwise or clockwise, a specified number of bits, of a 16 bit word.

426

(b) Multiply two 8 bit binary integers that can be either positive or negative.

Incorporate these functions into suitable test harnesses and run the programs.

[3]. A survey is to be carried out about the marital status of women in employment. Part of the data being collected will use the following variant record:

```
typedef struct    {
                boolean   marital_status;
                status    STATUS;
                } matrimony;
```

where status is defined as:

```
typedef union    {
                not_married SINGLE;
                married     MARRIED;
                } status;
```

If a woman is not married then only the surname of the woman is recorded, otherwise the current surname, maiden name and date of marriage are all recorded.

Write a program to create a binary file containing variant records having the format shown. After the file has been written display the contents of the file.

4. Modify the program c16_dpp\ex_06.c to contain a function to return both the maximum and minimum values from a set of integers. Hint - return these values as two fields of a record.

[5]. In compiler writing it is more convenient to evaluate arithmetic expressions written in reverse Polish notation than it is to evaluate arithmetic expressions written in infix notation. The following algorithm can be used to convert infix notations to reverse polish notations. For example, the expression a*(b+c/d) in infix notation is written as abcd/+* in reverse Polish notation. The algorithm uses operator priorities as defined in figure 16.1.

operator	priority
^	6
*	5
/	4
+	3
-	2
(	1
[	0

figure 16.1

The operators [and] are used to delimit the infix expression. For example, the expression a*(b+c/d) will be coded as [a*(b+c/d)].

Use figure 16.2 in the following explanation of the algorithm.

If brackets [or (are encountered, each is pushed on to the stack. All operands that are encountered, for example a, b and c, are displayed on the screen. When an operator is encountered its priority is compared with that of the operator priority at the top of the stack. If when comparing priorities the operator encountered is not greater than the operator on the stack, the stack operator is popped and displayed. This process is repeated until the encountered operator has a higher priority than the stack top operator. The encountered operator is then pushed on to the stack. When a) is encountered all the operators up to, but not including (, are popped from the stack one at a time and displayed. The operator (is then deleted from the stack. When the operator] is encountered all the remaining operators, up to but not including [, are popped from the stack one at a time and displayed. The string of characters that is displayed will be the reverse Polish string.

Modify the header file c16_dpp\ex_07.h and the corresponding file c16_dpp\ex_07.c to cater for a stack that contains single characters.

Using the techniques of data abstraction write a program that includes the new header file for the character stack to implement the reverse Polish algorithm.

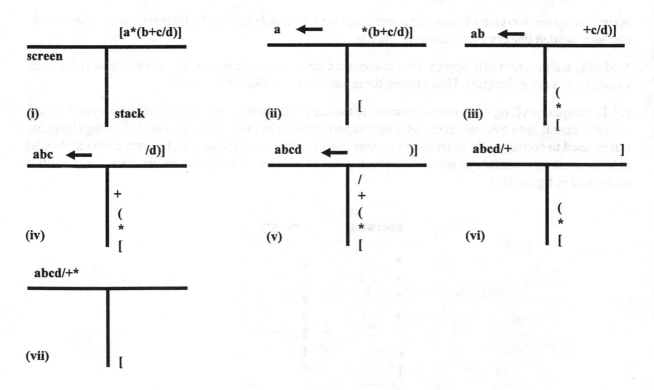

figure 16.2

Appendix A - Syntax of ANSI C

The following notation is used in the ANSI/ISO 9899-1990 standard to define the syntax of ANSI C.

Non-terminal syntactic categories are indicated by *italic* type.

Terminal symbols - literal words and character set members are indicated by **bold** type.

A colon : following a non-terminal symbol introduces its definition.

Alternative definitions are listed on separate lines, except when prefaced by the words "one of ".

An optional symbol is indicated by the subscript "$_{opt}$" so that { *expression $_{opt}$* } indicates an optional expression enclosed in braces.

A.1 Lexical grammar

A.1.1 Tokens

token:
> *keyword*
> *identifier*
> *constant*
> *string-literal*
> *operator*
> *punctuator*

preprocessing-token:
> *header-name*
> *identifier*
> *pp-number*
> *character-constant*
> *string-literal*
> *operator*
> *punctuator*
> each non-white-space character that cannot be one of the above

A.1.2 Keywords

keyword: one of

auto	**double**	**int**	**struct**
break	**else**	**long**	**switch**
case	**enum**	**register**	**typedef**
char	**extern**	**return**	**union**
const	**float**	**short**	**unsigned**
continue	**for**	**signed**	**void**
default	**goto**	**sizeof**	**volatile**
do	**if**	**static**	**while**

A.1.3 Identifiers

identifier:

> *nondigit*
> *identifier   nondigit*
> *identifier   digit*

nondigit: one of

```
_   a  b  c  d  e  f  g  h  i  j  k  l  m
    n  o  p  q  r  s  t  u  v  w  x  y  z
    A  B  C  D  E  F  G  H  I  J  K  L  M
    N  O  P  Q  R  S  T  U  V  W  X  Y  Z
```

digit: one of

```
0  1  2  3  4  5  6  7  8  9
```

A.1.4 Constants

constant:

> *floating-constant*
> *integer-constant*
> *enumeration-constant*
> *character-constant*

floating-constant:

> *fractional-constant exponent-part* opt *floating-suffix* opt
> *digit-sequence exponent-part floating-suffix* opt

fractional-constant:

> *digit-sequence* opt . *digit-sequence*
> *digit-sequence* .

exponent-part:

> **e** *sign* opt *digit-sequence*
> **E** *sign* opt *digit-sequence*

sign: one of

> + -

digit-sequence:

> *digit*
> *digit-sequence digit*

floating-suffix: one of

> **f l F L**

integer-constant:

> *decimal-constant   integer-suffix* opt
> *octal-constant   integer-suffix* opt
> *hexadecimal-constant   integer-suffix* opt

decimal-constant:

> *nonzero-digit*
> *decimal-constant   digit*

octal-constant:
>   **0**
>   *octal-constant   octal-digit*

hexadecimal-constant:
>   **0x** *hexadecimal-digit*
>   **0X** *hexadecimal-digit*
>   *hexadecimal-constant   hexadecimal-digit*

nonzero-digit: one of
>   **1 2 3 4 5 6 7 8 9**

octal-digit: one of
>   **0 1 2 3 4 5 6 7**

hexadecimal-digit: one of
>   **0 1 2 3 4 5 6 7 8 9**
>   **a b c d e f**
>   **A B C D E F**

integer-suffix:
>   *unsigned-suffix   long-suffix* opt
>   *long-suffix   unsigned-suffix* opt

unsigned-suffix: one of
>   **u U**

long-suffix: one of
>   **l L**

enumeration-constant:
>   *identifier*

character-constant:
>   ' *c-char-sequence* '
>   **L** ' *c-char-sequence* '

c-char-sequence:
>   *c-char*
>   *c-char-sequence   c-char*

c-char:
>   any member of the source character set except
>   the single quote ' backslash \ or new-line character
>   *escape-sequence*

escape-sequence:
>   *simple-escape-sequence*
>   *octal-escape-sequence*
>   *hexadecimal-escape-sequence*

simple-escape-sequence: one of
>   \' \" \? \\
>   \a \b \f \n \r \t \v

octal-escape-sequence:

> \ *octal-digit*
> \ *octal-digit octal-digit*
> \ *octal-digit octal-digit octal-digit*

hexadecimal-escape-sequence:

> \x *hexadecimal-digit*
> *hexadecimal-escape-sequence hexadecimal-digit*

A.1.5 String literals

string-literal:

> " *s-char-sequence* $_{opt}$ "
> L " *s-char-sequence* $_{opt}$ "

s-char-sequence:

> *s-char*
> *s-char-sequence s-char*

s-char:

> any member of the source character set except
> the double quote " backslash \ or new-line character
> *escape-sequence*

A.1.6 Operators

operator: one of

[	]	(	)	.	->	++
--	&	*	+	-	~	!
sizeof	/	%	<<	>>	<	>
<=	>=	==	!=	^	|	&&
||	?	:	=	*=	/=	%=
+=	-=	<<=	>>=	&=	^=	|=
,	#	##				

A.1.7 Punctuators

punctuator: one of

[	]	(	)	{	}
*	,	:	=	;	...
#					

A.1.8 Header names

header-name:

> < *h-char-sequence* >
> " *q-char-sequence* "

h-char-sequence:

> *h-char*
> *h-char-sequence h-char*

h-char:

> any member of the source character set except
> the new-line character and >

q-char-sequence:

> *q-char*
> *q-char-sequence   q-char*

q-char:

> any member of the source character set except
> the new-line character and "

A.1.9 Preprocessing numbers

pp-number:

> *digit*
> *.   digit*
> *pp-number digit*
> *pp-number nondigit*
> *pp-number* **e** *sign*
> *pp-number* **E** *sign*
> *pp-number .*

A.2 Phase structure grammar

A.2.1 Expressions

primary-expression:

> *identifier*
> *constant*
> *string-literal*
> (*expression*)

postfix-expression:

> *primary-expression*
> *postfix-expression* [*expression*]
> *postfix-expression* (*argument-expression-list* ₒₚₜ)
> *postfix-expression* .   *identifier*
> *postfix-expression* -> *identifier*
> *postfix-expression* ++
> *postfix-expression* --

argument-expression-list:

> *assignment-expression*
> *argument-expression-list , assignment-expression*

unary-expression:

> *postfix-expression*
> ++ *unary-expression*
> -- *unary-expression*
> *unary-operator   cast-expression*
> **sizeof** *unary-expression*
> **sizeof** (*type-name*)

unary-operator: one of

> & * + - ~ !

cast-expression:

> *unary-expression*
> (*type-name*) *cast-expression*

multiplicative-expression:
> *cast-expression*
> *multiplicative-expression* ***** *cast-expression*
> *multiplicative-expression* **/** *cast-expression*
> *multiplicative-expression* **%** *cast-expression*

additive-expression:
> *multiplicative-expression*
> *additive-expression* **+** *multiplicative-expression*
> *additive-expression* **-** *multiplicative-expression*

shift-expression:
> *additive-expression*
> *shift-expression* **<<** *additive-expression*
> *shift-expression* **>>** *additive-expression*

relational-expression:
> *shift-expression*
> *relational-expression* **<** *shift-expression*
> *relational-expression* **>** *shift-expression*
> *relational-expression* **<=** *shift-expression*
> *relational-expression* **>=** *shift-expression*

equality-expression:
> *relational-expression*
> *equality-expression* **==** *relational-expression*
> *equality-expression* **!=** *relational-expression*

AND-expression:
> *equality-expression*
> *AND-expression* **&** *equality-expression*

exclusive-OR-expression:
> *AND-expression*
> *exclusive-OR-expression* **^** *AND-expression*

inclusive-OR-expression
> *exclusive-OR-expression*
> *inclusive-OR-expression* **|** *exclusive-OR-expression*

logical-AND-expression:
> *inclusive-OR-expression*
> *logical-AND-expression* **&&** *inclusive-OR-expression*

logical-OR-expression:
> *logical-AND-expression*
> *logical-OR-expression* **||** *logical-AND-expression*

conditional-expression:
> *logical-OR-expression*
> *logical-OR-expression* **?** *expression* **:** *conditional-expression*

assignment-expression:
> *conditional-expression*
> *unary-expression* *assignment-operator* *assignment-expression*

assignment-operator: one of

     =   *=   /=   %=   +=   -=

     <<=   >>=   &=   ^= |=

expression:
> *assignment-expression*
> *expression , assignment-expression*

constant-expression:
> *conditional-expression*

A.2.2 Declarations

declaration:
> *declaration-specifiers init-declaration-list* opt ;

declaration-specifiers:
> *storage-class-specifier declaration-specifiers* opt
> *type-specifier declaration-specifiers* opt
> *type-qualifier declaration-specifiers* opt

init-declarator-list:
> *init-declarator*
> *init-declarator-list , init-declarator*

init-declarator:
> *declarator*
> *declarator = initializer*

storage-class-specifier:
> **typedef**
> **extern**
> **static**
> **auto**
> **register**

type-specifier:
> **void**
> **char**
> **short**
> **int**
> **long**
> **float**
> **double**
> **signed**
> **unsigned**
> *struct-or-union-specifier*
> *enum-specifier*
> *typedef-name*

struct-or-union-specifier:
> *struct-or-union identifier* opt { *struct-declaration-list* }
> *struct-or-union identifier*

struct-or-union:
> **struct**
> **union**

struct-declaration-list:
> *struct-declaration*
> *struct-declaration-list   struct-declaration*

struct-declaration:
> *specifier-qualifier-list   struct-declarator-list ;*

specifier-qualifier-list:
> *type-specifier   specifier-qualifier-list $_{opt}$*
> *type-qualifier   specifier-qualifier-list $_{opt}$*

struct-declarator-list:
> *struct-declarator*
> *struct-declarator-list , struct-declarator*

struct-declarator:
> *declarator*
> *declarator $_{opt}$: constant-expression*

enum-specifier:
> **enum** *identifier $_{opt}$*   { *enumerator-list* }
> **enum** *identifier*

enumerator-list:
> *enumerator*
> *enumerator-list , enumerator*

enumerator:
> *enumeration-constant*
> *enumeration-constant = constant-expression*

type-qualifier:
> **const**
> **volatile**

declarator:
> *pointer $_{opt}$ direct-declarator*

direct-declarator:
> *identifier*
> (*declarator*)
> *direct-declarator* [*constant-expression $_{opt}$*]
> *direct-declarator* (*parameter-type-list*)
> *direct-declarator* (*identifier-list $_{opt}$*)

pointer:
> * *type-qualifier-list $_{opt}$*
> * *type-qualifier-list $_{opt}$ pointer*

type-qualifier-list:
> *type-qualifier*
> *type-qualifier-list   type-qualifier*

436

parameter-type-list:
> *parameter-list*
> *parameter-list* , ...

parameter-list:
> *parameter-declaration*
> *parameter-list* , *parameter-declaration*

parameter-declaration:
> *declaration-specifiers declarator* .
> *declaration-specifiers abstract-declarator* opt

identifier-list:
> *identifier*
> *identifier-list* , *identifier*

type-name:
> *specifier-qualifier-list abstract-declarator* opt

abstract-declarator:
> *pointer*
> *pointer* opt *direct-abstract-declarator*

direct-abstract-declarator:
> (*abstract-declarator*)
> *direct-abstract-declarator* opt [*constant-expression* opt]
> *direct-abstract-declarator* opt (*parameter-type-list* opt)

typedef-name:
> *identifier*

initializer:
> *assignment-expression*
> { *initializer-list* }
> { *initializer-list* , }

initializer-list:
> *initializer*
> *initializer-list* , *initializer*

A.2.3 Statements

statement:
> *labelled-statement*
> *compound-statement*
> *expression-statement*
> *selection-statement*
> *iteration-statement*
> *jump-statement*

labelled-statement:
> *identifier* : *statement*
> **case** *constant-expression* : *statement*
> **default** : *statement*

compound-statement:
> { *declaration-list* _{opt} *statement-list* _{opt} }

declaration-list:
> *declaration*
> *declaration-list declaration*

statement-list:
> *statement*
> *statement-list statement*

expression-statement:
> *expression* _{opt} ;

selection-statement:
> **if** (*expression*) *statement*
> **if** (*expression*) *statement* **else** *statement*
> **switch** (*expression*) *labelled-statement*

iteration-statement:
> **while** (*expression*) *statement*
> **do** *statement* **while** (*expression*) ;
> **for** (*expression* _{opt} ; *expression* _{opt} ; *expression* _{opt}) *statement*

jump-statement:
> **goto** *identifier* ;
> **continue** ;
> **break** ;
> **return** *expression* _{opt} ;

A.2.4 External definitions

translation-unit:
> *external-declaration*
> *translation-unit external-declaration*

external-declaration:
> *function-definition*
> *declaration*

function-definition:
> *declaration-specifiers* _{opt} *declarator declaration-list* _{opt} *compound-statement*

A.3 Preprocessing directives

preprocessing-file:
> *group* _{opt}

group:
> *group-part*
> *group group-part*

438

group-part:

    pp-tokens _{opt}   *new-line*
    if-section
    control-line

if-section:

    if-group   *elif-groups* _{opt} *else-group* _{opt} *endif-line*

if-group:

    # if   *constant-expression new-line group* _{opt}
    # ifdef   *identifier new-line group* _{opt}
    # ifndef *identifier new-line group* _{opt}

elif-groups:

    elif-group
    elif-groups elif-group

elif-group:

    # elif *constant-expression new-line group* _{opt}

else-group:

    # else *new-line group* _{opt}

endif-line:

    # endif *new-line*

control-line:

    # include *pp-tokens new-line*
    # define   *identifier replacement-list new-line*
    # define   *identifier lparen identifier-list* _{opt} *) replacement-list new-line*
    # undef   *identifier new-line*
    # line   *pp-tokens new-line*
    # error   *pp-tokens* _{opt} *new-line*
    # pragma *pp-tokens* _{opt} *new-line*
    #   *new-line*

lparen:

    the left-parenthesis character without preceding white space

replacement-list:

    pp-tokens _{opt}

pp-tokens:

    preprocessing-token
    pp-tokens preprocessing-token

new-line:

    the new-line character

Appendix B - Summary of ANSI C Standard Library Functions

The ANSI C library is divided into fifteen sections, with each section being described by one of the following header files.

<assert.h>	<ctype.h>	<errno.h>	<float.h>	<limits.h>
<locale.h>	<math.h>	<setjmp.h>	<signal.h>	<stdarg.h>
<stddef.h>	<stdio.h>	<stdlib.h>	<string.h>	<time.h>

Many of the header files contain function declarations, type definitions, constant definitions and/or macro definitions. If a source file contains a reference to any of these items then the appropriate header file should be included using **#include** at the beginning of the source file.

Within this appendix the contents of all the header files have been described. Further references and a more detailed explanation of the contents of some of the headers can be found throughout the book.

B.1 <assert.h> Diagnostics

void assert(expression);

This header contains only the **assert** macro which enables a program to perform self-checks. If *expression* is zero (false), assert prints a message to *stdout* and calls **abort**. The message has the format:

`Assertion failed: expression, file filename, line linenumber`

Note - If #define NDEBUG 1 occurs prior to #include <assert.h> the call to assert is ignored.

```
/*
appendix B - program (P1.c) to demonstrate the assert function
*/

#include <stdio.h>
#include <assert.h>

void test(char character)
{

    /* assertion character is lower case letter or digit */
    assert(islower(character) || isdigit(character));
    printf("character %c lower case or digit\n", character);
}

main()
{
    test('3');
    test('a');
    test('!');
}
```

Results from program P1.c being run

```
character 3 lower case or digit
character a lower case or digit
Assertion failed: islower(character)||isdigit(character),file p1.c,line 12
Abnormal program Termination
```

B.2 <ctype.h> Character handling

The header contains functions for testing and converting characters. In the following list, the declaration of each function is followed by a description of the value returned by each function. Note - a return value of !=0 (non-zero) implies *true* when used in a conditional statement.

int isalnum(int c);	!=0 if c is an alphanumeric character in range 'A'-'Z', 'a'-'z', or '0'-'9'
int isalpha(int c);	!=0 if c is an alphabetic character in range 'A'-'Z' or 'a'-'z'
int iscntrl(int c);	!=0 if c is a control character in range 0x0-0x1F or 0x7F
int isdigit(int c);	!=0 if c is a digit in range '0'-'9'
int isgraph(int c);	!=0 if c is a printable character (excluding space) in range 0x21-0x7E
int islower(int c);	!=0 if c is lower case letter in range 'a'-'z'
int isprint(int c);	!=0 if c is a printable character in range 0x20-0x7E
int ispunct(int c);	!=0 if c is a punctuation character in range 0x21-0x2F, 0x3A-0x40, 0x5B-0x60, 0x7B-0x7E
int isspace(int c);	!=0 if c is a white space character in range 0x9-0xD or 0x20
int isupper(int c);	!=0 if c is upper case letter in range 'A'-'Z'
int isxdigit(int c);	!=0 if c is a hexadecimal digit in range '0'-'9', 'A'-'F' or 'a'-'f'
int tolower(int c);	return lower case value of character c in range 'a'-'z'
int toupper(int c);	return upper case value of character c in range 'A'-'Z'

B.3 <errno.h> Errors

If this header is included in a program, then it is possible to detect whether an error has occurred during calls to certain library functions. After an error occurs the system variable **errno** will contain information about the error. The following symbolic constants are defined in the header file <errno.h> in response to either the DOS or UNIX error codes.

/* Dos Error Codes */

EZERO	0	/* No Error */
EINVFN	1	/* Invalid function code */
ENOENT	2	/* File not found */
ENOPATH	3	/* Path not found */
EMFILE	4	/* Too many open files */
EACCES	5	/* Access denied */
EBADF	6	/* Invalid handle */
E2BIG	7	/* Memory blocks destroyed */
ENOMEM	8	/* Insufficient Memory */
EINVMEM	9	/* Invalid memory block address */
EINVENV	10	/* Invalid environment */
EINVFMT	11	/* Invalid format */
EINVACC	12	/* Invalid access code */
EINVDAT	13	/* Invalid data */
ENODEV	15	/* Invalid drive */
ECURDIR	16	/* Attempt to remove CurDir */
ENOTSAM	17	/* Not same device */
ENMFILE	18	/* No more files */

```
/* RTL error codes */
EINVAL        19      /* Invalid argument */
ENOTDIR       20      /* Not directory */
EISDIR        21      /* Is directory  */
ENOEXEC       22      /* Corrupted exec file */
EMLINK        32      /* Cross-device link */

EDOM          33      /* Math argument */
ERANGE        34      /* Result too large */
EDEADLOCK     36      /* file locking deadlock */
EEXIST        80      /* File exists MSDOS 3.0 + */

EFAULT        -1      /* Unknown error    */
EPERM         -1      /* UNIX - not in MSDOS */
ESRCH         -1      /* UNIX - not in MSDOS */
EINTR         -1      /* UNIX - not in MSDOS */
EIO           -1      /* UNIX - not in MSDOS */
ENXIO         -1      /* UNIX - not in MSDOS */
ECHILD        -1      /* UNIX - not in MSDOS */
EAGAIN        -1      /* UNIX - not in MSDOS */
ENOTBLK       -1      /* UNIX - not in MSDOS */
EBUSY         -1      /* UNIX - not in MSDOS */
ENFILE        -1      /* UNIX - not in MSDOS */
ENOTTY        -1      /* UNIX - not in MSDOS */
ETXTBSY       -1      /* UNIX - not in MSDOS */
EFBIG         -1      /* UNIX - not in MSDOS */
ENOSPC        -1      /* UNIX - not in MSDOS */
ESPIPE        -1      /* UNIX - not in MSDOS */
EROFS         -1      /* UNIX - not in MSDOS */
EPIPE         -1      /* UNIX - not in MSDOS */
EUCLEAN       -1      /* UNIX - not in MSDOS */

/*
appendix B - program (P2.c) to demonstrate header <errno.h>
*/

#include <stdio.h>
#include <errno.h>
#include <math.h>
#include <limits.h>

main()
{
    printf("%10.2G\n", sqrt(-1.0));
    printf("%d\n", errno);
    printf("%10.2G\n", exp(INT_MAX));
    printf("%d\n", errno);
}
```

Results from program P2.c being run

```
     0
33
  1.8E+308
34
```

Notice from the output that errno 33 (EDOM) indicates an error with the maths argument in sqrt(-1.0) and errno 34 (ERANGE) indicates that the result exp(INT_MAX) is too large.

B.4 <float.h> Characteristics of floating types - see also section 3.1

Supplies machine-dependent macros that define the range and accuracy of floating-point types.

DBL_DIG	15	/* number of decimal digits of precision */
DBL_MANT_DIG	53	/* number of bits in mantissa */
DBL_MAX_10_EXP	308	/* maximum decimal exponent */
DBL_MAX_EXP	1024	/* maximum binary exponent */
DBL_MIN_10_EXP	-307	/* minimum decimal exponent */
DBL_MIN_EXP	-1021	/* minimum binary exponent */
DBL_RADIX	2	/* exponent radix */
DBL_ROUNDS	1	/* addition rounding */
DBL_EPSILON	2.2204460492503131e-016	/* 1.0+DBL_EPSILON != 1.0 */
DBL_MAX	1.7976931348623151e+308	/* maximum value */
DBL_MIN	2.2250738585072014e-308	/* minimum positive value */
FLT_DIG	6	/* number of decimal digits of precision */
FLT_GUARD	0	
FLT_MANT_DIG	24	/* number of bits in mantissa */
FLT_MAX_10_EXP	38	/* maximum decimal exponent */
FLT_MAX_EXP	128	/* maximum binary exponent */
FLT_MIN_10_EXP	-37	/* minimum decimal exponent */
FLT_MIN_EXP	-125	/* minimum binary exponent */
FLT_NORMALIZE	0	
FLT_RADIX	2	/* exponent radix */
FLT_ROUNDS	1	/* addition rounding chops */
FLT_EPSILON	1.192092896e-07	/* smallest such that 1.0+FLT_EPSILON != 1.0 */
FLT_MAX	3.402823466e+38	/* maximum value */
FLT_MIN	1.175494351e-38	/* minimum positive value */
LDBL_DIG	19	/* number of decimal digits of precision */
LDBL_EPSILON	5.4210108624275221706e-20	
		/* smallest such that 1.0+LDBL_EPSILON != 1.0 */
LDBL_MANT_DIG	64	/* number of bits in mantissa */
LDBL_MAX	1.189731495357231765e+4932L	/* maximum value */
LDBL_MAX_10_EXP	4932	/* maximum decimal exponent */
LDBL_MAX_EXP	16384	/* maximum binary exponent */
LDBL_MIN	3.3621031431120935063e-4932L	/* minimum positive value */
LDBL_MIN_10_EXP	(-4931)	/* minimum decimal exponent */
LDBL_MIN_EXP	(-16381)	/* minimum binary exponent */
LDBL_RADIX	2	/* exponent radix */
LDBL_ROUNDS	DBL_ROUNDS	/* addition rounding */

B.5 <limits.h> Sizes of integral types - see also section 3.1

Supplies machine-dependent macros that define the range of integer and character types.

CHAR_BIT	8	/* number of bits in a char */
CHAR_MIN	(-128)	/* minimum if signed char, otherwise (0)*/
CHAR_MAX	127	/* maximum if signed char, otherwise (255) */
MB_LEN_MAX	1	/* multiple byte length - maximum 1 byte */

SCHAR_MAX	127	/* maximum signed char */
SCHAR_MIN	(-128)	/* minimum signed char */
UCHAR_MAX	255	/* maximum unsigned char */
SHRT_MAX	32767	/* maximum short integer */
SHRT_MIN	(-32767-1)	/* minimum short integer */
USHRT_MAX	65535U	/* maximum unsigned short integer */
INT_MAX	32767	/* maximum integer */
INT_MIN	(-32767-1)	/* minimum integer */
UINT_MAX	0xFFFFU	/* maximum unsigned integer */
LONG_MAX	2147483647L	/* maximum long integer */
LONG_MIN	(-2147483647L-1)	/* minimum long integer */
ULONG_MAX	4294967295UL	/* maximum unsigned long integer */

B.6 <locale.h> Localization

The header provides functions to control aspects of the library that depend upon the country or other geographical location. These include the character used as the decimal point, the currency symbol and the appearance of the date and the time.

struct lconv *localeconv(void);

The function localeconv returns a pointer to the structure specifying the current locale and is specified as follows in the header file <locale.h>

struct lconv   {

```
                char *decimal_point;
                char *thousands_sep;
                char *grouping;
                char *int_curr_symbol;
                char *currency_symbol;
                char *mon_decimal_point;
                char *mon_thousands_sep;
                char *mon_grouping;
                char *positive_sign;
                char *negative_sign;
                char int_frac_digits;
                char frac_digits;
                char p_cs_precedes;
                char p_sep_by_space;
                char n_cs_precedes;
                char n_sep_by_space;
                char p_sign_posn;
                char n_sign_posn;
            };
```

char *setlocale(int category, const char *locale);

The function setlocale may be used to set or query the program's current locale, where category specifies the action requested and can take one of the following values.

LC_ALL	specifies the entire locale
LC_COLLATE	specifies the behaviour of functions strcoll and strxfrm
LC_CTYPE	specifies the behaviour of the character and multi-byte functions
LC_MONETARY	specifies the formatting information returned by localeconv
LC_NUMERIC	specifies the decimal point character for the formatted I/O functions and string conversion functions
LC_TIME	specifies the behaviour of the strftime function

locale points to a specification for the locale. A value of "C" for locale specifies the minimal C environment; a value of "" specifies the native environment.

If a valid string is given for the locale argument, the area of the locale specified by category is changed to that value. If an error occurs a NULL value is returned. If the value of locale is "", the current setting for that portion of the locale is returned and the locale remains unchanged.

```
/*
appendix B - program (P3.c) to demonstrate <locale.h>
*/

#include <stdio.h>
#include <locale.h>
#include <limits.h>

main()
{
    struct lconv *current_locale;

    setlocale(LC_ALL, "C");
    current_locale = localeconv();

    printf("%s\n", current_locale->decimal_point);
    printf("%d\n", current_locale->frac_digits);
}
```

Results from program P3.c being run

127

B.7 <math.h> Mathematics - see also section 8.7

The header provides trigonometric, hyperbolic, exponential, logarithmic and several miscellaneous mathematical functions. These functions normally expect parameters of type double and return values of type double.

double acos(double x);	returns the arc cosine of x
double asin(double x);	returns the arc sine of x
double atan(double x);	returns the arc tangent of x
double atan2(double x, double y);	returns the arc tangent of y/x
double ceil(double x);	returns the result of rounding x towards infinity to the nearest integer
double cos(double x);	returns the cosine of x
double cosh(double x);	returns the hyperbolic cosine of x
double exp(double x);	returns the exponential result of x
double fabs(double x);	returns the absolute value of x
double floor(double x);	returns the result of rounding x towards zero to the nearest integer
double fmod(double x, double y);	returns the remainder after the division x/y
double frexp(double val, int *exptr);	function returns the mantissa and stores the exponent in the location pointed at by exptr
double ldexp(double x, int exp);	returns x multiplied by 2 raised to the power of exp
double log(double x);	returns the natural logarithm of x
double log10(double x);	returns the base 10 logarithm of x
double modf(double x, double *intptr);	returns the signed fractional part of x and stores the integer part at the location pointed at by intptr
double pow(double x, double y);	returns x raised to the power of y
double sin(double x);	returns the sine of x
double sinh(double x);	returns the hyperbolic sine of x

double sqrt(double x);   returns the square root of x
double tan(double x);   returns the tangent of x
double tanh(double x);   returns the hyperbolic tangent of x

B.8 <setjmp.h> Non-local jumps

If function main calls function A, and in turn function A calls function B, then control normally passes back to A upon exiting from B, and then to main upon exiting from A. However, it is possible to return from function B directly to main without returning via function A. Such a change in behaviour is possible by using the following functions.

void longjmp(jmp_buf env, int retval);
int setjmp(jmp_buf env);

The longjmp function restores the processor environment previously saved in env by setjmp. These functions provide a mechanism for executing inter-function gotos, and are usually used to pass control to error recovery code.

A call to setjmp causes the current processor environment to be saved in env. A following call to longjmp restores the saved environment and causes execution to resume at a point immediately after the corresponding setjmp call. Execution continues with retval as the return value from setjmp.

As long as longjmp is called before the function calling setjmp returns, all variables local to the routine will have the same value as when setjmp was called. However, register variables may not be restored. Use the *volatile* keyword to ensure that local variables are properly restored.

Essentially setjmp marks a place in a function so that longjmp can be used to return to that place later.

The function setjmp returns 0 after saving the processor environment. If setjmp returns after a call to longjmp, it returns the value argument of longjmp, which is guaranteed to be non-zero.

```
/*
appendix B - program (P4.c) to demonstrate the use of non-local jumps
*/

#include <stdio.h>
#include <setjmp.h>

typedef enum {false, true} boolean;

jmp_buf mark;

void B(void);

void A(void)
{
    printf("function A\n");
    B();
    printf("returned to function A\n");
}

void B(void)
{
    static boolean jump = false;

    if (jump)
        longjmp(mark, 1);
    else
        printf("function B\n");

    jump = true;
}
```

```
main()
{
    int counter = 0;

    for (; counter <= 1; counter++)
    {
        printf("function main\n");
        if (setjmp(mark))
            printf("jumped back to main from B\n");
        else
            A();
    }
}
```

Results from program P4.c being run

```
function main
function A
function B
returned to function A
function main
function A
jumped back to main from B
```

B.9 <signal.h> Signal handling

The header provides facilities for handling exceptional conditions including interrupts and run-time errors.

int raise(int sig);

The function raise sends a signal, sig to the current process. The default action for that signal will be taken unless a new action was defined previously by a call to signal. The return value is 0 if this call is successful and non-zero otherwise.

void (* signal (int sig, void(*func) (int))) (int);

The function signal sets the signal handler for signal sig to the value func. The function returns the previous value of the signal handler. If an error occurred, a value of SIG_ERR is returned and errno is set to EINVAL, indicating an invalid value for sig.

The argument sig can take any one of the following values defined in <signal.h>

```
SIGINT       /* interrupt - corresponds to DOS 3.x int 23H */
SIGILL       /* illegal op code */
SIGFPE       /* floating point error */
SIGSEGV      /* segment violation */
SIGTERM      /* Software termination signal from kill */
SIGABRT      /* abnormal termination triggered by abort call */
```

The argument func must be one of the following constants or the function address of a user defined signal handler.

```
SIG_DFL      /* default signal action */
SIG_IGN      /* ignore */
```

```
/*
appendix B - program (P5.c) to demonstrate the functions raise and signal
*/

#include <stdio.h>
#include <signal.h>

void warning(void)
{
    printf("interrupt - Ctrl C pressed\n");
}

void abort_program(void)
{
    printf("program termination - raised SIGABRT\n");
    exit(errno);
}

main()
{
    signal(SIGINT, warning);
    getchar();
    signal(SIGABRT, abort_program);
    raise(SIGABRT);
}
```

Results from program P5.c being run

```
^C
interrupt - Ctrl C pressed

program termination - raised SIGABRT
```

B.10 <stdarg.h> Variable arguments - see also section 16.4

The header provides functions that allow the programmer to write functions containing variable-length parameter lists. The variable argument list macros provide a portable method of accessing arguments to a function taking a variable number of arguments.

type va_arg(va_list argptr, type);	returns the current and succeeding arguments
void va_end(va_list argptr);	sets the argument pointer to NULL
void va_start(va_list argptr);	sets the argument pointer (argptr), declared as type va_list, to the first argument in the list passed to the function

B.11 <stddef.h> Common definitions

The header provides definitions of frequently used types and macros. A partial listing of the header illustrates definitions for the types ptrdiff_t, size_t, wchar_t and macros offsetof and NULL.

```
typedef int ptrdiff_t;
typedef unsigned size_t;
typedef unsigned char wchar_t;
#define offsetof(st, member) (size_t)(&((st*)0)->member)
#define NULL   0
```

B.12 <stdio.h> Input/ output - see also chapters 3 and 14

The header provides functions for text and binary I/O and file operations.

void clearerr(FILE *st); clears the error and EOF flags on stream st

int fclose(FILE *st); closes the stream st, flushing any buffer associated with the stream

int feof(FILE *st); returns -1 if a stream has reached the end of file

int ferror(FILE *st); returns non-zero if an error has occurred, otherwise 0

int fflush(FILE *st); flushes the stream st

int fgetc(FILE *st); returns the character read from stream st as an integer value

int fgetpos(FILE *st, fpos_t *fp); gets the current value of the stream's file position indicator and store this value in the object to which fp points if successful returns 0

char *fgets(char *string, int num, FILE *st); returns the string read from the stream st

int flushall(void); flushes all open streams and returns the number of open streams

FILE *fopen(const char *path, const char *type); opens the file specified by path and associates a stream with that file; if successful returns a pointer to the open stream, otherwise returns a NULL pointer

int fprintf(FILE *st, const char *format, ...); provides formatted output to the stream st

int fputc(int c, FILE *st); writes a character to the current position of stream st, and increments the stream pointer; if successful returns the character written as an integer value, otherwise returns -1 indicating an error or end of file condition

int fputs(const char *string, FILE *stream); writes a string to the specified stream at the current position in the stream; the null terminator is not copied; if successful the function returns the last character written, otherwise the function returns EOF

size_t fread(void *buffer, size_t size, size_t nritems, FILE *stream); reads a specified number of data elements from a stream; returns the number of complete items read

void free(void *buffer); de-allocates a block of memory previously allocated with malloc, calloc or realloc.

FILE *freopen(const char *path, const char *type, FILE *stream); closes the file specified by stream and then reassigns the stream to the file specified by path

int fscanf(FILE *stream, const char *format, [arguments] ...); reads data from the current position in the specified stream; returns the number of fields successfully converted and assigned

int fseek(FILE *stream, long offset, int origin); moves the file pointer associated with the specified stream to a location that is offet bytes from the specified origin - the next operation on the stream will take place at the new location; if successful returns 0.

int fsetpos(FILE *st, const fpos_t *fp); sets the current value of the stream st's file position indicator to the value pointed to by fp; if successful returns 0.

long ftell(FILE *st); returns the current position of the file pointer relative to the beginning of the file associated with stream st;

int fwrite(const void *buffer, size_t size, size_t num, FILE *st); writes up to num blocks, each of size bytes, from buffer to stream st; the stream pointer is incremented by the number of bytes written; returns the number of complete items actually written

int getc(FILE *st); reads a character from the current position of stream st and increments the stream pointer; returns the character read as an integer value

int getchar(void); reads a character from stdin; returns the character read as an integer

char *gets(char *buf); reads a string from the stream stdin and stores it at buf; returns buf if successful, otherwise returns NULL

void perror(const char *message); prints an error message to stderr

int printf(const char *format[, argument] ...); formats and prints a series of arguments to stdout; returns the number of characters printed

int putc(int ch, FILE *st); writes a character ch on to the stream st at the current position and increments the stream pointer; returns the character written as an integer

int putchar(int ch); writes a character ch on the steam stdout; returns the character written as an integer

int puts(const char *s); writes the string s to stdout, replacing the string's terminating null character with a new line character

int remove(const char *path); deletes the file specified by path; returns 0 is the file was successfully deleted, otherwise returns -1

int rename(const char *oldname, const char *newname); changes the name of the file or directory specified by oldname to newname - oldname must exist

void rewind(FILE *st); sets the file pointer associated with st to the beginning of the file and clears the error and end of file indicators

int scanf(const char *format, [arguments] ...); reads characters from stdin and stores the converted data in the locations given by arguments; returns the number of fields converted and assigned

void setbuf(FILE *st, char *buffer); allows the user to control buffering for stream st - st refers to an open stream before it has been read or written; if buffer is not NULL it must point to a character array of at least BUFSIZ defined in <stdio.h>

int setvbuf(FILE *st, char *buffer, int type, size_t size); allows the user to control buffering for stream st; the arguments st and buffer are the same as for setbuf; type specifies the buffering mode and size specifies the size of the buffer to be used

int sprintf(char *s,const char *format, ...); provides formatted output to a character string

int sscanf(const char *s, const char *format, ...); provides formatted input, taking its input from a character string

FILE *tmpfile(void); creates a temporary file, opening it for updating in a binary mode; the file is automatically deleted when it is closed or when the current process terminates; returns a pointer to the temporary file's stream

char *tmpnam(char *sptr); creates a unique file name which can be used as a temporary file; sptr is a pointer to an array of characters; returns a pointer to the newly created filename

int ungetc(int c, FILE *st); puts the character c, converted to an unsigned integer char, back on to stream st

B.13 <stdlib.h> General utilities

The header provides functions for converting numbers to strings and strings to numbers, random number generation, memory management, searching, sorting, operations upon multi-byte characters and strings, and miscellaneous functions.

void abort(void); writes the message Abnormal Program Termination to stderr and calls raise(SIGABRT)

int abs(int num); returns the absolute value of num

int atexit(void (*func)(void)); places the function pointer func onto a stack to be called from the function exit when the process terminates; returns 0 if the function was successfully placed on the stack

double atof(const char *s); converts the string argument to double precision; returns the result of the conversion

int atol(const char *s); converts the string input s to an integer value; returns the result of the conversion

void *bsearch(const void *key,
                const void *base,
                size_t num,
                size_t width,
                int (*compare)(const void *e1, const void *e2));
performs a binary search on a sorted array

void *calloc(size_t number, size_t size); returns a pointer to the allocated storage, otherwise returns NULL to indicate insufficient storage

div_t div(int num, int den); divides num by den, returning the quotient in the div_t structure member quot and the remainder in the structure member rem

void exit(int status); terminates the calling process

char *getenv(const char *name); returns a pointer to the environment variable containing the string value of name; if the variable is not defined the return value will be NULL

long labs(long num); returns the absolute value of its long integer argument num

struct ldiv_t ldiv(long num, long den); divides num by den, storing the quotient in the structure member quot and the remainder in the structure member rem; returns a structure of type ldiv_t which contains members for quotient and remainder

void *malloc(size_t size); allocates a block of at least size bytes from the heap; returns a void pointer to the allocated space, otherwise returns NULL

int mblen(const char *s, size_t n); determines the number of bytes comprising the multi-byte character to which s points

size_t mbstowcs(wchar_t *pwcs, const char *s, size_t n); converts a sequence of multi-byte characters pointed to by s and stores them as codes at the addresses to which pwcs points; returns the number of characters copied

int mbtowc(wchar_t *pwc, const char *s, size_t n); converts up to n bytes comprising the multi-byte character pointed to by s to a code representing that character and stores this code at pwc, provided that pwc is not NULL

void qsort(const void *base,
            size_t num,
            size_t width,
            int(*compare)(const void *e1, const void *e2));
qsort is an implementation of the quick sort algorithm for sorting an array

int rand(void); returns a pseudo-random number in the range 0 - RAND_MAX

void *realloc(void *buffer, size_t size); changes the size of a memory block (buffer) previously allocated from the heap by a call to calloc, malloc or realloc; size is the new number of bytes requested; returns a void pointer to the allocated space

void srand(unsigned seed); sets the starting point for the pseudo random number generator

double strtod(const char *s, char **endptr); converts a string to a double precision floating-point value

long strtol(const char *s, char **endptr, int base); converts a string to a long integer value

unsigned long strtoul(const char *s, char **endptr, int base); converts a string to an unsigned long integer value

size_t wcstombs(char *s, const wchar_t *pwcs, size_t n); converts the codes stored at the location to which pwcs points; these codes are converted to multi-byte characters and stored at the location to which s points; returns the number of characters created

int wctomb(const char *s, wchar_t wchar); returns the number of bytes needed to represent the code wchar as a multi-byte character and stores the multi-byte character at s

B.14 <string.h> String handling

The header provides functions that perform string operations.

void *memchr(const void *buf, int c, size_t num); searches for character c in the first num bytes of buf; if c found returns a pointer to the first occurrence, otherwise returns NULL

int memcmp(const void *s1, const void *s2, size_t num); compares the first num bytes of s1 and s2; returns an integer indicating the relationship of s1 and s2

void *memcpy(void *dest, const vid *source, size_t num); copies num bytes from source to dest; does not ensure that overlapping regions of memory are correctly copied; returns a pointer to dest

void *memmove(void *dest, const void *source, size_t num); copies num bytes from source to dest; if regions of memory overlap, these regions are copied before being overwritten

void *memset(void *s, int c, size_t num); sets the first num bytes of s to a specified character; returns a pointer to s

void *strcat(char *dest, const char *source); appends source to dest, terminating the new string with a null character

char *strchr(const char *s, int c); returns a pointer to the first occurrence of character c in string s

int strcmp(const char *s1, const char *s2); compares strings s1 and s2 and returns a value representing their relationship

int strcoll(const char *s1, const char *s2); similar to strcmp

char *strcpy(char *dest, const char *source); copies string source to dest

size_t strcspn(const char *s1, const char *s2); returns the index of the first character in s1 that belongs to the set of characters in s2

char *strdup(const char *s); allocates storage space for a copy of string s and copies string s to this new location; returns a pointer to the new copy of s

char *strerror(int errnum); maps errnum to an error message, returning a pointer to a string

size_t strlen(const char *s); returns the length of string s

char *strncat(char *dest, const char *source, size_t num); appends up to num characters from string source to string dest, terminating the new string with a null character; returns a pointer to the new string

int strncmp(const char *s1, const char *s2, size_t num); compares up to num characters from strings s1 and s2 and returns a value representing their relationship

char *strncpy(char *dest, const char *source, size_t num); copies up to num bytes from string source to string dest; returns a pointer to dest

char *strnset(char *s, int ch, size_t num); sets up to num bytes of string s to character ch

char *strrchr(const char *s, int c); returns a pointer to the last occurrence of character c in string s

char *strrev(char *s); reverses the order of the characters in string s (except for the terminating null character); returns a pointer to string s

char *strset(char *s, int ch); sets the bytes of string s to character ch
size_t strspn(const char *s1, const char *s2); returns the index of the first character in s1 that does not belong to the set of characters in s2

char *strstr(const char *s1, const char *s2); returns the address of the first occurrence of string s2 in s1

char *strtok(char *s1, const char *s2); separates string s1 into a series of tokens, with string s2 as the set of delimiters for the tokens; returns a pointer to a token

size_t strxfrm(char *s1, const char *s2, size_t n); copies up to n bytes from string s2 to string s1; returns a pointer to s1

B.15 <time.h> Date and time

The header provides functions for manipulating the date and time.

char *asctime(const struct tm *time); converts time as a structure to a formatted character string containing exactly 26 characters; returns a pointer to the character string result

time_t clock(void); returns a number that gives the number of seconds elapsed since the start of the current process if divided by the macro CLOCKS_PER_SECOND

char *ctime(const time_t *tt); converts time tt seconds, stored as a time_t to a formatted character string; returns a pointer to a formatted character string

double difftime(time_t t1, time_t t2); calculates the difference between two times t1 and t2; returns the elapsed time in seconds t1-t2

struct tm *gmtime(const time_t *tt); converts the time value stored at tt to a structure tm; returns a pointer to the structure result

struct tm *localtime(const time_t *tt); converts time stored at tt to a structure; the function uses global variables timezone and daylight to calculate local time; returns a pointer to the structure result

time_t mktime(struct tm *timeptr); converts the local time, stored in the structure timeptr, into the format that would have been returned by a direct call to the function time; returns the encoded time

size_t strftime(char *s, size_t maxsize, const char *format, const struct tm *timeptr); places characters into the array pointed to by s according to the format string format. No more than maxsize characters are output. Where s - specifies the location into which characters are to be placed; maxsize - specifies the maximum number of characters to place into the s array; format - specifies the format for the output and timeptr is a pointer to the structure containing the time. The format string consists of zero or more conversion specifiers and ordinary characters. Each conversion specifier is replaced by characters as specified in the following list. Other characters are output directly.

char	meaning
%a	abbreviated weekday name
%A	full weekday name
%b	abbreviated month name
%B	full month name
%c	date and time representation
%d	day of month as a decimal number 00 - 31
%H	hour as a decimal number 00 - 23
%I	month as a decimal number 01 - 12
%j	day of the year as a decimal number 001 - 366
%m	month as a decimal number 01 - 12
%M	minute as a decimal number 00-59
%p	AM or PM
%S	second as a decimal number
%U	week number of the year, with Sunday as day 1 - 00 - 53
%w	week day as a decimal number, with Sunday = 0 - 0 - 6
%W	week number of the year, with Monday as day 1 - 00 - 53
%x	date representation
%X	time representation
%y	year without century 00 - 99
%Y	year with century
%%	is replaced by %

time_t time(time_t *tt); returns the number of seconds elapsed since 00:00:00 Greenwich Mean Time, January 1st 1970

In a listing of the <time.h> file the following definitions are available

```
typedef long   time_t;
typedef long   clock_t;
#define CLOCKS_PER_SEC 100
```

```
struct tm {
            int tm_sec;
            int tm_min;
            int tm_hour;
            int tm_mday;
            int tm_mon;
            int tm_year;
            int tm_wday;
            int tm_yday;
            int tm_isdst;
         };
```

```
/*
appendix B - program (P6.c) to demonstrate the functions asctime,
clock, gmtime, localtime, strftime and time
*/

#include <stdio.h>
#include <time.h>

#define max_size 64

main()
{
    time_t      time_now;
    struct tm *time_ptr;
    char        string[max_size];

    time(&time_now); /* get time in seconds */

    /* display local time */
    printf("%s\n\n", asctime(localtime(&time_now)));

    /* custom build the format of the date/ time */
    time_ptr = gmtime(&time_now);
    strftime(string, max_size, "%H:%M %p", time_ptr);

    /* display new format string */
    printf("%s\n\n", string);

    getchar(); /* introduce a delay */

    /* display elapsed time in seconds since start of program */
    printf("%d\n\n", (int) clock() / CLOCKS_PER_SEC);
}
```

Results from program P6.c being run

```
Fri Feb 10 18:59:32 1995

18.59 PM

10
```

Appendix C - C programming in a UNIX environment

C.1 Compilation

Normally a C program is composed of one or more program text files, which can be header files and/or program files. Under UNIX, program files are compiled with the **cc** command. This command does not invoke the C compiler but invokes a driver program that initiates the phases of macro preprocessing, compiling, linking and loading. The format of the **cc** command is:

cc options file_1 file_2 ...

where the options are distinguished by a leading hyphen, and have the effect of altering the effect of the **cc** command.

A program that is created as one source file *ex_01.c*, say, may be compiled, linked and loaded using the command:

cc ex_01.c -o run

where the object filename is given to the compiler command by the **-o** option which is followed by the name of the destination file *run*.

Consider a program split over two files, *first.c* and *second.c*. The two files can be compiled and combined to produce an executable file called *run* by using the command

cc first.c second.c -o run

The source program *first.c* is processed up to and including the compilation phase. An object file named *first.o* is created. Similarly, the source program *second.c* is processed and an object file named *second.o* is created. The two object files are then linked together to produce the executable program file *run*. The two files *first.o* and *second.o* are then automatically deleted after the linking phase.

The object files can, however, be retained if the **-c** option is used. For example, object files may be retained that correspond to the source files *first.c* and *second.c* by using the commands

cc -c first.c

cc -c second.c

The two object files can be linked to produce the executable file named *run* with the command

cc first.o second.o -o run

The advantage of the separate compilation and linking is that if changes are made to one file, first.c say, then only this file need be re-compiled and the new object file first.o linked in with the second.o as before.

C.2 Linking specified libraries

In the compilation of those programs in the book that required the <math.h> header file it was necessary to specify the option **-lm** in the **cc** command line, otherwise, the functions of the maths library could not be reconciled.

For example in chapter 8, program ex_04.c was compiled and linked using the command

cc ex_04.c -lm -o run

The general format of the **-l** option is

-lname

where *name* is the name of the library to be searched.

457

C.3 Program execution

No separate command is available for program execution. The executable program created after linking and loading is complete, and is activated by using the name of the run-time file. In these examples the run-time file has deliberately been given the name *run* to mimic a hypothetical command *run*, to execute the program.

C.4 Makefiles

The basic operation of the command **make** is to update a target file by ensuring that all of the files on which it depends exist and are up to date. To illustrate, consider the contents of the *makefile* for the final example in chapter 16. A program named *run* is made by compiling and loading two C-language files *ex_07.c* and *ex_08.c*. Files *ex_07.c* and ex_08.c also requires declarations from the header file *ex_07.h*. The following text describes the contents of the file named *makefile*.

```
run : ex_07.o ex_08.o
    cc ex_07.o ex_08.o -o run
ex_07.o ex_08.c : ex_07.h
```

The command **make** will perform the operations needed to recreate the file *run* after any changes have been made to any of the files ex_07.c, ex_08.c or ex_07.h.

Make operates using three sources of information: the contents of the makefile, file names and time stamps from the file system and built in rules. In the example, the first line states that run is dependent upon two object files ex_07.o and ex_08.o. Once these object files are current the second line describes how to create run. The third line shows the dependence of the files.

If none of the source or object files had changed since the last time run was created, all the files would be current, and the make command would announce this fact and stop. If, however, the ex_07.h file had been changed then ex_07.c would be re-compiled and then run created from the new .o files.

In the example from chapter 12 it was necessary to create such a file for execution with the MAKE command in JPI TopSpeed C and Microsoft Visual C++. The equivalent file in UNIX is coded as follows:

```
ex_02: _initial.o _entrant.o _data.o _count.o _fastest.o _region.o _current.o _results.o _main.o
    cc _initial.o _entrant.o _data.o _count.o _fastest.o _region.o _current.o _results.o _main.o -o ex_02
_initial.o _entrant.o _data.o _count.o _fastest.o _region.o _current.o _results.o _main.o : header.h
```

Note - the tabulation before the cc command in the makefile is mandatory.

C.5 Redirection

Redirection of the standard output, normally to a screen, can be altered using the redirection operators > and >> , where > overwrites the contents of a file and >> appends data to a file.

Redirection of the standard input, normally from a keyboard, can be altered using the redirection operator <, where input is taken from a named file.

For example the demonstration program ex_02.c given in chapter 14, can input data from a text file *numbers.txt* and output the results to a file *results.txt* after the run-time file has been created using:

cc ex_02.c -o run

using the command line

run <numbers.txt >results.txt

It is assumed that the files run, numbers.txt and results.txt are to be found in the same sub-directory.

C.6 File manipulation

make (or create) a directory - **mkdir** *directory-name*

list a file on the screen - **cat** *filename* or **more** *filename*

print a file - **lpr options** *filename*

list files and directories

    ls for listing a current directory
    ls *directory-name* for listing a specified directory

move (or rename) files and directories
    mv *source-filename destination-filename*
    mv *source-filename destination-directory*
    mv *source-directory-name destination-directory-name*

copy files

    cp *source-filename destination-filename*
    cp *source-filename destination-directory*

remove (or delete) file

    rm *filename*
    rmdir *directory-name*
    rm ~r *directory-name*

change working directory

    cd to change directories to your home directory
    cd *directory-name* to change directories to another directory

find name of current directory - **pwd**

pathnames

    simple   one filename or directory name to access local file or directory
    absolute   list of directory names from root directory (first /) to desired filename or directory name, each name separated by /
    relative   list of directory names from current position to desired filename or directory name, each name separated by /

Warning! Before attempting to run the demonstration programs from chapters 12, 14, 15 and 16 you will probably need to change the pathnames in these programs to conform to your programming environment. If each data file is stored in the same sub-directory as the respective program to which it belongs then the pathnames can omitted and only the name of the file declared. For example in chapter 14, the demonstration program ex_01.c contains the line

#define filename "a:\\c14_dpp\\data.txt"

Provided that the executable image file was in the same subdirectory as the file *data.txt* the line could be modified to

#define filename "data.txt"

directory abbreviation

    ~ home directory
    ~username another user's home directory
    . working directory
    .. parent of working directory

timesavers

> to alias or abbreviate a command string with an alias - **alias** *alias-string command-string*
> **!!** repeat the entire last command line at any point in the current command line
> **!$** repeat the last word of the last command line at any point in the current command line

online documentation - **man** *command-name*

Appendix D - Answers

Chapter 1 - section 1.10

1.

The activities associated with programming include:
Designing and testing an algorithm as a solution to a problem.
Coding the algorithm into a computer program using an appropriate language.
Testing the computer program to prove that it solves the problem.
Documenting the computer program so that it can be maintained by others at a later time.

2.

Central processing unit, main memory, secondary storage units, input and output units.

In a personal computer the CPU and main memory are represented using micro-chip technology.
Typical secondary storage units are the internal hard disk, and floppy drives.
A common input unit is a keyboard with a pointing device known as a mouse.
A common output unit would be a printer.

Main memory storage capacity is typically of the order of Mbytes, for example 8 Mb.
Hard disk storage capacity varies from say 100 Mb to 1000 Mb.
Floppy disk storage is typically small in comparison to a hard disk, for example 1.4 Mb is common.

3.

Input units include keyboard, mouse, magnetic tape or disk, light pen.
Output units include screen, printer, plotter.
Common input/ output units in a C development environment are the keyboard, monitor (screen) and printer.

4.

The advantages of networking computers together is to enable software to be distributed over the network without the need for each user to possess a personal copy of the software. Similarly common hardware resources such as printers and plotters can be shared by all users of the network, without the need to provide each user with a separate item of hardware.

5.

C is a high-level language, therefore, the instructions are not in a machine recognisable form (machine code). A C program must be translated into machine code using a compiler.

6.

Phase 1 - creation of a C program, in text mode, using an editor.
Phase 2 - translation of the program into a machine recognisable form using a compiler.
Phase 3 - linking extra routines to allow the program to run (for example routines that permit input and output), and loading the program into the main memory of the computer.
Phase 4 - program running on a computer (program execution).

7.

The same program written in C for one computer architecture, can be compiled without modification using a compiler for a different computer architecture. The program when executed on both computer architectures must produce exactly the same results for true portability. Note that in C, incompatibility between dialects of C is most likely to be caused through the variation in libraries between different compilers and the different word sizes between computers. In ANSI C the contents and functionality of the libraries are pre-defined.

Low-level language statements are not portable between computers since the language statements relate to the specific architecture of the CPU.

Chapter 2 - section 2.9

1.

The data in the 'Used Cars for Sale', figure 2.16, are the details about each car and the price of each car. In C this might be described as:

```
char   details[44];
int    price;
```

In declaring the price of the car as being type int, it is assumed that there will be no price greater than £32767 on a 16-bit machine.

The data in the 'World forecasts', figure 2.17, are the names of the cities, the high and low temperatures and the type of weather. For example Acapulco, high 90 degrees, low of 79 degrees, s - sunny.

```
char   city[13];
int    high_temp;
int    low_temp;
char   weather[3];
```

Note in defining the number of characters for city, the city with the longest name, Buenos Aries, contains 12 characters, therefore, 13 characters are needed to store this name allowing for the null delimiter to be appended to the string.

The data in the 'Statement of Account', figure 2.18, will cover such items as the name of the account, the year, the sheet number, the account number, the date of the transaction, the description of the transaction, the amount of the transaction, the balance and whether the balance is in credit or debit.

```
char   name_of_account[80];
int    year;
int    sheet_number;
char   account_number[80];
char   date[6];
char   transaction[80];
float  amount;
float  balance;
char   credit_debit;
```

Note - the sizes of the strings for the name_of_account, account_number and transaction have been an arbitrary choice.

2.

Illegal variable name   reason for illegality

(b) net-pay   hyphen
(d) cost of paper   embedded spaces
(f) ?X?Y   question marks
(g) 1856AD   variable name must start with a letter or underscore
(h) float   reserved word

3.

(a) string
(b) char
(c) signed integer
(d) long integer
(e) float
(f) long double float
(g) octal integer
(h) hexadecimal integer
(i) unsigned integer
(j) single precision float

4.

	character	ASCII code	8-bit value
(a)	A	65	01000001
(b)	M	77	01001101
(c)	*	42	00101010
(d)	a	97	01100001
(e)	m	109	01101101
(f)	NUL	0	00000000
(g)	9	57	00111001

5.

(a) -8.74458E+02
(b) 1.23456E-03
(c) 1.23456789E+08

6.

(a) Exponent too large - overflow. Note 3.016E+39 is too large to store. Remedy is to change the type to double.
(b) Accuracy of the number will be lost, however, the approximation can be stored 1.23456789012E+09. Remedy to improve the accuracy of the representation is to change the type to long double
(c) Exponent too small - underflow. Note -4.56E-43 is too small to store. Remedy is to change the type to double.

7.

+7384 = 0001110011011000
-7384 = 1110001100101000 (2's complement)

8.

(a) 0.37948E+17
(b) -0.263948E+01   loss of accuracy
(c) 0.739462E+03   loss of accuracy
(d) -0.176943E40   overflow
(e) 0.471E-40   underflow - result may be represented as zero

9.

(a) 0234 in octal is 156 decimal
(b) 0x56ABC in hexadecimal is 355004 in decimal
(c) 10110111 in binary is -73 in decimal

10.

octal-constant:

       0

       octal-constant octal-digit

octal-digit: one of

       0 1 2 3 4 5 6 7

hexadecimal-constant:

       0x hexadecimal-digit

       0X hexadecimal-digit

       hexadecimal-constant hexadecimal-digit

hexadecimal-digit: one of

       0 1 2 3 4 5 6 7 8 9

       a b c d e f

       A B C D E F

Chapter 3 - section 3.11

1.

When program *ex_04.c* was run on a Digital Personal DECStation the only significant difference was the storage space allocated for integers. Since this is a 32-bit machine the contents of <limits.h> specified the following:

char unsigned max:	4294967295	int min:	-2147483648
int max:	+2147483647	int unsigned max:	4294967295

The contents of <float.h> remained the same as for a 16-bit machine.

When the same program was compiled on a PC compatible using Microsoft Visual C++ the following changes appeared to have been made to the <limits.h> file.

char min: -127   int min: -32767   long int min: -2147483647

2.

In the following text the underscore (_) represents the position of the screen cursor after the instruction had been executed.

```
(a)     Hello World_
(b)        name: _
(c)        name: Mickey Mouse

(d)     a=3    b=4    c=5

(e)     area covered      635.87

(f)     alpha=      1675    beta= 1.3456E+16

        _
```

3.

(a) Type d represents a decimal integer yet alpha is real - should be scanf("%f", &alpha)

(b) Address of beta required - should be scanf("%f", &beta)

(c) Too few type descriptions in the control string - should be scanf("%2d%2d%2d", &day, &month, &year)

(d) Address of name is wrong, since name is a string - should be scanf("%s", name)

(e) Type declaration is wrong, since gamma is declared as long int - should be scanf("%d", &gamma)

(f) This is wrong on two counts. The type declaration for an unsigned integer is wrong, and the address of alpha is required - should be scanf("alpha = %-5u\n", &alpha);

5.

```
/* c3_dpp\ans_05.c */

#include <stdio.h>

main()
{
        char    message[80];

        printf("input a message ");
        gets(message);

        printf("My message to the World is %s\n", message);
}
```

Chapter 4 - section 4.7

1.

(a)	A	B	C	D
	36	36	36	36

(b)	A	B	C	D
	10	14	29	89

(c)	A	B
	48	50

(d)	X	Y
	19	-13

(e)	X	Y	Z
	18	3	54

(f)	A	B
	12.5	2.0

(g)	A	B	X
	16	3	5

(h)	C	D	Y
	19	5	4

(i)	D
	35

2.

(a) (A+B)/C
(b) (W-X)/(Y+Z)
(c) (D-B)/(2*A)
(d) (A*A+B*B)/2
(e) (A-B)*(C-D)

(f) B*B-4*A*C

(g) X*X*(A+B)+C

3.

(a) A .B

   ^ illegal operator

(b) X*-Y

   ^ combined operators - does NOT produce an error, however, clearer to write X*(-Y)

(c) (64+B)/-6

   ^ combined operators - does NOT produce an error, however, clearer to write (64+B)/(-6)

(d) (A-B) (A+B)

   ^ no operator between parenthesis

(e) -2/A+-6

   ^ combined operators - does NOT produce an error, however, clearer to write -2/A+(-6)

(f) 1*(X-Y)

   -

   2

   ^ illegal division operator

4.

(a) X + 2 + 4

       -

       Y

(b) A.B

   ———

   C+2

(c) U.W

   ———

   V.X

(d) $B^2 - 4.A.C$

(e) A + C ÷ E

   -   -   -

   B   D   F

5.

```
/* c4_dpp\ans_05.c */

#include <stdio.h>

main()
{
        int     A = 5;
        int     B = 9;
```

```
        printf("A+B=%d\n", A+B);
        printf("A-B=%d\n", A-B);
        printf("AxB=%d\n", A*B);
        printf("A/B=%d\n", A/B);
        printf("A%%B=%d\n", A%B);
}
```

6.

```
/* c4_dpp\ans_06.c */

#include <stdio.h>

main()
{
        const   float   inch_cm = 2.54;
        const   float   pounds_kg = 0.4546;

                char    name[80];
                float   height_inch, height_cm;
                float   weight_pounds, weight_kg;

        printf("name? "); gets(name);
        printf("height (inches)? "); scanf("%f", &height_inch);
        printf("weight (pounds)? "); scanf("%f", &weight_pounds);

        height_cm = inch_cm * height_inch;
        weight_kg = pounds_kg * weight_pounds;

        printf("\n\nPERSONAL DETAILS\n");
        printf("NAME: %s\n", name);
        printf("HEIGHT (cm): %3.0f\n", height_cm);
        printf("WEIGHT (Kg): %3.0f\n", weight_kg);
}
```

7.

```
/* c4_dpp\ans_07.c */

#include <stdio.h>

main()
{
        const   float   border = 1.0;
        const   float   turf_cost = 2.00;
                float   length;
                float   width;
                float   lawn_area;
                float   cost;

        printf("length? "); scanf("%f", &length);
        printf("width? "); scanf("%f", &width);

        lawn_area = (length - 2 * border) * (width - 2 * border);
        cost = lawn_area * turf_cost;
        printf("area of lawn =  %-10.2f\n", lawn_area);
        printf("cost of turf = £%-10.2f\n", cost);
}
```

8.

```
/* c4_dpp\ans_08.c */

#include <stdio.h>

main()
{
        unsigned int money, twenty, ten, five, one;

        printf("input an amount of money ");
        scanf("%u", &money);

        twenty = money / 20; money = money % 20;
        ten = money / 10; money = money % 10;
        five = money / 5; one = money % 5;

        printf("£20 = %u\t£10 = %u\t£5 = %u\t£1 = %u\n",twenty, ten, five, one);
}
```

10.

```
/* c4_dpp\ans_10.c */

#include <stdio.h>

main()
{
        unsigned int char_code;
        unsigned int octal_2, octal_1, octal_0;
        unsigned int remainder;

        printf("input a letter of the alphabet? ");
        char_code = getchar();

        octal_2 = char_code / 64; remainder = char_code % 64;
        octal_1 = remainder / 8;
        octal_0 = remainder % 8;

        printf("ASCII code for %c is:\n\n", char_code);
        printf("octal %u%u%u\n", octal_2, octal_1, octal_0);
        printf("decimal %u\n", char_code);
}
```

Chapter 5 - section 5.10

1.

(a) false
(b) true
(c) true
(d) false
(e) true
(f) true
(g) true

2.

(a) X==Y
(b) X != Y
(c) A <= B
(d) Q <= T
(e) X >= Y
(f) (X <= Y && A != B)
(g) (A > 18 && H > 68 && W > 75)
(h) (G < 100 && G > 50)
(i) (H < 50 || H > 100)

3.

	A	B	C	output
(a)	16	16	32	y
(b)	16	-18	32	x
(c)	-2	-4	16	z

4.

```
/* c5_dpp\ans_04.c */

#include <stdio.h>

main()
{
        const    char female = 'F';

        char     sex;
        char     name[20];
        int      age;
        int      height;

        printf("input name of suspect "); gets(name);
        printf("input sex - [M]ale or [F]emale "); sex = getchar();
        if ('a' <= sex && sex <= 'z') sex = sex - 32;

        if (sex != female)
        {
            printf("age? "); scanf("%d", &age);
            printf("height? "); scanf("%d", &height);

            printf("%s", name);

            if (age < 20 || age > 25 || height < 66 || height > 70)
                printf(" is not a suspect and should be released\n");
            else
                printf(" is a suspect and should be interrogated\n");
        }
        else
            printf("%s is female and can be released\n", name);
}
```

469

5.

```
/* c5_dpp\ans_05.c */

#include <stdio.h>

main()
{
        const   float   normal_hours = 35.0;
        const   float   threshold = 60;
        const   float   rate_1 = 12.00;
        const   float   rate_2 = 16.00;

                float   hours_worked;
                float   overtime_pay;

        printf("input number of hours worked ");
        scanf("%f", &hours_worked);
        if (hours_worked > threshold)
           overtime_pay = (threshold - normal_hours) * rate_1
                        + (hours_worked - threshold) * rate_2;
        else
           if (hours_worked > normal_hours)
              overtime_pay = (hours_worked - normal_hours) * rate_1;
           else
              overtime_pay = 0.0;

        printf("overtime pay is £%-7.2f\n", overtime_pay);
}
```

7.

```
/* c5_dpp\ans_07.c */

#include <stdio.h>

main()
{
        enum{STORM=1, RAIN=2, CHANGE=3, FAIR=4, DRY=5};

        const     char    yes = 'Y';

        unsigned int      code;
        char              reply;

        printf("1 STORM\n");
        printf("2 RAIN\n");
        printf("3 CHANGE\n");
        printf("4 FAIR\n");
        printf("5 DRY\n\n");
        printf("input code 1..5 corresponding to barometer reading ");
        scanf("%u", &code); getchar();

        switch (code)
        {
        case STORM  : printf("wear overcoat and hat\n"); break;
        case RAIN   : printf("wear raincoat and take umbrella\n"); break;
        case CHANGE : printf("did it rain yesterday - [Y]es or [N]o? ");
                      reply = getchar();
```

```
                    if ('a' <= reply && reply <= 'z') reply = reply - 32;

                    if (reply == yes)
                        printf("wear jacket and take umbrella\n");
                    else
                        printf("wear raincoat and take umbrella\n");

                    break;

        case FAIR   : printf("wear jacket and take umbrella\n"); break;
        case DRY    : printf("wear jacket\n"); break;
        default     : printf("ERROR - CODE NOT IN RANGE 1..5\a");
        }
}
```

9.

```
/* c5_dpp\ans_09.c */

#include <stdio.h>

main()
{
        unsigned int char_code;
        unsigned int hex_1, hex_0;

        printf("input a letter of the alphabet? ");
        char_code = getchar();

        hex_1 = char_code / 16;
        hex_0 = char_code % 16;

        /* convert hex digits to A..F or 0..9 */
        hex_1 = (10 <= hex_1 && hex_1 <= 15) ? hex_1 + 55 : hex_1 + 48;
        hex_0 = (10 <= hex_0 && hex_0 <= 15) ? hex_0 + 55 : hex_0 + 48;

        printf("ASCII code for %c is:\n\n", char_code);
        printf("hexadecimal %c%c\n", hex_1, hex_0);
}
```

Chapter 6 - section 6.8

1.

```
/* c6_dpp\ans_01.c */

#include <stdio.h>

main()
{
        int     counter;

        for (counter = 0; counter < 10; counter++)
            printf("Hello World\n");

}
```

2.

```
/* c6_dpp\ans_02.c */

#include <stdio.h>

main()
{
        int     counter = 0;
        int     repeat;
        char    message[80];

        printf("message? "); gets(message);
        printf("repeated? "); scanf("%d", &repeat);

        for (; counter < repeat; counter++)
            printf("%s\n", message);

}
```

3.

```
/* c6_dpp\ans_03.c */

#include <stdio.h>

main()
{
        const    float    conv_factor = 1.609344;

        unsigned int      miles = 1;
                 float    kilometres;

        printf("MILES\t\tKILOMETRES\n\n");
        for (; miles <= 50; miles++)
        {
                if (miles % 20 ==0)
                    printf("\nMILES\t\tKILOMETRES\n\n");

                kilometres = miles * conv_factor;
                printf("%d\t\t%-12.2f\n", miles, kilometres);
        }
}
```

4.

```
/* c6_dpp\ans_04.c */

#include <stdio.h>

main()
{
        int     counter = 1;
        int     sum;
        char    letter;

        while (counter <= 29)
```

```
        {
                printf("%3d", counter);
                counter = counter + 2;
        }

        printf("\n");
        counter = 2;
        while (counter <= 20)
        {
                printf("%5d", counter*counter);
                counter = counter + 2;
        }
        printf("\n");
        counter = 1;
        sum = 0;
        while (counter <= 13)
        {
                sum = sum + counter * counter;
                counter = counter + 2;
        }
        printf("sum of squares of odd integers from 1..13 %d\n", sum);

        letter = 'A';
        while (letter <= 'Z')
        {
                printf("%c", letter);
                letter++;
        }

}
```

7.

```
/* c6_dpp\ans_07.c */

#include <stdio.h>

main()
{
        int     sum = 0;
        int     counter = 0;
        int     number;
        float   mean;

        printf("number? - terminate with zero "); scanf("%d", &number);
        while (number != 0)
        {
                sum = sum + number;
                counter++;
                printf("number? - terminate with zero "); scanf("%d", &number);
        }

        if (counter != 0)
        {
                mean = (float) sum / counter;
                printf("mean of %d numbers is %-10.2f\n", counter, mean);
        }
}
```

8.

```
/* c6_dpp\ans_08.c */

#include <stdio.h>

main()
{
        const   float   overtime_rate = 12.0;
        const   int     normal_hours = 40;
        const   int     max_employees = 10;

                int     hours_worked;
                int     employee = 1;
                float   overtime_pay;
                float   total_overtime_pay = 0.0;


        for (; employee <= max_employees; employee++)
        {
            printf("hours for employee %d ", employee);
            scanf("%d", &hours_worked);

            if (hours_worked > normal_hours)
            {
                overtime_pay = (hours_worked - normal_hours) * overtime_rate;
                total_overtime_pay = total_overtime_pay + overtime_pay;
            }
            else
                overtime_pay = 0.0;

            printf("overtime due is £%-8.2f\n", overtime_pay);
        }

        printf("total overtime paid £%-10.2f\n", total_overtime_pay);
}
```

9.

```
/* c6_dpp\ans_09.c */

#include <stdio.h>

main()
{
        const   char    LF = 10;
                int     char_code;

        printf("input a phrase\n\n");
        char_code = getchar();
        while (char_code != LF)
        {
            printf("ASCII code for %c is %d\n", char_code, char_code);
            char_code = getchar();
        }
}
```

10.

```
/* c6_dpp\ans_10.c */

#include <stdio.h>

main()
{
        int     largest, number;
        int     counter = 1;

        printf("integer? "); scanf("%d", &number);
        largest = number;

        while (counter != 10)
        {
            printf("integer? "); scanf("%d", &number);
            if (number > largest)
                largest = number;

            counter++;
        }

        printf("largest integer input was %d\n", largest);
}
```

Chapter 7 - section 7.8

1.

The output from this program are the characters **cba**.

2.

The values of x are 100, 110 and 120. Despite x initially declared as static by default, and having file scope with a value of 68, the re-declaration of x has block scope and hides the original value of x. The output from the program is **dnx**.

3.

(a) float
(b) double

4.

(a) False - variables of register storage class have similar attributes to variables of auto storage class.

(b) False - external variable storage has storage allocated only once.

(c) True - unless the variables in the block are specifically classified as static or register.

(d) False - variables in a block are assumed to be auto, unless otherwise specified; variables that are defined externally to a block, yet only have file scope, are by default static.

(e) False - a function can only take on static or external storage classes.

5.

(a) No actual parameter list in the function call. No types in the formal parameter list.

(b) Function declaration incorrect - name of function should not be enclosed in parenthesis and formal parameter list is missing.

(c) No comma separator between arguments in the actual parameter list of the function call.

(d) Actual parameters of wrong type and too few in number. Formal parameter list contains a syntax error. The three formal parameters must be declared with separate types.

6.

false, true, false.

7.

```
/* c7_dpp\ans_07.c */

#include <stdio.h>

const float pi = 3.14159;

float diameter(float radius)
{
    return 2*radius;
}

float circumference(float radius)
{
    return 2*pi*radius;
}

float area(float radius)
{
    return pi*radius*radius;
}

main()
{
    float radius_of_circle;

    printf("input radius of circle ");
    scanf("%f", &radius_of_circle);
    printf("diameter\t %6.2f\n", diameter(radius_of_circle));
    printf("circumference\t %6.2f\n", circumference(radius_of_circle));
    printf("area\t %8.2f\n", area(radius_of_circle));
}
```

8.

```
/* c7_dpp\ans_08.c */

#include <stdio.h>

typedef enum{false,true} boolean;
```

```
boolean convert(int octal_digit)
{
    boolean error = false;

    switch (octal_digit)
    {
    case 0 : printf("zero");   break;
    case 1 : printf("one");    break;
    case 2 : printf("two");    break;
    case 3 : printf("three");  break;
    case 4 : printf("four");   break;
    case 5 : printf("five");   break;
    case 6 : printf("six");    break;
    case 7 : printf("seven");  break;
    default: error = true;
    }
    return error;
}


main()
{
    int octal_digit;

    do
    {
        printf("\ninput octal digit ");
        scanf("%d", &octal_digit);
    }
    while (!convert(octal_digit));
}
```

9.

```
/* c7_dpp\ans_09.c */

#include <stdio.h>

typedef enum{false,true} boolean;

boolean vowel(char letter)
{
    boolean error = false;

    letter = ('a'<=letter && letter <='z') ? letter-32 : letter;
    switch (letter)
    {
    case 'A': case 'E': case 'I': case 'O': case 'U': break;
    default : error = true;
    }

    return error;
}

main()
{
    char character;
```

```
    do
    {
        printf("\ninput character ");
        scanf("%c", &character);
        getchar();
    }
    while (!vowel(character));
}
```

Chapter 8 - section 8.9

1.

```
/* c8_dpp\ans_01.c */

#include <stdio.h>

#define FALSE 0
#define TRUE 1
#define to_upper(c) ('a'<=(c) && (c) <='f' ? (c) - 32 : (c))
#define digit(x) ('0'<=(x) && (x)<='9' ? TRUE : FALSE)
#define letter(y) ('A'<=to_upper(y) && to_upper(y) <= 'F' ? TRUE : FALSE)
#define hex_digit(h) (digit(h) || letter(h) ? TRUE : FALSE)


main()
{
    char character;

    do
    {
        printf("input hexadecimal digit - error will terminate ");
        character =getchar(); getchar();
    }
    while (hex_digit(character));
}
```

2.

```
/* c8_dpp\ans_02.c */

#include <stdio.h>

#define FALSE 0
#define TRUE 1
#define maxima(X,Y,Z) ((Y > X) && (Y > Z) ? TRUE : FALSE)

main()
{
    int A,B,C;

    printf("input three integers ");
    scanf("%d%d%d", &A,&B,&C);

    if maxima(A,B,C) printf("%d is a maxima\n", B);
}
```

3.

```
/* c8_dpp\ans_03.c */

#include <stdio.h>
#include <math.h>
#define pi 3.14159



#define area_of_triangle(a,b,C)  (0.5*a*b*sin(C*pi/180.0))

main()
{
    int a,b,C;

    printf("input lengths of two sides and included angle of triangle\n");
    scanf("%d%d%d",&a, &b, &C);

    printf("area of triangle is %6.2f\n", area_of_triangle(a,b,C));
}
```

4.

```
/* c8_dpp\ans_04.c */

#include <stdio.h>

#define pi 3.14159
#define diameter(r) 2.0*r
#define circumference(r) 2.0*pi*r
#define area(r) pi*r*r
#define input(r) printf("input " #r " "), scanf("%f",&r)
#define output(macro,r) printf(#macro " = %8.2f\n", macro(r))

main()
{
        float radius;

        input(radius);
        output(diameter,radius);
        output(circumference,radius);
        output(area,radius);
}
```

Chapter 9 -section 9.7

1(a).

```
/* c9_dpp\ans_01a.c
program to input numbers into a one-dimensional array and display the contents of the array
*/

#include <stdio.h>

void input_data(int array[], int N)
{
```

```
        int index;

        printf("input %d integers, one per line\n\n", N);
        for (index = 0; index < N; index++)
        {
            printf("cell %d ", index);
            scanf("%d", &array[index]);
        }
        printf("\n\n");
}

void display_data(int array[], int N)
{
        int index;

        printf("contents of array\n\n");
        for (index = 0; index < N; index++)
            printf("cell %d\t%d\n", index, array[index]);
}

main()
{
        int vector[100];
        int size;

        printf("input the size of the array "); scanf("%d", &size);
        input_data(vector, size);
        display_data(vector, size);
}
```

1(b).

```
/* c9_dpp\ans_01b.c
program to input numbers into a one-dimensional array and find and display the largest number
in the array
*/

#include <stdio.h>

int largest(int array[], int N)
{
        int index;
        int maximum = array[0];

        for (index = 1; index < N; index++)
            if (array[index] > maximum) maximum = array[index];

        return maximum;
}

main()
{
        int numbers[100];
        int size;
        int index;

        printf("input size of the array "); scanf("%d", &size);
        printf("input %d integers, one per line\n\n", size);
```

```
        for (index = 0; index < size; index++)
        {
            printf("cell %d ", index);
            scanf("%d", &numbers[index]);
        }
        printf("\nlargest number in array is %d", largest(numbers, size));
}
```

1(c).

```
/* c9_dpp\ans_01c.c
program to find the length of a string
*/

#include <stdio.h>

int length(char array[])
{
        int  size = 0;
    const char null = 0;

    while (array[size] != null) size++;
    return size;
}

main()
{
    char data[255];

    printf("input a line of text\n"); gets(data);
    printf("length of text is %d characters\n", length(data));
}
```

1(d).

```
/* c9_dpp\ans_01d.c
program to change every alphabetic character in a string to upper case
*/

#include <stdio.h>
#define to_upper(c)  ('a'<=(c) && (c)<='z' ? (c)-32:(c))

void capitalize(char array[])
{
        const char null = 0;
            int  index;

        for (index = 0; array[index] != null; index++)
            array[index] = to_upper(array[index]);
}

main()
{
        char  text[255];

        printf("input a line of text\n"); gets(text);
        capitalize(text);
        printf("capitalized text\n%s", text);
}
```

481

2.

```
/* c9_dpp\ans_02.c */

#include <stdio.h>

main()
{
        int index;
    const char alphabet[] = "abcdefghijklmnopqrstuvwxyz";

    printf("%s\n\n", alphabet);

    for (index=0; index < 6; index++)
        printf("%c", alphabet[index]);
    printf("\n\n");

    for (index=16; index < 26; index++)
        printf("%c", alphabet[index]);
    printf("\n\n");

    printf("%c", alphabet[9]);
}
```

4.

```
/* c9_dpp\ans_04.c */

#include <stdio.h>

int  sunshine [12] = {100,90,120,150,210,250,300,310,280,230,160,120};
char months[12][4] = {"JAN","FEB","MAR","APR","MAY","JUN","JUL","AUG",
                      "SEP","OCT","NOV","DEC"};

float average(void)
{
    int index;
    int total_sunshine = 0;

    for (index=0; index < 12; index++)
        total_sunshine = total_sunshine + sunshine[index];

    return (float) total_sunshine / 12.0;
}

int highest(void)
{
    int index;
    int maximum = sunshine[0];
    int month   = 0;

    for (index=1; index < 12; index++)
        if (sunshine[index] > maximum)
        {
            maximum = sunshine[index];
            month = index;
        }
```

```
        return month;
}

int lowest(void)
{
        int index;
        int minimum = sunshine[0];
        int month   = 0;

        for (index=1; index < 12; index++)
            if (sunshine[index] < minimum)
            {
                minimum = sunshine[index];
                month = index;
            }

        return month;
}

main()
{
        printf("average sunshine %6.2f\n", average());
        printf("maximum sunshine was in %s\n", months[highest()]);
        printf("minimum sunshine was in %s\n", months[lowest()]);
}
```

Chapter 10 - section 10.6

1.

```
/* c10_dpp\ans_01.c */

#include <stdio.h>
#include <string.h>

typedef struct {
                char   name[14];
                float  price;
            } food;

float cost(char item[], food prices[])
/* function to search array for the price of an item of food,if the item cannot be found
returns the value zero */
{
        int index;

        for (index=0; index < 11; index++)
            if (strcmp(item, prices[index].name)==0)
                return prices[index].price;

        return 0.0;
}

void search(float amount, food prices[])
/* function to serach array and display the items of food and prices that are equal to or
below an amount of money */
{
        int index;
```

```
        for (index=0; index < 11; index++)
            if (amount >= prices[index].price)
                printf("%s %4.2f\n", prices[index].name, prices[index].price);
}

main()
{
        food prices[11] = {{"eggs",1.50},{"bacon",2.00},{"sausages",1.75},
                            {"black pudding",0.95},{"tomatoes",1.00},
                            {"baked beans",0.50},{"toast",0.75},{"cerial",1.00},
                            {"tea",0.75},{"coffee",0.75}, {"hot chocolate",0.95}};

        char  menu_item[14];
        float charge, amount;

        do
        {
            printf("input name of food "); gets(menu_item);
            charge = cost(menu_item, prices);
            printf("price of food £%4.2f\n", charge);
        }
        while (charge != 0.0);

        printf("input an amount of money "); scanf("%f",&amount);
        search(amount, prices);
}
```

2.

```
/* c10_dpp\ans_02.c */

#include <stdio.h>
#include <string.h>

#define size 10

typedef struct {
                char   town[13];
                char   area_code[6];
            } STD;

int search(char code[], STD towns_and_codes[])
/* function to search array for the telephone code of an town/city, if the search is
successful the function returns the index, otherwise the function returns the size of
the array */
{
        int index;

        for (index=0; index < size; index++)
            if (strcmp(code, towns_and_codes[index].area_code)==0)
                return index;

        return size;
}

main()
{
        STD codes[size] = {{"Aberdeen",    "01224"},
                           {"Ayr",         "01292"},
                           {"Dundee",      "01382"},
```

```
                    {"Edinburgh",     "0131"},
                    {"Falkirk",       "01324"},
                    {"Fort William","01397"},
                    {"Glasgow",       "0141"},
                    {"Inverness",     "01463"},
                    {"Perth",         "01738"},
                    {"Stirling",      "01786"}};

    char   area_code[6];
    int    index;

    do
    {
       printf("input area code "); gets(area_code);
       index = search(area_code, codes);
       if (index != size)
           printf("town/ city %s\n", codes[index].town);
    }
    while (index != size);
}
```

6.

```
/*
c10_dpp\ans_06.c
program to build a crossword
*/

#include <stdio.h>
#define to_upper(c) ('a'<=(c) && (c) <='z' ? (c)-32 : (c))

        char crossword[15][15];
const   char yes = 'Y';
const   char space = 32;

void clear(void)
/* function to clear the board */
{
        int down, across;

        for (down=0; down<15; down++)
        {
            for (across=0; across<15; across++)
                crossword[down][across]=space;
        }
}

void get_word(void)
/* function to get a word from the user and store it at a
set position on the crossword */
{
        int index, col_index, row_index; /* indices */
        int s_row, s_col, f_row, f_col;  /* co-ordinates */
        char word[16];

        printf("start? "); scanf("%d%d", &s_row, &s_col);
        printf("finish? "); scanf("%d%d", &f_row, &f_col);
        getchar(); /* clear keyboard buffer */
        printf("word? "); gets(word);
```

```
        index = 0;
        if (s_row == f_row)      /* word in same row */
            for (col_index = s_col; col_index <= f_col; col_index++)
            {
                crossword[s_row-1][col_index-1] = word[index];
                index++;
            }
        else
            for (row_index = s_row; row_index <= f_row; row_index++)
            {
                crossword[row_index-1][s_col-1] = word[index];
                index++;
            }
}

void display(void)
/* function to display the contents of the crossword */
{
        int down, across;

        printf("\n\n    1  2  3  4  5  6  7  8  9 10 11 12 13 14 15");
        for (down=0; down<15; down++)
        {
            printf("\n%-3d", down+1);
            for (across=0; across<15; across++)
                printf("%-3c", crossword[down][across]);
        }
        printf("\n\n");
}

main()
{
        char reply;

        clear();
        display();
        do
        {
                get_word();
                display();
                printf("another word? y(es) or n(o) ");
                reply = getchar(); getchar();
                reply = to_upper(reply);
        }
        while (reply == yes);
}
```

Chapter 11 - section 11.9

1.

```
/* c11_dpp\ans_01.c */

#include <stdio.h>
#include <stdlib.h>

int   *P;
float *Q;
char  *R;
```

```
main()
{
    P=malloc(sizeof(int));
    Q=malloc(sizeof(float));
    R=malloc(sizeof(char));

    printf("input data of the types int, float and char respectively\n");
    scanf("%d",P);
    scanf("%f",Q);
    getchar();
    scanf("%c",R);
    printf("values input are \n%d\n%f\n%c\n",*P,*Q,*R);

    free(P);
    free(Q);
    free(R);
}
```

3.

```
/* c11_dpp\ans_03.c */

#include <stdio.h>

void calculate(float *length, float size, int *pieces)
{
    *pieces = 0;

    while (*length >= size)
    {
        *length = *length - size;
        *pieces = *pieces + 1;
    }
}

main()
{
    float length, total_waste = 0;
    int   L5, L2, total_L5 = 0, total_L2 = 0;
    printf("input length of wood "); scanf("%f",&length);
    while (length > 0)
    {
        calculate(&length, 5.0, &L5);
        total_L5 = total_L5 + L5;
        calculate(&length, 2.0, &L2);
        total_L2 = total_L2 + L2;
        total_waste = total_waste + length;

        printf("5m %d\t2m %d\twaste %f\n", L5, L2, length);
        printf("input length of wood "); scanf("%f",&length);
    }

    printf("\ntotals\n");
    printf("5m %d\t2m %d\twaste %f\n", total_L5, total_L2, total_waste);
}
```

Chapter 12 - section 12.12

2.

```
/* c12_dpp\ans_02.c */

#include <stdio.h>

typedef enum{false, true} boolean;

void input_data(int *angle,float *side1, float *side2, float *side3, float *side4)
/* function to input one angle and the length of four side */
{
    do
    {
        printf("input the size of one internal angle ");
        scanf("%d",angle);
    }
    while (*angle <=0 || *angle >= 180);

    do
    {
        printf("input the lengths of the four sides ");
        scanf("%f%f%f%f",side1,side2,side3,side4);
        getchar();
    }
    while (*side1 <= 0 && *side2 <= 0 && *side3 <= 0 && *side4 <= 0);
}
char *analyse_shape(int angle,float sideA, float sideB, float sideC, float sideD)
/* function to return the name of the quadrilateral */
{
    if (sideA==sideB && sideB==sideC && sideC==sideD)
        if (angle==90)
            return "square";
        else
            return "rhombus";
    else
        if (sideA==sideC && sideB==sideD)
            if (angle==90)
                return "rectangle";
            else
                return "parallelogram";

        else
            return "irregular";

}

boolean more_data(void)
/* function to return true if more data is required otherwise
return false */
{
    char reply;

    printf("continue? - answer Y[es] or N[o] ");
    reply = getchar();

    if (reply=='Y' || reply=='y')
        return true;
    else
```

```
        return false;
}

main()
{
    int    angle;
    float sideA, sideB, sideC, sideD;

    do
    {
        input_data(&angle, &sideA, &sideB, &sideC, &sideD);
        printf("%s\n", analyse_shape(angle, sideA, sideB, sideC, sideD));
    }
    while (more_data());
}
```

4.

```c
/* c12_dpp\ans_04.c */

#include <stdio.h>
#include <stdlib.h>
#include <time.h>

typedef enum{false, true} boolean;

char minefield[10][10];

void initialise(int *last_row, int *last_column)
/* plant the mines in the minefield */
{
    const char space = ' ';
    const char mined = 'M';
    const char arrow = '^';
        int row, column;
        int mines;
        int mine_count;
    static int seed;
    time_t tt;



    /* clear minefield */
    for (row=0; row <= 9; row++)
        for (column=0; column <= 9; column++)
            minefield[row][column]=space;

    /* generate new random number */
    time(&tt);
    srand((unsigned)tt);

    /* generate starting position */
    *last_row=9; *last_column=rand()%10;
    minefield[*last_row][*last_column]=arrow;

    /* generate number of mines to lay */
    mines=rand()%10 + 1;

    /* generate positions of mines */
```

489

```
    mine_count=0;
    do
    {
        row=rand()%10;
        column=rand()%10;
        if (minefield[row][column]==space)
        {
            minefield[row][column]=mined;
            mine_count++;
        }
    }
    while (mine_count != mines);
}

boolean mine(int row, int column)
/* return true if a mine found at the coordinates */
{
    if (minefield[row][column]=='M')
    {
        printf("\n\nB O O M !!\n\n");
        return true;
    }
    else
    {
        minefield[row][column]='^';
        return false;
    }
}

void display(boolean reveal)
/* function to display the current state of the minefield */

{
    const char mined='M';
    const char space=' ';
        int row, column;

    printf("          NORTH\n");
    printf("   0 1 2 3 4 5 6 7 8 9\n");
    for (row=0; row<=9; row++)
    {
        printf("%2d",row);
        for (column=0; column<=9; column++)
        {
            if (minefield[row][column]==mined && reveal)
                printf(" %c",mined);
            else if (minefield[row][column]==mined)
                printf("%c%c", space, space);
            else
                printf(" %c", minefield[row][column]);
        }
        printf("\n");
    }
}

main()
{
    int     row, column;
    int     last_row, last_column;
    boolean boom;
```

```
        initialise(&last_row, &last_column);
        display(false);

        do
        {
            do
            {
                printf("input coordinates of next step ");
                scanf("%d%d",&row, &column);
            }
            while (((row < 0 || row > 9) || (column < 0 || column > 9)) ||
                    ((row != last_row) && (row!=last_row-1) && (row!=last_row+1)) ||
                    ((column!=last_column) && (column!=last_column-1) &&
                    (column!=last_column+1)));

            last_row=row; last_column=column;
            boom = mine(row,column);
            if (boom)
                display(true);
            else
                display(false);
        }
        while (! boom && row!=0);

        if (! boom)
        {
            printf("Congratulations!!\n");
            printf("You made it to the North through the following minefield\n\n");
            display(true);
        }
}
```

Chapter 13 - section 13.8

1(a).

```
/* c13_dpp\ans_01a.c */

#include <stdio.h>
#define max_array 100

int input_data(int array[])
/* function to input numbers into the array
and return the size of the array */
{
    int index = 0;
    int datum;

    printf("input positive integers - terminate with negative value\n");
    scanf("%d", &datum);
    while (datum > 0)
    {
        array[index] = datum;
        index++;
        scanf("%d", &datum);
    }
    return index;
}
```

```
int sum(int array[], int max_index)
/* recursive function to sum the contents of the array of integers */
{
    if (max_index < 0)
        return 0;
    else
        return array[max_index]+sum(array, max_index-1);
}

main()
{
    int array[max_array];
    int size;

    size = input_data(array);
    printf("sum of integers in array is %d\n", sum(array, size-1));
}
```

1(b).

```
/* c13_dpp\ans_01b.c */

#include <stdio.h>

long int power(int X, int n)
/* function to raise X to the power of n and return the result */
{
    if (n==0)
        return 1;
    else
        return X * power(X,n-1);
}

main()
{
    int X, n;

    printf("input a value for X "); scanf("%d", &X);
    printf("input a value for n "); scanf("%d", &n);
    printf("X raised to the power of n is %ld", power(X,n));
}
```

1(c).

```
/* c13_dpp\ans_01c.c */

#include <stdio.h>

int Fibonacci(int n)
/* recursive function to generate n terms in a Fibonacci sequence */
{
    if (n==1 || n==2)
        return 1;
    else
        return Fibonacci(n-2)+Fibonacci(n-1);
}
```

```
main()
{
    int n;

    for (n=1; n<=15; n++)
        printf("%4d", Fibonacci(n));
}
```

2.

```c
/* c13_dpp\ans_02.c */

#include <stdio.h>
#include <stdlib.h>
#define max_array 100

int input_data(int array[])
/* function to input numbers into the array and return the size of the array */
{
    int index = 0;
    int datum;

    printf("input positive integers - terminate with negative value\n");
    scanf("%d", &datum);
    while (datum > 0)
    {
        array[index] = datum;
        index++;
        scanf("%d", &datum);
    }
    return index;
}

int odd(int number)
/* function to return true if a number is odd, otherwise return false */
{
    return number % 2;
}

int compare(const void *n1, const void *n2)
{
    return *((int *)n1) - *((int *)n2);
}

main()
{
    int    array[max_array];
    int    size;
    float median;

    size = input_data(array);
    qsort(array, size, sizeof(int), compare);

    if (odd(size))
        median = (float) array[size / 2];
    else
        median = (float) (array[(size-1)/2] + array[size/2])/2;
    printf("%8.2f\n", median);
}
```

Chapter 14 - section 14.9

2.

```c
/* c14_dpp\ans_02.c */

#include <stdlib.h>
#include <stdio.h>
#include <errno.h>

#define input_file  "a:\\answers\\c14_dpp\\booze.txt"
#define output_file "a:\\answers\\c14_dpp\\stock.txt"
#define read "r"
#define write "w"
#define string_length 20

main()
{
    FILE  *booze;
    FILE  *stock;
    int   quantity;
    float price;
    char  description[string_length];
    float value;
    float total = 0;

    /* attempt to open files */
    booze = fopen(input_file, read);
    stock = fopen(output_file, write);

    if (booze == NULL)
    {
        printf("file cannot be opened\n");
        exit(errno);
    }

    /* print headings */
    fprintf(stock, "          BAR STOCK REPORT\n\n");
    fprintf(stock, "QUANTITY PRICE   VALUE DESCRIPTION\n\n");

    /* read every line in the file and write the report */

    while (! feof(booze))
    {
        fscanf(booze, "%d%f", &quantity, &price);
        fgets(description, string_length, booze);
        value = price * quantity;
        total += value;

        fprintf(stock, "%-9d%5.2f%8.2f%s",
                        quantity, price, value, description);
    }

    fprintf(stock, "\n\nTOTAL          £%8.2f", total);

    /* close data files */
    fclose(booze);
    fclose(stock);
}
```

4.

```c
/* c14_dpp\ans_04.c program to read a file of data, compress the data and write it back to a
new file, followed by reading the compressed data and decoding it back to the original form */
#include <stdlib.h>
#include <stdio.h>
#include <string.h>
#include <errno.h>

#define file_1 "a:\\answers\\c14_dpp\\data.txt"
#define file_2 "a:\\answers\\c14_dpp\\new_data.txt"
#define read "r"
#define write "w"
#define string_length 80

FILE *open_file(char filename[], char mode[])
/* function to open a file in a specified mode */
{
    FILE *file;

    file = fopen(filename, mode);
    if (file == NULL)
    {
        printf("%s cannot be opened\n", filename);
        exit(errno);
    }
    else
        return file;
}

int read_line(FILE *file, char string[])
/* function to read a line from the data file and return
the number of characters in the line */
{
    fgets(string, string_length, file);
    return strlen(string);
}

void encode(char string[], int *size, char new_string[], int *new_size)
/* function to encode the string */
{
    const char null = 0;
    char character, new_character;
    int  index=0, new_index=0, counter;

    while (index < *size)
    {
        character     = string[index];
        new_character = character;

        /* scan string counting characters that are the same */
        counter = 0;
        while (character == new_character && index < *size)
        {
            index++;
            counter++;
            new_character = string[index];
        }

        /* compression phase */
        if (counter > 3 && counter < 10)
```

495

```
              {
                  new_string[new_index]   = '@';
                  new_string[new_index+1] =   (char) (48 + counter);
                  new_string[new_index+2] =   character;
                  new_index = new_index+3;
              }
          else if (counter > 9)
              {
                  new_string[new_index]   = '@';
                  new_string[new_index+1] = (char) (48 + counter / 10);
                  new_string[new_index+2] = (char) (48 + counter % 10);
                  new_string[new_index+3] = character;
                  new_index = new_index+4;
              }
          else
              {
                  while (counter != 0)
                  {
                      new_string[new_index] = character;
                      new_index++;
                      counter--;
                  }
              }
      }
      new_string[new_index] = null;
      *new_size = strlen(new_string);
}


void decode(char new_string[])
/* function to decode a string and display the information */
{
      const char null = 0;
      int  new_index = 0, counter;
      char character;
      char digit_1, digit_2;

      character = new_string[new_index];
      while (character != null)
      {
         if (character != '@')
            printf("%c", character);
         else
         {
            new_index++;
            digit_1 = (int) new_string[new_index] - 48;

            if (new_string[new_index+1] >= '0' &&
                new_string[new_index+1] <= '9')
            {
                digit_2 = (int) new_string[new_index+1] - 48;
                counter = 10 * digit_1 + digit_2;
                new_index++;
            }
            else
            {
                counter = digit_1;
            }

            new_index++;
            character = new_string[new_index];
            while (counter != 0)
```

```
                {
                    printf("%c", character);
                    counter--;
                }
            }
            new_index++;
            character = new_string[new_index];
        }
    }

main()
{
    FILE *data, *new_data;
    char string[string_length], new_string[string_length];
    int  size, new_size;
    int  total_size = 0, total_new_size = 0;

    data     = open_file(file_1, read);
    new_data = open_file(file_2, write);

    printf("\n<<compressed data>>\n\n");
    while (! feof(data))
    {
        size = read_line(data, string);
        encode(string, &size, new_string, &new_size);
        total_size += size;
        total_new_size += new_size;
        fprintf(new_data, "%s", new_string);
        printf("%s", new_string);
    }

    printf("\n\n<<compression %4.1f%>>\n",
    100.0 * ((float) total_size - (float) total_new_size) / (float) total_size);

    fclose(data);
    fclose(new_data);

    data = open_file(file_2, read);

    printf("\n<<uncompressed data>>\n\n");
    while (! feof(data))
    {
        fgets(string, string_length, data);
        decode(string);
    }

    fclose(data);
}
```

6(a).

```
/* c14_dpp\ans_06a.c program to build a random access binary file */
#include <stdlib.h>
#include <stdio.h>
#include <errno.h>
#include <string.h>

#define max_records 20
#define null 0
```

```
#define names_file "a:\\answers\\c14_dpp\\names.bin"
#define write_bin "wb"

typedef struct {
                    char first_name[20];
                    char dob[20];
              } information;

FILE *open_file(char filename[], char mode[])
{
    FILE *file;

    file = fopen(filename, mode);
    if (file == NULL)
    {
        printf("%s cannot be opened\n", filename);
        exit(errno);
    }
    else
        return file;
}


int hash(char name[])
/* function to receive a name and generate a record position */
{
    int sum = 0;
    int index;

    for (index=0; name[index] != null; index++)
        sum += name[index];

    return sum % max_records;
}

main()
{
    information data[max_records];
    char        name[20];
    char        birthday[20];
    int         index;
    FILE        *names;

    for (index=0; index < max_records; index++)
    {
        strcpy(data[index].first_name, "");
        strcpy(data[index].dob, "");
    }

    printf("name? [quit to exit] "); gets(name);
    while (strcmp(name, "quit") != 0)
    {
        index = hash(name);
        if (strcmp(data[index].first_name, "") == 0)
        {
            printf("birthday? "); gets(birthday);
            strcpy(data[index].first_name, name);
            strcpy(data[index].dob, birthday);
        }
        else
            printf("data collision - try again\n");
```

498

```
        printf("name? [quit to exit] "); gets(name);
    }

    for (index=0; index < max_records; index++)
        printf("%d\t%s\t%s\n", index, data[index].first_name, data[index].dob);

    names = open_file(names_file, write_bin);
    fwrite(data, sizeof(information), max_records, names);
    fclose(names);
}
```

6(b).

```
/* c14_dpp\ans_06b.c program to read a random access binary file */
#include <stdlib.h>
#include <stdio.h>
#include <errno.h>
#include <string.h>

#define max_records 20
#define null 0
#define names_file "a:\\answers\\c14_dpp\\names.bin"
#define read_bin "rb"

typedef struct {
                char first_name[20];
                char dob[20];
            } information;

FILE *open_file(char filename[], char mode[])
{
    FILE *file;

    file = fopen(filename, mode);
    if (file == NULL)
    {
        printf("%s cannot be opened\n", filename);
        exit(errno);
    }
    else
        return file;
}

int hash(char name[])
/* function to receive a name and generate a record position */
{
    int sum = 0;
    int index;

    for (index=0; name[index] != null; index++)
        sum += name[index];

    return sum % max_records;
}

main()
{
    char        name[20];
```

499

```
FILE        *names;
long int    record_no;
information buffer[1];

names = open_file(names_file, read_bin);

printf("name? [quit to exit] "); gets(name);
while (strcmp(name, "quit") != 0)
{
    record_no = (long int) hash(name);
    fseek(names, record_no * sizeof(information), SEEK_SET);
    fread(buffer, sizeof(information), 1, names);
    if (strcmp(name, buffer[0].first_name) == 0)
        printf("%s\n", buffer[0].dob);
    else
        printf("no data in file\n");

    printf("name? [quit to exit] "); gets(name);
}

    fclose(names);
}
```

Chapter 15 - section 15.9

1.

```
/*
c15_dpp\ans_01.c
*/


#include <stdio.h>
#include <stdlib.h>

#define random_no (rand() % 100)
#define max_numbers 10

struct record {
                int         number;
                struct record *link;
            };

typedef struct record node;

node *build_circular(node *head)
/* function to build a circular linked list containing max_number
random numbers */
{
    node *temp, *last_node;
    int   counter;

    /* build first node */
    head = malloc(sizeof(node));
    head->number = random_no;
    head->link   = head;
    last_node    = head;
```

```
        /* build subsequent nodes */
        for (counter=2; counter <= max_numbers; counter++)
        {
            temp = malloc(sizeof(node));
            temp->number = random_no;
            temp->link = head;
            head = temp;
            last_node->link = head;
        }
        return head;
}

void list_out(node *head)
/* function to display the contents of a linked list */
{
        node *current;

        current = head;

        do
        {
            printf("%d\n", current->number);
            current = current->link;
        } while (current != head);

        printf("\nback to the beginning with the next node\n");
        printf("%d\n", current->number);
}

main()
{
        node    *head = NULL;

        head = build_circular(head);
        printf("circular list of random numbers\n");
        list_out(head);
}
```

2.

```
/*
c15_dpp\ans_02.c
*/

#include <stdio.h>
#include <stdlib.h>

#define random_no (rand() % 100)
#define max_numbers 10

struct record {
                int             number;
                struct record *link;
        };
```

```
typedef struct record node;


node *create_node(node *next)
/* function to create a node and return a pointer to it */
{
        next=malloc(sizeof(node));
        next->number = random_no;
        next->link = NULL;
        return next;
}


node *create_list(node *head)
/* function to create a linked list of max_number random numbers
and return a pointer to the head of the linked list */
{
        node *last;
        int  counter;

        for (counter=1; counter <= max_numbers; counter++)
        {
            if (head == NULL)
            {
                head = create_node(head);
                last = head;
            }
            else
            {
                last->link = create_node(last->link);
                last = last->link;
            }
        }
        return head;
}

int largest(node *head)
/* function to return the largest integer in a linked list */
{
        node *current;
        int  maximum;

        maximum = head->number;
        current = head->link;
        while (current != NULL)
        {
            if (current->number > maximum)
                maximum = current->number;

            current = current->link;
        }
        return maximum;
}

node *build(node *head, int maximum)
/* function to build a new linked list inserting new nodes at
the head of the list, thereby creating a list of numbers sorted
into ascending order */
{
    node *temp;

    if (head == NULL)
```

```
        {
            head = malloc(sizeof(node));
            head->number = maximum;
            head->link   = NULL;
        }
        else
        {
            temp = head;
            head = malloc(sizeof(node));
            head->number = maximum;
            head->link   = temp;
        }
        return head;
    }

node *delete_node(node *head, int maximum)
/* function to delete the node containing the number maximum */
    {
        node *current, *last;

        current = head;
        last    = head;

        while (current->number != maximum)
        {
            last = current;
            current = current->link;
        }

        if (head == current)
            head = head->link;
        else
            last->link = current->link;

        free(current);
        return head;
    }


void list_out(node *head)
/* function to display the contents of a linked list */
    {
        node *current;

        current = head;
        if (current == NULL)
            printf("list empty\n");
        else
        {
            while (current != NULL)
            {
                printf("%d\n", current->number);
                current = current->link;
            }
        }
        printf("\n");
    }

main()
    {
        node    *head     = NULL;
        node    *new_head = NULL;
```

```
        int     number;

        head = create_list(head);
        printf("list of random numbers\n");
        list_out(head);

        while (head != NULL)
        {
            number = largest(head);
            new_head = build(new_head, number);
            head = delete_node(head, number);
        }

        printf("sorted list of random numbers\n");
        list_out(new_head);
}
```

4.

```c
/* c15_dpp\ans_04.c */

#include <stdio.h>
#include <stdlib.h>
#include <string.h>
#include <float.h>

#define yes 'Y'

struct record_1 {
                float           operand;
                struct record_1 *link;
            };

typedef struct  {
                char            operand;
                float           value;
            } operand_value;

struct record_2 {
                operand_value   contents;
                struct record_2 *link;
            };

typedef struct record_1 stack_node;
typedef struct record_2 list_node;
typedef enum {false, true} boolean;

boolean stack_empty(stack_node *stack_top)
/* function to test and return whether a stack is empty */
{
    if (stack_top != NULL)
        return false;
    else
        return true;
}
```

```
stack_node *pop(stack_node *stack_top, float *number)
/* function to remove a node from the top of a stack and return a pointer for the new stack
top */
{
    stack_node *temporary;

    if (! stack_empty(stack_top))
    {
        *number = stack_top->operand;
        temporary = stack_top->link;
        free(stack_top);
        return temporary;
    }
    else
        return NULL;
}


stack_node *push(stack_node *stack_top, float number)
/* function to insert a node into the top of the stack and return a pointer to the new stack
top */
{
    stack_node *temporary;

    temporary = malloc(sizeof(stack_node));
    temporary->operand = number;
    temporary->link = stack_top;
    return temporary;
}


list_node *build(list_node *next, char character, float number)
/* function to build a linked list of operands and their respective values and return the
head of the linked list */
{
    next = malloc(sizeof(list_node));
    next->contents.operand = character;
    next->contents.value   = number;
    next->link             = NULL;
    return next;
}


list_node *input_string(list_node *head, char Polish_string[])
/* function to input a string, build a linked list of operands and return the head of the
list */
{
    const char      null = 0;
          int       index;
          float     value;
          list_node *last;
          char      character;

    printf("input reverse Polish string ");
    gets(Polish_string);
    for (index=0; Polish_string[index] != null; index++)
    {
        character = Polish_string[index];
        switch (character)
        {
        case '+': case '-': case '*': case '/' : break;
        default : printf("%c ? ", Polish_string[index]);
                  scanf("%f", &value);
                  if (head == NULL)
                  {
```

```
                        head = build(head, character, value);
                        last = head;
                    }
                    else
                    {
                        last->link = build(last->link, character, value);
                        last = last->link;
                    }
            }
    }
    return head;
}

float search(list_node *head, char character)
/* function to search a linked list for a character operand and return the respective value */
{
    list_node *current;

    current = head;
    while (current->contents.operand != character)
            current = current->link;

    return current->contents.value;
}

main()
{
    const char null = 0;
    stack_node *stack = NULL;
    list_node  *head;
    char       Polish_string[80];
    int        index;
    char       character;
    float      first, second, answer;
    char       reply;

    do
    {
        head = input_string(NULL, Polish_string);

        for (index=0; Polish_string[index] != null; index++)
        {
            character = Polish_string[index];
            if (character == '+' || character == '-' ||
                character == '*' || character == '/')
            {
                stack = pop(stack, &first);
                stack = pop(stack, &second);

                switch(character)
                {
                case '+': answer = second+first; break;
                case '-': answer = second-first; break;
                case '*': answer = second*first; break;
                case '/': if (first != 0)
                                answer = second/first;
                          else
                                answer = FLT_MAX;
                }
                stack = push(stack, answer);
            }
            else
```

```
                        stack = push(stack, search(head, character));
                }
            stack = pop(stack, &answer);
            printf("evaluation of reverse Polish string %s is %6.2f\n\n",
                    Polish_string, answer);

            printf("\nmore? [Y]es or [N]o "); getchar();
            reply = getchar(); getchar();
            reply = toupper(reply);

    } while (reply == yes);
}
```

Chapter 16 - section 16.7

1(a).

```
/* c16_dpp\ans_01a.c */

#include <bios.h>
#include <stdio.h>

main()
{
    unsigned int equipment;
    unsigned int mask = 1;

    equipment = biosequip();
    /* examine individual bits */

    if (equipment & mask) printf("system boots from disk\n");

    mask = mask << 1;
    if (equipment & mask) printf("coprocessor installed\n");

    mask = 0x000C;
    printf("motherboard RAM ");
    switch ((equipment & mask) >> 2)
    {
    case 0 : printf("16K\n"); break;
    case 1 : printf("32K\n"); break;
    case 2 : printf("48K\n"); break;
    case 3 : printf("64K\n");
    }

    mask = mask << 2;
    printf("initial video mode ");
    switch ((equipment & mask) >> 4)
    {
    case 0 : printf("unused\n"); break;
    case 1 : printf("color card 40x25 BW mode\n"); break;
    case 2 : printf("color card 80x25 BW mode\n"); break;
    case 3 : printf("monochrome card 80x25 BW mode\n");
    }

    mask = mask << 2;
    printf("number of disk drives ");
    switch((equipment & mask) >> 6)
```

```
    {
    case 0 : printf("1\n"); break;
    case 1 : printf("2\n"); break;
    case 2 : printf("3\n"); break;
    case 3 : if (equipment & 1) printf("4\n");
    }

    mask = mask << 1;
    if (equipment & mask) printf("DMA\n");

    mask = 0xE00;
    printf("number of serial ports %u\n", (equipment & mask) >> 9);

    mask = 0x1000;
    if (equipment & mask) printf("game port attached\n");

    mask = mask << 1;
    if (equipment & mask) printf("serial printer attached\n");

    mask = 0xC000;
    printf("number of parallel printers installed %u\n",
           (equipment & mask) >> 14);
}
```

1(b).

```
/* c16_dpp\ans_01b.c */

#include <bios.h>
#include <stdio.h>
typedef struct {
                unsigned int bit_0        : 1;
                unsigned int bit_1        : 1;
                unsigned int bits_2_3     : 2;
                unsigned int bits_4_5     : 2;
                unsigned int bits_6_7     : 2;
                unsigned int bit_8        : 1;
                unsigned int bits_9_11    : 3;
                unsigned int bit_12       : 1;
                unsigned int bit_13       : 1;
                unsigned int bits_14_15   : 2;
            } data;

typedef union {
                    data f1;
                    unsigned int  f2;
            } alternative;

main()
{
    alternative word;

    word.f2 = biosequip();

    /* examine individual bits */

    if (word.f1.bit_0) printf("system boots from disk\n");
```

```
        if (word.f1.bit_1) printf("coprocessor installed\n");

        printf("motherboard RAM ");
        switch (word.f1.bits_2_3)
        {
        case 0 : printf("16K\n"); break;
        case 1 : printf("32K\n"); break;
        case 2 : printf("48K\n"); break;
        case 3 : printf("64K\n");
        }

        printf("initial video mode ");
        switch (word.f1.bits_4_5)
        {
        case 0 : printf("unused\n"); break;
        case 1 : printf("color card 40x25 BW mode\n"); break;
        case 2 : printf("color card 80x25 BW mode\n"); break;
        case 3 : printf("monochrome card 80x25 BW mode\n");
        }

        printf("number of disk drives ");
        switch(word.f1.bits_6_7)
        {
        case 0 : printf("1\n"); break;
        case 1 : printf("2\n"); break;
        case 2 : printf("3\n"); break;
        case 3 : if (word.f1.bit_0) printf("4\n");
        }

        if (word.f1.bit_8) printf("DMA\n");
        printf("number of serial ports %u\n", word.f1.bits_9_11);


        if (word.f1.bit_12) printf("game port attached\n");

        if (word.f1.bit_13) printf("serial printer attached\n");

        printf("number of parallel printers installed %u\n",
                word.f1.bits_14_15);
}
```

2(a).

```
/* c16_dpp\ans_02a.c */

#include <stdio.h>

int right(int number, int bits)
/* function to right rotate a 16-bit number by a set number of bits and return the new value
of the number */
{
        /* masks to check the sign bit and least significant bit (lsb)
           and clear the sign bit */
        int sign = 0x8000;
        int lsb = 0x0001;
        int clear = 0x7FFF;

        for ( ; bits != 0 ; bits--)
```

```
            {
                if ((number & lsb) && ((number & sign) >> 15))
                    number >>= 1;
                else if (!(number & lsb) && ((number & sign) >> 15))
                {
                    number >>= 1;
                    number &= clear;
                }
                else if (number & lsb)
                {
                    number >>= 1;
                    number |= sign;
                }
                else
                    number >>= 1;
            }
        return number;
}


int left(int number, int bits)
/* function to left rotate a 16-bit number by a set number of bits
   and return the new value of the number */
{

        int sign = 0x8000;
        int lsb = 0x0001;

        for ( ; bits != 0; bits--)
        {
                if ((number & sign) >> 15)
                {
                        number <<= 1;
                        number |= lsb;
                }
                else
                        number <<=1;
        }
        return number;
}.


main()
{

        printf("%X\n", right(0x0F3C,3));
        printf("%X\n", right(0xF000,3));
        printf("%X\n", right(0x00FF,5));
        printf("%X\n", right(0xC01F,5));

        printf("%X\n", left(0x8F21,1));
        printf("%X\n", left(0xF01B,5));
        printf("%X\n", left(0x00F0,4));
}
```

2(b).

```c
/* c16_dpp\ans_02b.c */

#include <stdio.h>

int sign(int number)
/* function to return the sign bit of a number */
{
        if ((number & 0x8000) >> 15)
            return 1;
        else
            return 0;
}

int complement(int number)
/* function to return the two's complement of a number */
{
        return ~number+1;
}

int multiply(int a, int b)
/* function to multiply two 8-bit integers */
{
        int sum;
        int bit = -8;
        int lsb = 0x0001;
        int negative=0;

        if (sign(a))
        {
            a=complement(a); negative++;
        }
        if (sign(b))
        {
            b=complement(b); negative++;
        }
        sum=0;
        for (; bit != 0; bit++)
        {
                if (b & lsb)
                    sum = sum + a;

                b >>= 1;
                a <<= 1;
        }

        if (negative != 1)
            return sum;
        else
            return complement(sum);
}

main()
{
        printf("%d\n", multiply(15,15));
        printf("%d\n", multiply(150,18));
        printf("%d\n", multiply(-25, 50));
        printf("%d\n", multiply(-25, -60));
        printf("%d\n", multiply(-256, 127));
}
```

4.

```c
/* c16_dpp\ans_04.c demonstration of a function with a variable number of arguments */

#include <stdio.h>
#include <stdarg.h>

typedef struct {
                int max;
                int min;
             } results;

results max_min(int number, ...)
/* function to return the maximum and minimum values for any number of parameters */
{
    va_list      args;
    int          arg;
    int          count;
    results      values;

    va_start(args, number);
    arg = va_arg(args, int);
    values.max = arg;
    values.min = arg;

    for (count=1; count < number; count++)
    {
        arg = va_arg(args, int);
        if (arg > values.max)
           values.max = arg;
        else if (arg < values.min)
           values.min = arg;
    }
    va_end(args);
    return values;
}

main()
{
    results answer;

    answer = max_min(2,20,10);
    printf("max %4d\tmin %4d\n", answer.max, answer.min);
    answer = max_min(5,20,10,50,99,1);
    printf("max %4d\tmin %4d\n", answer.max, answer.min);
    answer = max_min(10,56,99,32,8,3,101,4,77,-5,17);
    printf("max %4d\tmin %4d\n", answer.max, answer.min);

}
```

Bibliography

Ammeraal, L   C++ for Programmers, Wiley, 1991

Barclay, K.A   ANSI C Problem Solving and Programming, Prentice Hall, 1990

Holmes, B.J   Convert to C and C++, DP Publications, 1992

Holmes, B.J   Modula-2 Programming - 2nd Edition, DP Publications, 1994

Jensen & Partners International TopSpeed C - Language Tutorial, 1990

Jensen & Partners International TopSpeed C - Language Reference, 1990

Jensen & Partners International TopSpeed C - Library Reference, 1990

Lowell, J.A   UNIX - Shell programming, Wiley, 1990

Manger, J.J   UNIX - The Complete Book, Sigma Press, 1992

Microsoft Corporation   Visual C++ User Guide, 1993

Schildt, H   The Annotated ANSI C Standard, Osborne McGraw-Hill, 1990

Index